The Blue Willow Inn

BIBLE OF SOUTHERN COOKING

Louis and Billie Van Dyke

Rutledge Hill Press

Nashville, Tennessee

A Division of Thomas Nelson Publishers

www.ThomasNelson.com

Published by Rutledge Hill Press, a Division of Thomas Nelson, Inc., P.O. Box 141000, Nashville, Tennessee 37214.

The authors and publisher of this book assume no liability for, and are released by readers from, any injury or damage resulting from the strict adherence to, or deviation from, the directions and/or recipes herein. All yields are approximations.

Rutledge Hill Press books may be purchased in bulk for educational, business, fund-raising, or sales promotional use. For information, please e-mail SpecialMarkets@ThomasNelson.com.

Library of Congress Cataloging-in-Publication Data

Van Dyke, Louis, 1947–
    The Blue Willow Inn bible of southern cooking / Louis and Billie VanDyke.
      p. cm.
    Includes index.
    ISBN 1-4016-0227-4 (hardcover)
    1. Cookery, American—Southern style. 2. Blue Willow Inn. I. VanDyke, Billie, 1937– II. Title.
TX715.2.S68V36 2005
641.5975—dc22   2005025294

Printed in the United States of America

05 06 07 08 09—5 4 3 2 1

To our family, staff, and customers, we dedicate this book. Without the assistance and tolerance of our family, the Blue Willow Inn Restaurant would not be a success. Our staff is our most valuable asset. Their dedication and professionalism have played a major role in the success of the Blue Willow Inn Restaurant. And to our customers, we have some of the best customers in the world. They have made our labors, our efforts, and our lives blessed.

Table of Contents

Acknowledgements	*7*
Foreword	*9*
Introduction	*11*
Appetizers	37
Beverages & Punches	61
Jellies, Jams, Preserves, & Spreads	79
Soups & Salads	89
Relishes & Pickles	123
Gravies & Sauces	129
Breads	139
Side Dishes	163
Main Dishes	211
Desserts & Sweets	261
Kids Korner	357
Charts & Tables	*363*
Index	*377*

Acknowledgments

There are many people who have helped make this cookbook a reality. We particularly want to thank Patsy Joiner, who has spent long hours editing our recipes, correcting our spelling and grammar, and assisting us in getting the information to our publisher on time in the acceptable format.

We want to thank our neighbor Sophia DeMoss, who has been one of our dearest friends for almost thirty years. Sophia has assisted in testing dozens of the recipes and has made comments on each recipe. Special thanks to Dominick Stella and Chip Edgerly (our son) at the Blue Willow Inn Restaurant for their assistance in testing recipes. Thank you also goes to Peggy Hawkins, the general manager of Magnolia Hall (Blue Willow Inn's catering and special events facility), for her assistance in testing appetizers and serving them to our guests for customer comments. We thank Denise Cardella and Mae Morrow at Journey's End Restaurant, our facility in Loganville, Georgia, for their time spent testing recipes and their comments. Without friends and staff assisting us in testing recipes, this book would have taken many more months to complete.

Thanks go to Michael and Jane Stern, cookbook authors and food columnists, for their work on *Louis and Billie Van Dyke's Blue Willow Inn Cookbook,* which was published in 2002, and for all we have learned from them. They introduced us to the publisher, Rutledge Hill Press, who is now our publisher. We appreciate the faith and support Rutledge Hill has placed in us by publishing *The Blue Willow Inn Bible of Southern Cooking.*

A special appreciation goes to the great cooks from all over the South who sent us their favorite family recipes. These great cooks responded to a recipe contest as we were seeking the best of the South. Winners were chosen in each category of the book as well as a first place winner. The winning recipes and many more great family recipes are included throughout the book.

We are especially indebted to the gracious kindness of First Ladies from all over the South who sent us the governor's and their family's favorite recipe, and a special thanks to the governor of Louisiana for her family recipe.

A very special thanks goes to the people who have worked for us over the years. We have learned a great deal from them. They have helped us refine recipes and introduced us to new recipes that we have added to our menu at the Blue Willow Inn.

We would most certainly be remiss if we did not thank our customers. Some of them have been brutally frank in their critiques of our cooking, but often their suggestions have made us a better restaurant. We have some of the best customers a restaurant could possibly have, and we would not trade them for any others.

Most importantly, we want to thank our Heavenly Father, Jesus Christ, and the Holy Spirit for the blessings and the strength They have given us. We thank Them for Their past and future blessings.

— LOUIS AND BILLIE VAN DYKE

Foreword

If we go to heaven when we die, we expect meals up there to be served at a celestial branch of the Blue Willow Inn. For now, though, the earthly one in Social Circle, Georgia, is quite heavenly enough. It is a place where divine food is presented with gracious hospitality in elegant surroundings. Having spent our adult lives traveling several million miles around the country looking for memorable regional restaurants, we can say without hesitation that the fare on those pretty Blue Willow plates in the grand mansion on Cherokee Road is some of best there is. These are meals that define Southern eating at its best, from hot biscuits to fried green tomatoes to tables crowded with desserts.

The only problem for us has been that we live over a thousand miles away, so we can't do what so many people in the region do, which is to drive to Social Circle for Sunday supper, which is what's served seven days a week. But now, thanks to this big, beautiful volume, we can enjoy the delicious food and high spirits of a visit to the Blue Willow Inn just by turning the pages. Louis and Billie Van Dyke's collection of recipes is a treasure trove of dishes we want to cook for friends and family; and among the recipes are hints, tips, suggestions, and just plain funny culinary Southernisms that make poring over this book like sitting down and listening to grandma share not only her cooking secrets but also her advice and good humor. This is so much more than a lavish cookbook. It truly is a Bible of cooking, eating, and entertaining.

— Jane and Michael Stern

Introduction

HISTORY OF SOUTHERN COOKING AND HOSPITALITY

Visitors to the Blue Willow Inn Restaurant in Social Circle, Georgia, frequently ask us why southerners act the way they do, talk the way they do, and cook the way they do—and why they do all things *slowly*. Perhaps not even the most learned scholars of southern culture can answer these questions with certainty, but the fact remains that southerners are known for their hospitable treatment of visitors and friends, their slow pace of life, their manner of talking, and their delicious style of cooking. Although few can explain the southern hospitality phenomenon, few would deny its existence. It is common in areas such as Social Circle, Georgia, to hear a visitor from another state or country remark that southern hospitality is truly alive and well today.

For example, after the 1996 Olympic Games in Atlanta, Georgia, with all of the traffic congestion and scheduling problems, visitors could be overheard marveling at the hospitable acts of native Georgians rather than complaining about the crowds or the heat. One man was overheard recounting the tale of an Atlanta resident lending his cellular phone to someone in the crowd in desperate need to contact the rest of his party. Another was heard boasting of a young woman allowing a family with small children to board the already crowded MARTA (Atlanta mass transit) train ahead of her. Although these examples of southern hospitality boast a modern age twist of mobile phones and mass transit systems, southern hospitality is not a myth perpetuated by the

Hollywood version of life in the South—it is a reality and a way of life for most southerners.

Some speculate that this way of life (and it *is* a way of life, not merely an attitude to exhibit on special occasions or for special company) is a function of the southern colonies traditionally being more rural and agricultural. In rural societies people had to travel quite a distance to visit with one another and stayed for a while once they arrived at their destination.

Others speculate that the impeccable manners of southern inhabitants were simply passed down from the original settlers of the area, chiefly the English and the French, two cultures known for their codes of manners. English colonists began the establishment of Jamestown in 1607, which by 1700 had grown into a colony of 70,000 settlers. In addition, in 1670 English colonists established the first European colony in the Low Country, which eventually came to be called Charleston. Not long after this, the Low Country was settled by immigrants from Barbados and the French Huguenots.

The hospitality and manners of the Old South are alive and well in the modern South. For example, studies have shown that most southern parents teach their children to address adults as "Ma'am" and "Sir." In addition, studies have also shown that helpful behaviors are more frequent in the South.

Most southerners and visitors to the South, however, do not need a poll to tell them that hospitality and helpfulness are a natural part of the southern experience. The comments overheard from those visiting from other regions testify to the surprising fact that friendliness and openness characterize the behavior of southerners—whether it is the act of holding the door open for someone, taking food to the family of one who is sick or in the hospital, or the modern-day kindness of lending someone your cellular phone. To experience this kindness is to experience the South.

A characteristically southern trait that goes hand-in-hand with hospitality is the trademark slower pace for which the South is known. To experience the South is to experience a pace of life that is less frenetic, patterns of speech that are more melodic, and attitudes that are more relaxed. This slow pace seems to lend itself to the attitude of hospitality; if you are not always in a hurry, you are more likely to offer someone a cold drink, to invite someone in to visit awhile, or to pick up someone's dropped pencil and return it.

Although the pace of life in the South may indeed be slower, southerners would no doubt emphasize that this slower pace does not mean that they do not work so hard as those in other regions. Harper Lee, author of *To Kill A Mockingbird,* explained away the perception that because southerners do not move so quickly they do not work so hard: "We work hard, of course, but we do it in a different way. We work hard in order not to work. Any time spent on business is more or less wasted, but you have to do it in order to be able to hunt and fish and gossip."

In addition to the perception that southerners move more slowly than others is the perception that southerners speak more slowly. Surprisingly, studies have shown that southerners speak nearly as many words per minute as others—they merely draw the words out longer. Novelist Reynolds Price noted, "Southerners employ more notes of the scale than other Americans; they need them for their broader reach of expression." Or as Mark Twain said, "The southerner talks music." Regardless of the results of studies, many southerners would beg to differ with the finding that southerners do not actually talk more slowly, but just sound as if they do. Any southerner who has been to the local drugstore or café and for the fourth time that week has patiently listened to Junior explain how he reeled in the ten-pound, ornery catfish from Lake Hoosawatchie would no doubt firmly insist that southerners do, in fact, speak more slowly.

The manner of southern speech patterns is not so controversial—most everyone would agree that southerners have speech patterns and vocabulary peculiar to the South. Not only do southerners use different words, but they pronounce the same words differently. For example, southerners frequently omit the "*r*" sound when it follows a vowel, so that *pardon* becomes *pahden* and *butter* become *buddah*. Mark Twain remarked that "the educated southerner has no use for an *R*, except at the beginning of a word."

Contrary to the belief of some, pure Elizabethan English has not been preserved in areas of the South. Linguists believe, however, that the speech patterns of the Lower South resemble those of London and counties of southern England, while the speech patterns of the Upper South resemble those of Northern England, Scotland, and Northern Ireland.

Other cultures have contributed to our present day southern vocabulary. For example, the phrase most commonly liked with the South, "you all" or "y'all" appears to be a modern day replacement for the second-person plural no longer present in the English language. And that is why southerners become so offended when non-southerners attempt to poke fun at them and misuse the term by referring to one person, when any self-respecting southerner knows that you use "y'all" only when speaking to more than one person. African contributions to the present-day southern vocabulary include *banjo* and *okra*.

Another term peculiar to the South is the use of *dinner* to mean the midday meal, which was the main meal of the day in agricultural societies such as the South. The evening meal was often much lighter and was dubbed *supper*. Although the practice of eating the heavier meal at noon has all but vanished, except on Sundays, southerners still often refer to a noonday meal as *dinner* and an evening meal as *supper*.

One thing is for certain—whether southerners are eating dinner or supper—they enjoy a cuisine and a style of cooking native to the South and for which the South is famous. A definition of what makes food *southern* requires some explaining, because Southern food is a different thing to different people. To some it is bending over vines on hot August days picking the peas, okra, and squash that will grace the table on cold winter nights. To some it is sitting on a front porch in the cool of the evening shelling those same peas and passing the time with family and loved ones. To some it is the first real tomato sandwich of summer—the one when the first tomato vine is ripe and pulled by hand—heavy on the salt, pepper, and mayonnaise. To some the term conjures up notions of elegant restaurants in Charleston, New Orleans, and Savannah—places with white linen napkins and sterling silver tableware. To others it is paper plates and sawdust floors and barbecue sauce dripping down the chin. Still others hear Southern food and think of slices of ice-cold watermelon or ice cream made in an oak bucket and churned by hand. Others recall platters of crisply fried chicken served only for company. Sadly, there are people in the world who have no notion whatsoever of true Southern cooking.

Although southern food conjures up different images, down-home Southern cuisine traditionally uses what southern farms have historically and can easily produce. Thus, corn and pork, two products easily cultivated in the southern climate, have served as the mainstay of Southern cuisine. Pork has been the meat of choice (or at least availability) in the South since well before the Civil War. History shows that hogs came to Jamestown with the first English settlers and then traveled across the South with the pioneers. Pork soon became a staple to both high and low Southern cuisines; almost every part of the hog was used—meat was eaten, lard was used for cooking, lighting, soap, and ointments. Raising hogs was relatively easy, since farmers could either turn the hogs loose to forage the land until they were ready for slaughter or feed the hogs on corn, a crop indigenous to the South and also a crucial element of Southern cooking.

Corn was already being grown by southern Native Americans when the colonists first arrived, and this crop they called "maize" soon became a mainstay for southern hogs, horses, mules, and people. Even after the Civil War, southern households purchased two and a half times more cornmeal than other Americans. Corn, although delicious on the cob, takes many forms in Southern cooking—hominy, grits, cornmeal, cornbread, hushpuppies, and much to the prohibitionists' dismay—corn whiskey and bourbon.

Native Americans also provided southerners with a popular delicacy, one for which the Blue Willow Inn is famous—fried green tomatoes. Native Americans are said to have introduced this dish to colonists who were so taken by the dish that they exported it to Europe as early as the 1500s. The Catholic Church banned eating red ripe tomatoes because the texture of a ripe tomato's skin was similar to the texture of the human skin, and thus, the red tomato was considered an aphrodisiac. When the tomatoes were in season, however, you can bet that more than a few of even the most devout individuals hid in armoires or pulled the curtains shut in order to delight in the forbidden fruit. The consumption of green tomatoes was permitted, however, and that may be one of the reasons that the most popular type of tomatoes used for this dish is the green tomato. The earliest recorded history of fried green tomatoes is in Northern Italy, and the cook probably used olive oil for frying them.

In addition to corn and fresh vegetables such as tomatoes, other staples of the southern kitchen include other meats and crops easily obtained or grown. For example, poultry, game, and catfish were, and still are, popular meats used in Southern cooking. Other crops grown easily in the southern climate are black-eyed peas, greens, okra, rice, tomatoes, Vidalia onions (grown in and around Vidalia, Georgia, where the soil makes them as sweet as molasses), and watermelon.

The method for preparing these foods is similar to the nature of the foods themselves—southerners have traditionally used the ingredients on hand to enhance the staples on hand. For example, a traditional southern method of cooking is to deep-fry everything from catfish to sliced green tomatoes—the lard and cornmeal are an ever present help to combat a tiresome menu. Novelist Reynolds Price described the southern lunch as "chicken and cured ham, corn pudding, green beans, spring onions, tomatoes, small limas, hot rolls, corn sticks, iced tea, and lemon pie (with all the ingredients but the tea and lemons grown no more than twenty miles off)."

Recently a new phenomenon known as "New Southern Cuisine" has been popping up around the South in an attempt to lighten the traditionally high-calorie southern dishes while incorporating ingredients not traditionally used in Southern cooking. This new Southern-cooking style has been extolled and practiced in many modern

Southern cookbooks and trendy restaurants. Whether you prefer traditional "down home" Southern cuisine or the New South recipes, it is probable that the notion of Southern cuisine—old or new—cannot be easily defined and conjures up different images to different folks.

Southern food, whatever the definition, was not created; it has evolved. It epitomizes the southern spirit in that southerners have always taken what they might have on hand and gone well beyond making do—turning very modest fare into delectable culinary treasures. It is served with pride and eaten with great relish. It adds joy to any celebration, absorbs tears better than a sponge, and is usually the very first thing offered when southerners need to help one another deal with grief.

Recipes of Southern dishes have been passed down from generation to generation, changing with the times when necessary, adapted and improved upon. Some foods have even been glamorized to the point of legend. Sadly, many Southern recipes have been changed drastically to suit our modern lifestyle of hurry, hurry, hurry, not to mention the twenty-first century notion that anything that tastes good must be bad for you. Many southerners have lost the art of preparing fresh food from scratch, seasoning it with just the right combination of salt, pork, and butter, and serving it up hot in enormous helpings to grateful crowds of hungry family and friends. New generations of children in the South are growing up without knowing the joy of sitting down to a scrumptious meal of true Southern victuals. The old recipes are not being passed down, and yet another part of our heritage may soon be gone with the same wind that is sweeping away so many other facets of our culture.

We are dedicated at the Blue Willow Inn to serving authentic Southern dishes, prepared in the same manner in which they have been prepared for generations—with a few special touches belonging only to us. It is always our hope that our customers will experience Southern hospitality and charm at its best and leave fully satisfied and eager to visit again. By publishing these recipes, we hope to pass along a little bit of the southern culture to future generations and to enable people from all areas to open this cookbook, experiment with these delicious recipes and . . . experience the South.

STORY OF BLUE WILLOW CHINA

The Blue Willow china pattern was first introduced in England in 1780 and was designed and engraved by Thomas Minton. The pattern was produced primarily by

English potters during the first 150 years of its existence. Japan began producing the pattern in the early twentieth century.

Once one of the most popular china patterns in the world, the china was widely used in the United States during the middle of the twentieth century. The term "blue-plate special" used by restaurants all over America is said to have originated from the common use of the Blue Willow pattern.

The Van Dykes have been collectors of Blue Willow china since the early 1970s. Their love of the pattern resulted in their decision to use the china in their restaurant, hence the name, Blue Willow Inn Restaurant.

The design illustrates the Chinese legend of a romance between Koong-se, daughter of a wealthy mandarin, and Chang, the mandarin's lowly secretary. To keep the two young lovers apart, Koong-se's father erected a fence so they could not see each other. However, Koong-se found a way to contact Chang. She wrote a poem and placed it in a seashell, floating it downstream to Chang.

Koong-se's father had promised her in marriage to a noble duke. Wearing a disguise, Chang crept into the palace during the wedding banquet and eloped with Koong-se. Only at the last minute did the mandarin see them crossing a bridge, Koong-se carrying a box of jewels that were to have been her wedding dowry.

The lovers found a hideout with a maid who protected them, and later they moved to a distant island to spend their lives together. But time did not stop the mandarin's search for the couple. Eventually he found the couple and put them to death. According to the legend, God was so touched by their love that he immortalized Chang and Koong-se as two doves flying together in the sky.

In the Blue Willow pattern are illustrations of the story such as the palace, bridge, lovers running to safety, the distant island, and two doves flying together in the sky.

History of the Blue Willow Inn

The Blue Willow Inn Restaurant is housed in a neoclassical, Greek Revival mansion featuring a wide portico porch supported by four fluted columns with Corinthian capitals. Above the front door is a balcony supported by ornate brackets. The house was built in 1917 by John Phillips Upshaw, Jr., for his wife, Bertha, and daughter, Nell. This was the second home built by Mr. Upshaw. His first home, on the same five-acre tract of land now the site of the Blue Willow Inn, was a two-story Victorian cottage built in

1899. The five-acre tract had previously been the site of a tannery owned by his father, John Phillips Upshaw, Sr.

The construction of the mansion was prompted by the building of a neoclassical mansion directly across the street from the Victorian cottage by John's younger brother, Sanders Upshaw, in 1916. Sanders in part owed his fortune to his brother, John, who loaned him money to purchase a cotton farm in the early 1900s. Not to be outdone by his younger brother, John and Bertha measured Sanders' home inside and out during the final phase of construction and then drew plans to build their house a little grander than Sanders' house.

In order to do this, the Victorian cottage had to be moved. Trees were felled, and the cottage was rolled on logs to the lot south of John's five-acre tract. After moving the cottage, numerous wagonloads of dirt were brought in to raise the building site to the same height as the Sanders' land. There was a natural slope, and by filling the site with dirt, the new home for John and Bertha would be directly across from Sanders' home and on the same level.

Several improvements were made in John's version of the house to better Sanders' house. For example, John's house was built with cream brick instead of wood; the roof on John's house was red tile, a roof that was far superior to Sanders' slate roof. Sanders' house had only one side porch, while John's house had two. The double windows on Sanders' house were outdone by the triple windows with granite sills and beveled and leaded crystal-glass fanlights on John's house. The oak floors in John's house were laid with a decorative pattern as opposed to Sanders' flooring, which was laid in the typical side-by-side pattern. John Upshaw's house had to be just a little larger and a little better. In spite of the "one-upmanship" by John Upshaw over his younger brother, it is said that the families had a close and cordial relationship all of their lives.

A frequent visitor to the Upshaw's new home was Margaret Mitchell, author of *Gone with the Wind*. Ms. Mitchell stayed at the relocated Victorian cottage while dating Redd Upshaw, her first husband. Redd Upshaw was a cousin of John Upshaw and lived nearby in Between, Georgia, and was reportedly the model for the character of Rhett Butler. The marriage of Redd and Margaret Upshaw was short, ill-fated, and ended in divorce.

Having constructed what was generally considered the finest and best-built house in the county, John and Bertha Upshaw lived there until their deaths. Mr. Upshaw made arrangements to bequeath the property to the clubs in Social Circle to be used as a community house after the death of his daughter, Nell. In 1952 Nell Upshaw Gannon deeded her life interest in the property to the clubs of Social Circle since she had no interest in maintaining the home.

From 1952 until the late 1960s, the house was the center of cultural, civic, and social activities. Weddings, birthdays, school proms, graduation dances, and most of the social activities in the community were held at the clubhouse. In the 1950s a baseball diamond was constructed behind the property.

During the late 1960s and early 1970s desegregation was taking place in the South, and Social Circle was no exception. Lawsuits were filed over the use of the community swimming pool since it had been constructed with city tax money. During the turmoil of the era, the clubs abandoned the property and renounced title to the property. With the death of Nell Upshaw Gannon in 1974, ownership of the house and property went into the courts for clarification.

In 1985 the Georgia Supreme Court ruled that title to the property belonged to the heirs of the estate of Nell Upshaw Gannon. Reverend Homer Harvey, a Church of God minister, purchased the property from the heirs in 1985 and established the Social Circle Church of God in the mansion. In the late 1980s construction began at the rear of the five-acre tract on a church, and in 1990 the Social Circle Church of God moved from the mansion to the church at the rear of the property. Reverend Harvey then deeded the church-occupied property to the church trustees and sold the main house and the remaining property to Louis and Billie Van Dyke.

The fifteen years during which the property had been abandoned and tied up in the courts had taken its toll on the grand old mansion. Reverend Harvey had already spent large sums of money renovating the exterior of the house, replacing rotting wood and repairing the roof. Louis and Billie Van Dyke took up where Reverend Harvey left off. The house needed more roof repairs, extensive repairs to the columns, and renovations inside. After repairing the main level, updating the wiring and plumbing, and expanding the kitchen, the Van Dykes were ready to open their dream—the Blue Willow Inn Restaurant. The restaurant opened on Thanksgiving Day, 1991.

During the next year, the second floor was renovated and transformed into dining rooms for banquets and group dining. In 1993 renovations began on the pool house and the pool, which had not been drained since the late 1960s. The pool house was expanded and converted into a gift shop to complement the restaurant, while the pool was refurbished and accented with fountains. The pool and gift shop compound were then enclosed with wrought-iron fencing.

The Blue Willow Inn Restaurant hosts some close to five thousand customers weekly, serving a Southern buffet often proclaimed the best in the South. As guests enter the grand hall with the crystal chandeliers, they are escorted to one of the many dining rooms: the Savannah Room with its warm fireplace; the Garden Room, which was formerly part of the back porch; the Sun Porch; the Charleston Room, which is reminiscent of old southern charm; the Lewis Grizzard Room, which was named for the famous author and columnist who wrote about the Blue Willow Inn; and the Walton Room, which is the largest room on the main level. The Walton Room is the buffet service area, and the southern buffets served in the Walton Room are served in a catered style. Guests choose from an array of four or five meats; nine or ten vegetables prepared southern style; soup and chicken and dumplings; salad fixings; and homemade biscuits, muffins, and cornbread. Last, but not least, is a delicious spread of pies, cobblers, puddings, and cakes.

The second floor houses the Magnolia Room, which is used for large functions and banquets. With seating for about seventy, it is the largest dining room in the house. Two smaller rooms, the Blue Room and the Tea Room, are also open to guests and small parties on the second floor.

The mansion is decorated in deep greens and burgundies, which are complemented by antique furnishings and accessories. The walls are adorned with fine art and part of the Van Dyke's Blue Willow dish collection. The Van Dykes have been collectors of the Blue Willow pattern china since the early 1970s, and their fondness for this pattern resulted in the name of the restaurant, the Blue Willow Inn. The tables are set with Blue Willow china and adorned with fresh-cut flowers.

Guests at the Blue Willow Inn Restaurant are encouraged to absorb and enjoy the slower pace of the Old South. A visit to the Blue Willow Inn should be an experience in both dining and relaxing. From being welcomed by greeters attired in antebellum dress, to sipping lemonade while rocking on the front porch, guests are treated to genuine southern hospitality of a bygone era.

Enjoy the gardens. Enjoy the Southern food. Enjoy the ambiance of the old southern mansion. Relax for just a moment and let the world pass by. This is the Blue Willow Inn experience.

"FEAR YE NOT, NEITHER BE AFRAID:" THE STORY OF LOUIS AND BILLIE VAN DYKE

From the time Billie Van Dyke was a small child she had an interest in cooking and helping in the kitchen. As a small child, her mother, Nita Jane Baker, used to "scoot" her out of the kitchen and out of her way so she could prepare family meals. When time allowed, however, Nita did teach Billie some of her cooking skills. Growing up on the banks of the Wilmington River in Savannah, Billie spent many hours with her father and brothers fishing, shrimping, and digging oysters in Savannah's salt waters. When Billie was eleven years old, her father, Herman "Pop" Baker, suddenly died of a heart attack. Gone were the fishing days with her dad. Hard times set in for her family, now consisting of her mother, one sister, and three brothers. Billie, the oldest, had to help raise the younger siblings, ranging in age from six weeks to nine years old.

Serious illness beset her mother, and the family was scattered. Her brothers Dennis and Jimmy were adopted and moved out of the Savannah area. Her sister, Dot, was raised in a boarding school, and brother Charles was sent to Bethesda Orphanage in Savannah, where he stayed until joining the Marines upon graduation from high school. Since Billie was the oldest, she was "less adoptable" than the younger siblings. Billie was placed in a children's home and also spent some time with her mother, whose health had improved. She spent her last years in high school with her foster parents, Marvin and Annie Laura Exley, in Garden City, a suburb of Savannah.

While living with the Exley's, Billie developed her cooking, entertaining, and sewing skills. Mr. Exley taught Billie how to make biscuits and cornbread, and how to have them look just like the pictures on the packages of flour and cornmeal. Mr. Exley was always clipping recipes from the newspaper and magazines and trying new dishes. Billie helped prepare and cook the new recipes for company that was always coming to the Exley's house and the minister and his family who usually ate Sunday dinner with the Exley family. During this time she met her first husband, William "Bill" Edgerly Jr., a student at Benedictine Military Academy in Savannah.

A courtship in high school blossomed into marriage when Billie was eighteen. From the time Billie and Bill were married, her home became the center of family activities with her brother Charles, her sister, Dot, and their grandmother, "BaBa." Billie made friends with everyone she met. She always found herself entertaining friends and family. Cooking for large groups became a natural way of life for her.

In the first five years of her marriage her three children were born—William III, "Chip", then her second son, Dale, and finally a daughter, Donna. Billie involved herself in church work, school activities, and the American Red Cross, volunteering with the swimming program. She taught swimming, which proved to be her needed outlet from homemaking that could include her children. Having received many awards from the Red Cross for volunteer work, she took over the swimming instruction and lifeguard program at the Port Wentworth, Georgia, swimming pool. It was during this time that she met Louis Van Dyke, a volunteer swimming instructor. Louis became good friends with Billie's husband and a friend of the family. No one would have ever dreamed that a tragic event would eventually lead to Billie and Louis' marriage.

In 1967 Billie's first husband, Bill, suddenly died in a tragic accident. Billie was now facing the same situation that her mother had faced many years earlier. Left alone with three small children, she was determined to keep her family together. Times had changed since her father had died. Social Security now provided survivor's benefits, and with the Social Security benefits and a part-time job Billie continued to make a home for her children.

At the time of Bill Edgerly's death, Louis was entering active duty in the U.S. Navy. After being discharged from the navy Louis renewed his friendship with Billie and the children. From fixing screens to hanging gutters and painting, Louis became the "handyman" around Billie's house. He also became a "big brother" to Chip, Dale, and Donna. After a couple of years the friendship between Billie and Louis grew into love, and Billie and Louis were married on May 1, 1970.

Billie soon again adjusted to married life and became a full-time mother and homemaker. Also she was back to entertaining friends and family. It seemed as though social and family events always took place at Billie and Louis' house. Just prior to the wedding, Billie's brother, Dennis, who had been adopted twenty-eight years earlier, showed up at Billie's sister Dot's door with his wife and family. He was making the U.S. Army his career and had recently been transferred to Ft. Stewart Army Base near Savannah. Dennis had remembered living as a small child on Wilmington Island and brought his family to Savannah to search for his "roots" and family. Seeing a familiar house, Dennis discovered an aunt he did not know he had. She directed him to his sister Dorothy in Garden City. After visiting, Dorothy directed Dennis to Billie's house.

Soon Billie was entertaining Dennis and his wife, Liz, and their children, along with Billie's brother, Charles, and sister, Dot, and their families. There was never a dull or boring time around the Van Dyke house.

In 1973 tragedy again struck Billie. Her son Dale was accidentally shot and killed by his best friend. He was buried the day after what would have been his seventeenth birthday. Entertaining and the thoughts of entertaining were over. Dark clouds settled over Billie, Louis, and the children. In 1974 Louis left a business in which he had invested everything he and Billie had (including borrowing against their house), and the business went bankrupt shortly thereafter. After the loss of Dale and then the business and their house, Louis and Billie packed Chip and Donna and everything they owned in the back of a rented moving van and moved to Atlanta.

Louis began a career in operations with a major Atlanta trucking firm, and both Billie and Louis became active in their church. Billie was again entertaining often, and in order to help with family income, she began a small catering business out of her home. The year was 1978 and Billie was soon doing weddings and parties. For the first few years Billie limited herself to church friends and their referrals. In 1979 Louis and Billie were tiring of the typical suburban, sub-division life of small lots and little privacy. They began looking for several acres outside of Atlanta to build a house. In the latter part of 1979 they purchased land in Walton County just outside of Social Circle. They still joke that they had to move forty miles from Atlanta in order to afford a few acres of land. They completed the home, but Billie's part-time catering business became too busy to continue operating out of the home.

In the summer of 1985 Louis and Billie decided that it was time to move the catering out of the house and into a catering facility. A small restaurant in an old house in Social Circle had recently gone out of business. One of Billie's friends, Susan Pressley, upon hearing that she was looking at the former restaurant, suggested that Billie open a restaurant so the "girls" could get together for morning coffee. After looking at the house, both Louis and Billie agreed that it would make an ideal catering facility. And with some work, it would probably make a good restaurant too. A restaurant? Neither Louis nor Billie had ever given any thought to opening a restaurant. After talking over the idea several times, they decided, "Yes, we can open a restaurant. Anybody can open a restaurant."

The plan was that Louis and Billie would spend all of their spare time fixing up the house, decorating, and cleaning the kitchen. Since Billie was a good cook and Louis was good at fixing things, this would work. Louis would continue to work at his job and Billie would run the restaurant and catering. After the restaurant opened, Louis was to spend his spare time helping run the restaurant. After all, someone had to wash the dishes and clean the floors.

Louis had consulted with a good friend whom he respected for his business skills, and the friend had been frank with Louis. "You do not have enough cash for a venture like this," he advised. He further added that Louis was "under capitalized and was risking losing his savings." Louis listened intently to this advice but decided to open the restaurant anyway. After all "anyone can open a restaurant."

After spending most of their savings and working three months getting the restaurant ready to open, Billie and Louis opened "Billie's Classic Country Dining" during Thanksgiving week 1985. They both knew that they *had* to make a go of it. They had spent more than they had thought it would take to get the restaurant ready and had only eight hundred dollars left on opening day. But they figured that's okay; they still had Louis' income from the trucking company.

Serving lunch and supper six days a week (the restaurant was closed on Mondays) began to take its toll on both of them. With only two employees Billie was working sixteen-hour days and Louis was getting only four to five hours of sleep nightly between his job and the restaurant. But they needed Louis' paycheck. After being opened three and a half weeks Louis fell asleep on the way home from working in Atlanta and almost hit a car head-on just a couple of miles from home. Still this did not wake him up and he fought sleep just to make the next two miles to the house. The following day Louis gave notice at the truck line. His boss suggested that if his interest was no longer with the trucking company and was now with the restaurant maybe he should not work through the notice period. Louis agreed.

The following day when Billie asked Louis what time he had to be at work, Louis told her that he had good news and bad news. The good news was that he could spend all of his time helping her in the restaurant; the bad part was that there would be no more paychecks. They both knew this time that they had some rocky roads ahead of them. Over the next several months while the restaurant was struggling to make a profit, both of them learned that restaurant bills and employees get paid first. They learned that if anyone went without a paycheck it had to be the two of them. They learned that they could live at home without electricity for a few days, but the restaurant couldn't. The same went for gas and telephone.

Slowly the business began to show a profit. What had happened was that this small restaurant in Social Circle had begun to attract customers from Atlanta, some forty-five miles away. After being open for eighteen months, the 68 seats in the restaurant could no longer accommodate the business. There was no way to add on to the restaurant since there was no place to park any additional cars. A restaurant in Covington, ten miles from Social Circle, closed due to poor business. This restaurant had 220 seats. It had previously been a chain steakhouse and a family restaurant. In late April of 1987 Louis and Billie closed Billie's Classic Country Dining and opened Billie's Family Restaurant in Covington, Georgia. From the beginning, business was good. Although the Van Dykes lost a lot of their Atlanta customers who came for the small-town atmosphere and the setting of the old-country cottage, they had moved to an area with fifteen times the population of Social Circle. They had developed a reputation for excellent Southern cooking served buffet style and business was good.

The good fortune was short lived. The building that housed the restaurant was in very poor condition. Termite infestations closed the restaurant the first time the termites swarmed and ruined the food. When it rained, more than three-fourths of the dining room had to be closed due to a leaking roof. Utility bills were tremendous due to poor planning when the building was built. After eighteen months in a deteriorating facility with escalating costs, the Van Dykes closed Billie's Family Restaurant in Covington. All efforts to have the property owner maintain the roof and building had failed.

Several months prior to closing the Covington restaurant, the American Legion Post in Monroe, Georgia, had contacted Louis and Billie and asked them to operate the restaurant in the American Legion Hall, which had been originally established in the 1950s. The American Legion restaurant had fallen on hard times the past few years, and the current operator had decided not to renew the lease. The commander of the American Legion made an offer too attractive for Louis and Billie to refuse, and in September of 1987 they opened "Billie's at the American Legion." While Louis ran the day-to-day operations at the Covington restaurant, Billie and her son, Chip, ran the restaurant in Monroe. When they closed the Covington restaurant, Louis joined Billie in their Monroe restaurant and ran the kitchen as head cook while Billie handled the dining room.

What had been a foundering restaurant, serving thirty to thirty-five meals at lunch Monday thru Friday and 50 to 60 people on Sundays, was soon serving 200 to 250 people for weekday lunch and up to 500 people on Sundays. At nights and on weekends the facility stayed busy with banquets, parties, wedding receptions, and other catered events. It was during this time that the Blue Willow dream began to come true.

THE BLUE WILLOW DREAM

From the time that the Van Dykes moved from the crowded confines of Atlanta to their land outside of Social Circle, they had admired the grand, yet dilapidated, old mansion in Social Circle that had been known as the Bertha Upshaw Club House. A few of the old homes in Social Circle were in varying degrees of disrepair, but the mansion that was to eventually become the Blue Willow Inn Restaurant was abandoned and neglected. After inquiring among the locals, they discovered that the mansion had at one time been the center of civic and cultural activity in Social Circle but had fallen on hard times in the late 1960s and became the subject of a lawsuit until 1985, when the Georgia Supreme Court ruled that the property was to revert to the estate of the original owners, the Upshaw family.

While the Van Dykes were struggling to make their first restaurant a success, Billie and Louis dreamed of one day owning this grand old mansion just three blocks away. Of course they knew this was just a dream. While struggling to keep the doors open in the small cottage restaurant, how could they possibly ever have the means to purchase and restore such a place.

One day during lunch at the restaurant Billie met the Rev. and Mrs. Homer Harvey. The Harveys began telling Billie how much they enjoyed their lunch and that they would soon become regular customers. Homer Harvey, a Church of God minister, then told Billie that he had just purchased the Bertha Upshaw Club House and was starting the Social Circle Church of God in the old mansion. Billie said, "You mean the old Bertha Upshaw clubhouse I've always wanted?" Homer Harvey was not sure it was the same house, but Billie knew that it was.

Even after closing the restaurant in Social Circle, moving to Covington, and opening the restaurant in Monroe, Billie still loved and dreamed of one day owning the old mansion, all the time knowing it was just was a dream. Soon Louis and Billie began attending fund-raising dinners and yard sales at the church just to see the inside. Each time Billie was in the old mansion she would mentally lay out the house for a restaurant and fancy herself opening the massive front door to customers and guests.

While Billie was at the church/mansion for a spaghetti supper hosted by the ladies of the church, Pastor Harvey mentioned to her that the house would make a nice restaurant.

"Don't tease me!" Billie exclaimed.

"We're not teasing," replied Pastor Harvey. "We wanted to restore this old house, but we're just getting too old. We plan to sell the mansion when we finish the new church on the back of the property."

Billie was elated. She could barely wait until Louis got home from the restaurant in Monroe so she could share the news.

"Pastor Harvey is selling the mansion, and he said we could purchase it for a restaurant!" Billie excitedly told Louis as he pulled into their driveway at home. Louis told Billie not to tease him and told her, "We can't afford it anyway. What would we do for money?"

Billie was not giving up this easily. She insisted that Louis go to the bank and try to borrow the money. Over Louis' protests that they had just finally finished paying off the losses at the Covington restaurant and had very little money, she insisted that he at least ask.

Several days later as Billie was mentally placing tables, furnishings, and the kitchen in the mansion, Louis told her that he had gone to the bank and asked about financing to purchase the mansion. Pastor Harvey was asking around $200,000 for the property, and this is what Louis told the bank. Louis shared the bad news with Billie. The banker had said "You want to do what?! With our money?! Where? You must be kidding! You'll never serve enough meals in Social Circle to pay for the purchase, much less the repairs!" Louis took this as a "No."

That was 1990. Louis and Billie had struggled, made mistakes, paid off losses, and still had a dream. The restaurant at the American Legion in Monroe was successful, but the dining room was a big lunch-room-style dining hall. They both missed the charm and decor of their first restaurant, the small cottage in Social Circle. Both of them wanted a permanent location in an old house and both of them wanted the old mansion in Social Circle. If there were a way, they would find it.

When Billie told Pastor Harvey that the bank had turned Louis down flat, he told her that he might consider financing the purchase. When she told him that they did not have the money to make a down payment on a purchase that size, Pastor Harvey told her that he would finance 100 percent of the purchase price. Billie was ecstatic!

As soon as she saw Louis, she shared the good news. Louis was hesitant. Although the Harveys had partially restored the old mansion, a lot of money was needed to finish the repairs, add a kitchen, rewire, decorate, and so forth. The whole project seemed overwhelming.

"Restorations like this take tens of thousands of dollars," Louis thought out loud.

"We can do it!" Billie countered. "We'll take extra parties and banquets at the restaurant in Monroe and we'll do more catering. With the extra money we can buy supplies and materials and do the work ourselves."

They both agreed that this was an almost overwhelming project without bank financing. It was time for prayer.

When Louis had first opened the restaurant in Covington, everything was going great. Money was coming in and for the first time since opening the first restaurant, the Van Dykes had a cash reserve. Louis wanted more. He wanted to get rich and open more restaurants. He had taken the business out of God's care and decided he could do it on his own.

Louis said, "What a fool I was. Since the 1970s I have depended on the Lord for guidance and leading. I walked away from him and decided I would get rich. And I learned a lesson from God. If it could go wrong at the Covington restaurant, it would, and did, go wrong."

After closing the restaurant in Covington, Louis realized that he had just learned a hard lesson. He lost his desire to "get rich," and as a result of this he would not make a decision about the old mansion until he had prayed and sought God. For Billie this was part of her daily life. For Louis it was part of a roller coaster ride with God.

Louis and Billie both agreed that they needed a word from the Lord before signing the papers to purchase the mansion. They both went to prayer. The day before they were to sign the papers, there was still no answer to their prayers. After agreeing together that they would not pursue their "dream," Louis began to read the Bible. The Lord answered the prayer. The scripture was Isaiah 44: 8 and 9 (KJV).

Fear ye not, neither be afraid: have I not told thee from that time, and have declared it? ye are even my witnesses. Is there a God beside me? Yea, there is no God; I know not any. They that make a graven image are all of them vanity; and their delectable things shall not profit; and they are their own witnesses; they see not, nor know; that they may be ashamed.

After sharing this with Billie, they both agreed that this was a powerful word from the Lord and that they had best not make the new restaurant their god. Louis did not want to learn the same lesson twice.

In the summer of 1990 Louis and Billie signed the papers to purchase their dream. They decided to place their home up for sale in order to help finance the renovations. Almost overnight they had a signed contract to sell their house. But the Gulf War buildup had just begun and the housing market collapsed. The Van Dykes were still confident that the house would sell and the money could be used for renovations. The mansion was large enough that they would live on the second floor, and the first floor would be the restaurant.

After getting the proper zoning to operate a restaurant in the house, the hard work started. Every free hour for ten months was spent scraping paint, wiring, plumbing, finishing floors, and so forth. With the help of family and friends and several all-nighters, the Blue Willow Inn Restaurant opened on Thanksgiving Day 1991. And what a day it was!

The used kitchen equipment that had been purchased to save money rebelled at cooking on Thanksgiving Day. If it could go wrong, it did. With a lot of improvising and patching they got through the first day. Both Louis and Billie still advise against opening a new restaurant on Thanksgiving Day.

With the opening of the Blue Willow Inn Restaurant behind them, Louis and Billie concentrated on finishing the renovations of the Blue Willow Inn and operating both restaurants. They knew that they only had a few months left on the lease on the American Legion restaurant in Monroe. They also knew that the lease would not be renewed because the new officers of the American Legion in Monroe had indicated that they wanted the restaurant closed so the building could be turned into a dance hall and bingo parlor. Although there was a year left on the lease, the Van Dykes agreed to terminate the lease six months early after experiencing three arson attempts and a break-in with acid poured into their cash register and lamp oil used to contaminate all of the food. By the time the Monroe restaurant was closed in June of 1992, the Blue Willow Inn Restaurant had become profitable. But there had been some rough times getting to that point.

By January 1992, the Van Dykes were experiencing serious financial problems. While the restaurant in Monroe was operating profitably (in spite of the break-ins and fires), the Blue Willow had a mountain of start-up bills that remained unpaid. With the collapse of the housing market as a result of the Gulf War buildup, their house never sold. Their lawyer and accountant both told them that they should consider bankruptcy. Louis and Billie had been in tight spots before and did not consider bankruptcy an option. Somehow they would make it all work.

On March 9 Louis got some particularly bad news. That night as he and Billie exhaustedly prepared to get some sleep, Louis roared, "Life's lousy! I wish I were dead." As Louis slept, Billie stayed awake all night praying. She prayed, saying that she and Louis had worked hard and were trying to follow the Lord's will. She told the Lord that she had prayed for miracles for others before, but had never prayed for a miracle for herself.

"But," she told the Lord, "we need a miracle."

The following evening a writer, Marty Godbey, was dining at the Blue Willow and asked to meet the owners. After she introduced herself to Billie and Louis, she told them that she was writing a book titled *Dining in Historic Georgia*. She told them that she had previously dined at the Blue Willow Inn and had decided to include the Blue Willow in her book. Billie and Louis were both very pleased and proud to be part of a few select restaurants that would be featured in the book. Louis thought to himself that this was nice, but by the time the book came out the Blue Willow Inn might be history. (As it turns out the Blue Willow remained open and was featured on the cover of the book.)

On the following day, Wednesday, March 11, while Louis was cooking, a friend and customer came to the kitchen with good news. "Lewis Grizzard is dining with you today," he exclaimed.

Louis was excited. He had recently read one of Mr. Grizzard's columns criticizing an un-named Southern restaurant in Atlanta that, in addition to other misdeeds with Southern cooking, had served mashed potatoes out of a box. Having read all of Lewis Grizzard's books, Louis knew that he was always searching for just the right restaurant with authentic Southern cooking. When Louis went to the dining room to welcome Mr. Grizzard to the Blue Willow Inn, he found him sitting in front of a heaping plate of food. Mr. Grizzard ate as he talked with Louis, heaping praises on the food, particularly the fried green tomatoes. Remembering Mr. Grizzard's comments about mashed potatoes from a box, Louis moaned to himself that he did not have mashed potatoes on the buffet line that day. Then he remembered that he had a bowl of leftover mashed potatoes from the day before. After the leftover mashed potatoes were quickly heated, they were served to Mr. Grizzard. When Mr. Grizzard had finished his lunch he complimented the food and said, "Watch the paper."

Louis could barely contain himself. Some of the customers and most of the staff thought he had lost his mind as he jumped, hooted, hollered, and laughed for the next few minutes. On the following Friday in the Atlanta paper, Lewis Grizzard's column featured the Blue Willow Inn Restaurant and its fried green tomatoes. Mr. Grizzard ended his column with the following:

I am a connoisseur of authentic Southern cooking, which is getting more and more difficult to locate. Half the time you think you've stumbled upon it, they serve mashed potatoes that come out of a box, but not at the Blue Willow Inn in Social Circle. If I gave ratings for Southern cooking, I'd have to give the Blue Willow my absolute highest mark—five bowls of turnip greens. Every dish was authentic and delicious, including the banana pudding I had for dessert. I shall return.

Return he didn't. Shortly after writing the column he began to suffer problems with his heart. The Van Dykes enclosed and extended one of the side porches to expand the seating. Although Mr. Grizzard gave permission to name the new room the "Lewis Grizzard Room" in his honor, his health did not allow him to return to dedicate the room.

The Grizzard column was syndicated in almost three hundred newspapers throughout the country. The Van Dykes got phone calls, visitors, and letters from all over the country as a result of the column. And that weekend they made their first profit since opening the Blue Willow Inn Restaurant. Lewis Grizzard may have never known it, but he was their miracle. All of the start-up bills were paid off in just a few weeks.

Since that time the Blue Willow Inn Restaurant and the Van Dykes have been featured in such magazines as *Southern Living, Gourmet, A Taste of Home,* and on Cable News Network's travel show. In June of 1996 *Guideposts* magazine featured Billie in a story titled "The Inn of My Dreams." In the spring of 1996 the Blue Willow Inn Restaurant was awarded the *Southern Living Magazine* Reader's Choice Award for being voted the best small-town restaurant in the South. The restaurant was voted best in the South for six years in a row until *Southern Living* retired the category. In 2003 and 2004 the Blue Willow Inn Restaurant was featured on *USA Today*'s "Top 10" lists of restaurants. *Gourmet* magazine included the Blue Willow Inn in its 2004 guide of America's top 100 restaurants worth the drive. In 2004, the restaurant was featured in the Food Network's Top 5 show as one of the top five "Bodacious Buffets" in America.

Having served guests from all 50 states and over 180 countries, the Blue Willow Inn Restaurant has established itself as one of the South's premier Southern restaurants—all as a result of a dream, hard work, a miracle, and the blessings of the Lord.

HOLIDAYS AND SPECIAL OCCASIONS IN THE SOUTH

New Years' Day

New Years' Day dinner is traditionally served at noon in the South. To start the year off right, specific dishes must be served to insure prosperity, good health, and good luck. New Years' dinner is a family affair that both ends the holiday season and starts the New Year. A typical menu includes:

Waldorf Salad (apple salad)

Pork Roast or Baked Ham (for good health)

Greens, Turnip or Collard (for prosperity)

Black-eyed Peas with Ham (for good luck), also known as Hoppin' John

Candied Yams or Sweet Potato Soufflé

Buttered Rice

Corn Pudding

Cornbread and Biscuits

Desserts

Sweetened Iced Tea

Easter Sunday

In the South, Easter Sunday is considered the most holy religious day of the year. Churches are filled to overflowing and everyone is adorned with their new spring outfits. Easter dinner is a family occasion celebrated after church. In many parts of the country lamb is the main meat of Easter dinner. However, few southerners eat lamb; instead ham is their choice. A typical southern Easter dinner includes:

Salad (mixed greens or congealed salad)	*Macaroni & Cheese*
Baked Ham	*Corn on the Cob*
Butter Peas	*Biscuits and Cornbread*
Italian cut Green Beans with New Potatoes	*Desserts*
Baked Sweet Potatoes	*Sweetened Iced Tea*

Mother's Day

Mother's Day is the single busiest day of the year for restaurants across America. This is the day to give mothers a break from cooking dinner. Menus for Mother's Day should be planned with considerations given to the mother's favorite dishes. The secret to a successful Mother's Day is for the family to do the cooking. In the South, a sample Mother's Day menu is:

Garden Salad

Orange Pecan Glazed Chicken with Wild Rice or Chicken Devine

Roasted New Potatoes

Steamed Buttered Squash or Squash Casserole

Fresh Buttered Carrots

Green Bean Amandine

Broccoli Casserole

Cornbread and Biscuits

Desserts

Sweetened Iced Tea

Father's Day

Father's Day, like Mother's Day, is a day for families to reminisce and celebrate. The menu should be planned around Dad's favorite dishes. A menu that would satisfy the palate of most dads is:

Potato Salad	*Baked Beans*
BBQ Pork Ribs	*Corn on the Cob*
Fried Chicken	*Texas Toast*
Macaroni & Cheese	*Desserts*
Italian-cut Green Beans	*Sweetened Iced Tea*
	(followed by an afternoon nap)

Fourth of July

Our celebration of Independence Day is a time for gathering with family and friends with a traditional cookout. Everyone brings a dish and everyone helps with the preparation and cooking. Bring the lawn chairs and food and enjoy! Typical dishes in a southern Fourth of July cookout include:

Potato Salad	*Baked Beans*
Cole Slaw	*Deviled Eggs*
Watermelon	*Macaroni & Cheese*
BBQ Ribs	*Scalloped Potatoes*
BBQ Chicken	*White Bread*
Grilled Fish	*Desserts*
Brunswick Stew	*Sweetened Iced Tea*
Corn on the Cob	*Lemonade*

Thanksgiving Dinner

Thanksgiving dinner in the South rivals Christmas as one of the biggest family days of the year. Oftentimes couples will have Thanksgiving dinner with one spouse's family and Christmas dinner with the other spouse's family. Several days are spent planning and preparing for the feast. The host usually prepares the meats and guests often bring the side dishes and desserts. In the South, a Thanksgiving feast often includes:

Blueberry Congealed Salad	*Sweet Potato Soufflé or Candied Yams*
Ambrosia	*Butter Beans or Butter Peas*
Waldorf Salad	*Collard Greens*
Roast Turkey	*Macaroni & Cheese*
Baked Ham	*Corn Pudding*
Cornbread Dressing with Giblet Gravy	*Yeast Rolls*
Italian-cut Green Beans with New Potatoes	*Desserts such as cakes, pies*
Buttered Rice	*(coconut cream), and puddings*
Black-eyed Peas	*Sweetened Iced Tea*

Christmas Dinner

It goes without saying that Christmas Day is the biggest family day of the year. Family, fellowship, gifts, and good food all make Christ's birthday the largest celebration day of the year also. Families in the South celebrate Christmas with different menus according to their family traditions. However, the most popular Christmas menus are very similar to Thanksgiving menus in the South. A typical Christmas dinner could include:

Ambrosia

Blueberry Congealed Salad

Roast Beef and Gravy

Roast Turkey

Pork Tenderloin or Baked Ham

Cornbread Dressing with Giblet Gravy

Sweet Potato Soufflé

Creamed Potatoes

Collard Greens

Macaroni & Cheese

Butter Beans

Corn Casserole

Orange-glazed carrots

Yeast Rolls or Biscuits

*Desserts such as cakes, including fruit cake, pies,
    and Louis' Brownies to complement the ambrosia*

Sweetened Iced Tea

Appetizers

Cocktail is purely American both in the word and the mixture—an appetizer. At one time it was made almost entirely of liquors. Today, appetizers can comprise any number of dishes at the hostess's discretion. The use of fruits, vegetables, and meats is a delight to the palate whether it is prior to a dinner party or a casual gathering.

Asparagus Sandwiches

1   loaf sandwich bread
1   (15-ounce) can asparagus, drained and mashed
1   tablespoon mayonnaise
½   cup chopped pecans
¼   cup chopped onion
    Dash of soy sauce
    Dash of garlic salt
    Dash of seasoned salt
1   (8-ounce) package cream cheese, softened
    Lemon pepper (optional)

Cut the crust from the bread and cut the bread into rounds or shapes with a cookie cutter. In a medium-size mixing bowl mix the asparagus, mayonnaise, pecans, onion, soy sauce, garlic salt, seasoned salt, and cream cheese. Add the lemon pepper if desired and mix all together until well blended and smooth. Spread on the sandwich rounds and serve on a pretty platter.

YIELD: 15 TO 20 SANDWICHES

Bacon-Chestnut Appetizers

15   slices quality bacon
1   cup whole water chestnuts (about 30)

Preheat the oven to 350°. Cut the bacon in half lengthwise and wrap each piece around a water chestnut. Secure with a toothpick. Place them on a cookie sheet.

Bake for 25 to 30 minutes, turning once. Drain on paper towels before serving.

YIELD: 30 SERVINGS

Bacon, Lettuce, and Tomato Dip

This dip is great for summer cookouts and celebrations, especially when tomatoes are garden fresh.

1   (8-ounce) package cream cheese, softened
½   cup ranch salad dressing
1   teaspoon granulated sugar
1   medium tomato, seeded and diced (about ¾ cup)
6   bacon slices, crisply cooked, drained, and chopped
½   cup finely chopped celery
2   tablespoons finely chopped onion
    Lettuce leaves
    Crackers

In a medium-size bowl combine the cream cheese, ranch dressing, and sugar. Mix well. Add the diced tomato, bacon, celery, and onion. Toss with a fork. Cover and refrigerate at least 3 hours (this will allow the flavors to blend). Line a small serving platter with the lettuce leaves. Fill with the dip. Serve with party crackers

YIELD: 2 CUPS

Cherie Powell
Newborn, Georgia

Bacon Roll-Ups

½ cup water

¼ cup (½ stick) butter

1½ cups herb-seasoned breadcrumbs

1 egg, lightly beaten

¼ pound hot or mild bulk pork sausage

⅔ pound bacon

Preheat the oven to 375°. In a saucepan heat the water over medium heat. Melt the butter in the water. Put the breadcrumbs in a large mixing bowl. Remove the saucepan from the heat and stir the mixture into the breadcrumbs. Add the egg and sausage to the bread-crumb mixture and blend thoroughly.

Place in the refrigerator and chill for 1 hour. Remove from the refrigerator and shape into balls the size of wal-nuts. Cut the bacon strips into thirds and wrap the sausage balls with the bacon, securing the bacon with a toothpick. Place the roll-ups on a cookie sheet with sides. Bake for 35 to 40 minutes, turning once. Drain on paper towels prior to serving. Serve hot.

YIELD: 3 DOZEN ROLL-UPS

Bacon-Tomato Cocktail Rounds

1 cup mayonnaise

1 tablespoon minced garlic

2 tablespoons finely chopped onion

1 teaspoon salt

12 plum or Italian tomatoes

36 thin slices fresh white bread

¼ pound chopped cooked bacon

¼ cup finely chopped scallions

In a small bowl combine the mayonnaise, garlic, onion, and salt. Chill. Cut the tops off the tomatoes. Slice lengthwise into thin slices. Cut the bread into rounds with a biscuit cutter or glass. Spread the bread with the mayonnaise mixture. Top with a tomato slice. Sprinkle with the bacon and then the scallions.

YIELD: 36 ROUNDS

Cheese Ball

1 (8-ounce) jar soft cheddar cheese

1 (8-ounce) package cream cheese, softened

1 (8-ounce) package blue cheese

1 rounded teaspoon dry onion flakes, soaked in a little water

1 teaspoon Worcestershire sauce

1 bunch parsley, washed and chopped

1 cup finely chopped pecans

In a medium-size mixing bowl mix the cheddar cheese, cream cheese, blue cheese, onion flakes, and Worcestershire sauce together with a mixer and shape into a ball.

This mixture can be stored in the refrigerator for several weeks or can be frozen. When ready to serve, bring to room temperature and roll the ball in the chopped parsley and pecans. Place on a platter or cheese board and serve with crackers.

YIELD: 15 TO 20 SERVINGS

Cheese Cookies

This is a favorite recipe of Petra Broberg, who was a second grandmother to the Van Dyke children as they were growing up. Cheese cookies or cheese straws are a "must" at any southern special occasion such as teas, receptions, baby showers, or bridal showers.

3	cups all-purpose flour
½	cup chopped pecans
1	cup (2 sticks) butter
1	pound (16 ounces) longhorn or sharp cheddar cheese
	Dash of cayenne pepper
1	cup pecan halves

In a medium-size mixing bowl combine the flour, chopped pecans, butter, cheese, and pepper. Mix well. On a lightly floured surface shape the dough into a roll about the diameter of a quarter. Wrap the roll in plastic wrap, place in the refrigerator, and chill.

Preheat the oven to 350°. Remove the dough from the refrigerator. Slice and place the slices on an ungreased sheet pan about ⅛-inch apart. Place a pecan half in the center of each cookie. Bake for 10 to 15 minutes. Do not brown.

Hint: This dough can be put in a cookie press and used for cheese sticks. The baked cookies or cheese sticks freeze well. Place them in a tight tin with wax paper between each layer.

YIELD: 125 BITE-SIZE COOKIES

Cheese Mold

This cheese mold serves well as an appetizer with assorted crackers before a meal or as one of several hors d'oeuvres at a reception. It can be made ahead and frozen and complements both alcoholic and non-alcoholic beverages.

1½	pounds (24 ounces) grated sharp cheddar cheese
3	(8-ounce) packages cream cheese, softened
1	large onion, finely chopped
3	drops Tabasco
1	cup finely chopped pecans
1	cup strawberry preserves

Allow the cheddar cheese and cream cheese to come to room temperature. In a large mixing bowl combine the cheddar cheese, cream cheese, chopped onions, Tabasco, and chopped pecans. Work the ingredients together using your hands (the heat from your hands should soften the cheeses and allow them to blend together). Once thoroughly mixed, the mixture can then be pressed into a mold.

Either lightly grease the mold or cover the inside of the mold with plastic wrap. When pressing the mixture into the mold, be sure to press into all of the cavities.

Chill 2 to 3 hours before serving or you can freeze for later use. When you are ready to serve, remove from the mold, place on a platter, and pour the desired amount of strawberry preserves over the top. Also, the sides of the cheese mold can be garnished with coarsely chopped pecans gently pressed into its sides.

If you have frozen the cheese mold, allow it to defrost and soften before serving.

Hint: Generally cheeses should be served at room temperature, about 70°, to bring out the flavors.

YIELD: 20 TO 25 SERVINGS

Chicken Bites with Sweet-Hot Tomato Chutney

2 skinless, boneless chicken breast halves, about 8 ounces each
¼ teaspoon lemon pepper seasoning
12 precooked bacon slices
½ cup hot mango chutney
½ cup salsa

Preheat the oven to 450°. Cut each chicken breast into 12 cubes. Sprinkle with the lemon pepper seasoning. Cut the bacon slices in half crosswise. Wrap a bacon piece around each chicken cube. Secure with wooden toothpicks. Arrange on a lightly greased rack in a broiler pan. Bake the cubes for 10 to 12 minutes or until the bacon is crisp.

Process the chutney and salsa together in a blender or food processor until smooth. Serve with the chicken bites.

YIELD: 6 TO 8 SERVINGS

Chocolate Chip Cheese Ball

This is a great recipe for those who like a "sweet" cheese ball.

1 (8-ounce) package cream cheese, softened
½ cup (1 stick) butter (no substitutes)
¼ teaspoon vanilla extract
¾ cup confectioners' sugar
2 tablespoons light brown sugar
¾ cup miniature semisweet chocolate chips
¾ cup finely chopped pecans
Graham crackers

In a mixing bowl beat the cream cheese, butter, and vanilla until fluffy. Gradually add both the confectioners' and light brown sugar and beat until combined. Stir in the chocolate chips. Cover and refrigerate for 2 hours. Place the cream cheese mixture on a large piece of plastic wrap. Shape into a ball. Refrigerate for at least 1 hour. Just before serving, roll the cheese ball in the pecans. Serve with the graham crackers (regular or chocolate).

YIELD: 15 TO 20 SERVINGS

Vivian Beasley
Monroe, Georgia
First Place Winner—Appetizers and Hors d'Oeuvre
Blue Willow Inn Restaurant Recipe Contest, 2004

Crab Dip

1   (8-ounce) can crabmeat, drained and flaked

1   (8-ounce) package cream cheese, softened

3   tablespoons mayonnaise

1   teaspoon Dijon mustard

¼   teaspoon salt

2   tablespoons dry white wine

Drain and flake the crabmeat. In the top of a double boiler over simmering water, combine the cream cheese, mayonnaise, mustard, and salt. Stir constantly until smooth and well blended. While stirring, gradually add the wine. Stir in the crabmeat until well mixed.

Serve hot in a chafing or fondue dish with crackers or toast points.

YIELD: 12 TO 15 SERVINGS

Cream Cheese and Pineapple Finger Sandwiches

I have served these finger sandwiches for years. They are a family favorite and are easy to make. My daughter now makes them when she entertains.

1   (8-ounce) package cream cheese, softened

1   (8-ounce) can crushed pineapple, drained

½   cup sugar

1   cup chopped pecans

1   loaf white sandwich bread

In a mixing bowl combine the softened cream cheese and pineapple. Add the sugar and pecans to this mixture. Trim the crust from the bread slices. Spread the cheese mixture on the bread slices and make into sandwiches. Place the sandwiches on a tray and cover with plastic wrap. Chill.

When you are ready to serve, cut the sandwiches into thin slices about 1 inch in width and place a on decorative tray.

Hint: Tea sandwiches should be made of bread that is at least 24 hours old and preferably from a sandwich loaf. This gives better slices since the grain is closer than in an ordinary loaf of bread. Brown, white, and sometimes nut breads are those that are generally used. Whatever bread is chosen, all the crust should be removed. Tea sandwiches can be cut in a variety of fancy shapes with various cutters. If cutters are used, keep them damp by dipping them in warm water so the slices will not be ragged around the edges.

YIELD: 20 TO 25 SERVINGS

Joyce Dina
Gainesville, Florida

Cream Puffs

1   cup water
½   cup (1 stick) margarine or butter
1   cup all-purpose or self-rising flour
4   eggs

Preheat the oven to 375°. In a saucepan heat the water and butter to a rolling boil. Bring the heat down to low and stir in the flour. Stir vigorously over low heat about 1 minute or until the mixture forms a ball. Remove from the heat. Add the eggs, one at a time, and continue beating until smooth. Drop the dough by the ¼ cupful 3 inches apart on an ungreased baking sheet. Bake for 35 to 40 minutes or until puffed and a golden color.

Cool the puffs away from any draft. Cut off the tops and pull out any filaments of soft dough. Carefully fill the puffs with a desired filling. Replace the tops. Dust with confectioners' sugar, if desired. Refrigerate until ready to use. These cream puffs may be filled with chicken salad, tuna salad, vanilla pudding, ice cream, or frosted with chocolate icing.

Hint: If smaller puffs are desired, drop the dough on an ungreased baking sheet by the rounded teaspoonful and bake only 25 to 30 minutes.

YIELD: 16 TO 18 PUFFS

Yvonne McMillan
Red Springs, North Carolina

Cucumber Party Sandwiches

Note the hint on page 42 concerning tea sandwiches.

1   to 2 loaves sandwich bread, crusts removed
2   to 3 tablespoons garlic & herb or ranch dry dressing mix
1   (8-ounce) package cream cheese, softened
4   to 6 tablespoons milk
2   large cucumbers, peeled and thinly sliced
     Paprika

Use a small biscuit cutter or a small glass to cut the bread into rounds the same diameter as the cucumber slices.

In a small mixing bowl blend the dressing mix and the cream cheese well. Add the milk to thin to a spreading consistency. Spread the bread rounds with a thin layer of the cream cheese mixture. Top the round with a cucumber slice and sprinkle lightly with paprika. Arrange on a pretty tray with lettuce and cherry tomatoes.

YIELD: 30 TO 60 ROUNDS

Double Oink Roll-Ups

It's no secret that pigs rule on southern menus. For breakfast, lunch, and supper; from streak o' lean to country ham; and from barbecue to Brunswick stew, pork is the meat of choice. That's a fact well reflected in these hors d'doeuvres, which combine a good mouthful of bacon and sausage in one piggy wallop!

1	cup (2 sticks) butter
½	cup water
1½	cups seasoned breadcrumbs
1	egg, lightly beaten
⅓	pound bulk mild or hot sausage
⅔	pound bacon strips

In a saucepan, melt the butter in the water over medium-high heat. Pour the breadcrumbs into a bowl. Remove from the heat and stir into the breadcrumbs. Add the egg and sausage and blend thoroughly. Chill for 1 hour in the refrigerator.

Preheat the oven to 375°. Remove the mixture from the refrigerator and form into pecan-size balls. Cut the bacon strips into thirds and wrap around the balls, securing each with a wooden toothpick. Place them on a shallow baking pan and bake for 35 to 40 minutes, turning once. Drain on paper towels before serving.

YIELD: ABOUT 30 ROLL-UPS

Dried Beef Dip

2	(8-ounce) packages cream cheese, softened
1	(8-ounce) container soft cream cheese
½	(16-ounce) bottle ranch-style dressing
1	small onion, grated
2	(2.25-ounce) jars chopped dried beef
1	head cabbage
	Assorted crackers
	Chopped pecans (optional)

In a medium-size mixing bowl beat the softened cream cheeses, ranch dressing, and onion until blended. Stir in the chopped beef. Serve in a hollowed head of cabbage with the crackers. Sprinkle with the pecans, if desired.

YIELD: 4 CUPS

Famous Tomato Sandwiches

This recipe was printed in Southern Living *magazine some ten years ago. These are pretty sandwiches when cut with seasonal cookie cutters. It's a great way to serve a tomato sandwich at church luncheons or showers. This is a different way to enjoy a southern favorite.*

2	large ripe tomatoes, peeled
1	large white onion
16	slices white sandwich bread
¼	cup mayonnaise

1   tablespoon mustard
     Salt and pepper

Slice the tomatoes and onion and layer them in a plastic container. Cover and refrigerate for 8 hours. Cut the bread into circles (I use a pineapple can). Spread each slice generously with a mixture of mayonnaise and mustard. Discard the onion, drain the tomatoes, and place one slice of tomato on a bread round. Sprinkle generously with salt and pepper to taste. Top with another bread round. When sandwiches are complete, place in a pan or tray and cover with slightly damp paper towels and plastic wrap. Refrigerate 1 to 2 hours before serving.

YIELD: ABOUT 15 SERVINGS

Robin Smith
Buchanan, Georgia

Flamingo Floyd's Spinach Dip

This recipe came from the kitchen of Columba Bush, the first lady of Florida. She notes that it is delicious when served with different colorful vegetables, corn chips, or a nice crusty bread.

1   (10-ounce) box frozen chopped spinach, thawed
1   (8-ounce) package cream cheese, softened
2   cups shredded cheddar cheese
1   medium tomato, chopped
1   medium onion, chopped

In a large microwavable bowl place the thawed spinach, cream cheese, cheddar cheese, tomato, and onion. Microwave for 2 to 3 minutes until the cheeses are softened. Remove from the microwave and stir. Return to the microwave and heat until the cheeses are melted. Remove and stir the ingredients until they are well mixed.

YIELD: ABOUT 6 CUPS

Fruit Cheese Ball

2   (8-ounce) packages cream cheese, softened
1   (8-ounce) can crushed pineapple, drained
1   small bell pepper, finely chopped
1   small onion, finely chopped
1   cup chopped nuts

In a mixing bowl combine the cream cheese, pineapple, pepper, and onion. Mix until all are well blended. Cover and refrigerate to chill. Before serving, form the mixture into a ball and roll in the nuts. Serve with crackers.

YIELD: 15 TO 20 SERVINGS

Chris Franks
Stone Mountain, Georgia

Fruit Dip

This is delicious with apples. It can be doubled for more people. It is really good with all fruits.

4	Skor candy bars
1	(8-ounce) package cream cheese, softened
¾	cup packed light brown sugar
½	cup granulated sugar
1	teaspoon vanilla extract

Finely crush the candy bars. In a medium-size mixing bowl with a mixer, combine the candy bars, cream cheese, brown sugar, granulated sugar, and vanilla until thoroughly blended. Cover, place in the refrigerator, and chill overnight.

Hint: In testing we had difficulty finding Skor candy bars, so we substituted Heath candy bits. We used 2 (8-ounce) bags of the bits. The dip was delicious.

YIELD: ABOUT 2 CUPS

Elaine Harrison
Covington, Georgia

Cheeses should be served
at room temperature,
approximately 70 degrees.

Marshmallow Fruit Dip

Dipped strawberries are especially yummy.

1	(7-ounce) jar marshmallow crème
1	(8-ounce) package cream cheese, softened
1	(8-ounce) cup sour cream
1	(14-ounce) can sweetened condensed milk

In a blender combine the marshmallow crème, cream cheese, sour cream, and sweetened condensed milk until smooth. Chill for 1 hour.

YIELD: ABOUT 5 CUPS

Alma K. Smith
Foley, Alabama

Glorified Grapes

This is a very different recipe that Billie has often used when catering special events. In fact, when Louis was helping Billie make them for an event, Billie caught Louis eating almost as many as he prepared. Louis loves these, and you will love them too.

1	(10-ounce) package toasted almonds, pecans, or walnuts
1	(8-ounce) package cream cheese, softened
⅛	pound (2 ounces) Roquefort cheese
2	tablespoons heavy cream

1 pound seedless green or red grapes, washed and dried

Preheat the oven to 275°. Spread the nuts on a baking sheet. Bake until toasted. In a food processor or by hand, coarsely chop the toasted nuts. Spread them on wax paper or on a platter. In a small bowl, preferably with an electric mixer, combine the cream cheese, Roquefort cheese, and cream. Beat these ingredients until they are smooth. Roll the grapes in the cheese mixture and gently press the cheese mixture around each grape. Then roll the cheese-coated grapes in the toasted nuts. Place the grapes on a wax paper-lined tray. Chill until ready to use. Any extra cheese mix can be frozen and reused.

YIELD: 12 TO 13 SERVINGS

Granny Smith Apples with Caramel Fondue

12 to 15 (½-ounce) pieces caramel candy
1 (14-ounce) can sweetened condensed milk
8 Granny Smith apples

Place the candy in a medium-size microwave-safe bowl. Microwave the candy on medium heat until melted, stirring 2 to 3 times. Remove from the microwave oven and add the sweetened condensed milk. Stir to mix well. Microwave just long enough to blend the caramel and the condensed milk, stirring two or three times.

Wash and slice the apples and arrange them on a tray with a chafing or fondue dish in the center. Place the caramel mixture in the dish over medium heat.

Hint: If possible, the apples should be cut immediately prior to serving to prevent browning. If the apples are not served immediately, place them in cold water with a small amount of lemon juice. Caramel fondue can be prepared ahead, refrigerated, and reheated before serving.

YIELD: 20 TO 25 SERVINGS

Ham and Cheese Tarts

2 (3-ounce) packages cream cheese, softened
½ cup French onion dip
1 tablespoon milk
¼ teaspoon ground mustard
¼ teaspoon grated orange peel
½ cup finely chopped fully cooked ham
1 (12-ounce) can refrigerated buttermilk biscuits
¼ teaspoon paprika

Preheat the oven to 375°. In a small mixing bowl beat the cream cheese, onion dip, milk, mustard, and orange peel until well blended. Stir in the ham. Split each biscuit into thirds and press into lightly greased miniature muffin cups. Spoon 1 tablespoonful of the ham mixture into each cup. Sprinkle with the paprika. Bake for 12 to 17 minutes or until golden brown. Serve warm.

YIELD: 2½ DOZEN

Hot Artichoke Dip

2   (14-ounce) cans artichoke hearts
¾   plus ¾ cups freshly grated Parmesan cheese
1½   cups mayonnaise
     Dash of Worcestershire sauce
     Garlic powder
     Crackers

Preheat the oven to 350°. Chop and drain the artichoke hearts. Mix ¾ of the cup Parmesan cheese with the mayonnaise, Worcestershire sauce to taste, and garlic powder to taste. Place this mixture in a small casserole dish. Sprinkle the top with the remaining ¼ cup Parmesan cheese. Bake for 20 minutes or until bubbly. Serve with party crackers.

YIELD: 15 TO 20 SERVINGS

Becky Dally
Social Circle, Georgia

Hot Beef Dip

1   tablespoon margarine
¼   cup chopped onions
1   (8-ounce) package cream cheese, softened
1   cup milk
1   tablespoon chopped parsley
1   (4-ounce) can drained mushrooms
1   (2½-ounce) package chipped smoked beef
½   cup grated Parmesan cheese
     Potato chips

In a small skillet melt the margarine over low heat and sauté the onions. Add the cream cheese and milk and cook, stirring continuously over low heat until the cheese is melted. After the cheese is melted, add the parsley, mushrooms, beef, and Parmesan cheese. Heat thoroughly. Serve hot with chips.

YIELD: 20 TO 30 SERVINGS

Hot Shrimp Dip

This was always a hit when my mother, Louise Wainwright, entertained.

1½   (8-ounce) packages cream cheese
2   (4-ounce) cans shrimp, drained and shredded
     Dash of Tabasco
1   teaspoon paprika
     Juice of half a lemon
¾   cup half-and-half
     Juice of 1 garlic clove or ½ teaspoon garlic powder
3   tablespoons catsup
     Dash of cayenne pepper

In a saucepan over low heat combine the cream cheese, shrimp, Tabasco sauce, paprika, lemon juice, half-and-half, garlic, catsup, and cayenne pepper. Heat thoroughly until the cheese is completely melted and smooth. Serve in a chafing dish with crackers.

YIELD: 15 TO 20 SERVINGS

Nancy Posner
Social Circle, Georgia

Hot Spinach Artichoke Dip

This is a crowd-pleasing appetizer served by Peggy Hawkins, our events manager at Magnolia Hall, during many weddings and special events.

1	(14-ounce) can marinated artichoke hearts, drained
1	(10-ounce) package frozen spinach, thawed and drained
½	cup mayonnaise
1	cup freshly grated Parmesan cheese (not shredded)
1	cup Monterey Jack cheese
1	cup sour cream
1	(8-ounce) package cream cheese, softened
	Crackers

Preheat the oven to 350°. Chop the artichokes. In a medium-size mixing bowl blend the spinach, mayonnaise, Parmesan cheese, Monterey Jack cheese, sour cream, and cream cheese. Mix well. Gently stir in the artichoke hearts. Transfer the mixture to a 2-quart greased baking dish. Place in the oven and bake for 20 to 30 minutes until golden brown. Serve warm with party crackers.

Hint: Do not use shredded Parmesan cheese because it tends to make the dip greasy, and do not use mozzarella cheese as a substitute either because it tends to simply make the dip stringy.

YIELD: 25 TO 30 SERVINGS

Jalapeño and Pimiento Squares

These squares are great for an afternoon outdoor get-together. Be sure to accompany them with cold lemonade.

4	cups (16 ounces) shredded cheddar cheese
4	large eggs, beaten
3	canned jalapeño peppers, seeded and chopped
1	(12-ounce) jar pimientos, diced and drained
1	teaspoon minced onion

Preheat the oven to 350°. In a medium bowl combine the cheddar cheese, eggs, jalapeño peppers, pimientos, and onion. Stir until all the ingredients are well mixed. Spread the mixture into a lightly greased 8-inch square baking pan. Bake for 30 to 40 minutes. Let stand 10 minutes. Cut into squares and serve immediately.

YIELD: 3 DOZEN

Jezebel Sauce and Cream Cheese

Billie's friend Nancy brought this recipe to a garden club Christmas party and what a hit it was. She got the recipe from her brother-in-law's niece, Toni, of West Palm Beach, Florida, who served this appetizer at an outdoor dinner for out-of-town family at the wedding of her niece, Kelly. It was a big hit there too.

1   (18-ounce) jar pineapple preserves
1   (18-ounce) jar apple jelly
½   (1.37-ounce) jar dry mustard
1   (5-ounce) jar horseradish
1   teaspoon coarsely ground pepper
1   (8-ounce) package cream cheese
     Crackers

In a medium-size mixing bowl mix the pineapple preserves, apple jelly, mustard, horseradish, and pepper together. Chill. Place the cream cheese on a serving tray and pour the sauce over the cheese. Serve with the crackers.

YIELD: 20 TO 25 SERVINGS

Killer Sausage Balls

These have been holiday "musts" for about thirty years at our house. They never go to waste, and they make great "goody" gifts. My kids swear by them. Once they have baked, you can reheat them in the microwave for just a few seconds. These make Christmas morning snacks a cinch.

3   pounds hot sausage
     Salt and pepper
3   (10-ounce) packages extra sharp cheddar cheese, grated
6   cups baking mix
¼   teaspoon cayenne pepper

Cook the sausage, crumbling well, and season with a little salt and pepper to taste. While the sausage is cooking, put the grated cheese in a large bowl. Add the baking mix and sprinkle the cayenne pepper on top. Mix together. Preheat the oven to 375°.

Drain the sausage in a colander. When the sausage is cool enough to handle, squeeze it through lots of paper towels before adding it to the remainder of the ingredients. Add the warm sausage to the cheese mixture, fluffing through with a fork.

Roll the mixture into small balls about the size of a walnut. Place on a cookie sheet and bake until golden brown, 8 to 10 minutes. You can form the balls and freeze uncooked. When you like, take out a few to bake without thawing.

Hint: I use Wampler's sausage and add a little cayenne, black pepper, and salt. Hot sausage usually is not what it used to be.

YIELD: ABOUT 15 SERVINGS

Anne Galbraith
Knoxville, Tennessee

Lemon Tea Sandwiches

These are very unusual and delicious sandwiches for an afternoon tea. See hints for tea sandwiches on page 42.

3   egg yolks
½   cup sugar
2   tablespoons lemon juice
    Grated rind of 2 lemons
1   (8-ounce) package cream cheese, softened
1   cup finely chopped pecans
    Mayonnaise
20 thin slices whole-wheat bread

In a saucepan over medium heat cook the egg yolks, sugar, lemon juice, and lemon rind until thick, stirring constantly. Remove from the heat. Add the cream cheese and pecans. Stir until smooth. Refrigerate. Remove from the refrigerator 30 minutes before making the sandwiches.

Spread mayonnaise on the bread. Spread the filling on ten of the bread slices and top with the other ten bread slices. Trim the crusts from the sandwiches and cut into triangles, squares, or rectangles before serving. Place on pretty decorative platter or plate.

YIELD: 10 SERVINGS

Olive Spread Tea Sandwiches

1   (7.5-ounce) jar pimiento-stuffed olives, drained and chopped
½   small onion, diced
2   hard-cooked eggs, chopped
1   cup chopped toasted pecans
1   cup mayonnaise
36 slices day-old white bread

In a large mixing bowl, stir together the olives, onion, eggs, pecans, and mayonnaise. Cover and chill for 1 hour. Trim the crusts from the bread. Spread 18 of the slices with the olive mixture. Top with the remaining 18 slices. Cut each sandwich into triangles or squares. The bread can be cut with decorative cookie cutters and then spread with the olive mixture.

YIELD: 18 SERVINGS

Oyster Dip

2   (8-ounce) packages cream cheese, softened
1   teaspoon Worcestershire sauce
2   teaspoons lemon juice
1   cup sour cream
1   (3½-ounce) can smoked oysters

In a medium bowl blend the cream cheese, Worcestershire sauce, lemon juice, and sour cream. Mix well. Combine this mixture with the oysters. Serve with chips.

YIELD: ABOUT 8 CUPS

Picadillo with Capers

This dip is a family favorite. It can be served with chips as an appetizer or over rice as a main dish.

½   cup olive oil
2   pounds lean ground beef
1   small onion, finely chopped
½   medium green bell pepper, finely chopped
1   (14.5-ounce) can diced tomatoes
1   garlic clove, minced
1   (3¼-ounce) jar capers
1   bay leaf
1   teaspoon dried oregano
8   pimiento stuffed olives
2   tablespoons wine vinegar
3   tablespoons tomato sauce
¼   cup burgundy wine
2   to 3 drops hot sauce
½   teaspoon brown sugar
    Dash of nutmeg
½   cup water
    Salt (optional)

In a large covered skillet, heat the oil over medium heat and brown the ground beef. In a small mixing bowl, combine the onion, pepper, tomatoes, garlic, capers, bay leaf, and oregano. Add to the meat in the skillet. Mix well. Cook for 10 minutes. Cut the olives into thin rounds. Add to the meat. Add the vinegar, tomato sauce, wine, hot sauce, sugar, and nutmeg to the meat. Stir well and cook for 5 minutes uncovered. Add the water and mix well. Correct the seasonings and add salt if needed. Turn the heat to low, cover, and cook for 30 minutes or until most of the liquid is absorbed. Cook uncovered until the liquid evaporates. Serve with corn chips or nacho chips.

YIELD: 25 TO 30 SERVINGS

Salmon Ball

1   (14.75-ounce) can salmon
1   (8-ounce) package cream cheese, softened
2   tablespoons lemon juice
3½ teaspoons grated onion
2½ teaspoons horseradish
¾   teaspoon salt
    Dash of Worcestershire sauce
    Cayenne pepper
¼   teaspoon liquid smoke
¾   cup chopped pecans
3   tablespoons minced fresh parsley

Drain the salmon, remove the bones, and flake. In a small bowl, beat the cream cheese. Blend in the lemon juice, onion, horseradish, salt, Worcestershire sauce, cayenne pepper to taste, and liquid smoke. When well blended, gently stir in the flaked salmon. Shape into a ball and chill. When ready to serve, combine the pecans and parsley. Roll the salmon ball in this mixture until well coated. Place on a pretty dish and serve with crackers.

YIELD: 20 TO 25 SERVINGS

Sausage Balls in Cheese Pastry

These sausage balls can be prepared ahead and frozen. Simply reheat on low heat in the oven.

1	pound (16 ounces) mild or hot bulk pork sausage
¾	cup dry breadcrumbs
⅓	cup chicken broth
⅛	teaspoon ground nutmeg
¼	teaspoon poultry seasoning
1½	cups all-purpose flour
¼	teaspoon salt
1	teaspoon paprika
2	cups shredded sharp cheddar cheese
½	cup (1 stick) butter, softened

Preheat the oven to 300°. In a medium-size mixing bowl combine the sausage, breadcrumbs, chicken broth, nutmeg, and poultry seasoning. Mix thoroughly. Shape the sausage mixture into 1-inch balls. Place them on a baking pan and bake until brown. Drain on paper towels and allow to slightly cool.

Raise the oven heat to 350°. In a medium bowl combine the flour, salt, paprika, and cheese. Mix well. Cut in the butter with a pastry blender. Mix with your hands until smooth. Shape about 1 tablespoon of dough around each sausage ball, completely covering the ball. Place on a greased baking pan and bake for 15 to 20 minutes or until golden brown.

YIELD: 4 DOZEN

Shrimp Dip

This recipe was sent to us by the first lady of Florida, Columba Bush. It is the favorite snack dip of Governor Jeb Bush, who says there is nothing better after a long day than relaxing with the family. Hopefully your family will enjoy this recipe as much as the Bush family.

1	(8-ounce) container sour cream
1	(8-ounce) package cream cheese, softened
½	cup chopped celery
½	cup chopped onion
	Juice of 1 lemon
	Cayenne pepper
	Salt and pepper
1	(4½-ounce) can shrimp, drained

In a medium-size bowl blend the sour cream and cream cheese until smooth. Fold in the celery and the onion. Add the lemon juice. Add the cayenne pepper, salt, and pepper to taste. Mash the shrimp and add them to the mixture. Cover and refrigerate for several hours before serving. Serve with crackers or chips of your choice. This recipe can be prepared two days in advance.

YIELD: 4 CUPS

Shrimp Mold

This mold can be made a day ahead to enhance the seasoned flavor and then served with an assortment of crackers. It also prevents the rush of preparation just before the party is to begin.

2   (3-ounce) packages unflavored gelatin
½   cup water
1   pound cooked shrimp
2   cups mayonnaise
1   small onion, grated
2   tablespoons horseradish
3   to 4 drops red food coloring to make mixture light pink
     Juice of 1 lemon

Sprinkle the gelatin in the water and place it in the top of a double boiler over simmering water to dissolve. When the gelatin has dissolved, remove it from the heat. Add the shrimp, mayonnaise, grated onion, horseradish, food coloring, and lemon juice. Pour the mixture into a mold. Place in the refrigerator and chill for 2 to 3 hours. Remove from the mold to serve. Turn it out on an attractive platter and serve with crackers.

YIELD: 20 TO 25 SERVINGS

Shrimp Wrapped in Bacon

This recipe works best with jumbo and medium-size shrimp. Also flash-frozen shrimp rather than fresh shrimp can be used if preferred.

24   large shrimp
1   (16-ounce) bottle French dressing
12   strips bacon, halved

Peel, clean, and devein the shrimp. Marinate the shrimp in the French dressing for 2 hours. Preheat the oven to 350°. Wrap each shrimp with a half strip of bacon and secure with a toothpick. In a shallow baking pan bake the bacon-wrapped shrimp for 20 minutes, turning once. Drain on paper towels before serving.

YIELD: 12 SERVINGS

Spiced Olives

We have found that ladies are delighted with these at our teas. They are also a tasty side dish for hamburgers, barbeque, or hot dogs.

½   cup juice from olives
⅓   cup olive oil
1   tablespoon minced garlic
½   teaspoon crushed oregano
2   cups large pitted green olives

Combine the olive juice with the oil, garlic, and oregano. Place the olives in a container and cover with this mixture. *Must* refrigerate for 24 hours before serving.

YIELD: ABOUT 15 SERVINGS

Spinach Balls

2   (10-ounce) packages frozen chopped
    spinach
½   cup (1 stick) butter
5   eggs
1   tablespoon black pepper
½   cup grated Parmesan cheese
1   medium onion, chopped
1   (12-ounce) package chicken-flavor
    stuffing mix

Preheat the oven to 325°. Cook the spinach according to package directions and drain. In a small saucepan melt the butter over low heat. In a small mixing bowl, beat the eggs. Combine the spinach, melted butter, eggs, pepper, Parmesan cheese, onion, and stuffing mix and mix well. Form the mixture into walnut-size balls. Bake on a non-stick cookie sheet for 20 minutes.

YIELD: 15 SERVINGS

Spinach Dip

This is another delicious recipe served at Magnolia Hall by our events manager, Peggy Hawkins. We have used it prior to rehearsal parties, Christmas gatherings, and numerous other functions.

2   (10-ounce) packages frozen spinach,
    thawed and well drained
1   (8-ounce) package sour cream

1   cup mayonnaise
1   (8-ounce) can water chestnuts,
    chopped
1   onion, finely chopped

Drain the spinach until dry. In a medium-size mixing bowl mix the spinach, sour cream, mayonnaise, water chestnuts, and onion. Place the mixture in the refrigerator and chill overnight. Serve cold with crackers.

YIELD: 15 TO 20 SERVINGS

Spinach Roll-Ups

2   (10-ounce) packages frozen chopped
    spinach
1   cup mayonnaise
½   cup sour cream
1   (3-ounce) package cream cheese,
    softened
6   chopped green onions
⅓   cup crumbled cooked bacon
1   envelope ranch salad dressing mix
6   (8-inch) flour tortillas

In a colander thaw the spinach and squeeze it dry. In a bowl combine the mayonnaise, sour cream, cream cheese, onions, bacon, and salad dressing mix. Stir in the spinach until well blended. Spread over the tortillas and roll up tightly jelly-roll style. Wrap in plastic wrap. Refrigerate for at least 5 hours. With a serrated knife cut the roll into ½-inch slices. Refrigerate any leftovers.

YIELD: 12 TO 14 SERVINGS

Strawberries
with Fluffy Cream Cheese Dip

1	(8-ounce) package cream cheese, softened
2	cups confectioners' sugar
2	teaspoons vanilla extract
1	cup whipped cream
	Fresh whole strawberries

With an electric mixer at medium speed beat the cream cheese, sugar, and vanilla until fluffy. Fold in the whipped cream. Serve with the strawberries.

Hints: For a delightful citrus cream cheese dip add 1 tablespoon grated lime, lemon, or orange rind to the cream cheese mixture while beating. Another option is to add ¼ cup orange liqueur to the cream cheese mixture for an orange-flavored cream cheese, or 1/2 cup of orange marmalade could be beaten with the cream cheese mixture for another great flavor.

YIELD: 20 TO 25 SERVINGS

Strawberries
with Mint Yogurt Dip

A dip using yogurt or sour cream will have a thicker consistency if the excess liquid is removed from the yogurt or sour cream. This procedure takes a minimum of 24 hours, but the result is perfect for dipping fresh fruit.

Place a coffee filter in a fine wire-mesh strainer. Place the strainer over a small bowl. Spoon the yogurt or sour cream into the filter. Cover the strainer and the bowl with plastic wrap. Place in the refrigerator and chill for at least 24 hours. The yogurt or sour cream may be chilled for up to 72 hours. It gets thicker the longer it chills. The yogurt or sour cream in the filter is ready to use. Discard the liquid in the bowl.

1	quart (4 cups) thickened vanilla yogurt
1	tablespoon minced fresh mint
¼	teaspoon grated lemon rind
2	to 3 tablespoons honey
	Fresh mint sprig for garnish
	Fresh whole strawberries

In a small bowl whisk together the thickened yogurt, mint, lemon rind, and honey until well blended. Garnish with a spring of mint and serve with the strawberries.

YIELD: 4 CUPS

Stuffed Cherry Tomatoes

This is a colorful and tasty dish on its own but can also be used to accent any appetizer tray or to add to a finger-sandwich display.

24	cherry tomatoes
2	cups shrimp (page 109), tuna, or chicken salad (page 104)
5	to 7 green lettuce leaves

Wash the cherry tomatoes. Scoop out and discard the centers of the tomatoes. With a pastry bag or spoon, fill the centers of the tomatoes with your favorite prepared salad mixture. To serve, cover a serving dish or tray with fancy leaf lettuce.

Hint: If tomatoes will not stay upright, simply square off the bottom of the tomato by removing a small portion with a sharp knife.

YIELD: 12 SERVINGS

Sugared Nuts

Margaret Hale, who gave us the following recipe, is the daughter of Sanders Upshaw. She told us the story of Miss Bertha and the cloth measuring tape and also the delightful history of the two houses.

2½   cups pecan halves
½   cup water
1   cup granulated sugar
1   teaspoon ground cinnamon
1   teaspoon salt

Preheat the oven to 375°. Toast the pecans in the oven for 15 minutes. In a small saucepan cook the water, sugar, cinnamon, and salt to a soft boil stage without stirring. Add the pecans to the mixture and mix well. Pour onto waxed paper and separate the pecans immediately. Cool before serving.

Hint: Shelled and unshelled seeds and nuts keep best and longest when stored in the freezer. These can be used directly from the freezer. Unshelled nuts will crack more easily when frozen.

YIELD: 10 TO 15 SERVINGS

Sweet and Sour Meatballs

These are great toothpick snacks to make for a buffet or cocktail party, especially because they taste even better if made a day ahead, refrigerated overnight, and reheated. A word to the wise: Don't use fancy or exotic grape jelly in this recipe. Regular Welch's is all that is needed.

2   pounds ground beef
2   eggs, lightly beaten
½   cup breadcrumbs
½   cup water
      Salt
      Pepper
      Garlic powder
1   (12-ounce) bottle chili sauce
1   (16-ounce) jar grape jelly

Preheat the oven to 350°. In a medium-size mixing bowl combine the ground beef, eggs, breadcrumbs, and water. Add the salt, pepper, and garlic powder to taste. Mix well. Shape into walnut-size balls. Bake on an ungreased baking pan for 15 to 20 minutes or until lightly browned. Drain on paper towels.

In a small saucepan on low heat combine the chili sauce and grape jelly. Bring to a slow boil. Add the cooked meatballs and allow them to simmer for 8 to 10 minutes. Serve hot in a chafing dish.

YIELD: ABOUT 4 DOZEN

Tea Sandwiches

This is a fruity, elegant, and satisfying delight with afternoon tea or simply as a snack. The sandwiches can be cut into shapes to fit the occasion by using the appropriate cookie cutters. Be sure to cut the crusts off of each slice of bread. See the hints for tea sandwiches on page 42.

½ cup orange juice

1 tablespoon lemon juice

1 apple, cored and cut into small pieces

1 cup raisins

1 cup chopped pecans

   Dash of seasoned salt

   White bread, crust trimmed

In a food processor blend the orange juice, lemon juice, apple, raisins, pecans, and salt to a spreadable consistency. Do not process the mixture until completely smooth. Spread the mixture onto the trimmed bread and cut into desired shapes.

YIELD: 3 TO 4 CUPS

Tuna Salad Mini Sandwiches

I have been serving these appetizer sandwiches for years. They are always a hit.

1 (6-ounce) can solid white tuna in water, well drained

4 tablespoons mayonnaise

4 tablespoons apricot preserves

3 tablespoons raisins

2 tablespoons chopped onion

   Cocktail-size breads, dark or rye

In a medium-size mixing bowl combine the tuna, mayonnaise, apricot preserves, raisins, and onion. Mix thoroughly. Serve on cocktail-size breads.

YIELD: ABOUT 1½ CUPS

Joyce Dina
Gainesville, Florida

Virginia's Vidalia Onion Dip

Virginia is known for her fabulous parties and currently holds the title "best cook in the neighborhood." Her guests tend not to eat breakfast and lunch so they can "save room" for her enormous spreads. They especially look for her Vidalia Onion Dip and scoop it out by the spoonfuls.

2 large Vidalia onions, chopped

1 cup grated Parmesan cheese

½ cup mayonnaise

Preheat the oven to 350°. In a large bowl mix the onions, cheese, and mayonnaise. Bake in a 1-quart casserole dish until bubbly. Serve with Melba toast or Ritz crackers.

YIELD: 3½ CUPS

Watercress Dip or Spread

1   tablespoon lemon juice
1   tablespoon prepared horseradish
1   garlic clove, minced
½   teaspoon salt
¼   teaspoon white pepper
1   bunch (about 6 cups) trimmed watercress
4   green onions, quartered
1   (8-ounce) package cream cheese, cubed

In a food processor or blender combine the lemon juice, horseradish, garlic, salt, pepper, watercress, and green onions. Cover and process until finely chopped. Add the cream cheese and process until creamy and blended. Refrigerate until serving.

Hint: This can be used as a dip or spread. It can be used on tea sandwiches or spread on crackers. It is really pretty if put in a pastry bag and piped onto the cracker and garnished with watercress.

YIELD: 1¾ CUPS

Beverages & Punches

Punches are a great part of southern entertaining. They are mostly used for special occasions such as weddings, teas, showers, receptions, and on special holidays. A favorite punch or lemonade or sweet tea is often served at an outdoor cookout for the guests to sip on while the meal is grilling. Use your imagination. Use various flavors of ginger ale combined with different fruits or sherbets. One important note for beverages and punches is always to chill juices or sodas before adding them to beverage recipes. Your punch can be garnished not only with an attractive ice ring but also with edible flowers, such as snapdragons, pansies, or hibiscus.

Another tip: The way to answer guests' questions such as "Is the tea sweet or unsweet?" or "Does this have alcohol?" is with beverage labels. Make your own labels and attach them to the beverages, including water, by using a pretty ribbon to hold a paper label or small card. Use a pretty sticker to attach the ribbon to the label.

Bellini

1   (16-ounce) bottle chilled peach nectar
1   (750-milliliter) bottle chilled sparkling
    wine or 1 (2-liter) bottle ginger ale
    Fresh raspberries for garnish

Fill each of six champagne flutes with 2 ounces peach nectar and 4 ounces sparkling wine. Garnish with raspberries if desired. Serve immediately.

YIELD: 6 SERVINGS

Cherry Cordial Hot Chocolate

5½   cups milk
1½   cups half-and-half
1½   cups chocolate syrup
7   plus 1 tablespoons (½ cup) maraschino
     cherry juice
1¾   cups whipping cream
1   tablespoon confectioners' sugar
     Maraschino cherries with stems
     (optional)

In a Dutch oven over medium-low heat, stirring often, heat the milk, half-and half, chocolate syrup, and 7 tablespoons of the cherry juice. With an electric mixer at medium speed beat the whipping cream until foamy. Gradually add the confectioners' sugar and the remaining 1 tablespoon cherry juice. Continue beating until the cream forms soft peaks. Serve the cream with each cup of hot chocolate and top each serving with a cherry if desired.

YIELD: ABOUT 8 CUPS

Cherry Jubilee Splash

4   cups orange juice
4   cups chilled ginger ale
1   cup maraschino cherry juice
4   cups ice cubes
    Maraschino cherries with stems
    Fresh mint

In a large pitcher combine the orange juice, ginger ale, and cherry juice. Pour into eight tall glasses filled with the ice. Garnish with cherries and mint.

YIELD: 8 SERVINGS

Seeds and nuts, both shelled and unshelled, keep the best and the longest when stored in the freezer. Unshelled nuts crack more easily when frozen. Nuts and seeds can be used directly from the freezer.

Chocolate Iced Coffee

To keep the drink from diluting, freeze cubes of leftover coffee and half-and-half to use in place of ice.

3½	cups water
1	cup ground coffee
2	tablespoons granulated sugar
¾	teaspoon ground cinnamon
2	cups half-and half
⅓	cup chocolate syrup

In a saucepan over medium heat bring the water and coffee to a boil. Remove from the heat and let stand for 10 minutes. Pour the mixture through a fine wire-mesh strainer into a bowl, discarding the coffee grounds. Stir the sugar and cinnamon into the coffee until the sugar dissolves. Let the coffee cool. Stir in the half-and-half and the syrup. Chill for 2 hours. Serve over ice.

YIELD: 2 QUARTS

Classic Cola Float

This is "the" soda fountain drink of the South—especially Atlanta, Georgia. Everyone can talk with you about sitting at his or her favorite "soda shoppe" and sipping a cola float.

	Vanilla ice cream
	Cola soft drink
¼	teaspoon vanilla extract

Fill a tall glass about half full of scoops of vanilla ice cream. Pour your favorite cola soft drink over the ice cream. Gently stir in the vanilla extract. Serve immediately.

Hint: Add cherry syrup or a flavored soda to your float. You can even top the drink with a maraschino cherry.

YIELD: 1 SERVING

Coffee-House Slush

6	cups strong-brewed coffee
2	cups granulated sugar
2	quarts (8 cups) milk
1	quart (4 cups) half-and-half
4	teaspoons vanilla extract
	Whipped cream

In a 5-quart freezer container stir the coffee and sugar until the sugar is dissolved. Stir in the milk, half-and-half, and vanilla. Cover and freeze overnight. Before serving, thaw the mixture in the refrigerator for 8 to 10 hours or until slushy. When ready to serve, spoon into glasses and garnish with the whipped cream, or serve from a punch bowl and garnish.

YIELD: 5 QUARTS

Holiday or Spiced Tea

My great aunt, Clarine Ivey, would bring this tea for us to enjoy at the family Christmas get-together. We would sip on the tea while catching up on family news and waiting on the meal.

8   plus 2 cups water
2   (family-size) large tea bags
2   cups sugar
3   or 4 sticks cinnamon
1   teaspoon ground cloves
1   (46-ounce) can pineapple juice
1   (12-ounce) can frozen orange juice, prepared
1   (6-ounce) can frozen lemonade, prepared

In a large saucepan bring 8 cups of the water to a boil. Add the tea bags and allow them to steep for 5 minutes. Remove the tea bags. Add the sugar to the hot tea and stir until the sugar is completely dissolved. In a medium saucepan combine the remaining 2 cups water with the cinnamon and ground cloves. Bring this mixture to a boil, turn the heat down to low, and simmer for 10 minutes. Remove the cinnamon sticks and pour this mixture into the hot tea. Add the pineapple juice, orange juice, and lemonade. Mix well. Place in a pitcher and store in the refrigerator.

When you are ready to serve, put in mugs and heat in the microwave or heat desired amount in a saucepan on the stove and pour into mugs.

YIELD: ABOUT 5 QUARTS (20 CUPS)

Juanita Muse
·Calhoun, Georgia

Hot Chocolate

6   tablespoons unsweetened cocoa
     Pinch of salt
6   tablespoons granulated sugar
2½   cups milk
2½   cups light cream
     Pinch of ground cinnamon
½   teaspoon vanilla extract
     Whipped cream
     Fine orange zest

In a saucepan mix the cocoa, salt, and sugar. Turn the heat to medium-low and add the milk, light cream, cinnamon, and vanilla. Heat to just below boiling, stirring to mix the ingredients well. Pour into warm mugs. Top with a dollop of whipped cream, cinnamon, and orange zest.

Hint: The basic recipe for hot chocolate can have numerous additions to tempt your taste buds. For a cool and refreshing taste place fresh or dried mint in the bottom of the cup.

YIELD: ABOUT 5 CUPS

Low-Fat Cappuccino Cooler

Use fresh-brewed, double-strength, dark-roast coffee in iced drinks to ensure plenty of flavor and aroma when the coffee is diluted. For a greater coffee kick try coffee or mocha ice cream in place of the whipped topping.

1½ cups chilled brewed coffee
1½ cups low-fat chocolate ice cream
¼   cup chocolate syrup
    Reduced-fat frozen whipped topping, thawed (optional)

In a blender process the coffee, ice cream, and chocolate syrup. Serve immediately over crushed ice. Top with the whipped topping if desired.

YIELD: 3 CUPS

Lemonade

Lemonade is served daily at the Blue Willow Inn Restaurant. While our guests are waiting to be seated, our ladies dressed in antebellum gowns serve lemonade on the porches and grounds. This lemonade is refreshing anytime. We have left the sugar to your judgment because some southerners like it tart and others like it syrupy sweet.

Country Time lemonade mix
Granulated sugar
Fresh lemons

A shortcut to lemonade is to use Country Time lemonade mix as a base for lemonade. Follow the directions on the carton for the desired amount of lemonade. For each 8 ounces (1 cup) lemonade, use 2 teaspoons sugar and the juice of 1 lemon. Squeeze each lemon into a small bowl and remove the seeds. In a pitcher stir the lemon juice and the lemon pulp into the lemonade mix. For a pretty addition place mint sprigs along the sides of the pitcher and float snapdragons or lemon balm on top.

Hint: For freshly squeezed lemonade use 2 to 3 lemons per 8 ounces of water and 2 teaspoons of sugar. Use more or less lemon and sugar for desired taste.

Variations: For Peachy Lemonade add 2 (5½-ounce) cans peach or apricot nectar and 1 cup frozen peach slices. For Pink Lemonade add ¼ cup grenadine and ½ pint fresh or frozen strawberries or raspberries.

Magnolia Blossoms

Serve this at a special occasion brunch for a delightfully delicious drink.

1   (6-ounce) can frozen orange juice concentrate, thawed
3   cups Chablis
1½ cups water
½   cup Triple Sec
    Orange slices (optional)

In a large pitcher combine the orange juice concentrate, Chablis, water, and Triple Sec. Mix well. Serve over ice. Garnish with orange slices, if desired.

YIELD: 6 CUPS

Mimosa

Chilled fresh orange juice
Champagne
Orange slice

Using a champagne flute, pour equal parts of chilled fresh orange juice and champagne into the flute. Garnish with an orange slice and an orange blossom sprig, if desired.

YIELD: 1 SERVING

Mint Julep

Mint Juleps were first made in Georgia; however, Virginia lays claim to this distinction also. Kentucky must take credit for the julep's popularity since it is the official drink of the Kentucky Derby. Mint Juleps are a traditional southern favorite and are great for sipping while sitting on the front porch on a warm summer afternoon.

2   sprigs fresh mint
1   rounded teaspoon confectioners' sugar
2   to 3 drops water
1   plus 1 jiggers bourbon whiskey
    Ice, finely crushed

Put the sprigs of fresh mint in the bottom of a tall, thin glass. Add the sugar and a few drops of water. Using a wooden muddler (or wooden spoon), thoroughly bruise the mint with the sugar and water. Pour in 1 jigger bourbon whiskey. Pack the glass to the brim with finely crushed ice. Add the remaining 1 jigger whiskey and let it trickle down to the bottom of the glass. Put a sprig of fresh mint in the top of the glass and serve with two straws.

Hint: If desired, dampen the top sprig of mint with bourbon and dip it in confectioners' sugar.

YIELD: 1 SERVING

Shirley Smith Bowyer
Foley, Alabama

First Place Winner—Beverages and Punches
Blue Willow Inn Restaurant Recipe Contest—2004

Poppa's Eggnog

My daughter, Mandy, called my father "Poppa," and when the holidays rolled around we would make "Poppa's Eggnog" to toast the holidays. My daughter would get so excited because she would be allowed to sip the foam and make a foam mustache. However, my dad's mother was the originator of this recipe as far as my dad could recall. (My dad passed away March 16, 2005, on his eighty-seventh birthday.) He remembered his mother serving this eggnog at family holidays, especially Christmas. She also used it for "medicinal purposes."

When we were growing up, we would travel each Christmas to the family farm located in North Carrollton, Mississippi, and gather at my grandparents' farm on Christmas Eve to celebrate the season with a bit of cheer. The children were allowed to sip the foam on the top of the glass, and I remember it made me feel so adult.

After my grandmother died, we continued the tradition in my parents' home, and I have since carried on this tradition with my family.

3   eggs, separated
2   tablespoons granulated sugar
1½ to 2 shots whiskey
1½ to 2 cups whole milk

In a medium-size mixing bowl whisk the egg yolks and sugar together until light. Add the whiskey and mix well. Add the milk. Beat the egg whites until they are thick but not dry. Add them to the whiskey mixture and lightly work in with a spoon. The eggnog should look foamy. Pour and serve.

YIELD: 2 TO 3 CUPS

Marilyn Goucher
Oxford, Georgia

Swamp Breeze

1   (6-ounce) can frozen limeade concentrate
1   cup spiced rum
¾   cup dark rum
⅓   cup orange liqueur
    Ice cubes
2   to 3 fresh mint sprigs
    Fresh mint sprigs for garnish

In a blender process the frozen limeade, spiced rum, dark rum, and orange liqueur until smooth. Add ice to the 5-cup level and process until smooth. Add the mint and process until smooth. Pour into glasses and garnish with a sprig of mint if desired.

YIELD: 5 CUPS

Dissolve old-fashioned lemon drops or hard candy in your tea for a nice flavor. They melt quickly and keep the tea brisk!

Bourbon-Tea Punch

2   cups water
3   regular tea bags
3   to 4 cups bourbon
2   cups orange juice
1   cup granulated sugar
1   cup lemon juice
1   cup Curaçao or other orange-flavored liqueur
3   (33.8-ounce) bottles chilled club soda

In a small saucepan over high heat bring the water to a boil. Put the tea bags in a large container and pour the water over the tea bags. Cover and let stand for 15 minutes. Discard the tea bags. Add the bourbon, orange juice, sugar, lemon juice, and orange liqueur, stirring until the sugar dissolves. To serve, pour into a punch bowl over a decorated ice ring. Add the club soda.

YIELD: 5½ QUARTS (22 CUPS)

Sweet Southern Tea

You know you are in a true southern restaurant when you are offered only one kind of tea—"sweet." If made in the true southern fashion, there will be no need to add sugar as the tea comes already sweetened. It is best when drunk from a tall, wide-mouth glass with clear, fresh ice cubes or heaps of crushed ice—lots and lots of ice. Southerners revel in their sweet tea and drink it by the pitcher-full at every meal. Grandmothers in the South never served their children tea until they were twelve years old. Until then it was milk, lemonade, or water—never soft drinks at the dinner table.

In the South you will have to specifically ask for unsweetened or even maybe try "half and half"—that is the modern way of having half sweet and half unsweet for those that can't handle the syrupy sweetness of the beverage that God intended parched southerners to drink. After all, it quenches the thirst, replenishes verve and vitality, and stimulates the appetite for a nice hot supper. Gourmet calls sweet tea the "Champagne of the South." You can experiment with Sunshine Tea, which is half sweet tea and half lemonade. This, too, is wonderful on a warm summer afternoon.

1   gallon water
4   to 5 family-size tea bags (each one is enough for a quart of tea)
3   cups granulated sugar (at a minimum)
    Lemon slices or mint sprigs for garnish

In a 1½-gallon saucepan, bring the water to a boil. Remove from the heat and add the tea bags. Cover and allow the tea to steep for 12 to 15 minutes. For stronger tea, let it steep longer, up to 20 minutes. Add the sugar while the tea is hot, stirring vigorously until the sugar is completely dissolved. Allow the tea to cool and then pour it over ice. Garnish as desired with lemon slices or a sprig of mint.

Hint: Although it is not truly southern, you can add various flavors, such as peppermint, peach, or raspberry, to your tea.

YIELD: 4 QUARTS (16 CUPS)

Three-Fruit Yogurt Shake

2   cups low-fat vanilla yogurt
1   cup frozen blueberries
1   cup frozen peach slices
1   (8-ounce) can unsweetened pineapple chunks, drained and frozen

In a blender process the yogurt, blueberries, peach slices, and pineapple until smooth, stopping occasionally to scrape down the sides. Serve immediately.

YIELD: 5 CUPS

Auntie Lucille's Punch

This punch recipe has been passed down from one family to another over the years and is always requested by everyone who is fortunate enough to try it. The refreshing taste of this truly southern concoction evokes wonderful "Old South" memories of ladies gathering on a warm summer afternoon under the shade of large oak trees, with laughter and gaiety in abundance.

12	sprigs fresh mint
6	pounds granulated sugar
3	dozen lemons, juice and hulls
3	quarts (12 cups) water
3	(46-ounce) cans pineapple juice
	Green food coloring
8	quarts (7½ liters) ginger ale
	Mint sprigs for garnish

In a 5-quart saucepan boil the mint, sugar, lemon juice, and the lemon hulls in the water. Strain and remove the mint springs and lemon hulls. Add the pineapple juice and several drops of food coloring. (You determine the richness of color, but pale green looks best.) Store the punch in the refrigerator. When ready to serve, add two parts of this mixture to one part ginger ale and one part water. Garnish with sprigs of mint.

Hint: This punch will last for months in the refrigerator, so it is an excellent "do-ahead" punch for teas, bridal parties, and large church functions.

YIELD: 70 TO 100 SERVINGS

Deborah P. Massey
Covington, Georgia

Strawberry Lemonade

The fondest memories of my childhood have always been Sunday dinners at my grandparents' home. When I think back to those times I'm reminded of my grandfather's smile, his sense of humor, and his lemonade. We would all gather on the front porch after those hearty meals, still sipping from our glasses. Neighbors would often come by to chat, but we knew it was for a taste of that homemade lemonade. We all loved my grandfather Buddy and he left this world too early. No one in the family ever knew his secret to such a refreshing drink, but over the years I've tried to copy it. Now that I've become a wife and mother, we've started a tradition of "Family Day" once a month. Whenever it's our month to host, or anyone else's month for that matter, the family wants my lemonade. While I'm sure there are some variations from my grandfather's lemonade, it always reminds me of him, and I love making it as much as I enjoy drinking it.

3	cups freshly squeezed lemon juice (about 12 lemons and pulp)
½	pint fresh strawberries, hulled and halved
12	cups water
4	to 5 cups granulated sugar

Pour the lemon juice into a large pitcher. In a blender purée the strawberries. Add the water to the strawberries and pour this mixture into the pitcher. Add the sugar and stir until it dissolves. Chill in the refrigerator for at least 1 to 2 hours before serving.

YIELD: 10 TO 12 SERVINGS

Sherrie Sommerville
Decatur, Georgia

Champagne Punch

3   to 3½ cups granulated sugar
    Juice of 12 lemons
    Juice of 12 oranges
1   quart (4 cups) strong black tea, cooled
1   pint (2 cups) maraschino liqueur
1   pint (2 cups) whiskey (bourbon or rye)
1   cup Bénédictine liqueur
⅔   cup rum
5   bottles well-chilled champagne

In a gallon container, dissolve the sugar in the lemon juice. Stir in the orange juice. Stir in the tea. Add the maraschino liqueur, whiskey, Bénédictine, and rum. Stir until thoroughly blended. Chill. Pour the chilled mixture into a punch bowl and add an ice mold. When ready to serve, pour the chilled champagne into the punch mixture.

YIELD: 5 GALLONS

Chatham Artillery Punch

The Chatham Artillery of Savannah, Georgia, the oldest military organization of record in Georgia, hosted Presidents George Washington and James Monroe. This famous punch, thought to be a combination of mild ingredients designed by the ladies with the addition of harder spirits by the artillery members, was probably served to both presidents. The recipe was kept jealously secret for years and was unobtainable by an outsider. It is said that this is the punch that knocked out Admiral Schley when he visited Savannah in 1899 after the Spanish War. The brave American admiral went unharmed by Admiral Cervera's Spanish shells, but Artillery Punch scored a direct hit that put him out for two days. This punch is often served for large gatherings in Savannah and known to be a "knockout" in more ways than one.

1½   gallons Catawba wine
½   gallon St. Croix rum
1   quart gin
1   quart brandy
½   pint Bénédictine D.O.M
2   quarts maraschino cherries
1½   quarts rye whiskey
1½   gallons strong tea
2   pounds brown sugar
1½   quarts orange juice
1½   quarts lemon juice
1   case champagne

In a large container mix the wine, rum, gin, brandy, Bénédictine, cherries, rye whiskey, tea, sugar, orange juice, and lemon juice. Store in the refrigerator for 36 to 48 hours to allow the flavors to blend. Add the case of champagne just before serving.

YIELD: 100-PLUS SERVINGS (OR ENOUGH FOR 10 ADMIRALS)

Coffee Punch

This punch is always served by Billie at her Epiphany parties. It is a delightfully refreshing punch for coffee lovers.

PUNCH

6	cups strong, hot, brewed coffee
2	cups milk
1	cup granulated sugar
1	tablespoon vanilla extract
1	quart vanilla ice cream
1	quart coffee ice cream

WHIPPED CREAM

1	quart whipping cream
5	tablespoons granulated sugar
5	tablespoons vanilla
	Shaved semisweet chocolate for garnish
	Ground cinnamon or nutmeg for garnish

For the **punch:** In a large bowl, combine the coffee, milk, sugar, and vanilla. Stir until the sugar is dissolved. Chill thoroughly. Pour into a punch bowl, stirring gently. Scoop the ice creams into the bowl.

For the **whipped cream:** In a medium bowl with an electric mixer beat the whipping cream until stiff peaks form, adding the sugar and vanilla as you whip.

To serve, ladle the punch into mugs and add a dollop of whipped cream on top. Sprinkle the shaved chocolate and cinnamon or nutmeg on top.

YIELD: 4½ QUARTS (18 CUPS)

Georgia Peach Champagne Punch

This is a wonderful punch served by Peggy Hawkins, our events manager at Magnolia Hall.

2	(11.5-ounce) cans peach nectar
1	quart (4 cups) lemonade (not lemon drink)
¾	cup peach brandy
3	bottles chilled champagne or other sparkling wine
	Edible flower garnish

In a large pitcher combine the peach nectar, lemonade, and peach brandy. Chill well. When ready to serve, pour the punch into a large punch bowl. Add the champagne and garnish with edible flowers.

YIELD: 3 GALLONS

Magnolia Punch

This punch is a local favorite for receptions, teas, and gatherings of all kinds.

2   cups granulated sugar

2   cups water

1½ cups orange juice

¼   cup lemon juice

1   (48-ounce) can pineapple juice

3   mashed ripe bananas

3   quarts ginger ale

In a large bowl mix together the sugar, water, orange juice, lemon juice, pineapple juice, and bananas. Freeze into a slush. When ready to serve, pour the mixture into a punch bowl and add the ginger ale.

> Hints: Garnish with an ice ring made with orange and lemon slices and mint leaves. Garnish the punch bowl tray with magnolia leaves and flowers if they are in bloom.

YIELD: 6 QUARTS (24 CUPS)

Minted Tea Punch

4   cups boiling water

4   family-size decaffeinated tea bags

½   cup loosely packed fresh mint leaves

¾   cup granulated sugar

1   (6-ounce) can frozen lemonade concentrate, thawed and undiluted

4   cups cold water

     Lemon slices and fresh mint sprigs for garnish

In a large pitcher pour the boiling water over the tea bags and mint leaves. Cover the tea and allow it to steep for 3 minutes. Remove and discard the tea bags and the mint. Stir in the sugar until dissolved. Stir in the lemonade concentrate and cold water. Place in the refrigerator to chill. Serve in a pretty punch bowl over ice or an ice ring. Garnish with lemon slices and fresh mint sprigs if desired.

YIELD: 9 CUPS

Make your own spiced tea or cider. Place orange peels, whole cloves, and cinnamon sticks in a 6-inch square piece of cheesecloth. Gather the corners and tie with a string. Steep in hot cider or tea for 10 minutes or longer if you want a stronger flavor.

Ice Mold

To cool your punch, float an ice ring made from the punch rather than using ice cubes. This is a beautiful way to keep your punch cold and is especially nice when used in champagne or fruit punches. Not only is the ice ring or mold more decorative, but it also inhibits melting and diluting the punch.

3   to 4 fresh peaches (canned peach halves may be used)
    Strawberries or red maraschino cherries
    Mint leaves
    Lemonade or water
    Ring mold
    Green seedless grapes

Peel the peaches. Cut them into halves and remove the pits. Spray the bottom of the ring mold lightly with a nonstick coating. Place the peach halves around the mold cut side down. (If the centers of the peaches are not red, place a strawberry or a maraschino cherry in each half to add the red color). Arrange the mint leaves on the bottom between each peach half. Pour enough lemonade or water in the mold to cover the bottom, about ½-inch. Place the mold in the freezer. When this layer is frozen, add the seedless grapes in small bunches between the peaches and continue to layer lemonade or water and freeze until the mold is full. Unmold the frozen ring and place in a punch bowl with the punch.

Hint: An ice ring may be composed of any number of fruit selections, or try edible flowers for another decoration addition.

YIELD: 1 ICE RING

Miss Betty Rob's Southern Punch

Miss Betty Rob Golson's son, Henry, and I were schoolmates in Fort Deposit, Alabama, until my parents and I moved to Foley in 1966 when I was beginning the eleventh grade. Miss Betty Rob and my mother were best friends, and my mother and I continued to keep in touch by visits, phone calls, and mail until Miss Betty Rob passed away at the age of ninety in September 2003. My mother and I always looked forward to sitting with Miss Betty Rob and her son in their huge family room looking out the glass doors into a beautiful, green pecan orchard, where we caught up on news and sipped Miss Betty Rob's Southern Punch that she always served when we came. She was a dear friend to both my mother and me, and she taught me everything I know about the Bible when she was my Sunday school teacher. Because of her, I can still name in order all of the books of the Old and New Testaments, and I can still repeat from memory many of the Bible verses she taught us.

1   (12-ounce) can frozen pink lemonade
1   (12-ounce) can frozen orange juice
½   container Crystal Light iced tea mix
    Water

In a large pitcher mix the lemonade, orange juice, and iced tea mix. Add water to taste. Chill for at least 2 hours prior to serving. Serve over ice and add a sprig of mint if desired.

YIELD: 1½ TO 2 QUARTS (6 TO 8 CUPS)

Alma K. Smith
Foley, Alabama

Peppermint Punch

*Peggy Hawkins, our events manager, often serves this
delicious punch for special holiday events at Magnolia
Hall. It is a favorite every time it is served.*

1   quart (4 cups) eggnog
1   (1-liter) bottle chilled club soda
½   gallon softened peppermint ice cream
     Hard peppermint candies, crushed

In a punch bowl, stir together the eggnog, club soda, and
peppermint ice cream. Sprinkle with the crushed peppermint candies and serve immediately. The punch may
be made ahead without the crushed peppermint candies;
chill for 2 hours, stir well, and sprinkle with the candies
just before serving.

Hint: Hang peppermint candy canes on the rim of the
punch bowl, if desired, and sprinkle with shaved semisweet chocolate.

YIELD: ABOUT 3 GALLONS

Punch for a Crowd

3   (.16-ounce) packages lemon-lime Kool-
     Aid
5   quarts (20 cups) water
1½   (6-ounce) cans frozen sweetened
     lemonade concentrate
3   cups granulated sugar
1   quart (4 cups) ginger ale

In a large 2-gallon container mix the Kool-Aid, water,
lemonade concentrate, and sugar. Chill for 1 to 2 hours.
To serve, put in a punch bowl and add the ginger ale.

YIELD: ABOUT 7 QUARTS (28 CUPS)

Request Punch

3   (46-ounce) cans Hawaiian punch
3   quarts (12 cups) ginger ale
1   (46-ounce) can apple juice
1   gallon softened raspberry sherbet (or
     any flavor)

In a 3 to 5-gallon punch bowl, mix the Hawaiian punch,
ginger ale, and apple juice. Add scoops of the sherbet.

YIELD: 50 SERVINGS

Sweet Tart Punch

This is, without a doubt, the best punch ever. It is a slightly tart punch, which people seem to find more refreshing than a sweet punch. I make it for church affairs, woman's clubs, showers, etc. People are always asking me to make it. Citric acid is purchased at drugstores or the pharmacy department of grocery stores. You can make the base ahead of time, pour it into a plastic gallon jug, freeze it, and add the juices and ginger ale when serving.

2   plus 1 quarts (8 plus 4 cups) water

2   tablespoons citric acid powder

3   cups granulated sugar

1   (12-ounce) can frozen orange juice concentrate, thawed

1   (12-ounce) can frozen limeade or lemonade, prepared

1   (46-ounce) can pineapple juice

1   (2-liter) bottle ginger ale

    Crushed ice

In a medium-size saucepan bring 1 quart of the water to a boil. In a 2-quart glass pitcher combine the citric acid powder, sugar, and the boiling water. Cover and allow this to sit out overnight. Do not refrigerate.

Add the remaining 2 quarts water to the above mixture. When ready to serve, add the can of orange juice concentrate, the prepared limeade or lemonade (whichever you prefer), pineapple juice, and ginger ale to the base. Fill a large punch bowl with crushed ice and pour the prepared punch over the ice.

Hint: You can change the color or change the punch by adding other fruit juices (grape, cranberry, etc) or frozen punch.

YIELD: 50 TO 60 SERVINGS

Jeanne Smith
Covington, Georgia

Syllabub

Recipes for syllabub have been handed down from seventeenth, eighteenth, and early nineteenth-century England. It was popular for celebrations, special occasions, and holidays due to its festive appearance. One could always detect the drinker of the beverage by the thick white mustache left behind. This recipe is particularly southern because bourbon is the liquor ingredient.

2   pints whipping cream

1   cup half-and-half

1   cup granulated sugar

⅔   cup bourbon

In a medium-size bowl mix the whipping cream, half-and-half, and sugar. Stir until the sugar is dissolved. Add the bourbon and stir. Churn the mixture with a syllabub churn and skim off the froth. Serve the froth in glasses or cups.

Hint: Garnish with a sprig of mint or a sprinkling of grated nutmeg.

YIELD: 12 TO 16 SERVINGS

Texas Governor's Mansion Summer Peach Tea Punch

This recipe comes from Anita Perry, First Lady of the State of Texas. She says that her remarkable chef, Sarah Bishop, has made hundreds of gallons of this delicious summer tea for receptions and events at the mansion. It is incredibly popular, and the recipe, though somewhat complicated, is well worth the effort. Sarah's torch has now been passed to Dean Peterson, who now makes the punch for various mansion events.

4	cups water
3	family-size tea bags
4	cups fresh mint
1	(12-ounce) can lemonade concentrate, undiluted
2	bottles Knudsen's Peach Nectar (no substitutes)
2	liters ginger ale, chilled
2	liters club soda
½	to 1 cup simple syrup (2 parts sugar to 1 part water slowly boiled for about 4 minutes)

In a saucepan on high heat boil the water to steep the tea and the mint. Steep for about 15 minutes. Remove the tea bags. Leave the mint in the solution until it cools. Strain into a 2-gallon container. Add the lemonade, peach nectar, and the simple syrup to taste. Add the ginger ale and the club soda.

YIELD: 2 GALLONS

Veranda Tea Punch

This punch is a sweet alternative to tea or lemonade for sipping in the swing or maybe just sitting and swinging your feet on those hot, southern, summer afternoons on the porch.

⅔	cup granulated sugar
⅔	cup water
	Juice of 4 oranges
2	cups strong-brewed hot tea
1	quart (4 cups) chilled soda water
1	quart (4 cups) chilled cola or ginger ale
	Lemon and orange slices for garnish

In a large saucepan combine the sugar and water. Bring to a boil and boil for 10 minutes to make a sugar syrup. Remove from the heat and allow the sugar syrup to cool. After it has cooled, mix the orange juice with the cooled sugar syrup. Add the hot tea to the mixture and allow it to cool. Just prior to serving, add the soda water and cola or ginger ale. Pour into a punch bowl with an ice ring and garnish with the lemon and orange slices.

YIELD: 3 QUARTS (12 CUPS)

Winter Wassail

This delightfully festive punch will fill the house with the aromas of the holidays and will certainly let guests know that the holidays have arrived.

2	teaspoons whole allspice
2	teaspoons whole cloves
6	cinnamon sticks
2	quarts (8 cups) apple cider
2	cups granulated sugar
2	cups orange juice
1½	cups lemon juice
1	cup water

Tie the allspice, cloves, and cinnamon sticks in a piece of cheesecloth. In a large saucepan over medium heat, bring the cider and sugar to a boil. Add the spice bag and reduce the heat to low. Cover and simmer for 10 minutes. Remove and discard the spice bag. Stir in the orange juice, lemon juice, and water. Simmer for 5 minutes or until heated. Serve hot.

YIELD: 13 CUPS

Jellies, Jams, Preserves, & Spreads

When one thinks about Southern cooking it is important to remember that in our early history there was no electricity or refrigeration. Also the South has a long growing season, so the home cook put much thought into preserving foods for the winter months. Many methods such as canning, pickling, or preserving were used. The industrious cook would work diligently to stock her pantry or larder with jars of jams and preserves made from the bounty of the summer gardens. Even today you will find Southern cooks preserving fruits and making luscious jams, jellies, and preserves for their families and friends to enjoy after the growing season is long over.

Apple Butter

This makes a delicious condiment to serve with biscuits or on toast.

- 3 quarts (12 cups) applesauce (make your own or use canned)
- 3 cups granulated sugar
- 7 cups firmly packed dark brown sugar
- ½ cup apple cider vinegar (5% acidity)
- 1 cup red hot cinnamon candies
- 2 teaspoons ground cinnamon
- 1 tablespoon butter
- 1½ (1¾-ounce) packages powdered fruit pectin

In a heavy saucepan on medium heat combine the applesauce, granulated sugar, brown sugar, vinegar, cinnamon candies, ground cinnamon, and butter. Stir them together and continue to cook and stir until the mixture is warm throughout. Add the pectin. Heat to a rolling boil and continue to cook for 2 minutes.

Remove from the heat and put into sterilized jars. Fill the jars to about ¼-inch from the top. Wipe off the tops and seal the jars. Immediately turn them upside down and allow them to sit for 3 minutes. Quickly flip them up and allow them to sit for 8 hours without bothering them.

YIELD: ABOUT 6 PINTS (12 CUPS)

Joyce Lee
Good Hope, Georgia

Apple-Mint Jelly

- 1½ cups finely chopped, firmly packed mint leaves
- 4 cups apple juice
- 1 (1¾-ounce) package powdered fruit pectin
- ½ cup lemon juice
- 5 cups granulated sugar

In a saucepan on medium heat combine the mint leaves and apple juice. Bring to a boil. Remove from the heat. Cover and let stand for 10 minutes. Strain the juice and pour it into a large heavy saucepan. Discard the mint.

In the saucepan on high heat, stirring constantly, stir the pectin and lemon juice into the apple juice and bring to a boil. Stir in the sugar all at once. Continue to stir and bring to a full rolling boil (a boil that cannot be stirred down) and boil hard for 1 minute, stirring constantly. Remove from the heat and skim off the foam with a metal spoon.

Quickly pour the jelly into hot sterilized jars, leaving ¼-inch headspace; wipe the jar rims. Cover at once with metal lids, and screw on the bands. Process the jars in a boiling water bath for 5 minutes.

YIELD: ABOUT 6 HALF PINTS

Blueberry Jam

1½ cups slightly crushed fresh blueberries

7 cups granulated sugar

2 tablespoons lemon juice

2 (3-ounce) packages liquid pectin

In a large Dutch oven on high heat combine the blueberries, sugar, and lemon juice. Bring the mixture to a rolling boil. Boil for 1 minute, stirring constantly. Remove from the heat and immediately stir in the pectin. Stir, and alternately skim off, the foam with a metal spoon for 5 minutes.

Quickly pour the jam into hot sterilized jars, leaving a ¼-inch space from the top of the jar. Cover at once with metal lids and screw on the bands. Process the jars in a boiling water bath for 10 minutes.

YIELD: ABOUT 9 HALF-PINTS

Fig Preserves

These preserves are great with hot biscuits and are an old southern specialty. Figs can be found from late June through October. Handle the fresh ones gently. They can be stored in the refrigerator for two or three days. Count yourself blessed if a neighbor or a friend offers you some of his fig harvest.

2 quarts fresh ripe figs (about 4 pounds)

3 cups granulated sugar

Wash, stem, and quarter the figs. In a Dutch oven layer the figs and the sugar. Cover and let the figs stand for 8 hours. Cook over medium heat for 2 hours, stirring occasionally, until the syrup thickens and the figs are clear.

Pack the hot figs into hot, sterilized jars, filling the jar to ½-inch from the top. Cover the fruit with the boiling syrup, making sure to fill no higher than ½-inch from the top. Remove the air bubbles. Wipe the jar rims. Cover at once with the metal lids and screw on the bands. Process the jars in a boiling water bath for 15 minutes. Cool completely and chill if desired.

YEILD: 4 QUARTS

Fig-Strawberry Preserves

3 cups granulated sugar

1 (6-ounce) package strawberry gelatin

4 cups water

3 cups crushed figs

In a bowl mix together the sugar and strawberry gelatin. Add the water and mix until the gelatin and sugar dissolve. Place the figs in a stockpot on medium-high heat. Pour the gelatin mixture over the figs. Mix well. Bring the mixture to a boil. Cook for 20 minutes. Pour the preserves into sterilized jars and seal.

YIELD: 2 PINTS

Green Tomato Marmalade

1   cup water

2   thinly sliced oranges

1   thinly sliced lemon

6   large green tomatoes (about 4 pounds), chopped

4   cups granulated sugar

½   teaspoon salt

In a Dutch oven over medium heat cook the water, oranges, and lemon for 17 to 20 minutes or until the fruits are tender. Add the tomatoes, sugar, and salt, stirring until the sugar dissolves. Bring to a boil, stirring constantly. Reduce the heat to low and simmer, stirring occasionally, for 3 hours and 30 minutes or until the mixture thickens.

Pour the hot mixture into hot sterilized jars, filling each to about ¼-inch from the top. Remove the air bubbles. Wipe the jar rims. Cover at once with metal lids and screw on the bands. Process the jars in a boiling water bath for 10 minutes. Remove from the heat and allow them to cool.

YIELD: 3 PINTS

Guava Jelly

This is a backwoods recipe for guavas, which grow in Florida. This jelly is wonderful on toast and is also a great appetizer served on a block of cream cheese with crackers. Guava paste can also be used. Guava paste comes in blocks, and the taste is a little stronger than jelly. The paste block comes in a box and is found in the Spanish section of the grocery store.

1   pound tart cattley guavas (ordinary guavas require the addition of some citric acid)

1   quart (4 cups) cold water

2   cups granulated sugar

Wash the guavas, remove the blossom end, and slice thinly. In a large saucepan on medium heat, combine the guavas and water and boil until very soft, about 30 minutes. Remove from the heat and allow the guavas to cool. Strain the guava mixture, pressing through cheesecloth, then through flannel without pressing. In a medium-size saucepan on medium heat bring the juice to a boil, and for each cup of juice add 1 cup sugar, stirring slowly. Boil until the jellying point is reached. Remove from the heat and skim off the foam with a metal spoon.

Quickly pour the jelly into hot sterilized jars, filling the jars to ¼-inch from the top. Wipe the jar rims. Cover at once with metal lids and screw on the bands. Process the jars of jelly in a boiling water bath for 5 minutes. Remove and cool on wire racks.

YIELD: ABOUT 6 HALF PINTS

Kudzu Blossom Jelly

One summer while visiting my college friend Mildred, we drove around in the country looking for pink-purple kudzu blossoms. Mildred made a wonderful kudzu blossom jelly. The jelly is great on toast for breakfast. It can be spooned over cream cheese and used as an appetizer. It can be melted to serve over waffles or ice cream. Her recipe for the jelly was originally obtained from Nancy Basket, a Cherokee Indian, from Walhalla, South Carolina. Nancy is an artist who makes gifts from nature. She does basket weaving and teaches classes in basket making—some woven from kudzu vines. She learned her skills from her Cherokee grandmother, Margaret Basket. Nancy can cook an entire meal using kudzu in every dish.

4 cups kudzu blossoms
4 cups boiling water
1 tablespoon lemon juice
1 (1¾-ounce) package powdered pectin
5 cups granulated sugar

Wash the kudzu blossoms with cold water and place them in a large bowl. Pour the boiling water over the blossoms and refrigerate for 8 hours or overnight.

Pour the blossoms and liquid through a colander into a Dutch oven. Discard the blossoms. Add the lemon juice and pectin, and over high heat bring the mixture to a rolling boil while stirring constantly. Stir in the sugar and return to a full rolling boil. Allow the mixture to boil for 1 minute while stirring constantly. Remove from the heat and skim off the foam with a metal spoon.

Quickly pour the jelly into hot sterilized jars, filling them to ¼-inch from the top. Wipe the jar rims. Cover at once with metal lids and screw on bands. Process the jars of jelly in a boiling water bath for 5 minutes. Remove and cool on wire racks.

YIELD: 6 HALF PINTS

Nancy Posner
Social Circle, Georgia
First Place Winner—Jellies and Sauces
Blue Willow Inn Restaurant Recipe Contest, 2004

Peach Preserves

8 cups fresh ripe peaches
5 cups granulated sugar
1 cup water

Peel and cut up the peaches. Place the peaches in a heavy stockpot and cover with the sugar. Allow the peaches and sugar to sit for 1 hour for the juices to develop. Add the water and place on low heat. Bring to a slow simmer. Cook for about 2 hours, stirring often to prevent scorching. Remove the peaches from the heat and allow them to cool. Refrigerate.

If canning, spoon the hot peaches into hot sterilized canning jars. Cover at once with metal lids and screw on bands. Process the jars of jelly in a boiling water bath for 5 minutes. Remove and cool on wire racks.

YIELD: ABOUT 6 QUARTS

Muscadine Marmalade

3   plus 4 pounds muscadine grapes
4   cups water
2   (1¾-ounce) packages powdered fruit pectin
14 cups granulated sugar

Remove the skins from 3 pounds of muscadines and reserve. Set the pulp aside. Pulse the reserved skins in a food processor at least five times or until thoroughly chopped. Cover and chill.

In a Dutch oven over medium-high heat bring the muscadine pulp, the remaining 4 pounds of muscadines, and the water to a boil. Reduce the heat to low. Simmer, stirring occasionally, for 1 hour (skins should be tender and the liquid a plum color). Remove from the heat and allow the muscadine juice to cool.

Pour the muscadine juice through a triple thickness of damp cheesecloth into a pot. Discard the solids. Stir in the powdered fruit pectin until blended. Bring the mixture to a boil over medium-high heat, stirring constantly. Stir in the sugar. Return to a boil and cook, stirring constantly, for 1 minute. Remove from the heat and skim off the foam with a metal spoon.

Add ½ cup of the chopped muscadine skins to each hot, sterilized jar, and pour hot marmalade into the jars quickly, filling the jars to ¼-inch from the top. Wipe the jar rims. Cover at once with metal lids and screw on bands.

Process the jars in a boiling water bath for 5 minutes. Remove from the heat and set aside to cool.

YIELD: 8 PINTS

Oven Apple Butter

The tradition of making apple butter has long been a symbol of fall. The methods and tastes are as varied as the cooks themselves. Nothing can beat tender flaky biscuits hot from the oven slathered with freshly made apple butter.

8   large Granny Smith apples, peeled and diced
1   cup apple juice
1   cup granulated sugar
1   teaspoon ground cinnamon

In a Dutch oven over medium heat cook the diced apples and apple juice for 30 minutes or until the apples are tender. Stir until the apples are mashed. Stir in the sugar and cinnamon. Preheat the oven to 275°. Pour the apple mixture into a lightly greased 11 x 7-inch baking dish. Bake the apple butter for 4½ hours, stirring every hour, or until of a spreading consistency. Cover and chill.

Hint: For spicy apple butter, increase the cinnamon to 2 teaspoons and add ½ teaspoon ground cloves and ¼ teaspoon ground allspice.

YIELD: 3 CUPS

Scuppernong Jelly

4   cups scuppernong juice
2   teaspoons lemon juice
1   (3-ounce) package liquid pectin
7   cups granulated sugar

In a Dutch oven over medium-high heat bring the scuppernong juice, lemon juice, and liquid pectin to a boil, stirring constantly. When boiling, stir in the sugar. Return to a boil and boil, stirring constantly, for 1 minute. Remove from the heat. Skim off the foam.

Quickly pour the hot jelly into hot sterilized jars, filling each jar to ¼ inch from the top. Wipe the jar rims. Cover at once with metal lids, and screw on the bands. Process the jars in a boiling water bath for 5 minutes. Remove from heat and set aside to cool.

YIELD: 8 HALF PINTS

Scuppernong Juice

3   **pounds crushed scuppernongs**
1   **cup water**

In a large saucepan over medium-high heat bring the scuppernongs and water to a boil. Cover and reduce the heat to medium low. Simmer for 10 minutes.

Pour the mixture through a double thickness of damp cheesecloth and discard the solids. Use the juice in the scuppernong jelly.

Hint: To serve as a juice to drink, stir in 1¼ cups granulated sugar and chill.

YIELD: 3½ CUPS

Strawberry Preserves

6   **cups strawberries**
6   **cups granulated sugar**

Wash, stem, and drain the strawberries well. In a large saucepan crush the berries. Add the sugar and mix well. Over medium heat bring the strawberry and sugar mixture to a boil. Boil for 10 minutes after it begins to boil, stirring often. Pour into hot sterilized jars. Seal while hot.

YIELD: 3 TO 4 PINTS

Cheese Spread

8   **ounces sharp cheddar cheese**
1   **cup evaporated milk**
1   **cup mayonnaise**
    Garlic powder

Grate the cheese and combine with the evaporated milk. Heat the mixture in a saucepan on low heat until the cheese is melted. Remove from the heat and allow the mixture to cool. Add mayonnaise and the garlic powder to taste. Place in a small serving bowl, cover, and chill until ready to serve. Serve on crackers.

YIELD: 20 TO 25 SERVINGS

Chutney-Onion Cheese Spread

2 (8-ounce) packages softened cream cheese

½ cup Tomato Chutney (page 127)

⅓ cup chopped green onions

⅓ cup coarsely chopped dry-roasted peanuts or roasted pecans

Spread the cream cheese into a 6 inch circle on a serving plate. Spread the chutney over the cream cheese. Sprinkle with the green onions and the peanuts or pecans. Serve immediately, or cover and chill up to 1 hour. Serve with assorted crackers.

YIELD: 3 CUPS

Cranberry-Ambrosia Cream Cheese Spread

2 (8-ounce) packages cream cheese, softened

¾ cup confectioners' sugar

1 (6-ounce) package sweetened dried cranberries, divided

1 (15½-ounce) can crushed pineapple

1 (11-ounce) can mandarin oranges

1 (3½-ounce) can shredded coconut, divided

1 cup toasted chopped pecans

8 toasted pecan halves
   Gingersnaps

Stir together the cream cheese and sugar until blended. Add ½ cup dried cranberries. Drain the pineapple and oranges and put them between layers of paper towels. Set the oranges aside. Stir the pineapple and a little more than ½ cup coconut into the cream cheese mixture. Stir in the chopped pecans. Spoon the mixture into a serving bowl. Sprinkle the remaining cranberries around the edges of the bowl. Arrange the orange sections around the inside edge of the cranberries. Sprinkle the remaining coconut in the center and top with the pecan halves. Serve with the gingersnaps.

YIELD: 24 SERVINGS

Garlic Cheese Spread

This was a favorite recipe of Anne Van Dyke, Louis' mom. She and Louis' dad had a favorite restaurant in Savannah where a garlic cheese spread was served, but the owners refused to give Mom the recipe. She went home and kept toying with various ingredients until she created her own recipe, and everyone though it was much better than the restaurant's.

2 (8-ounce) packages softened cream cheese

1 (16-ounce) jar Cheez Whiz

10 ounces shredded sharp cheddar cheese

1 teaspoon minced fresh garlic

In a food processor or mixer blend together the cream cheese and the Cheez Whiz until smooth. Add the cheddar cheese and the minced garlic. Blend until smooth.

Place in a serving dish, cover, and refrigerate overnight. Serve with crackers or toast points.

Hint: This is delicious served on warm French bread and also as a condiment with steaks.

YIELD: 5 CUPS

Pimiento Cheese Spread

This recipe comes from Marvin Exley, Billie's foster father. This is a versatile recipe that is a good addition to any refrigerator. It can be made into sandwiches and is great for fishing trips, hiking trips, or other excursions. It is ideal for ladies' socials or afternoon teas—make open-face tea sandwiches and garnish with a bit of parsley or a slice of stuffed olive. It is wonderful as a quick appetizer on Ritz crackers or as a side dish stuffed into celery ribs. It can also be a great "sport-mom" snack.

1   pound (4 cups) cheddar cheese
1   (7-ounce) jar pimientos, diced and drained
1   (8-ounce) package softened cream cheese
1   tablespoon Worcestershire sauce
2   tablespoons mayonnaise

Grate the cheddar cheese and place it in a medium-sized mixing bowl. Add the pimientos and cream cheese. Mix at low speed with an electric mixer. Slowly add the Worcestershire sauce and mayonnaise. After the mixture is blended, increase the speed of the mixer and continue to mix until it is smooth.

YIELD: 5 TO 6 CUPS

FOR LARGE QUANTITIES

3   pounds cheddar cheese
3   (7-ounce) jars pimientos, diced and drained
3   (8-ounce) packages softened cream cheese
⅓   cup Worcestershire sauce
¼   cup mayonnaise

YIELD: ABOUT 4 QUARTS

Nasturtium Spread

This is a fun recipe to try as in the South flowers and their leaves are often used in cooking and as garnishes.

1   (8-ounce) package softened cream cheese
¼   cup chopped nasturtium flowers or pansies
¼   cup prepared horseradish
     Crackers or snack rye bread
     Cherry tomatoes

In a small mixing bowl, beat the cream cheese, nasturtium flowers, and horseradish until well blended. Serve with crackers or bread and cherry tomatoes.

YIELD: 1½ CUPS

PICKLING AND CANNING FRUITS AND VEGETABLES

You should always pickle fruits or vegetables within twenty-four hours after they are picked. If you cannot do it immediately, then refrigerate or spread out the produce in a well-ventilated area.

Whether pickling, canning, or freezing, you should wash and sort your fruits and vegetables first. Then thinly slice the blossom end of the vegetables.

When canning, use standard canning jars with pretreated lids for pickling; *leftover food jars are not safe to use.* Discard any cracked or chipped jars and any lids with blemished sealing surfaces. Thoroughly wash and then boil the jars and lids for about 10 minutes to sterilize before filling. The jars should be hot when filled. Before filling the jars, skim off any foam that collects during the boiling process.

Fill the jars with your desired fruit or vegetables. Be sure to leave about a half inch of head room at the top.

Place the filled jars in a canner or large Dutch oven with a cooling rack. A boiling-bath canner has a tight-fitting lid and a metal rack to keep the jars off the bottom of the kettle. Cover with at least 1 inch of water. Bring the water to a boil and boil for about 10 minutes (15 minutes at altitudes of 1000 to 6000 feet and 20 minutes over 6000 feet). Start timing as soon as the water begins to boil.

Make sure the lids have sealed properly before storing pickled food. When the jars are sealed, you should feel a downward curve to the center of the lids. Examine the jars closely before opening homemade relishes and jams. A bulging lid, leakage, disagreeable odor, spurting liquid, or change in color of vegetables may mean the contents are spoiled. Do not taste the contents.

Pepper Jelly Spread

This is an easy and quick spread for snacks or hors d'oeuvres. For a variation, use peach chutney in place of the pepper jelly.

1   (10-ounce) jar green or red pepper jelly
1   (8-ounce) package softened cream cheese
    Crackers

Pour the pepper jelly over the top of the softened cream cheese. Serve with crackers.

YIELD: 20 TO 25 SERVINGS

Soups & Salads

In the Southern home there was always a pot of soup simmering on the back burner of the stove. Soups range from simple, clear bouillon and consommé to cream. The most commonly made soup in the South is of course either chicken and dumplings or vegetable. Vegetable is a big favorite because you can use up all of your leftovers. Chowders are a great favorite of coastal cities or those close to a river where fishing is easily accessible. Stews are meatier and are often used as a main course. A stew in earlier times was known as a "stick-to-your-ribs" spoon food.

Salads in the "Old South" weren't the tender greens we favor today. They were seasoned mixes of root vegetables such as cabbage, kale, dried peas, or fresh vegetables, which wintered well. Everyone had a root cellar where these precious vegetables were kept. Today a salad could include anything ranging from fresh greens or congealed fruits to meats or seafood. When mixing salads, though, don't used metal bowls. Use china, wood, or glass.

Ann Lowe's Chicken Stew

Add a little bit of love to this recipe. It is the secret ingredient that works to make one feel better. The Blue Willow Inn Restaurant's head cook, Ann Lowe, has been making this "feel good" stew for many years to comfort loved ones and friends when they're not feeling well or simply down in spirit. It's a true southerner's comfort food.

1   (3 to 4-pound) broiler-fryer chicken
1   quart (4 cups) water
1   quart (4 cups) milk
1   cup (2 sticks) butter
2   sleeves saltine crackers
    Salt and pepper

Thoroughly wash the chicken. In a stockpot on medium heat place the chicken in the water. Cook the chicken until tender. Remove the chicken from the pot, reserving the chicken broth. Add the milk to the broth and bring the mixture to a slow boil, stirring often to prevent scorching. Add the butter and melt. Crush the saltine crackers and add them to the stockpot. Add the salt and pepper to taste. Turn the heat to low and allow the mixture to simmer, stirring often, until it thickens. Remove the skin and the bones from the chicken. Tear the chicken into bite-size pieces. When the broth mixture in the pot has thickened, add the chicken. Serve hot.

YIELD: 8 TO 10 SERVINGS

Brunswick Stew

1   large onion, chopped
1   pound ground sirloin
2   (15-ounce) cans stewed tomatoes
2   (15-ounce) cans creamed corn
2   (13-ounce) cans chicken
2   (10-ounce) cans barbeque pork
1   (14-ounce) bottle catsup
1   teaspoon garlic powder
1   teaspoon apple cider vinegar
1   teaspoon salt
    Pepper

In a Dutch oven on medium heat sauté the onion and the sirloin. Mix in the tomatoes, corn, chicken, pork, catsup, garlic powder, vinegar, salt, and pepper to taste. Reduce the heat and simmer for 2 to 3 hours to blend the flavors.

YIELD: 13 TO 15 SERVINGS

Jeanette Allen
Loganville, Georgia

Chicken and Dumplings

A true favorite of our guests, Chicken and Dumplings is served at almost every meal at the Blue Willow Inn Restaurant. Although it may take a while to prepare, the final product is worth the effort. It is great on a cold winter night. Add a salad and some crackers or toast for a complete meal.

1   (3 to 4-pound) broiler-fryer chicken

2   quarts (8 cups) plus ¼ cup water

1   teaspoon salt

2   cups self-rising flour

¼   cup shortening

¼   cup cold water

½   cup (1 stick) butter, melted

2   teaspoons black pepper

In a stockpot on medium-high heat place the chicken in 2 quarts water. Cook until done, about 1 hour. Remove the chicken from the pot, reserving the chicken broth. Cool the chicken. After the chicken has cooled, remove the bones, skin, and fat. Cut the chicken into bite-size pieces.

In a medium-size mixing bowl combine the flour and salt. Cut the shortening into the flour mixture until the mixture forms coarse crumbs. Add the remaining ¼ cup cold water and mix well with your hands to form a dough.

Over medium-high heat bring the chicken broth back to a slow boil. Do not boil rapidly. With floured hands pinch off pieces of the dough about the size of a quarter and drop them into the slowly boiling chicken broth. Gently stir the broth after adding several pieces of dough. Repeat until all the dumpling mix has been used and stir gently. Add the butter and black pepper. Stir gently.

Turn the heat to low and allow the mixture to simmer for 8 to 10 minutes. Serve in soup bowls.

YIELD: ABOUT 10 SERVINGS

Corn Chowder

5   slices bacon, diced

2   medium onions, chopped

2   (10¾-ounce) cans chicken broth

2   (broth) cans water

3   large potatoes, peeled and diced

1   (15-ounce) can cream-style corn

2   cups evaporated milk
    Salt and pepper
    Cayenne pepper

In a large skillet or Dutch oven over medium heat sauté the bacon until crisp. Remove from the drippings. Sauté the onions in the drippings until soft. Add the chicken broth diluted with the water. Add the potatoes and cook until done, 15 to 20 minutes. Add the corn, evaporated milk, bacon, and salt and pepper to taste. Heat through. Sprinkle with the cayenne pepper to taste.

YIELD: 6 TO 8 SERVINGS

Jean Elder
Covington, Georgia

Crab Chowder

This is a favorite recipe of Mary Perdue, first lady of the state of Georgia.

1	tablespoon butter
¼	cup chopped onion
¼	cup diced green bell pepper
¼	teaspoon minced garlic
⅛	teaspoon cayenne pepper
2	(10¾-ounce) cans potato soup
1	(8-ounce) package cream cheese, cubed and softened
1½	(12-ounce) cans evaporated milk
6	to 7 ounces crabmeat
1	(15-ounce) can whole-kernel corn, not drained
2	tablespoons granulated sugar

In a medium saucepan on low heat melt the butter. Stir in the onion, green pepper, garlic, and pepper. Cook until the onions and peppers are soft. Turn the heat to medium and blend in the soup, cream cheese, and milk, stirring to prevent sticking. Continue to cook until the cream cheese is melted and the mixture is smooth. Stir in the crabmeat. Add the corn. Bring the mixture to a boil. Reduce the heat to low. Simmer for 10 minutes. Stir in the sugar.

YIELD: 6 TO 8 SERVINGS

Garbanzo Bean Soup (Chickpeas)

This soup was a favorite of a friend of Louis and Billie's who grew up in Miami, Florida. It will keep for two weeks in the refrigerator and the taste improves daily.

1	large ham bone (about 2 pounds with meat)
2	large onions, chopped
2	garlic cloves, minced
2	bay leaves
3	quarts (12 cups) water
2	tablespoons salt
½	teaspoon pepper
¼	teaspoon saffron
4	medium potatoes, peeled and cut into eighths
2	(16-ounce) cans garbanzo (chickpeas) beans
2	chorizo sausages (¼ pound), sliced

In a large stockpot on medium heat combine the hambone, onions, garlic, and bay leaves. Cover with the water and cook for 2 hours. Stir in the salt, pepper, and saffron. Add the potatoes and cook for 30 minutes. Add the beans and sausage. Remove the hambone from the pot. Remove the meat from the bone. Dice the meat and return it to the soup. Cook over low heat for another 30 minutes, checking the seasoning. Discard the bay leaves before serving.

Hint: You can use any well seasoned Spanish or Italian sausage in place of the chorizo.

YIELD: 10 TO 12 SERVINGS

Georgia Peach Soup

This is a delicious cold soup to serve as a first course for a luncheon or dinner party. It is a wonderful way to enjoy fresh Georgia peaches.

SIMPLE SYRUP

- 1 cup sugar
- 2 cups water

SOUP

- 10 fresh peaches
- 2 cups white wine
- 1 cup mineral water
- 1 cup simple syrup
  Mint leaves and chopped pecans for garnish

For the **simple syrup**, in a saucepan on medium heat bring the sugar and water to a boil and boil until syrupy.

For the **soup**, in a saucepan on high heat bring enough water to cover the peaches to a boil. Dip the peaches in the boiling water for 1 minute. Remove the skins and pits. Place the peaches in a blender. Add the wine, mineral water, and simple syrup. Blend until smooth. Chill for several hours. Garnish with little cubes of fresh peaches, mint leaves, and chopped pecans.

YIELD: 12 SERVINGS

Peanut Soup

- 2 tablespoons butter or margarine
- 2 tablespoons grated onion
- 1 celery rib, minced
- 2 tablespoons all-purpose flour
- 3 cups chicken broth
- ½ cup creamy peanut butter
- ½ cup half-and-half
- 2 tablespoons chopped roasted peanuts

Over medium heat in a large saucepan melt the butter. Add the onion and celery and sauté for 5 minutes. Stir in the flour. Cook for 1 minute, stirring constantly. Add the chicken broth. Stirring constantly, bring this mixture to a boil. Reduce the heat to low and simmer for 30 minutes. Stir in the peanut butter and the half-and-half. Continue to cook over low heat for 3 to 4 minutes or until heated, stirring constantly. Before serving, sprinkle with the chopped peanuts.

YIELD: 2 TO 3 SERVINGS

Fresh lemon juice will remove onion scent from hands.

Louis' Dad's North Carolina Brunswick Stew

This is a traditional "made-from-scratch" Brunswick Stew that Louis' father often cooked when he was growing up. There is a lot of love and time put into this recipe as you cook the meats, make the broth, and prepare the vegetables. Be prepared for large quantities and have two stockpots available to help you prepare this undeniably good stew for your friends and family.

1	(7 to 8-pound) baking hen
4	pounds boneless stewing beef, cut into small pieces
4	pounds ham hocks
6¼	pounds frozen shoepeg corn or equal amount of corn cut from the cob
1	(106 ounce or #10) can tomatoes, drained
4	pounds frozen baby lima beans
4	pounds frozen or fresh sweet peas
4	cups chopped onions
4	cups chopped celery
10	pounds peeled and sliced potatoes
	Salt and pepper
	Barbeque sauce (optional)
	Worcestershire sauce (optional)

In a 3-gallon stockpot combine the baking hen, stew beef, and ham hocks. Cover with enough water to make 2½ gallons. Cook on medium heat until the meats are fully done. Remove all the meat from the pot, leaving the broth in the pot. Remove the bones, fat, and skin from the meat. Chop the meat into small pieces. Skim the fat from meat broth.

Use a second 3-gallon stockpot and divide the broth and meat equally between the two pots. Divide the corn, tomatoes, lima beans, sweet peas, onions, celery, and potatoes equally between the two pots. (If you use canned tomatoes, be sure to drain the juice from them.) Cover both pots to retain the flavors. Put on medium-high heat and bring to a rapid boil, stirring often. Boil rapidly for 8 to 10 minutes, continuing to stir often to prevent sticking and burning. Turn the heat down to low and allow each pot to simmer for 3 to 4 hours. While cooking, add the salt and pepper as desired to season. If desired, add the sauces to flavor and season during cooking.

YIELD: 6 GALLONS, 64 SERVINGS

Jill's Vegetable Soup

3	tablespoons olive oil, divided
5	small red potatoes, diced
½	teaspoon garlic salt
4	yellow squash, chopped
2	zucchini squash, chopped
1	small bag baby carrots, chopped
2	garlic cloves, minced
1	medium onion, chopped
3½	cups water
2	(15¾ ounce) cans beef consommé

1 cup steamed cabbage

2 (15-ounce) cans diced seasoned tomatoes

1 cup fresh spinach

1 (10¾-ounce) can light red beans
Salt and pepper

In a large skillet heat 2 tablespoons of the olive oil over medium heat and sauté the red potatoes until they are browned and partially cooked. Sprinkle with the garlic salt. Remove from the skillet and set aside. Spray the skillet with a nonstick vegetable spray and add the remaining 1 tablespoon of olive oil. Sauté the squash, zucchini, and carrots, garlic, and onion on high for a few minutes. In a stockpot on medium-high heat, place the potatoes, squash, zucchini, carrots, garlic, onion, water, and consommé. Bring to a boil and boil for 3 minutes. Add the cabbage, tomatoes, spinach, beans, and salt and pepper to taste. Simmer for 1 hour and 15 minutes. Remove from the heat and let sit for 20 minutes before serving.

YIELD: 6 SERVINGS

Jill Nicholson
Loganville, Georgia

POPULAR SOUTHERN SAYING

I was running around like a chicken with its head cut off!

Maryland Vegetable Crab Soup

This recipe was sent to us by Kendel Ehrlich, first lady of the state of Maryland. She says this is a favorite at Government House, not only of the governor and herself, but of their guests as well. It is a regional treat, and she is sure all who try it will love it.

1 bunch celery, diced small

4 carrots, diced small

2 medium onions, diced small

1 gallon crab stock

1 gallon beef stock

½ cup Old Bay seasoning

½ cup hot sauce

1 pound fresh green beans, cut into bite-size pieces

6 potatoes, peeled and diced small

1 pound lima beans

1 pound corn

1 pound crabmeat (use fresh Maryland jumbo lump crab if possible)

In a Dutch oven on medium heat sauté the celery, carrots, and onions in the oil until they are soft. Add the crab stock and beef stock to the sautéed mixture. Add the Old Bay seasoning and hot sauce to the soup. Add the green beans, potatoes, lima beans, and corn to the soup. Bring the soup to a boil. Turn the heat down and simmer until all the vegetables are fully cooked. Season to taste with additional hot sauce. Add the crabmeat.

YIELD: 3 GALLONS, ABOUT 32 SERVINGS

Potato Soup

If you enjoy potato soup, this is one of the best ever.

8	red potatoes, peeled and diced
1	(10¾-ounce) can cream of chicken soup
1	(10¾-ounce) can cheddar cheese soup
1	(12-ounce) can evaporated milk
2	cups shredded cheddar cheese
1	(10¾-ounce) jar real bacon bits

Put the potatoes in a large saucepan with enough water to cover. Cook over medium-high heat until fork tender. In a medium-size saucepan over low heat, combine the soups and milk, stirring until smooth. Add the potatoes, cheese, and bacon bits. Stir constantly until the mixture is blended, about 5 minutes. Serve hot with rolls.

YIELD: ABOUT 4 SERVINGS

Minestrone Soup

This wonderful winter soup recipe was sent to us by Charlie and Gloria Norwood. Charlie is the congressman for the state of Georgia from the ninth district. This treat is enjoyed by family and friends throughout the holidays. It is very forgiving of added, changed, or omitted ingredients. Actually, Gloria says that is the description of her cooking technique. "If it isn't flexible, it has no place in my life. Should I ever have a cooking show, it would be named Look How She Made It This Time!"

½	pound sausage, cooked and drained
1	cup chopped onions
2	garlic cloves, minced
1	cup diced carrots
1	teaspoon dried basil
2	medium zucchini, sliced
1	(16-ounce) can diced tomatoes, not drained
2	cups shredded cabbage
2	(10-ounce) cans beef broth
	Salt and pepper
1	(15-ounce) can kidney or black beans, drained
½	cup uncooked rice
½	cup red wine

In a heavy stockpot on medium heat cook the sausage. Drain the grease from the sausage. Add the onions, garlic, carrots, and basil to the sausage and cook for 5 minutes. Add the zucchini, tomatoes, cabbage, beef broth, and salt and pepper to taste. Bring the mixture to a boil. Lower the heat and simmer for about 1 hour. Add the kidney beans, rice, and red wine. Cook for 20 minutes. When ready to serve, garnish with parsley and Parmesan cheese.

YIELD: 10 SERVINGS

Dip a spoon in hot water to measure shortening, butter, and other fats, and they won't stick as easily.

Quick-and-Easy Clam Chowder

This special chowder recipe comes from the kitchen of Louis' Aunt Dot.

1 (10¾-ounce) can New England clam chowder

1 cup whole milk

1 tablespoon butter

¼ cup breaded clam pieces

¼ cup shredded cheddar cheese

Salt and pepper

In a heavy saucepan on medium heat, combine the clam chowder, milk, butter, clam pieces, cheese, and salt and pepper to taste. Bring to a slow boil, stirring often. Turn the heat down to low and simmer for 10 to 15 minutes, continuing to stir often. Raise heat to medium and bring to a slow boil, stirring often. Serve hot.

YIELD: 4 SERVINGS

She-Crab Soup

1 quart whipping cream

⅛ teaspoon salt

⅛ teaspoon pepper

2 fish bouillon cubes

2 cups boiling water

¼ cup (½ stick) unsalted butter

½ cup all-purpose flour

2 tablespoons lemon juice

¼ teaspoon ground nutmeg

1 pound fresh crabmeat

Chopped parsley for garnish

⅓ cup sherry (optional)

In a heavy small saucepan over medium heat bring the whipping cream, salt, and pepper to a boil. Reduce the heat to low and simmer for 1 hour. Set aside. In a small mixing bowl dissolve the fish bouillon cubes in the boiling water, stirring until the cubes are completely dissolved. In a large, heavy saucepan over low heat, melt the butter. Add the flour to the melted butter, stirring until it is smooth. Cook for 1 minute, stirring continuously. Gradually add the hot fish broth. Turn the heat to medium and cook until the mixture thickens. Stir in the cream mixture and cook until the soup is thoroughly heated. Add the lemon juice, nutmeg, and crabmeat. When serving, garnish each bowl with parsley and a teaspoon of the sherry (*not* cooking sherry) if desired.

YIELD: 6 TO 8 SERVINGS

Sherry Soup

This is a very flavorful and colorful soup. It would be a wonderful accompaniment to any dinner. The rich ruby color of the soup is beautiful in a lovely white china bowl. It is also delicious as a sauce over pound cake with a dollop of whipped topping on top.

½   cup water
3   tablespoons quick-cooking tapioca
2   cups Concord grape juice
2   cups pineapple juice
½   cup granulated sugar
    Rind of 1 lemon, grated
1   (1 to 2-inch) stick of cinnamon
1   cup fresh raspberries
½   cup sherry

In a large saucepan on high heat bring the water to a rapid boil and stir in the tapioca. Reduce the heat to medium and cook until clear. Add the grape and pineapple juices. Bring to a boil. Add the sugar, lemon rind, and cinnamon. Reduce the heat to low and cook for 10 minutes. Remove from the stove and put in a large bowl. Add the raspberries and sherry. Put in the refrigerator to chill before serving.

YIELD: ABOUT 4 SERVINGS

Joyce Dina
Gainesville, Florida

Tomato-Basil Cream Soup

5   large fully ripened tomatoes
1   whole head garlic, smashed
     Salt
     Freshly ground black pepper
     Dash of lemon pepper
1½   tablespoons chopped basil
¼   cup (½ stick) butter
1½   cups cream
     Lemon juice

Peel the tomatoes, and in a large heavy saucepan on medium-high heat stew the tomatoes with just enough water to start them cooking. Add the garlic, salt and pepper to taste, lemon pepper, and basil. When the liquid reduces and the tomatoes are softened, purée the mixture with a blender (or just mash them right in the pan) until smooth. Strain the tomatoes to remove the seeds if you like and pour the tomato liquid back into the pan.

Over medium-high heat, melt the butter. Slowly pour in the cream, stirring as you pour. You have to judge by the thickness desired; you may need more cream. Taste the soup and adjust the seasoning. Give a good squirt of lemon juice. Serve in individual bowls and top with grated pecorino cheese mixed with small buttered croutons.

YIELD: 4 SERVINGS

Anne Galbraith
Knoxville, Tennessee

Vegetable Soup

Vegetable soup lends itself to a lot of flexibility to add your favorite ingredients. The traditional soup can include such vegetables as snap beans, butter beans, and lima beans. However, leftover vegetables are great additions and a nice way to get two meals out of one.

4	cups water
½	cup diced potatoes
½	cup sliced carrots
½	cup early June peas
¾	cup corn
1	cup mashed cooked whole tomatoes
½	cup fresh or frozen okra
¼	cup chopped celery
¼	cup sliced onions
1	pound cubed beef—for vegetable beef soup, (optional)
1	pound ham or ham hock—for vegetable ham soup, (optional)
	Salt and pepper

In a large stockpot over medium heat combine the water, potatoes, carrots, peas, corn, tomatoes, okra, celery, onions, and beef or ham if desired. Bring to a boil. Turn the heat down to low and allow the soup to simmer for 1 to 2 hours until seasoned and done, stirring occasionally. Season the with salt and pepper to taste.

YIELD: 8 SERVINGS

ABC Salad

½	cup vegetable oil
2	plus 1 tablespoons lemon juice
1	teaspoon granulated sugar
¼	teaspoon salt
1	cup dried cranberries
3	large red apples cut in ½-inch cubes
2	cups fresh broccoli florets
½	cup chopped walnuts

In a bowl whisk the oil, 2 tablespoons lemon juice, sugar, and salt. Add the cranberries. Let stand for 10 minutes. In another large bowl toss the apples with the remaining 1 tablespoon lemon juice. Add the broccoli, walnuts, and cranberry mixture. Toss to coat. Cover and refrigerate for 2 hours or until chilled. Toss before serving.

YIELD: 6 TO 8 SERVINGS

Almond and Orange Salad

This salad goes well with special dinners or luncheons.

CARAMELIZED ALMONDS

4	tablespoons granulated sugar
½	cup sliced almonds

DRESSING

¼	cup vegetable oil
2	tablespoons apple cider vinegar
2	tablespoons granulated sugar
5	drops Tabasco
½	teaspoon salt

SALAD

2	green onions, sliced
4	cups drained mandarin orange sections
2	tablespoons chopped fresh parsley
½	cup caramelized almonds
½	head endive, chopped (optional)

For the **caramelized almonds**: In a medium-size heavy saucepan on high heat mix the sugar and almonds. Stir for 3 minutes. Remove from heat and spread apart on wax paper. Allow to cool.

For the **dressing**: In a small jar mix the oil, vinegar, sugar, Tabasco, and salt. Shake all the ingredients together and refrigerate until ready to serve.

For the **salad**: In a large mixing bowl mix the onions, mandarin orange slices, parsley, caramelized almonds, and endive (if desired). Cover and refrigerate until ready to serve. Prior to serving, pour the dressing over the salad. Sprinkle the almonds on top of the salad.

YIELD: 4 SERVINGS

Mildred Tribble
Social Circle, Georgia

Al Fresco Watermelon Salad

This unique onion and watermelon salad makes its appearance at many of our family gatherings in the summer. The savory seasonings complement each and every bite of the sweet melon.

1	medium Vidalia onion
4	cups cubed and seeded watermelon
2	tablespoons minced fresh basil
¼	cup balsamic vinegar
	Salt and pepper

Peel, quarter, and thinly slice the onion. In a large bowl combine the onion, watermelon, and basil. Drizzle with the vinegar. Toss gently. Add the salt and pepper to taste. Refrigerate for up to 1 hour. Serve with a slotted spoon.

YIELD: 4 TO 6 SERVINGS

Ambrosia

8	medium navel oranges
1	(8-ounce) can crushed pineapple, drained

½ cup flaked coconut

1 cup whipping cream

2 tablespoons confectioners' sugar
Maraschino cherries

Peel and section the oranges over a bowl, reserving any juice. Stir together the orange sections, reserved juice, pineapple, and coconut. Cover and chill for 8 hours.

Beat the whipping cream until foamy. Gradually add the confectioners' sugar, beating until soft peaks form. Spoon the fruit mixture into individual dishes. Top each serving with the whipped cream and a cherry.

YIELD: 4 TO 6 SERVINGS

Amy's Salad

This salad recipe comes to us from a family friend, Amy Corasaniti. It is very tasty, and when we have pot luck get-togethers, Amy is always asked if she brought her salad. She now brings a double recipe and there are never any leftovers.

1 head romaine lettuce

1 bunch broccoli, chopped

4 green onions, chopped

4 teaspoons butter

1 cup chopped English walnuts

1 package Ramen noodles

DRESSING

1 cup vegetable oil

¼ cup red wine vinegar

1 cup granulated sugar

1 tablespoon soy sauce

In a large bowl place the lettuce, broccoli, and green onions. In a skillet on low heat melt the butter. Brown the walnuts and noodles in the melted butter. Remove from the heat and allow to cool. When cool, pour the mixture over the lettuce mixture and toss.

In a small saucepan on low heat mix the vegetable oil, vinegar, sugar, and soy sauce. Stir over low heat until the sugar is dissolved and the mixture is warm. Pour over the salad just before serving.

YIELD: 10 TO 12 SERVINGS

Apple Cole Slaw

1 to 2 Granny Smith or Rome apples, unpeeled, cored and diced

1 medium head white cabbage, quartered and shredded

¼ cup shredded purple cabbage (optional)

2 carrots, grated

¼ cup mayonnaise

1 tablespoon granulated sugar
Salt and pepper

In a large mixing bowl toss the apples, cabbages and carrots. Add the mayonnaise, sugar, and salt and pepper to taste. Stir all the ingredients together and mix well. Refrigerate until ready to serve.

Hint: If a creamier slaw is desired, add more mayonnaise.

YIELD: 4 TO 6 SERVINGS

Frozen Bing Cherry Salad

This is a beautiful salad for special occasions, bridal luncheons, and more. The recipe comes to us from Sandi McClain, who managed our Blue Willow Gift Shop for a number of years.

1   (8-ounce) package cream cheese, softened

1   (8-ounce) container sour cream

½   cup granulated sugar

1   cup chopped pecans

1½   cups miniature marshmallows

1   to 2 drops red food coloring

1   (16-ounce) can crushed pineapple

1   (16-ounce) can dark pitted cherries in their juice, drained

In a food processor mix the cream cheese, sour cream, sugar, pecans, marshmallows, and food coloring. Then pour the mixture into a medium-size mixing bowl and stir in the pineapple and cherries. Pour into a 9 x 13-inch casserole dish and freeze. When frozen, cut into squares and serve. This recipe also works well in individual molds for a brunch or luncheon.

YIELD: ABOUT 24 SERVINGS

Blueberry Salad

This dish can be served as a dessert or a salad, and is often prepared for holidays and special family gatherings. It is a great favorite of the Van Dyke's son, Chip.

1   (8-ounce) can crushed pineapple

1   (6-ounce) package blueberry gelatin (blackberry can be substituted)

3   cups boiling water

1   (16-ounce) can blueberries, drained

1   (8-ounce) container sour cream

1   (8-ounce) package cream cheese, softened

½   cup granulated sugar

½   cup chopped pecans

In a small bowl drain the pineapple and reserve the juice. In a medium bowl dissolve the gelatin in the boiling water. After the gelatin has dissolved, stir the pineapple juice into the gelatin mixture. Place in the refrigerator and chill until the consistency of unbeaten egg white.

Stir the pineapple and blueberries into the gelatin. Pour the gelatin and fruit mixture into two 6 x 10-inch pans and chill until firm.

In a medium bowl combine the sour cream, cream cheese, and sugar. Mix until smooth and well blended. Divide and spread the mixture evenly over the firmly set salad. Top with the chopped pecans.

YIELD: 8 SERVINGS

Bridge-Luncheon Frozen Fruit Salad

This is a typical salad served at ladies' bridge clubs in the South. Bridge clubs can meet once a week, once a month, or whatever schedule the ladies in the group agree upon. The day is devoted to bridge, possibly sipping a glass or two of wine, and a light luncheon served in the dining room with good silver, crystal, fine china, and linens. The ladies often agree on an amount to be put in the kitty for the day's winner, or the hostess for the day will have an appropriate gift for the winner. If one of the members is unable to be at bridge club, she must find a suitable substitute. In the South, bridge must go on!

2   (3-ounce) packages cream cheese, softened
1   cup mayonnaise
1   cup whipped cream (refrigerated whipped topping can be used; thaw and stir first to aerate)
1   (20-ounce) can crushed pineapple, drained
1½   cups mini marshmallows
1   (6-ounce) jar maraschino cherries, diced
1   cup diced strawberries
½   cup fresh (not canned) blueberries or peaches

Grease a 9 x 13-inch casserole pan. In a large mixing bowl combine the cream cheese, mayonnaise, whipped cream, pineapple, marshmallows, cherries, strawberries, and blueberries. Pour this mixture into the greased casserole pan. Freeze. When ready to serve, cut into squares and serve on a bed of lettuce.

YIELD: 12 SERVINGS

Broccoli Salad

1   (10-ounce) bunch fresh broccoli, chopped
½   cup chopped green onions
1   tablespoon bacon bits
¾   cup chopped English walnuts
½   cup slivered almonds
½   cup golden raisins

DRESSING
1   cup mayonnaise
¼   cup granulated sugar
2   tablespoons apple cider vinegar

In a large mixing bowl combine the broccoli, onion, bacon bits, walnuts, almonds, and raisins. Toss. In a small mixing bowl mix the mayonnaise, sugar, and vinegar. Pour the mayonnaise mixture over the salad and serve. This has a better flavor if chilled overnight in the refrigerator.

YIELD: 10 TO 12 SERVINGS

Lois Dalton
Covington, Georgia

Buttermilk Congealed Salad

This recipe, provided by Mae Morrow of our Journey's End Restaurant, can be found in the original Blue Willow cookbook and remains a favorite of customers to this day.

1   (3-ounce) package orange gelatin
1   (8-ounce) can crushed pineapple, not drained
2   cups buttermilk
1   (6-ounce) package whipped topping
2   cups chopped pecans

In a small saucepan combine the gelatin and the pineapple. Cook over low heat until the gelatin dissolves. Remove from the heat and allow the mixture to cool.

In a medium-size mixing bowl combine the buttermilk and whipped topping. Add the pecans and gelatin mixture. Pour into a mold or casserole dish and refrigerate. Serve when firm.

YIELD: 6 SERVINGS

Carrot-Raisin Salad

A delicious salad that is great for both picnics and luncheons.

8   to 10 carrots
½   cup raisins
½   cup chopped pineapple

¼   cup mayonnaise
1   teaspoon granulated sugar

In a food processor or with a hand grater shred the carrots and put in a medium-size mixing bowl. Add the raisins, pineapple, mayonnaise, and sugar. Stir to mix well. Refrigerate until ready to serve.

Hint: A peeled and chopped Red Delicious apple can be added for a different taste.

YIELD: 6 TO 8 SERVINGS

Chicken Salad

This salad works well as a sandwich filling when the chicken is chopped fine and it can be used for stuffing hollowed-out cherry tomatoes or served in puffed pastry shells for an appetizer.

3   cups cooked and chopped chicken
½   cup chopped celery
2   hard-cooked eggs, chopped
½   cup sweet pickle cubes
⅓   cup mayonnaise
     Salt

In a large mixing bowl combine the chicken, celery, eggs, pickles, mayonnaise, and salt to taste. Stir until all the ingredients are thoroughly mixed. Refrigerate the salad for at least 1 hour before serving.

YIELD: 8 TO 10 SERVINGS

Cole Slaw

1   large head green cabbage, shredded
¼   cup shredded purple cabbage
     (optional)
2   carrots, grated
1   heaping tablespoon sweet pickle relish
¼   cup mayonnaise
1   tablespoon granulated sugar
1   tablespoon white vinegar (optional)
     Salt and pepper

In a large mixing bowl combine the cabbages, and the carrots. Add the relish, mayonnaise, sugar, vinegar, and salt and pepper to taste. Stir to mix well. Refrigerate until ready to serve.

Hint: Add 1 large peeled and diced Red Delicious apple.

YIELD: 8 TO 10 SERVINGS

Corn Bread Salad

This is a perfect way to utilize any leftover corn bread that you might have, unless, of course, you would prefer to mix it in a glass of buttermilk for a midnight snack.

8   corn bread muffins (see page 154)
1   (8-ounce) can green peas, drained
1   (11-ounce) can Mexicorn
2   hard-cooked eggs, chopped

½   large green bell pepper, chopped
½   large onion, chopped
¾   cup mayonnaise
     Salt and pepper

In a large mixing bowl crumble the corn bread muffins. Add the peas, Mexicorn, eggs, bell pepper, onion, mayonnaise, and salt and pepper to taste. Toss lightly. Refrigerate and serve cold.

YIELD: 8 SERVINGS

Cottage Cheese Salad

This recipe is also fondly known as "Orange Stuff."

1   (12-ounce) container cottage cheese
1   (8-ounce) container whipped topping
1   (10-ounce) can mandarin orange
     sections, drained
1   (20-ounce) can crushed pineapple,
     drained
½   cup chopped nuts
1   (3-ounce) package orange gelatin

In a medium-size mixing bowl combine the cottage cheese and whipped topping and gently blend. Add the oranges, pineapple, and nuts and mix gently. Add the dry gelatin to the salad and mix well. Pour the mixture into a large Pyrex dish. Chill for 2 to 3 hours before serving.

YIELD: 6 TO 8 SERVINGS

Company Chicken Salad

My neighbor served this recipe thirty-two years ago at my bridesmaids' luncheon. I have made it hundreds of times for showers and many more times for my own family.

3	cups cooked and chopped chicken
1	tablespoon minced onion
1	teaspoon salt
2	tablespoons lemon juice
1	cup chopped celery
1	cup seedless grapes, halved
⅓	cup mayonnaise
1	(11-ounce) can mandarin oranges, drained
½	cup toasted slivered almonds
1	tablespoon horseradish
1	teaspoon granulated sugar

In a large mixing bowl combine the chicken, onion, salt, lemon juice, celery, grapes, mayonnaise, oranges, almonds, horseradish, and sugar. Put in the refrigerator and chill for at least 1 hour before serving.

YIELD: 8 TO 10 SERVINGS

Marilynn Walker
Loganville, Georgia

Crunchy Apple Salad

This salad is very pretty when made in decorative molds and served over a bed of fancy lettuce leaves and surrounded by apple slices.

1	(20-ounce) can crushed pineapple, not drained
⅓	cup granulated sugar
1	(3-ounce) package lemon gelatin
1	(8-ounce) package cream cheese, softened
1	cup diced unpeeled apples
½	to 1 cup chopped pecans
1	cup chopped celery
1	cup whipped topping

In a medium-size saucepan on medium heat combine the pineapple and sugar. Bring to a boil and boil for 3 minutes. Add the gelatin and stir until completely dissolved. Add the cream cheese and stir until the mixture is thoroughly combined. Set aside to cool. Fold in the apples, pecans, celery, and whipped topping. Pour into a 9-inch square pan. Chill until firm.

YIELD: 8 TO 10 SERVINGS

Dandelion Potato Salad

3	plus 1 hard-cooked eggs
1⅓	cups water
1	plus ½ teaspoon salt
4	cups cubed peeled potatoes
½	cup granulated sugar
4	teaspoons all-purpose flour
½	cup white vinegar
1	teaspoon prepared mustard
1½	cups diced onions
¼	cup mayonnaise
¾	teaspoon celery salt
¼	teaspoon garlic powder
¼	teaspoon black pepper
½	cup chopped green bell pepper
½	cup chopped sweet red pepper
½	cup sweet pickle relish
1	to 1½ cups snipped dandelion leaves or spinach leaves
	Paprika

Peel the eggs. Chop 3 eggs and slice 1 for garnish. In a saucepan over medium heat bring the water and 1 teaspoon salt to a boil. Add the potatoes. Cook until tender. While the potatoes are cooking, in another saucepan over medium heat combine the sugar, flour, vinegar, and mustard until smooth. Bring to a boil. Cook and stir for 2 minutes or until thickened. Add the onions. Cook 2 minutes longer. In a colander drain the potatoes and put them into a medium-size bowl. Add in the onion mixture and stir. In a small bowl combine the mayonnaise, celery salt, garlic powder, pepper, and the remaining ½ teaspoon salt. Add the mayonnaise mixture to the potato mixture. Toss to coat. Stir in the chopped eggs, green and red peppers, pickle relish, and dandelion leaves. Cover and refrigerate until serving. Garnish with the sliced egg and sprinkle with paprika to taste.

YIELD: 10 TO 12 SERVINGS

Curried Sweet Potato Salad

This makes an excellent tasty side dish for Thanksgiving or Christmas.

4	medium sweet potatoes
½	cup Hellmann's mayonnaise
2	teaspoons curry powder
1	teaspoon coarse-ground mustard
1	tablespoon brown sugar
½	cup cranraisins
½	cup slightly toasted chopped pecans
2	green onions, sliced
	Salt and pepper

Preheat the oven to 350°. Bake the sweet potatoes for 50 to 60 minutes, or until slightly firm but thoroughly cooked. Allow to cool; then peel and dice the potatoes. In a large bowl combine the mayonnaise, curry powder, mustard, and brown sugar. Add the sweet potatoes, craisins, pecans, and green onions. Season with the salt and pepper to taste. Chill overnight.

YIELD: 6 SERVINGS

Daylily Salad

2   cups (about 50 buds) sliced daylily buds
1   cup torn lettuce
½   medium cucumber, sliced
1   medium tomato, diced
2   celery ribs, sliced
¼   cup shredded red cabbage
3   radishes, sliced
    Salad dressing

In a large salad bowl combine the daylily buds, lettuce, cucumber, tomato, celery, cabbage, and radishes. Serve with the dressing of your choice.

YIELD: 4 TO 6 SERVINGS

Elegant Chicken Salad

This is a delicious chicken salad "for light luncheons and ladies' functions." It is suggested that the salad be served on a bed of lettuce with crackers on the side or stuffed into whole ripe tomatoes that have been cut into wedges but left intact at the bottom to form a cup.

3   cups cooked diced chicken
¾   cup halved seedless red or green grapes
1   (20-ounce) can pineapple chunks, drained
1   (11-ounce) can mandarin oranges, drained

¼   cup toasted chopped pecans
¼   cup chopped celery (optional)
¼   cup salad dressing
⅛   teaspoon salt
    Romaine lettuce leaves

In a large mixing bowl, toss the chicken, grapes, pineapple, oranges, pecans, and celery if desired together lightly. Gently mix the salad dressing and salt with the chicken mixture. Chill. Line a large glass bowl with the lettuce leaves. Add the chicken salad and garnish with more pecans if desired.

YIELD: 8 TO 10 SERVINGS

Family-Favorite Layered Salad

1   medium head of lettuce, shredded
½   cup thinly sliced green onions
1   cup thinly sliced celery
1   (8-ounce) can sliced water chestnuts
1   (10-ounce) package frozen peas, not thawed
2   cups mayonnaise
2   tablespoons granulated sugar
½   cup Parmesan cheese
¼   teaspoon garlic powder
1   teaspoon seasoned salt
3   hard-cooked eggs, chopped
½   to ¾ pound bacon, crisply cooked and crumbled
    Cherry tomatoes

Spread the shredded lettuce in a shallow dish. Top with a layer of green onions, a layer of celery, and a layer of water chestnuts and peas. Spread the mayonnaise over all. In a small mixing bowl combine the sugar, Parmesan cheese, garlic powder, and seasoned salt. Sprinkle on top of the layered ingredients. Cover and chill for at least 24 hours. Before serving, garnish the salad with the eggs, bacon, and cherry tomatoes.

YIELD: 10 TO 12 SERVINGS

Friendship, or Doug's Favorite, Salad

This is not a family recipe, but one I developed on a whim. I have used this recipe for the last fifteen years or so after having tweaked the ingredients a bit from the original. The name "Friendship Salad" came about after one of the ladies at church said she loved it, but made her husband go brush his teeth after eating it. For a fun idea this salad may be served in a large conch shell, and individual servings in smaller shells. It can be garnished with palm trees made from green onions and an island made from tomato wedges.

4	to 6 bunches green onions
1	(15-ounce) can early peas, rinsed and drained
1	(16-ounce) package imitation crabmeat, shredded
1½	pounds peeled and chilled salad-size shrimp
3	to 4 celery ribs, split and diced

1	tablespoon granulated sugar
½	cup mayonnaise
⅛	cup distilled white vinegar
1	large tomato, diced

Wash and drain the onions. Dice the green part into 1-inch pieces and dice the whites into ¼-inch pieces. In a large mixing bowl combine the onions, peas, crabmeat, shrimp, celery, sugar, mayonnaise, and vinegar and toss well. Add the tomato last so that it does not get mushy. Cover and refrigerate overnight. Serve cold on a bed of lettuce.

YIELD: ABOUT 20 SERVINGS

Buddy Logan
Lagrange, Georgia
First Place Winner—Soups and Salads
Blue Willow Inn Restaurant Recipe Contest, 2004

Grape Salad

This is a luscious, colorful salad that can be combined with a tuna plate for a lovely presentation at a ladies' luncheon. It is refreshing and we found it to be well received when served at Magnolia Hall.

1½	cups toasted coarsely chopped pecans
1	(1-pound) bag seedless green grapes
1	(1-pound) bag seedless red grapes
1	(1-pound) bag seedless black grapes
1	(8-ounce) package cream cheese, softened
1	(8-ounce) container sour cream
⅓	cup granulated sugar
1	cup packed light brown sugar

In a small skillet on medium heat toast the pecans. Wash and dry the grapes and place in a medium-size bowl. In a small bowl of an electric mixer beat the cream cheese, sour cream, and granulated sugar. Pour this mixture over the grapes and gently mix well. Place the mixture in a pretty serving bowl. In a small bowl mix the brown sugar and toasted pecans. Sprinkle them over the salad. Serve immediately or cover and refrigerate. This will last for several days.

YIELD: ABOUT 20 SERVINGS

Ariann Stone
Monroe, Georgia

Fresh Fruit and Cheese in Pineapple Wedges

This is a beautiful salad or fruit dish served at bridal luncheons and showers at Magnolia Hall. The fruits make this a very colorful presentation and everyone is delighted with the taste.

2	medium-size fresh pineapples
4	cups sliced fresh strawberries
2	cups cubed cantaloupe
2	cups cubed honeydew
1	cup seedless red grapes
1	cup fresh blueberries
2	peeled and sliced kiwifruit
1	cup cubed mild cheddar cheese
1	(8-ounce) container sour cream
⅓	cup strawberry preserves
½	teaspoon vanilla extract

Using a sharp chef's knife or an electric knife, cut the pineapple into quarters, keeping fronds (leaves) attached. Remove the core from each wedge. Cut out the pineapple, leaving a ¼-inch-thick shell. Cut the pineapple into small chunks and set aside 2 cups, reserving any remaining pineapple for other uses.

In a large bowl combine the 2 cups pineapple, strawberries, cantaloupe, honeydew, grapes, blueberries, kiwifruit, and cheese cubes. Stir gently. In a small bowl, combine the sour cream, strawberry preserves, and vanilla. Stir well.

When ready to serve, place the pineapple wedges on

individual serving plates. Spoon about 1½ cups of the fruit mixture onto each wedge. Spoon 2 tablespoons of the sour cream mixture beside each pineapple wedge.

YIELD: 8 SERVINGS

Peggy Hawkins, Events Manager
Magnolia Hall

Holiday Mincemeat Salad

This is a wonderful salad to serve for Thanksgiving and Christmas.

1 (8-ounce) can crushed pineapple
1 (¼-ounce) envelope unflavored gelatin
¼ cup cold water
2 (3-ounce) packages cherry gelatin mix
 Hot water (use the pineapple juice and add hot water to measure 3½ cups)
1 (20½-ounce) jar mincemeat
1 small apple with peel, cubed
1 cup chopped pecans

In a small mixing bowl drain the crushed pineapple and save the juice. In a small bowl soak the unflavored gelatin in the cold water, allowing it to dissolve. In a medium-size serving bowl dissolve the cherry gelatin in the pineapple juice and hot water mixture. Add the unflavored gelatin to the cherry gelatin mixture. Refrigerate until it is the consistency of egg whites. Add the crushed pineapple, mincemeat, apple, and pecans. This salad can be poured into a 7-cup mold sprayed with cooking oil.

YIELD: 14 SERVINGS

Hot Chicken Salad

This recipe comes from a good friend and customer of the Blue Willow Inn Restaurant, Scottie Sherrill, whose husband, Frank, was mayor of Social Circle for several years.

2 cups chopped, cooked boneless chicken
2 cups chopped celery
½ cup mayonnaise
½ teaspoon salt
2 tablespoons grated onion
½ (10¾-ounce) can condensed cream of mushroom soup
1 cup chopped green bell peppers
2 tablespoons lemon juice
3 tablespoons chopped pimientos
1 teaspoon Worcestershire sauce
¾ cup grated cheddar cheese
½ cup slivered almonds
2 cups crushed potato chips

Preheat the oven to 350°. In a large mixing bowl, mix the chicken, celery, mayonnaise, salt, onion, soup, peppers, lemon juice, pimientos, and Worcestershire. Pour into a 2-quart baking dish and top with the cheese, almonds, and potato chips. Bake for 30 minutes.

YIELD: 8 TO 10 SERVINGS

Horseradish Salad

This salad is delicious with roast beef or other beef dishes.

2	cups boiling water
1	(3-ounce) package lime gelatin
1	(3-ounce) package lemon gelatin
1	(20-ounce) can crushed pineapple, drained
2	(12-ounce) containers small curd cottage cheese
1	cup mayonnaise
1	cup finely chopped pecans
4	tablespoons horseradish
3	tablespoons lemon juice
¼	teaspoon salt
1	(14-ounce) can sweetened condensed milk

Topping

½	cup mayonnaise
½	cup sour cream
1	teaspoon horseradish

In a small saucepan on high heat bring the water to a boil. In a large mixing bowl dissolve the lime and lemon gelatins in the boiling water. Add the chilled pineapple.

In a medium-size mixing bowl combine the cottage cheese with the mayonnaise and mix until smooth. Add to the gelatin mixture. Add the pecans, horseradish, lemon juice, salt, and condensed milk to the mixture and stir until the mixture begins to congeal.

Pour into a mold or a 9 x 13-inch pan and refrigerate overnight. Prior to serving, in a small mixing bowl combine the mayonnaise, sour cream, and horseradish for the topping. Mix well. Serve the gelatin salad on a bed of lettuce with the topping spooned on.

YIELD: 24 SERVINGS

Marinated Vegetable Salad

2	to 3 cups broccoli florets
2	to 3 cups cauliflower florets
1	cup sliced squash
1	cup sliced cucumbers
1	pint cherry tomatoes
¼	cup black olives
¼	cup green olives
2	to 3 radishes, sliced
1	(16-ounce) bottle Italian salad dressing

In a large mixing bowl prepare 4 cups of the desired combination of broccoli, cauliflower, squash, cucumber, and cherry tomatoes. Mix in the black olives, green olives, and radishes. Pour the Italian dressing over the vegetables. Marinate in the refrigerator overnight.

YIELD: 10 TO 12 SERVINGS

Gourmet Potato Salad

This is a nice change from regular potato salad. I often use red potatoes and leave the skins on, giving it a different taste and color.

1   cup cottage cheese

1   cup sour cream

2   teaspoons mustard

2   teaspoons seasoned salt

4   cups sliced cooked potatoes

1   cup sliced green onions

1   cup sliced celery

½   cup diced green peppers

3   hard-cooked eggs, chopped

1   (1-ounce) package crumbled blue cheese

In a medium-size mixing bowl combine the cottage cheese, sour cream, mustard, and salt.

In a large mixing bowl combine the potatoes, onions, celery, green peppers, and eggs. Add the cheese mixture and stir carefully. Place in the refrigerator and chill for several hours to blend flavors. Fold in the blue cheese just before serving.

YIELD: 8 TO 10 SERVINGS

Karol Trammel
Monroe, Georgia

Pasta Salad

3   cups cooked spiral pasta

½   cup thinly sliced celery

1   cup par-boiled broccoli florets

½   cup thinly sliced carrots

¼   cup thinly sliced green onion

½   cup green bell pepper

½   to ¾ cup salad dressing

     Salt and pepper

     Hard-cooked eggs

Prepare the pasta according to package directions. Drain. In a large bowl combine the pasta, celery, broccoli, carrots, onion, pepper, salad dressing, and the salt and pepper to taste. Slice the hard-cooked eggs and garnish the top of the salad. Cover and chill before serving.

YIELD: 8 SERVINGS

Kraut Salad

1   (1-pint) container sauerkraut, chopped and drained

1   cup chopped onion

1   cup chopped celery

1   medium green bell pepper, chopped

1   cup granulated sugar

½   cup cider vinegar

½   cup salad oil

In a medium-size mixing bowl combine the drained sauerkraut, onion, celery, bell pepper, sugar, vinegar, and salad oil. Cover, refrigerate, and chill for at least 2 hours. This is best if prepared the day before and refrigerated overnight. Store in a sealed container.

YIELD: ABOUT 4 CUPS

Louis' Potato Salad

Louis does not favor any uncooked onion or relish in his potato salad, so Miss Billie always makes his potato salad separately. For those who enjoy onions and relish, you will find those ingredients listed below in a variation of the original recipe.

6	medium all-purpose potatoes
3	plus 1 hard-cooked eggs, sliced
¼	cup chopped green salad olives
¼	cup mayonnaise
1	tablespoon prepared mustard
	Salt and pepper
	Paprika (optional)
	Parsley sprigs (optional)

Peel and cut the potatoes into ½ to 1-inch cubes. In a stockpot cover the potatoes with warm water and bring to a boil. Cook until the potatoes are just beginning to test tender. Remove from the heat and cool in cold water to stop the cooking process. In a large mixing bowl combine the potatoes, slices of 3 eggs, olives, mayonnaise, mustard, and salt and pepper to taste. Mix gently and transfer the potato salad to a serving bowl. Layer the remaining egg slices on top. If desired, garnish with a small amount of paprika and fresh parsley sprigs. Cover and refrigerate until served.

Hint: For a tastier salad, add ¼ cup sweet pickle relish and/or ½ cup finely chopped onion.

YIELD: 8 TO 10 SERVINGS

Mama Smith's Pear Delight

1	(15-ounce) can pears
1	cup reserved pear syrup
1	(3-ounce) box lime gelatin
1	(3-ounce) package cream cheese, softened
1	cup whipping cream

In a small saucepan over medium heat bring the pear syrup to a boil. Remove from the heat immediately. In a medium-size mixing bowl dissolve the gelatin in the pear syrup. In a medium bowl thoroughly mix the pears and the cream cheese. In a small bowl beat the whipping cream. Add the whipped cream to the pear mixture and add the dissolved gelatin. Pour into a 9 x 13-inch casserole dish or a mold. Place in the refrigerator and allow the salad to congeal.

YIELD: ABOUT 16 SERVINGS

Jimmy Clack
Cordele, Georgia

Luscious Lemon Cream Salad

This pretty salad can be put into a mold. Its sunny yellow color will brighten any table. It is beautiful to use in the spring or summer with a centerpiece of yellow and white daffodils and daisies. This is also a wonderful addition to a pot luck dinner.

1   (10-ounce) bottle lemon-lime soda

1   cup miniature marshmallows

1   (8-ounce) package cream cheese,
    softened and cubed

2   (3-ounce) packages lemon gelatin

1   (20-ounce) can crushed pineapple, not
    drained

¾   cup chopped pecans

1   cup heavy whipping cream, whipped

In a small sauce pan over low heat, stirring constantly, combine the soda, marshmallows, and cream cheese and heat until the cream cheese melts. Remove from the heat. Add the gelatin, stirring until it dissolves. Stir in the pineapple and the pecans. Chill until the consistency of unbeaten egg whites. Fold in the whipped cream. Cover, refrigerate, and chill until firm.

YIELD: 12 TO 15 SERVINGS

Vivian Beasley
Monroe, Georgia

Ranch House Salad with Pecan Vinaigrette

1   (8-ounce) package mixed salad greens

1   cup finely shredded red cabbage

½   cup (2 ounces) shredded Monterey
    Jack cheese

1   tomato, cut into wedges

1   avocado, sliced

    Vegetable oil

2   corn tortillas, cut into thin strips
    Pecan Vinaigrette

PECAN VINAIGRETTE

¼   cup white wine vinegar

2   tablespoons Dijon mustard

2   garlic cloves

½   teaspoon salt

½   teaspoon pepper

2   tablespoons dry sherry (optional)

1   cup olive oil

¼   cup chopped toasted pecans

Divide the salad greens evenly among four salad plates. Top each with the cabbage and cheese. Arrange the tomato wedges and avocado over the greens. In a small skillet on medium-high heat pour the oil to a depth of ½-inch. Heat the oil to 350°. Fry the tortilla strips in the hot oil for 1 minute or until crisp. Drain on paper towels. Drizzle each salad with Pecan Vinaigrette. Top evenly with tortilla strips.

For the **pecan vinaigrette:** In a blender process the white wine vinegar, Dijon mustard, garlic, salt, pepper, and sherry, if desired, until smooth. Stop to scrape down the sides. Turn the blender on high and gradually add the oil in a slow, steady stream until thickened. Stir in the pecans.

YIELD: 4 SALADS AND 1¼ CUPS VINAIGRETTE

Millionaire Salad

This salad is well known in the South and is popular in the Midwest as well.

Due to the luxurious nature of its ingredients, it is mostly a special-occasion salad and is often used for dinner during the holidays.

2	cups mandarin orange slices, drained
2	cups crushed pineapple, drained
2	cups sour cream
2	cups shredded coconut
2	cups miniature marshmallows (white or multi-colored)
1	(6-ounce) jar halved maraschino cherries
½	cup chopped toasted pecans

In a medium-size bowl combine the oranges, pineapple, sour cream, coconut, and marshmallows. Add the cherries and pecans. Set in the refrigerator to chill.

Y IELD : 10 TO 12 SERVINGS

Molded Egg Salad

This is a wonderful recipe for a ladies' luncheon. Be sure to mold this in an attractive scalloped mold or individual molds and turn it out onto a bed of red lettuce leaves. It can be garnished with egg slices and pimientos. Placing pansies around the edges of the lettuce leaves makes a beautiful presentation.

1	(¼-ounce) envelope unflavored gelatin
½	cup water
1	cup mayonnaise
1	teaspoon salt
	Dash of pepper
2	tablespoons lemon juice
¼	teaspoon Worcestershire sauce
½	cup finely chopped parsley
¼	cup chopped pimiento
¼	cup chopped green bell pepper
	Dash of hot sauce
4	hard-cooked eggs, sliced
	Fancy red leaf lettuce (optional)

In a saucepan over low heat, sprinkle the gelatin over the cold water. Stir until dissolved (about 3 minutes). Set aside to cool. In a large bowl, combine the mayonnaise, salt, pepper, lemon juice, Worcestershire sauce, parsley, pimiento, bell pepper, hot sauce, and the gelatin. Mix well. Fold in the eggs. Chill until firm. Make ahead so that the flavors will blend. Serve on a bed of lettuce leaves.

Y IELD : 10 TO 12 SERVINGS

Kitty Jacobs
Atlanta, Georgia

North Georgia Caviar

This will keep refrigerated in a plastic sealed container for several days. It is great with corn bread or as a side item with hamburgers and hotdogs.

2   (15-ounce) cans black-eyed peas, drained and rinsed

1   (15-ounce) can shoe peg corn, drained

1   (10-ounce) can Rotel tomatoes, drained

1   medium green bell pepper, chopped

6   whole green onions, chopped

1   (16-ounce) bottle Italian dressing

In a large mixing bowl combine the black-eyed peas, corn, tomatoes, bell pepper, onions, and dressing. Mix thoroughly. Refrigerate until ready to serve.

YIELD: ABOUT 8 CUPS

Karol Trammel
Monroe, Georgia

Roasted Vidalia Onion Salad

5   medium Vidalia onions, peeled and cut into ½-inch-thick slices

¼   cup olive oil

8   cups gourmet mixed salad greens

½   cup chopped toasted walnuts

1   (4-ounce) package crumbled blue cheese
    Garlic Vinaigrette

GARLIC VINAIGRETTE

3   garlic cloves

2   shallots

¼   cup chopped fresh parsley

2   tablespoons white wine vinegar

½   teaspoon dried crushed red pepper

½   teaspoon salt

½   teaspoon freshly ground black pepper

⅔   cup olive oil

Preheat the oven to 450°. Arrange the onion slices in a lightly greased roasting pan. Drizzle evenly with olive oil. Bake for 12 to 15 minutes or until the onion slices are lightly charred. Cool for 5 minutes. In a salad bowl combine the salad greens, walnuts, and blue cheese. Toss gently. Top with the onion slices and drizzle with the Garlic Vinaigrette.

For the **garlic vinaigrette:** In a food processor pulse the garlic and shallots three or four times. Add the parsley, vinegar, red pepper, salt, and pepper. Process the vegetables for 20 seconds, stopping one time to scrape down the sides. With the processor running, gradually pour in the olive oil in a slow, steady stream through the food chute until blended.

YIELD: 8 SERVINGS

Rice-A-Roni Salad

This recipe was tested at a ladies' luncheon and there was not a bite left. It was delicious.

1   (6.5-ounce) box chicken Rice-A-Roni
1   (6-ounce) jar artichokes, drained and chopped
1   (5.75-ounce) jar stuffed olives, sliced
1   medium green bell pepper, chopped
⅛   teaspoon curry powder
3   green onions, sliced
2   celery ribs, thinly sliced (optional)
    Mayonnaise

Cook the Rice-A-Roni according to the package directions and set aside to cool. Once it has cooled, in a large mixing bowl combine the Rice-A-Roni, artichokes, olives, bell pepper, curry powder, green onions, celery, if desired, and mayonnaise to taste. Mix well and place in the refrigerator to cool.

Hint: Add 2 cups chopped cooked chicken for a hearty variation.

YIELD: ABOUT 8 SERVINGS

"Not Apple Salad!"

This is one of my mother's favorite salads. Although we all enjoyed it, she made it so often that we jokingly referred to it as "Not Apple Salad!" I like to combine several varieties of apples and leave some unpeeled.

⅓   cup all-purpose flour
¾   cup granulated sugar
1   cup heavy whipping cream
1   (15.2-ounce) can crushed pineapple, drained
¼   cup (½ stick) butter or margarine
½   cup sliced maraschino cherries
4   or more large apples, peeled and diced
1   cup chopped pecans

In a saucepan sift the flour and sugar together. Stir in the whipping cream and pineapple. Cook over medium heat until the mixture thickens. Remove from the heat and add the butter. Set the mixture aside to cool. In a bowl combine the cherries, apples, and pecans. Pour the cooled mixture over the fruit and mix well. Sprinkle some cherries on top if desired. Refrigerate for an hour before serving.

YIELD: 10 TO 12 SERVINGS

Barbara Sams
Social Circle, Georgia

POPULAR SOUTHERN SAYING

We get along like a house on fire! (Fondness—get along great)

Orange Fluff

Make this orange salad in a mold with a space in the center. When it is taken out of the mold, put the Millionaire Salad (page 116) in the middle for a delightful combination. It is a beautiful addition of color at a fall luncheon or for Thanksgiving dinner.

2   cups water
1   (6-ounce) box orange gelatin
2   cups miniature marshmallows
1   (11-ounce) can mandarin oranges, drained
1   pint orange sherbet, softened
1   (8-ounce) container whipped topping

In a medium-size saucepan on high heat bring the water to a boil. In a medium-size bowl thoroughly dissolve the gelatin in the water. After the gelatin is completely dissolved, add the marshmallows. Stir gently. Don't worry about stirring thoroughly—just a bit will do. Set the bowl in a sink with ice cubes and allow the mixture to cool. In a large bowl combine the gelatin mixture, the oranges, and the sherbet. Stir until the mixture begins to gel (it WILL get thick). Fold in the whipped topping.

Pour the mixture into a 2-quart dish or a mold and refrigerate until chilled and firmly set.

Hints: You can substitute strawberry gelatin, strawberries, and strawberry ice cream, or lime gelatin, drained pineapple, and lime sherbet.

YIELD: 10 TO 12 SERVINGS

Donna Page
Pelzer, South Carolina

Sexy Raspberry Salad

My husband says this is the sexiest gelatin salad he's ever had. It's sweet, it's tart, it's smooth, it's pink, and I make it in a heart-shaped mold. It makes a wonderful treat for your Valentine.

1¾ cups water
2   (3-ounce) packages raspberry gelatin
1   cup sour cream
1   (10-ounce) package frozen raspberries, not drained
1   (8-ounce) can crushed pineapple
1   banana, peeled, sliced lengthwise and then in half across
½   cup chopped pecans (optional)

In a small saucepan on high heat bring the water to a rolling boil. In a large mixing bowl dissolve the gelatin in the boiling water. Make sure the gelatin is completely dissolved. Whisk the sour cream into the gelatin. Add the raspberries, pineapple, banana slices, and pecans. Pour the ingredients into a mold or an 8 x 8-inch dish. Place in the refrigerator and chill for at least 4 hours or overnight, no longer or the bananas will darken.

YIELD: 16 SERVINGS

Janice "Sam" Sears
Atlanta, Georgia

Spinach-Strawberry Salad

This delicious salad makes a wonderful colorful salad for Christmas or Valentine's Day. We have tested it at a luncheon and at the restaurant where it was gobbled up.

1	(16-ounce) bag baby spinach leaves
1	quart fresh strawberries, sliced
10	to 12 cherry tomatoes
1	large purple onion, sliced
1	(16-ounce) bottle poppy seed salad dressing
	Bacon bits (optional)

In a large bowl lightly toss the spinach, strawberries, tomatoes, and onion. Add the dressing and mix thoroughly. Sprinkle with bacon bits.

YIELD: 6 TO 8 SERVINGS

Fran Stewart
Loganville, Georgia

Tomato Zucchini Salad

4	medium zucchini
3	medium tomatoes
⅓	cup vegetable oil
3	tablespoons white vinegar
1½	teaspoons lemon juice
1	teaspoon sugar
½	teaspoon salt
½	teaspoon ground mustard
½	teaspoon dried oregano
¼	teaspoon coarsely ground pepper
	Pitted ripe olives

Cut the zucchini and the tomatoes into ¼-inch slices. In a skillet on medium heat place the zucchini in 1 inch of water and bring to a boil. Reduce the heat. Cover and simmer for 2 to 3 minutes or until the zucchini is crisp-tender. Drain in a colander and pat dry with paper towels. Arrange the zucchini and tomatoes in alternating circles on a serving platter. In a jar with a tight-fitting lid combine the oil, vinegar, lemon juice, sugar, salt, mustard, oregano, and pepper. Shake well. Drizzle over the zucchini and tomatoes. Cover and refrigerate for at least 2 hours. Place the olives in the center of the vegetables to serve.

YIELD: 6 SERVINGS

Waldorf Salad

1   cup diced Red Delicious apples, unpeeled

1   cup diced Granny Smith apples, unpeeled

2   bananas, sliced crosswise

¾   cup chopped celery

¾   cup coarsely chopped pecans

⅔   cup raisins

¼   to ⅓ cup mayonnaise

In a large mixing bowl combine the apples, bananas, celery, pecans, raisins, and mayonnaise. Mix thoroughly. Place in the refrigerator to chill before serving.

Hint: If the salad won't be served immediately, toss the apples and bananas in ¼ cup water with 2 teaspoons lemon juice to keep them from turning brown.

YIELD: 8 SERVINGS

Watergate Salad (also known as Green Stuff)

This salad is a southern favorite, but is better known as "Green Stuff" than by its official name, "Watergate Salad." This recipe comes from the kitchen of Kim Unruh, who worked for the Van Dykes for several years as their salad and dessert person.

1   (3-ounce) package instant pistachio pudding

1   cup miniature marshmallows

1   (14-ounce) can crushed pineapple, drained

1   (9-ounce) package Cool Whip

⅓   cup chopped pecans

In a large mixing bowl combine the pudding, marshmallows, pineapple, Cool Whip, and pecans. Whip until fluffy. Refrigerate and serve cold.

YIELD: 6 TO 8 SERVINGS

Relishes & Pickles

Pickling is another way of preserving summer fruit and vegetables. In the Old South these were stored either in the pantry or the root cellar—anywhere that was dark and cool. Most Southern cellars always had a barrel of pickles. These delicious treats were used to complement pork, chicken, and seafood. They were often used as a side dish. Every Southern table had its own special bread and butter pickles.

Apple Chutney

This is a great accompaniment to pork tenderloin and pork roast. Also this is good in the winter as an appetizer served on cream cheese with crackers.

2	medium onions
1	large orange
5	cups pared firm apples
¾	cup crystallized ginger
⅓	cup cider vinegar
1	tablespoon ground cinnamon
2	tablespoons lemon juice
2½	cups packed brown sugar
½	cup seedless raisins
1	cup light corn syrup
1½	teaspoons salt
1½	cups water
	Dash of Tabasco

Grind the onions and the orange in a food processor. Add the apples, ginger, vinegar, cinnamon, lemon juice, brown sugar, raisins, corn syrup, salt, water, and Tabasco. Pulse a few more times to mix, pour into a saucepan, and simmer 2 hours or until the mixture becomes thick and dark. Seal in hot sterilized jars. This can be kept in the refrigerator for about 1 week without canning.

YIELD: ABOUT 3 PINTS

Bread and Butter Pickles

Billie got this is a recipe from my good friend Eleanor Stanhope of Port Wentworth, Georgia. The recipe is handed down from Eleanor's mother, Jimmie Hindman. Eleanor says that her dad grew the cucumbers in the garden, her mom made the pickles, and they always had bread and butter pickles on the table. Both her mom and dad liked their pickles on black-eyed peas and rice.

2½	pounds medium cucumbers, cut into ⅛-inch slices
3	medium onions, thinly sliced
¼	cup salt
2	cups vinegar (5% acidity)
1½	cups granulated sugar
2	teaspoons celery seed
1	teaspoon mustard seeds
1	teaspoon ground ginger

In a large glass container layer the cucumber, onion, and salt. Cover with ice and let it sit for 2 hours. Drain and rinse thoroughly. Drain again. In a large Dutch oven combine the vinegar, sugar, celery seed, mustard seed, and ginger. Bring to a boil. Add the cucumber and onion. Reduce the heat to low and simmer uncovered for 20 to 30 minutes or until tender. Pack the hot pickles in hot sterilized jars leaving ½-inch head space. Remove the air bubbles. Wipe the jar rims. Cover at once with metal lids, screw on the bands, and process in a boiling water bath for 10 minutes. Set aside to cool before storing.

YIELD: 4 PINTS

Cabbage Relish

This recipe is very good with barbeque.

1	head cabbage, diced
2	cucumbers, peeled and thinly sliced
1	green or red bell pepper, julienned
2	carrots, grated
1	onion, thinly sliced
¾	cup granulated sugar
1	cup cider vinegar
½	cup salad oil
1	teaspoon salt
1	teaspoon celery salt
	Garlic salt
	Pepper

In a large mixing bowl combine the cabbage, cucumbers, bell pepper, carrots, and onion. In a small bowl, mix the sugar, vinegar, salad oil, salt, celery salt, garlic salt, and pepper. Pour over the vegetables. Keep the relish refrigerated, and marinate one day before serving, stirring occasionally.

YIELD: 6 QUARTS

Kitty Jacobs
Atlanta, Georgia

Select tender vegetables and firm fruits for making relishes or pickles.

Chow-Chow

Chow-chow is a truly southern relish that goes great over beans, collards, and turnip greens to add a little extra flavor.

1	peck (8 quarts or about 40) green tomatoes, finely chopped
10	large onions, finely chopped
6	hot green peppers, finely chopped
2	small heads cabbage, finely chopped
1	green bell pepper, finely chopped
1	red bell pepper, finely chopped
6	cups water
2	cups salt
1	quart (4 cups) cider vinegar
2	cups granulated sugar

Combine the tomatoes, onions, hot peppers, cabbage, and bell peppers in a large mixing bowl and mix well. In a 2-quart saucepan on high heat combine the water and salt and bring to a boil to make brine. Pour the scalding brine over the vegetables. Let this mixture stand for 3 hours and then drain. In a medium saucepan over medium heat combine the vinegar and sugar and bring to a boil. Add the vegetables to the vinegar mixture. Turn the heat to low and simmer for 15 minutes. Remove from the heat. Pour the chow-chow into sterilized canning jars while hot, seal, and process in a boiling water bath for 10 minutes.

YIELD: 6 TO 8 PINTS

Corn Salsa

3   large ears fresh corn

1   large tomato, finely chopped

1   (7-ounce) jar roasted sweet red peppers, drained and chopped

2   green onions, finely chopped

1   jalapeño pepper, seeded and minced

3   tablespoons minced fresh cilantro

2   tablespoons fresh lime juice

1   tablespoon white wine vinegar

½   teaspoon salt

¼   teaspoon pepper

¼   teaspoon ground cumin

2   avocados, chopped (optional)

Cut the corn from the cob. In a mixing bowl stir together the corn, tomato, sweet red peppers, green onions, jalapeño pepper, cilantro, lime juice, vinegar, salt, pepper, cumin, and avocado, if desired. Cover and chill for at least 2 hours. Serve with tortilla chips.

YIELD: 2½ CUPS

Cranberry-Orange Relish

This is a beautiful and tasty side to roasted turkey or baked chicken.

1   (14-ounce) can whole cranberry sauce

1   (14-ounce) can jellied cranberry sauce

1   (8-ounce) jar orange marmalade

1   cup chopped pecans

1   tablespoon lemon juice

In a medium bowl mix the whole cranberry sauce, the jellied cranberry sauce, orange marmalade, chopped pecans, and lemon juice. Cover and refrigerate.

YIELD: 1 QUART

Pickled Peaches

Summer pickled peaches are a delight on the table at Thanksgiving or throughout the winter months accompanying poultry or pork dishes.

4   cups water

19 to 20 small peaches (6 pounds)

1   quart (4 cups) white vinegar (5% acidity)

6   cups granulated sugar

1   tablespoon whole cloves

4   (2½-inch) cinnamon sticks

In a Dutch oven on high heat bring the water to a boil. Remove from the heat and add the peaches. Let the peaches stand for 4 to 6 minutes. Drain, cool, and peel the peaches.

In a Dutch oven on medium heat bring the vinegar and sugar to a boil. Reduce the heat to low and simmer for 15 minutes. Place the cloves on a 6-inch square of cheesecloth and tie with a string. Add the bag and cinnamon sticks to the vinegar mixture.

Add half of the peaches and cook for 10 minutes. Remove the peaches with a slotted spoon and repeat the process with the remaining peaches. After removing the second batch of peaches, bring the remaining syrup to a boil. Remove from the heat. Add the peaches. Cover and let stand at room temperature for 8 hours. Remove the peaches with a slotted spoon and pack into hot, sterilized jars. Remove and discard the spice bag and the cinnamon sticks.

Bring the peach syrup to a boil and pour it over the peaches, filling the jars to ½-inch from the top. Remove the air bubbles. Wipe the jar rims. Cover at once with metal lids and screw on the bands. Process the jars in a boiling water bath for 20 minutes.

YIELD: 8 QUARTS

Red Cabbage and Cranberry Relish

You can serve this relish warm or cold and it complements pork dishes and ham.

1	tablespoon olive oil
¼	plus ¼ cup packed brown sugar
8	garlic cloves, minced
2	plus 1 cups fresh or frozen cranberries
½	cup red wine vinegar
1	medium head red cabbage, shredded (about 10 cups)
1	cup dry red wine or apple juice
½	teaspoon salt
⅛	to ¼ teaspoon cayenne pepper

In a Dutch oven or kettle over medium heat, heat the oil and ¼ cup brown sugar. Add the garlic and sauté for 2 minutes. Stir in 2 cups cranberries and the vinegar.

Cover and cook over medium heat for 3 to 4 minutes or until the berries have popped.

Add the cabbage and the wine or apple juice. Continue to cook over medium heat, stirring occasionally, for 15 minutes or until the cabbage is tender. Stir in the salt, cayenne, the remaining 1 cup cranberries, and the remaining ¼ cup brown sugar. Remove from the heat. Cover and let stand for 5 minutes or until the berries are tender.

YIELD: 8 SERVINGS

Tomato Chutney

This recipe is served with every meal at the Blue Willow Inn Restaurant. It is delicious with fried green tomatoes, green beans, and cooked greens. It can also be used as an appetizer served with cream cheese and crackers.

1	(14-ounce) can whole tomatoes, chopped, not drained
1	cup firmly packed light brown sugar
½	cup granulated sugar
2	green bell peppers, finely chopped
1	medium onion, finely chopped
2	tablespoons ketchup
6	drops Tabasco
1	teaspoon black pepper

In a saucepan or small stockpot on medium heat mix the tomatoes, brown sugar, granulated sugar, bell peppers, onion, ketchup, Tabasco, and pepper. Bring to a boil. Reduce the heat and allow the mixture to simmer for 2 hours or until cooked to a thick sauce.

YIELD: 6 CUPS

Tomato Relish

This is a great way to enjoy your garden-fresh tomatoes. It is great with beans and will keep for several weeks in the refrigerator.

1	quart ripe tomatoes, drained and chopped
1	green bell pepper
1	onion
1	hot pepper (optional)
	Salt
1	cup granulated sugar
1	cup cider vinegar
1	teaspoon mustard seed

In a large bowl combine the tomatoes, bell pepper, onion, and hot pepper if desired; mix well. Add salt to taste. In a saucepan over medium heat combine the sugar, vinegar, and mustard seed and bring to a boil, stirring often. Be sure the sugar is completely dissolved. Remove from the heat and pour over the tomato mixture. Allow to cool and then store in the refrigerator.

YIELD: 10 CUPS

Watermelon Pickles

These delicious pickles have been a favorite of our family for many years and can be served any time of the year with many entrées as well as given as gifts. After serving watermelon to guests, save all the watermelon rind for these pickles.

	Rind of 1 large watermelon
4	tablespoons salt
1	quart (4 cups) water
8	teaspoons whole cloves
16	cinnamon sticks
	Dash of mustard seed
8	cups granulated sugar
4	cups apple cider vinegar
	Red or green food coloring (optional)

Peel and remove all the green and pink portions from the rind of the watermelon. Cut the rind into 1-inch cubes. Place in a large bowl and soak overnight in a mix of the salt and water.

Drain the watermelon rind. Tie the cloves, cinnamon sticks, and mustard seed in a cheesecloth bag. In a saucepan on medium heat mix the sugar and vinegar into a syrup. Add the bag of spices and bring to a boil. Remove from the heat and allow the syrup to sit for 15 minutes. Add the drained watermelon rind, return to the heat, and cook 15 to 20 minutes or until the pickle is clear and transparent. Before removing from the heat, if desired add enough red or green food coloring to give color to the pickle.

Pack the pickles into hot, sterilized, half pint jars and seal at once. Process the jars in a boiling water bath for 5 minutes. Remove and turn upside down on wire racks until cool.

YIELD: ABOUT 10 HALF-PINT JARS

Bernice Wilson
Lawrenceville, Georgia

Outdoor Cooking
in the South

Southerners look forward to the first warm days of spring to begin their annual ritual of grilling, barbequing, and outdoor cooking. This migration to the outdoors is a favorite pastime until the first cold days of fall.

Outside cooking takes place lakeside, poolside, creekside, and in backyards. During the fall, tailgating is very popular in the South. The outside of motor homes and campers are lined with grills and propane-fueled cookers.

The recipes that follow can be used for small families to enjoy on their patio or deck or for large gatherings when all day cooking is the norm.

Summer Holidays in the South

Pit-Cooked Hog	4
Char Grilled Sucking Pig	6
Roasted Sweet Potato	7
Journey's End Cole Slaw	7
LeRoy's Green Beans	8
Potato Salad	8
Macaroni Salad	9

Barbeque in the South

Baby Back Ribs	10

Grilling

Grilled Shrimp	12
Sweet and Sour Grilled Ribs	13
Honey-Lime Grilled Chicken	14
Grilled Slaw	14
Grilled Vegetables	15
Garlic, Chive, and Cheese Bread	16
Sage Rub	16
Spicy Rub	17
Ginger Rub	17

Shish Kabobs for Family Reunion Fare

Grilled Shish Kabobs	19

THE ART OF CRABBING

Crab Boil   20
Clarified Butter   21
Garlic Butter   22
Cocktail Sauce   22

OYSTER ROAST

Roast Oysters   24

SAVANNAH LOW-COUNTRY BOIL

Orange-Seasoned Sweet Potato Packets   25
Low-Country Boil   26
Grilled Corn on the Cob   27
Cheesy Grilled Tomatoes   27
Roasted Mixed Peppers   28
Pecan-Stuffed Portobello Mushrooms   29
Watermelon Social   30

KIDS' WIENER ROAST

Raosting Marshmallows   31
Hot Dogs   32

Summer Holidays in the South (A Reason to Cook)

Billie's brother, Dennis, provided the pit-cooked hog recipe. The Fourth of July is not complete without experiencing one of Dennis' pit-cooked hogs with all the trimmings. The first and foremost rule of pit cooking is to forget about being in a hurry. Pit cooking requires time and patience, and a real desire to follow traditional methods to achieve mouth-watering flavor and tenderness. Generally speaking, you must allow 10 to 12 hours to cook a 100-pound hog. This will yield about 40 pounds of lip-smacking pork when done.

Pit-Cooked Hog

1   100 pound whole hog, gutted

The first step is **preparing the pit**. Choose a spot where you won't run into a lot of large tree roots and dig your pit approximately 6 feet long x 3 feet wide x 2 feet deep. The sides of the pit should not be sloped; they must be straight to provide proper heat to the hog. Keep the area around the pit clear, so that you have room to add wood and to check on the hog. "Dress" the edges of your pit with lumber (preferably 2 x 6's), brick, or you can even use split logs to line the sides and ends to prevent dirt from being knocked on top of your fire and to provide a solid surface to hold the hog. (This is part of the "art" of pit-cooking.)

Cover the pit with a grate that is free of dirt and rust. There are two options for cooking the hog: 1) use a metal "tent" to cover the pig while on the grate. (This cooks both sides of the hog so you don't have to turn it.) 2) place strong wire mesh under the hog and use a second piece of mesh on top to turn the hog several times during cooking.

The next step is **preparing the heat source**. There are as many choices here as there are trees in the forest. Our family favorite for cooking anything with wood is blackjack oak. Our second choice is hickory, and the third is any oak other than blackjack—white oak, water oak, live oak, and laurel oak. All of these are hard, dense woods that are not prone to flame-ups and fast burning. Whatever your choice, the wood should be seasoned, not freshly cut. This provides even burning and minimizes popping, which may cause flame-ups and grease fires. Line your pit on the sides with crumpled newspaper. You should have a row of balled-up newspaper along each side. Place a mound of twigs on top of the newspaper. The twigs should be one-quarter inch or less in diameter. On top of the twigs place small branches, one-half to two inches in diameter. Finally, place split wood, 4 to 6 inches in diameter, on top of the branches. Light the newspaper on each side, and your fire should be well on it's way. Do not put any wood on the ends, only on the sides of the pit. The heat reflecting off the sides of the pit will cook your hog.

The final step is **cooking the hog**. Once the logs have turned white, place the hog belly side down on the grate that is over the pit. Once the logs have burned down to two-thirds their original size, add more wood. Always place the new wood next to the sides, avoiding fire directly under the hog to prevent flame-ups from grease dripping into the pit. Keep a spray bottle at hand to quench any flame-ups.

Once the hog has been placed over the pit, use a 4 x 8-foot piece of corrugated tin to cover the pit. Wedge the edge of the tin on the inside of each side of the pit dressing to form a tent. This provides even heat and eliminates the need for turning the hog. Cooking time is 10 to 12 hours. The sure way to tell if your hog is done is to use a meat thermometer. Place it in the hams, the thickest part. When the temperature reaches 160° it is done. It is always better to plan on your hog being ready at least 2 hours before you actually want to serve. This gives you a comfortable margin for error, and you can keep it warm without drying it out by cutting back on your heat. Simply shovel some dirt on your fire to lower the temperature. Let the hog rest off the fire for 1 hour before serving. You can take the meat off the bone for your guests or put some tongs on the table and let them pull the meat off the bone for themselves.

Of course the hog is the star of this show, but you must have a supporting cast. If you want to keep it really simple, cut the silk end of fresh corn still in the husk and soak it in a washtub filled with water. After an hour of soaking, place the corn next to the hog. It will take the corn about 1 hour to cook. Two favorites to include with the pit-cooked hog are green beans and potato salad. Recipes for both follow. Be sure to have plenty of your favorite barbeque sauce available.

YIELD: 35 TO 40 SERVINGS

Char Grilled Suckling Pig

1	15 to 20-pound sucking pig	12	cups corn bread crumbs
	Water	6	cups biscuit crumbs
2	cups white vinegar	12	eggs, lightly beaten
		6	hard-cooked eggs
STUFFING		1½	cup chopped chicken or turkey giblets
1½	cups chopped onion	3	teaspoon sage
¾	cup chopped celery		Salt and pepper
¾	cup butter or margarine	6	cups chicken broth

Clean the pig well. Place pig in a large container. Cover the pig with water and add the vinegar. Stir to mix. Let it sit for 2 to 3 hours. (This can be done the day before cooking.)

For the **stuffing**, combine the onion, celery, butter, corn bread crumbs, biscuit crumbs, beaten eggs, hard-cooked eggs, chopped chicken giblets, sage, and salt and pepper to taste. Mix well. Add the chicken broth and mix well. Fill the cavity of the pig with the stuffing. Close the cavity using string. An ice pick can be used to make holes for the string. Tuck the front and back legs down and toward the center of the pig. If necessary, use string to keep the legs in place. Cover the ears with tin foil. –If you like, place a wooden peg in the pig's mouth so that at the end of cooking an apple can be inserted in the mouth.

Use a charcoal grill with a cooking area large enough to accommodate the pig. Heat the coals until they are white hot. Arrange the coals on either end of the grill and place a drip pan in the middle, under the pig, to catch the drippings and prevent flame-ups. Additional coals will need to be added during cooking and, if desired, add chips of hickory wood for additional flavor. Cover the pig and cook for 2 to 2½ hours and then turn lengthwise on the grill. Cook 1 hour more and insert a meat thermometer into the thickest part—the ham portion—of the pig. It is done when the internal temperature reaches 160° Cooking time will vary depending on the heat of the grill. Thirty minutes prior to removing the pig from grill remove the aluminum foil from its ears. At this time remove the wood peg from the pig's mouth and insert a red apple, if desired.

Serve the pig on a large platter. Corn on the cob, LeRoys Green Beans, and Journey's End Cole Slaw complement this meal.

YIELDS 8 TO 10 SERVINGS

Roasted Sweet Potato

6   sweet potatoes
6   tablespoons butter or ⅓ cup vegetable oil
6   tablespoons firmly packed brown sugar
    Ground cinnamon

Rub each sweet potato with butter or oil and wrap in aluminum foil. Bake over hot coals for 1 hour or until soft to the touch. In a small bowl mix the brown sugar and cinnamon to taste. Remove the potato from the coals and open the foil. Cut open the potato. Fill with butter and sprinkle liberally with the cinnamon sugar.

YIELD: 6 SERVINGS

Journey's End Cole Slaw

3½   large heads cabbage, shredded
2½   large carrots, grated
2   cups sweet pickle relish
1½   cups granulated sugar
5   cups mayonnaise
    Salt and pepper

In a large mixing bowl, combine the cabbage, carrots, relish, sugar, mayonnaise, and salt and pepper to taste.

YIELD: 50 SERVINGS

LeRoy's Green Beans

When Billie's brother Dennis cooks his whole pig, his wife, Elizabeth (LeRoy), always prepares her favorite green beans.

4	smoked ham hocks (sliced about ¾ inch thick)
	Water
3	gallon (#10) cans green beans (Blue Lakes), undrained
	Salt
8	slices bacon

Place the sliced ham hocks in a large stockpot over high heat and cover with 3 inches of water. Bring to a boil and cover. Reduce the heat to medium and cook for 20 minutes. Add the green beans and salt to taste. (start with about 4 tablespoons and adjust according as the beans cook). Cook for another 20 minutes. Fry the bacon in a skillet until lightly crisp. Add the fried bacon and the bacon grease to the beans. Turn the heat to low and cook for 20 minutes. Continue cooking until the desired tenderness is reached. Remove the beans from the heat and allow them to stand covered for 30 minutes before serving.

Yield: 40 servings

Potato Salad

20	pounds white or red potatoes
12	hard-cooked eggs, peeled, divided
4	celery stalks, finely chopped
¾	quart mayonnaise
8	heaping tablespoons yellow mustard
1	cup sweet pickle relish
	Salt and pepper
	Paprika
	Celery leaves

Peel and chop the potatoes. Put the potatoes in a large pot and cover with water. Place over medium-high heat and cook until the potatoes are done. (They are done when they easily drop off a fork when pierced.) *Do not overcook.* Drain the potatoes and allow them to cool completely. Place the cooled potatoes in a large mixing bowl. Coarsely chop 10 of the eggs and add them to the potatoes. Add the celery, mayonnaise, mustard, relish, and salt and pepper to taste. Mix lightly. Transfer to a serving bowl. Cut the remaining 2 eggs into slices or wedges and garnish the top of the salad. Sprinkle the top of the salad with paprika and add some celery leaves for flair. Serve immediately or cover and place in the refrigerator until ready to serve.

YIELD: 40 SERVINGS

Macaroni Salad

3	pounds macaroni
2½	large green bell peppers, diced
2½	large onions, chopped
1	cup pimientos
2	cups chopped celery
5	cups mayonnaise
6	hard-cooked eggs
	Salt and pepper

Cook the macaroni according to the package directions. Drain and transfer to a large mixing bowl and allow the macaroni to cool. While it is still slightly warm, add the peppers, onions, pimientos, celery, mayonnaise, eggs, and salt and pepper to taste. Stir to combine.

YIELD: 50 SERVINGS

Barbeque in the South

Barbeque is beef—no pork. How about chicken, goat, or mutton? Georgia has the best barbeque—no Texas. How about North Carolina or Memphis?

This debate goes on and on in the South. While y'all argue, I'll eat. In the South, we love barbeque; it's the one food that makes us different. It speaks of our Southern sense of comfort, of friends and family getting together to enjoy good food and company.

Growing up in the South meant outdoor cooking. Barbeque is a way of life for Southerners. It used to be an all day affair, but that's no longer the case. You can have the barbeques from the pit or the grill to the table in a short periord of time . Lots of slaw, white bread, french fries, and babreque sauce make for an enjoyable and delicious meal. Sweetened iced tea is always a must!

Baby Back Ribs

3   slabs baby back pork ribs (about 5½ pounds)

2   limes, halved

Rub

2	tablespoons ground ginger
½	teaspoon dried crushed red pepper
1	teaspoon salt
1	teaspoon black pepper

Barbeque Sauce

2	(10-ounce) bottles sweet and sour sauce
2	cups ketchup
½	cup cider vinegar
½	teaspoon ground ginger
2	teaspoons hot sauce

Rinse the ribs and pat them dry. Rub the lime halves over the ribs.

To prepare the **rub**, combine the ginger, red pepper, salt, and black pepper. Massage the rub into the ribs, covering all sides. Wrap tightly with plastic wrap and place in a zip-lock freezer bag or 13 x-9-inch baking dish; chill for 8 hours. Let the ribs stand at room temperature for 30 minutes before grilling. Remove plastic wrap.

Preheat or prepare a grill to medium-high heat. Place the ribs on the rack, cover, and grill for 1 hour. Reposition the ribs slabs, placing the one closest to the heat source away from heat moving other slabs closer. Grill for 1 more hour or until the ribs are tender. Prepare the barbeque sauce while the ribs are grilling.

For the **barbeque sauce**, stir together the sweet and sour sauce, ketchup, cider vinegar, ginger, and hot sauce in a saucepan over medium high heat. Bring the mixture to a boil, reduce heat, and simmer for 30 minutes.

Grill the ribs for a final 30 minutes over medium heat, basting with half of the barbeque sauce. Remove the ribs from the grill and let stand for 10 minutes. Cut the ribs, slicing between bones. Serve with the remaining barbeque sauce.

Yield: 6 servings

GRILLING

Grilling is a delightful warm-weather way of cooking for the family or for large groups. The numerous and varied types of grills available today make cooking outdoors fun and easy. Grills now come in many sizes from the table-top to the elaborate stainless steel, from charcoal to gas, and you can find them with rotisseries, side stoves, and sinks.

The most popular item for grilling is hamburgers, steaks, and hot dogs with chicken running a close second. However, cookout fans are learning that fish, other seafood, and vegetables are also delicious and easy to cook on the grill. Some favorite recipes we have enjoyed with friends and family follow. We hope you and your family will give them a try and have a wonderful time enjoying cooking them together.

Grilled Shrimp

4	pounds large unpeeled shrimp
½	cup olive oil
½	cup (1 stick) butter, melted
¼	cup Worcestershire sauce
2	lemons, sliced
4	garlic cloves, chopped
½	teaspoon hot sauce

Wash and drain the shrimp. In a large shallow dish combine the shrimp, olive oil, butter, Worcestershire sauce, lemons, garlic, and hot sauce. Toss until the shrimp are evenly coated. Cover and chill for 2 hours.

Heat the grill to medium. Spray a grill basket with nonstick cooking spray. Drain the shrimp and place them in the grill basket. Cook the shrimp 4 to 6 inches from the coals for 10 to 13 minutes or until pink. Shake the grill basket once or twice during cooking to turn the shrimp. Serve with Savannah Red Rice (recipe on page 198) and Journey's End Cole Slaw (recipe on special section page 7).

Hint: You can also bake the shrimp in an oven heated to 400°. Place the shrimp in an aluminum foil–lined broiler pan; cover and bake for 20 minutes or until the shrimp turn pink, turning once.

YIELD: 4 SERVINGS

Sweet and Sour Grilled Ribs

1	(11.5-ounce) bottle sweet and sour sauce
⅓	cup pineapple juice
2	garlic cloves, pressed
1	tablespoon firmly packed dark brown sugar
4	pounds beef ribs or spareribs
¼	teaspoon salt

In a mixing bowl stir together the sweet and sour sauce, pineapple juice, garlic, and brown sugar. Set the sauce aside.

Prepare the fire by piling charcoal or lava rocks on each side of the grill, leaving the center empty. Place a drip pan in the center of the coals. Coat the food rack with vegetable cooking spray and place on the grill.

Sprinkle the ribs with the salt. Arrange the ribs on the food rack over the drip pan. Cover with the grill lid or tinfoil. Cook for 2½ hours basting with the sauce every 30 minutes. Serve with Orange-Seasoned Sweet Potato Packets (recipe on special section page 25) or baked sweet potatoes.

YIELD: 4 SERVINGS

Honey-Lime Grilled Chicken

¾   cup honey
⅓   cup soy sauce
⅓   cup lime juice
¼   teaspoon salt
6   chicken leg and thigh quarters

In a large heavy-duty, zip-lock bag combine the honey, soy sauce, and lime juice. Sprinkle the salt on the chicken quarters and place them in the bag. Seal and shake to coat the chicken with the sauce. Place in the refrigerator and chill for 30 minutes.

Heat the coals to medium. Spray the cooking surface with nonstick cooking spray. Remove the chicken from the bag. Place the chicken on the grill and cover with a grill cover or aluminum foil "tent." Cook for 45 to 50 minutes or until a meat thermometer inserted in the thickest portion of the chicken reads 160°. Turn once during cooking to brown on both sides. Serve with Grilled Corn on the Cob (recipe on special section page 27) and Grilled Slaw (recipe below).

YIELD: 6 SERVINGS

Grilled Slaw

1   large head cabbage, cored and quartered
3   strips bacon, cut into ½-inch pieces
1   small onion, chopped
1   tablespoon granulated sugar
¼   teaspoon salt
¼   teaspoon pepper
2   tablespoons butter, cut into small pieces

Prepare a grill to low heat. Spray a cooking bag with nonstick cooking spray. Place the cabbage, bacon, onion, sugar, salt, pepper, and butter in the bag. Seal the bag and place it on the grill. Cook for 20 to 25 minutes, turning the bag often to evenly cook the cabbage. The cabbage is done when it is soft.

YIELD: 4 SERVINGS

Grilled Vegetables

3	tablespoons salted butter, melted
1	tablespoon olive oil
¼	teaspoons salt
⅛	teaspoon pepper
1	small zucchini, sliced
¼	pound (about 1 cup) fresh snow pea pods
½	small, sweet onion, sliced
1	small green bell pepper, cut into 1-inch pieces
½	small red bell pepper, cut into 1-inch pieces
1	medium yellow squash, sliced
3	tablespoons garlic powder

Heat the grill to medium heat. Spray a grill basket with nonstick cooking spray. In a mixing bowl combine the butter, oil, salt, and pepper and mix well. Add the zucchini, snow pea pods, onion, bell peppers, squash, and garlic powder and toss to coat. Transfer the coated vegetables to the grill basket. Place the basket on the grill and cook the vegetables for 13 to 15 minutes or until crisp-tender, shaking the grill basket once or twice to turn and mix.

Hint: You can add ½ pound sea scallops and cook until opaque in color or ½ pound shrimp and cook until pink.

YIELD: 4 SERVINGS

Garlic, Chive, and Cheese Bread

1   (8-ounce) container garden vegetable cream cheese
2   tablespoons chopped fresh chives
1   small garlic clove, minced
1   (16-ounce) loaf French bread, split lengthwise

Heat the grill to medium. In a small bowl combine the cream cheese, chives, and garlic. Mix well. When ready place the bread haves, cut side down, on the grill . Toast the bread for 1 to 2 minutes or until a light golden brown. Turn the bread halves and spread the cream cheese mixture on the toasted sides. Cook, cheese side up, for an additional 3 to 4 minutes or until thoroughly heated. This goes well with all of the grilled dishes.

YIELD: 16 SERVINGS

The following are sample rubs that can be used for grilling and barbequing.

Sage Rub

¼   pound (1 stick) butter, softened
2   tablespoons salt
1   tablespoon garlic powder
1   tablespoon onion powder
1   teaspoon dried thyme
1   teaspoon dried sage
1   teaspoon black pepper

In a small bowl combine the butter, salt, garlic powder, onion powder, thyme, sage, and pepper and mix well. Use to rub on meat to coat it well. Can be stored in an airtight container and refrigerated for later use.

YIELD: ⅓ CUP

Spicy Rub

1½	teaspoon dried oregano
¼	cup chili powder
1	tablespoon onion powder
1	tablespoon ground cumin
2	teaspoons salt
1½	teaspoon garlic powder
1	teaspoon ground red pepper

In a small bowl combine the oregano, chili powder, onion powder, cumin, salt, garlic powder, and red pepper. Mix thoroughly. Store in an airtight container in the refrigerator. Rub on the meat of your choice before smoking or grilling.

YIELD: ½ CUP

Ginger Rub

2½	tablespoons ground ginger
½	teaspoon crushed red pepper
1	teaspoon salt
1	teaspoon black pepper

In a small bowl combine the ginger, red pepper, salt, and black pepper. Mix well. Rub on the meat of your choice prior to grilling.

YIELD: ¼ CUP

Shish Kabobs for Family Reunion Fare

Shish kabobs are a perfect choice for family reunions. Kids particularly delight in picking their favorite ingredients and excitably threading them on skewers. The variety of ingredients can satisfy multiple palates making it a great crowd-pleaser. Kabobs can be prepared in advance, but the fun lies in creating a kebab from an array of marinated items to make your taste buds beg for more. Let you imagination run wild with different marinades and combinations of meats, fruit, and vegetables. There are no limits to what you can use. You can even make dessert kabobs.

Recently, our family enjoyed a tasty feast of shish kabobs by the ocean. Onion quarters, button mushrooms, cherry tomatoes, chunk of red peppers, green peppers, and pineapple were piled into individual serving bowls and placed in a circle on a large round table. In the middle were pre-cut cubes of beef and chicken marinated in equal parts of vinegar, olive oil, and soy sauce. Extra marinade was placed near the large communal grill for basting to taste.

While waiting for the kabobs to cook, everyone helped themselves to salad and crudités. There were three choices of rice˜yellow rice, steamed rice, or fried rice˜to make a bed for the kabobs. It was great fun for all! For dessert, try fruit kabobs with strawberries, pineapples, watermelon, grapes, and apples.

Grilled Shish Kabobs

MARINADE

⅓ cup soy sauce
¾ cup vegetable oil
⅛ cup Worcestershire sauce
1 tablespoon dry mustard
2 teaspoons salt
1 teaspoon dried parsley
1½ teaspoon freshly ground black pepper
1 garlic clove, crushed
¼ cup lemon juice

SHISH KABOBS

2½ pounds beef, cut into 2-inch cubes
12 cherry tomatoes
12 button mushrooms
12 small onions, coarsely chopped
2 green bell peppers, cut into 1-inch squares
12 slices bacon, halved twice
2 zucchini, cut into 1/4-inch slices

For the **marinade**, blend the soy sauce, oil, Worcestershire sauce, dry mustard, salt, parsley, pepper, garlic, and lemon juice in a blender for about 30 seconds. Pour into a jar with a tight lid and refrigerate until ready to use.

In a shallow bowl or zip-lock bag pour the marinade over the beef cubes and let them marinate for several hours or all day.

Prepare or preheat a grill to hot. To prepare the **shish kabobs**, arrange the meat and vegetables on skewers, brush with the marinade and grill over hot coals for 15 minutes or until cooked. Turn the skewers and brush with marinade during the cooking process.

Hint: Potato wedges and small new potatoes make great additions to kabobs. Parboil the potatoes in the microwave first. Brush lightly with oil and season with salt and pepper. Thread the potatoes on the skewer and grill until tender. You can also grill wedges of sweet potatoes sprinkled with ground cinnamon or ginger.

YIELD: 6 SERVINGS

THE ART OF CRABBING

You will need to have crab baskets, scoop nets, chicken necks, and 10-gallon wash tubs or bushel baskets. Tie the chicken neck securely in the middle of the crab basket. Lower the crab basket over the side of the boat or off the dock. Wait five to ten minutes if the crabs are running and if not wait a little longer. Pull the crab basket up to see if you have caught a crab. If so, bring the basket up quickly and dump the catch into the washtub. Check to make sure your chicken neck is still securely tied in the crab basket and lower the basket again for another catch. Continue the process until you have at least half a bushel of crabs. For a low-country crab boil be sure to have plenty of ice cold beer, paper towels, iced sweet tea, and good friends to make the time complete.

Crab Boil

1½	gallons water
¾	cup (3 ounces) crab boil seasoning
1	medium onion, sliced
1	lemon, quartered
⅓	cup salt
25	live blue crabs*

Pour the water into a large stockpot over high heat. Stir in the crab boil seasoning, onion slices, lemon, and salt. Cover the pot and bring to a boil. Using long-handled tongs place the crabs into the boiling water. Cover and cook for 15 minutes or until the crabs are bright read. Drain the water. Pour the crabs onto a table layered with newspaper. Serve with clarified butter, garlic butter, cocktail sauce, ketchup, hot sauce, saltine crackers, sweetened iced tea, and beer.

How to open crabs:

1. Twist and pull the legs and crab claws from the body of the crab.

2. Turn the crab on its back and lift the tab on its belly. This will "unlock" the shell from its body. Pull the shell off the body and discard or save for stuffing.

3. Clean the body by removing the sponge gills. (We called them dead man fingers.)

4. Remove the organs and the fat yellowish material.

5. Break the body in half at the middle.

6. Use a cocktail fork to remove the meat from the pockets.

7. Use a seafood cracker or mallet or nut cracker to remove the meat from the legs and claws.

*Hint: Always use live crabs. Discard any dead crab because bacteria grow rapidly in a dead crab.

YIELD: 6 SERVINGS

Clarified Butter

1   pound (4 sticks) unsalted butter

In a saucepan on medium heat, bring the butter to a boil, being careful not to allow it to brown. Place in the refrigerator for ½ hour or until the butter is separated. Pour off the clear liquid to use for seafood dipping.

YIELD: 1½ CUPS

Garlic Butter

½ pound (2 sticks) butter, softened
1½ teaspoons garlic powder or 2 garlic cloves, crushed
¼ cup minced onion
¼ cup finely chopped fresh parsley

Combine the butter, garlic, onion, and parsley. Mix thoroughly and chill.

YIELD: 1 CUP

Cocktail Sauce

This is a delicious sauce to serve with boiled shrimp, raw oysters, or at an oyster roast.

1½ cups ketchup
2 tablespoons bottled horseradish
1½ tablespoons Worcestershire sauce
2 cups chili sauce
3 tablespoons fresh lemon juice
¼ teaspoon Tabasco
Salt and pepper

In a mixing bowl combine the ketchup, horseradish, Worcestershire sauce, chili sauce, lemon juice, Tabasco, and salt and pepper to taste. Mix well. Cover and refrigerate until chilled.

YIELD: 4 CUPS

OYSTER ROAST

The fresh taste of a plump oyster roasted in it's own shell, dipped in butter is one of life's greatest pleasures to an oyster lover. When Louis and I go to an oyster roast, Louis shucks the oysters for me as he loves the art of shucking oysters. (He doesn't eat oysters; tube steaks—hot dogs—are available for people like Louis.)

As a child, my family home was on Wilmington Island on Turner Creek in Savannah. My father taught my siblings and me at an early age how to swim and handle a boat. His lessons also included throwing one of his homemade shrimp nets and digging for oysters. My sister, Dot, brother, Charles, and I would go out with the tide for a few hours of digging oysters. Before the tide turned we'd do some crabbing (see special section page 20). When the tide turned, Dot and I would take turns rowing the boat back to the dock while Charles casts the net for shrimp. What fun we all had.

Roast Oysters

Daddy and Charles were always in charge of roasting the oysters. Charles still does oyster roasts for our family reunions, and this is his recipe.

1   croaker (burlap) sack of fresh oysters in the shell (1 croacker sack equals 1 bushel)
      Cold beer or sweetened iced tea
      Melted butter (optional)
      Sliced lemons (optional)
2   boxes saltine crackers
      Sweet pickles (optional)
1   pair heavy cloth work gloves per guest for handling hot oyster shells
1   oyster knife per guest (screwdrivers work too)

Wash the oysters in the shell to remove all mud and debris. Drink a beer or glass of tea. Oysters can be roasted over a gas grill or charcoal or over wood fire coals. Charles prefers wood fire coals.

Dig a pit 2 feet by 4 feet by 12 inches deep. Build a fire in the pit using oak and hickory. Add more oak as needed and allow the fire to burn down to hot coals. Place a steel sheet 8 inches above the pit supported by concrete blocks. Drink another beer or glass of tea. Place the oysters in a single layer on the hot metal sheet; the metal must be hot. Cover the oysters with a wet croaker sack . Keep the croaker sack wet. When the oyster shells begin to open slightly remove them using a flat shovel. Place the oysters on a wooden table covered with newspaper. Drink another beer or glass of tea. Using an oyster knife, open the oysters and enjoy with melted butter and lemons if desired. Saltine cracker and pickles compliment the oysters. Serve with Potato Salad (recipe on special section page 8).

YIELD: 8 TO 10 SERVINGS

Savannah Low-Country Boil

Along the coast of South Carolina and Savannah when shrimp are coming in, it's time for a low-country boil. Famous in the marshy South Carolina low country and the Georgia coast, the boil is a great way to fellowship with friends and family.

Orange-Seasoned Sweet Potato Packets

4   small or 2 large dark orange sweet potatoes, peeled and thinly sliced
2   tablespoons margarine or butter, divided
1   small onion, chopped, divided
¼   cup orange juice, divided
1   teaspoon grated orange peel (optional)
⅛   teaspoon salt

Preheat or prepare a grill to medium heat. Cut four 18 x 12-inch pieces of heavy-duty aluminum foil; spray the foil with nonstick cooking spray. Divide the sweet potatoes in thin layers among each piece of sprayed foil. Top each with ½ tablespoon margarine, one-quarter of the onion, and 1 tablespoon of the orange juice. Sprinkle each with orange peel, if desired, and salt. Wrap each of the packets securely using double-fold seals, allowing room for heat expansion.

When ready to grill, place the packets, with the seam side up, on the grill. Cook for 30 to 35 minutes or until the potatoes and onions are tender. Rearrange the packets several times during the cooking time. Open the packets carefully to allow steam to escape.

Yield: 4 servings

Low-Country Boil

The Stanhope family in the Port Wentworth suburb of Savannah has been close and dear friends of ours since the 1960s. Our first low-country boil was with them. The following recipe is from Ernie Stanhope.

	Salt
2½	gallons water
2	to 3 bay leaves
1	small box seafood seasoning
½	cup (1 stick) butter or margarine
2	to 3 large lemons, halved
6	pounds kielbasa
20	whole red potatoes, unpeeled
8	small whole onions, cleaned
1	celery stalk, cut into 1-inch pieces
5	large ears corn, halved
6	pounds green headless shrimp
12	live blue crabs (optional)

Using a 24-quart stockpot or outdoor cooker with a basket insert, bring salted water to a boil. Add the bay leaves, seafood seasoning, butter, and lemons. Boil for 10 to 12 minutes. Add the kielbasa and boil for 10 minutes. Add the potatoes, onions, and celery; boil for 10 minutes. Add the corn and boil for 10 more minutes. Add the shrimp and crabs; boil for 5 minutes. Remove from heat and allow to stand 5 to 10 minutes. Remove from the water. Serve dry in a large bowl or drain and dump onto an outside table covered with newspaper. Serve with saltine crackers, cocktail sauce, ketchup, and lots of sweetened iced tea and beer.

Dishes that complement are coleslaw, dill pickles, and banana pudding for dessert.

Hint: When finished simply roll up the newspaper and dispose. Hose down the table. It's easy clean up.

YIELD 10 TO 12 SERVINGS

Grilled Corn on the Cob

6   ears corn in the husk
    String to tie the husks
1   tablespoon kosher salt
    Water
    Water bottle for spraying

Preheat or prepare a grill to medium hot. Carefully peel back the husks of the corn, without breaking them, and discard the silk. Fold the husks back into place and tie the ends together with kitchen string. In a large bowl soak the corn in water and salt for 10 minutes. Drain the corn and grill on a rack set 5 to 6 inches over the coals for 15 minutes, turning occasionally. Lightly spray the corn with water to help it to steam. The corn is done when the kernels are tender.

YIELD: 6 SERVINGS

Cheesy Grilled Tomatoes

2   large tomatoes
⅓   cup crumbled blue cheese
1   tablespoon olive oil
1   tablespoon chopped fresh basil
2   tablespoon grated Parmesan cheese

Preheat or prepare a grill to medium hot. Cut the tomatoes in half crosswise. Scoop out the seeds with a small spoon. Fill with blue cheese. Drizzle with olive oil; sprinkle with basil and Parmesan cheese. Place the tomatoes, cut sides up, in a foil pie pan or on a piece of heavy-duty aluminum foil. Place the pie pan on the grill and cook for 15 minutes or until the tomatoes are thoroughly heated and begin to soften. Serve with any grilled meal.

YIELD: 4 SERVINGS

Roasted Mixed Peppers

1   green bell pepper, quartered and seeded
1   red bell pepper, quartered and seeded
1   yellow bell pepper, quartered and seeded
1   sweet onion, cut into ¾-inch-thick slices
2   tablespoons olive oil

DRESSING

2   tablespoons balsamic vinegar
1   tablespoon chopped fresh oregano
1   garlic clove, minced
    Salt and pepper (optional)

Preheat or prepare a grill to medium heat. In a shallow bowl, combine the green, red, and yellow bell peppers and onion. Drizzle with olive oil; toss to coat.

When ready to grill, remove all the peppers and the onion from the oil with tongs; place on the grill and cook for 12 to 14 minutes or until crisp-tender, turning one time.

For the **dressing**, combine the vinegar, oregano, and garlic in a bowl; mix well. Cut the grilled peppers into 1/2-inch strips. Add the peppers and onion to the dressing; toss to coat. If desired, season with salt and pepper to taste.

YIELD: 4 SERVINGS

Pecan-Stuffed Portobello Mushrooms

¼   cup (½ stick) margarine or butter, divided
6   large Portobello mushroom cups
2   green onions, sliced
¼   cup chopped pecans
1   cup seasoned stuffing mix
½   cup apple juice or chicken broth

Melt the margarine or butter in a small saucepan over medium heat. Scoop out the gills from the under sides of mushroom caps. Brush all sides of the mushrooms with about 2 tablespoons of the melted margarine or butter. Set the mushrooms aside. Combine the onions and pecans with the remaining margarine or butter; cook in the saucepan over medium heat, stirring occasionally, for 4 to 5 minutes or until the onions are tender and the pecans are toasted. Add stuffing mix and apple juice or chicken broth and mix well.

When ready to grill, place the mushrooms, rounded side up, on the grill and cook for 5 minutes or until the mushrooms begin to soften. Turn the mushrooms. Spoon the stuffing mixture into the mushroom caps. Cook an additional 10 to 15 minutes or until the mushrooms are tender. These mushrooms complement any grilled steak.

YIELD: 6 SERVINGS

Watermelon Social

A watermelon social is a great opportunity to have a large group of friends over to share in a fun afternoon. Mark Twain said "When one has tasted watermelon, he knows what the angels eat." What a fun thing to do on a hot summer day between two o'clock and five o'clock in the afternoon. Have several containers of Petra's Pound Cake (recipe on page 301) and homemade ice cream on hand. And plan to play some old-fashioned games, such as badminton, volleyball, and horseshoes. A great location for a watermelon social is your favorite swimming hole.

1 ice cold watermelon

Set up long tables and cover with newspaper. Use a scooped out watermelon filled with wild-flowers for a centerpiece.

YIELD: 10 SERVINGS PER WATERMELON

Kids' Wiener Roast

Some of our fondest memories of outdoor cooking are the wiener roasts with our children and now our grandchildren. Everyone participates in building the fire and cooking their own wieners. Wiener roasts are best on cool fall evenings followed by sitting around the fire and telling stories.

Wiener roasts can be done over an open wood fire or over hot coals in a grill. Our preference, time permitting, is an open fire. Clear the desired location for the fire of leaves, grass, and debris. Build a small fire using balled up newspaper, small dry twigs, and logs three to four inches in diameter. Stack the logs in the form of a tent. Light the newspaper and allow the fire to burn to hot coals. Add more logs as needed.

Roasting Marshmallows

For eating by themselves or making s'mores.

1   large bag of large marshmallows
4   wooden sticks left over from wiener roast (see next page)

Place a marshmallow on the end of the wooden stick. Hold over hot coals until brown, continuously turning the stick to cook evenly. If the marshmallow flames up, blow it out. They are still good!

YIELD: VARIED

Hint: For S'mores, follow recipe on page 361 and use the cooked marshmallows.

Hot Dogs

4 (2½ to 3-foot long) wooden (hardwood) sticks
8 all beef hot dogs
8 hot dog buns
   Ketchup
   Mustard
   Pickle relish
   Chopped onions

The sticks should be about 2½ to 3 feet long. Using a knife, trim the last 6 inches of the stick to make a tapered end about the thickness of a small pencil. (Or you can use a coat hanger opened lengthwise.)

Spear the hot dog lengthwise with the tapered end of the wooden stick. Hold the hot dog over the fire until the it begins to turn dark, continuously turning the stick to cook evenly. Place the hot dog in a bun and dress with ketchup, mustard, relish, and onions to taste. Serve with baked beans, slaw, potato chips, and fruit drinks. For dessert, either cook s'mores (recipe on page 361) or roast marshmallows.

Hint: Make a couple extra wooden sticks as some may break. Also, have extra hot dogs on hand as they sometimes drop in the fire.

YIELD: 4 SERVINGS

Gravies & Sauces

Gravies are made from the brown juices of baked meats or the "pan drippings" of fried meats, and they can be made thick or thin. In the South they are used for any meal from breakfast over grits or biscuits to dinner where gravy can be served with beef, chicken, or pork. Gravy is a wonderful addition to creamed potatoes as any Southern child can tell you.

Southern cooks use a variety of sauces for meats, vegetables, and desserts. They enhance the flavor and make a tasty addition to numerous dishes. Sauces can be plain and simple or luscious with the addition of fruits, vegetable, and cheeses. Sauces are numerous in their consistency and usage. For example mint sauce with lamb, cranberry sauce with chicken or turkey, and barbeque sauce with pork.

Baked Cranberry Sauce

This is an elegant, easy sauce and can be made ahead of time.

1	(16-ounce) bag fresh cranberries, rinsed and picked over
⅔	cup granulated sugar
1	(8-ounce) jar orange marmalade
½	cup chopped nuts

Preheat the oven to 350°. Prepare a baking dish with nonstick cooking spray. In a medium-size mixing bowl mix the cranberries, sugar, marmalade, and nuts. Pour into the baking dish. Bake for 30 to 35 minutes until hot and bubbly. Serve warm. Refrigerate leftovers and serve reheated within a week.

YIELD: 3 CUPS

Jean Elder
Covington, Georgia

Blueberry Sauce

This sauce is certainly a flavorful accent to blueberry pancakes or to blueberry-banana nut bread. It is wonderful when served warm.

2	cups water
¾	cup granulated sugar
¼	cup cornstarch
24	ounces fresh or frozen blueberries

In a medium-size saucepan on medium heat combine the water and sugar and bring to a boil. In a small bowl combine the cornstarch with a small amount of water to dissolve. Stir the cornstarch mixture into the boiling mixture. Add the blueberries and continue to cook, stirring continuously, until thickened. Remove from the heat, cool, and serve.

YIELD: 1 QUART

Bourbon Sauce

Pour this sauce over bread pudding, rice pudding, and even ice cream. For a little variety, substitute Scotch whiskey for bourbon.

½	cup (1 stick) butter
1	cup granulated sugar
1	egg, well beaten
¼	cup bourbon

In the microwave oven heat the butter and sugar until the sugar is dissolved. Add the egg and whisk rapidly so that the egg does not scramble. Add the bourbon and mix. Cool and serve.

YIELD: ABOUT 1 CUP

Blueberries can be frozen
immediately after picking.
Just wash and freeze.

Cabernet Cranberries

1½   cups granulated sugar

1   cup Cabernet Sauvignon

1   (12-ounce) package fresh cranberries

2   teaspoons grated tangerine rind

1   (3-inch) cinnamon stick

In a medium saucepan over medium-high heat bring the sugar and wine to a boil. Add the cranberries, tangerine rind, and cinnamon stick. Return to a boil, stirring constantly. Reduce the heat and simmer, partially covered, for 10 to 15 minutes or until the cranberry skins pop. Remove from the heat and discard the cinnamon stick. Cool slightly and serve warm or chill for 2 hours if preferred.

Hint: This sauce may be stored in the refrigerator for up to 2 months.

YIELD: 3½ CUPS

Carolina Low Country Dressing

This is wonderful as an accompaniment with ham, turkey, or beef. It can be made for Christmas gifts and packaged in old collectible wire lid jars.

¼   cup prepared mustard

¼   cup granulated sugar

2   cups mayonnaise

1   medium onion, grated

In a small mixing bowl combine the mustard, sugar, mayonnaise, and onion. Mix well. Cover and refrigerate until ready to use.

YIELD: 2½ CUPS

Cheese Sauce

Normally used over steamed broccoli or baked potatoes, this sauce also lends itself as a great sauce with seafood au gratin, ham-potato casserole, and just about any dish calling for a cheese sauce.

¼   cup (½ stick) butter, melted

¼   cup all-purpose flour

2   cups milk

1   (16-ounce) jar Cheez Whiz

2½   cups grated cheddar cheese

½   teaspoon salt

¼   teaspoon black pepper

In a saucepan combine the butter and flour. Mix well to make a roux. Heat the milk. Add the milk to the butter mixture. Heat this mixture on medium heat, stirring often to prevent scorching. When the milk mixture is hot, add the Cheez Whiz and grated cheddar cheese. Continue to heat to melt the cheeses as you blend. Add the salt and pepper. Turn the heat to low and allow the cheese sauce to simmer for 5 to 6 minutes. Stir often.

YIELD: 8 CUPS

Chunky Cranberry Applesauce

Wonderful served with pork or ham.

6	cups chopped peeled apples
2	cups fresh or frozen cranberries
1	cup water
½	cup raisins
⅓	cup packed brown sugar
2	tablespoons red hot cinnamon candies
1	teaspoon ground cinnamon
⅛	teaspoon ground nutmeg

In a large saucepan over medium heat combine the apples, cranberries, and water. Cook until the berries pop, about 15 minutes. Reduce the heat. Simmer uncovered for 15 minutes or until the apples are tender.

Stir in the raisins, brown sugar, cinnamon candies, cinnamon, and nutmeg. Simmer uncovered for 5 to 10 minutes or until the candies are dissolved. Serve warm or refrigerate until serving.

YIELD: 5 CUPS

Classic Hollandaise Sauce

This is a rich egg-based sauce flavored with a bit of lemon or vinegar, butter and a hint of cayenne pepper. It can be served over vegetables, fish, or Eggs Benedict. A successful sauce is made in a double boiler. Be sure not to allow the water in the bottom of the double boiler to boil, just to remain hot and lightly simmering. A tablespoon of cold water can be added to reduce the heat of the water if it starts to boil. The sauce should be served immediately.

½	cup (1 stick) unsalted butter
2	tablespoons white-wine or tarragon vinegar or fresh lemon juice
4	tablespoons boiling water
3	large egg yolks
¼	teaspoon cayenne pepper
½	teaspoon salt

In a small saucepan on low heat, melt the butter and keep it warm. In another small saucepan on low heat, heat the vinegar or lemon juice until just warm. Have a small saucepan with boiling water and a measuring tablespoon ready. Place the top of a double boiler over (not in) hot water. Place the egg yolks in the top of a double boiler and whisk until they begin to thicken. Now add 1 tablespoon of the boiling water. Continue to beat the sauce until it begins to thicken. Repeat with the remaining water, 1 tablespoon at a time, beating the mixture after each addition. Add the warmed vinegar or lemon juice. Remove the double boiler from the heat. Beat the sauce briskly with a wire whisk. Continue to beat the mixture as you slowly pour in the melted butter. Add the salt and cayenne and beat the sauce until it is thick. Serve immediately.

YIELD: 1 CUP

Dijon Sauce

1   (8-ounce) container sour cream
3   tablespoons Dijon mustard
1   tablespoon white wine vinegar
1   teaspoon granulated sugar
¼   teaspoon salt
⅛   teaspoon pepper

In a small mixing bowl, whisk together the sour cream, mustard, vinegar, sugar, salt, and pepper. Chill before serving.

YIELD: 1¼ CUP

Dill Sauce

A standard sauce used for grilled, broiled, or baked fish, especially salmon.

¼   cup sour cream
¼   cup mayonnaise
1   tablespoon dill weed
¼   teaspoon lemon juice

In a medium-size mixing bowl combine the sour cream, mayonnaise, dill weed, and lemon juice. Mix well. Cover and refrigerate.

Hint: This sauce can be used as a dip. For variation, add 1 tablespoon dried onion flakes or chopped green onions, parsley, and seasoned salt to taste.

YIELD: 3 TO 4 SERVINGS

Ginger Sauce

This is a delicious sauce to serve with a pork loin or pork chops.

1   teaspoon dark sesame oil
1   garlic clove, minced
1   tablespoon minced fresh ginger
2   tablespoons light soy sauce
1   tablespoon rice wine vinegar
2   teaspoons teriyaki sauce
1   minced green onion

Heat the oil in a small saucepan on medium heat. Sauté the garlic and ginger in hot oil for 1 minute. Remove from the heat and quickly whisk in the soy sauce, rice wine vinegar, teriyaki sauce, and minced onion.

YIELD: ABOUT ⅓ CUP

Lemon Sauce

The Blue Willow Inn Restaurant serves this sauce on hot gingerbread. It is also delicious served over fritters that have been sprinkled with confectioners' sugar.

1	cup boiling water
1	pound granulated sugar
1½	teaspoons cornstarch
¼	teaspoon salt
2	tablespoons butter, melted
1½	teaspoons lemon juice
1½	teaspoons grated lemon rind
	Dash of ground nutmeg

In a large saucepan over medium heat combine the boiling water, sugar, cornstarch, salt, butter, lemon juice, lemon rind, and nutmeg. Stir until the ingredients are smooth and creamy. Bring the sauce to a boil, stirring often. Remove from the heat and cool.

YIELD: ABOUT 1½ CUPS

Marchand de Vin Sauce

Marsha Barbour, the first lady of the state of Mississippi, sent this recipe to us. She said Governor Haley Barbour's mother gave this recipe to her. It is the first one she attempted to prepare as a young bride. She said it has become a favorite of their two sons as well, and it is delicious served over beef and pork.

¾	cup (1½ sticks) butter
⅓	cup finely chopped mushrooms
½	cup minced ham
⅓	cup finely chopped shallots
½	cup finely chopped onion
2	tablespoons minced garlic
2	tablespoons all-purpose flour
½	teaspoon salt
⅛	teaspoon pepper
	Dash of cayenne
¾	cup beef stock
½	cup red wine

In a large skillet over medium heat, melt the butter and lightly sauté the mushrooms, ham, shallots, onion, and garlic. When the onion is golden brown, add the flour, salt, pepper, and the cayenne. Brown the base well for about 7 to 10 minutes. Blend in the stock and wine. Turn the heat to low and simmer for 35 to 40 minutes.

YIELD: 2 CUPS

Raisin Sauce

This sauce is a delicious complement to ham, other pork dishes, and turkey.

¼	cup firmly packed light brown sugar
¼	cup water
½	cup golden raisins
2	tablespoons cider vinegar
1	tablespoon butter
¾	teaspoon Worcestershire sauce

¼ teaspoon salt

⅛ teaspoon pepper

⅛ teaspoon ground cloves

⅛ teaspoon ground mace

½ cup jellied cranberry sauce

In a small saucepan over low heat stir together the brown sugar, water, raisins, vinegar, butter, Worcestershire sauce, salt, pepper, cloves, mace, and cranberry sauce. Stir until the cranberry sauce melts. Serve warm.

YIELD: 1½ CUPS

Raspberry Sauce

2 (14-ounce) packages frozen raspberries, thawed

1 cup granulated sugar

1 tablespoon cornstarch

2 tablespoons raspberry liqueur

Press the thawed raspberries through a fine wire-mesh strainer into a saucepan. Discard the solids. In a small bowl stir the sugar and cornstarch together. Stir this mixture into the raspberry juice until it is smooth. Cook over medium-high heat until the mixture comes to a boil, stirring constantly. Allow it to boil for 1 minute, stirring constantly. Remove from the heat. Stir in the liqueur. Set it aside to cool. Pour into a bowl, cover, and chill for 2 hours.

YIELD: 4 TO 5 SERVINGS

Shrimp Sauce for Vegetables

This sauce is very good over asparagus, broccoli, Brussels sprouts, cauliflower, or on a baked potato.

½ cup boiled shrimp, very finely chopped

1 (10¾-ounce) can cream of shrimp soup

1 (3-ounce) package cream cheese

1 tablespoon onion juice

1 tablespoon lemon juice

1 teaspoon Tabasco

½ teaspoon white pepper

In a medium-size saucepan over low heat mix the shrimp, soup, cream cheese, onion juice, lemon juice, Tabasco, and white pepper. Stir constantly until smooth and melted. Pour over vegetables to serve.

YIELD: 2 CUPS

Shirley Smith Bowyer

Foley, Alabama

Do not despair if you oversalt gravy. Stir in some instant mashed potatoes to repair the damage. Just add a little more liquid in order to offset the thickening.

Tartar Sauce

This is a complement to fish—baked, broiled, or fried.

- 1 cup mayonnaise
- 1 tablespoon dill pickle relish
- 1 tablespoon chopped pimiento-stuffed olives
- 1 tablespoon capers
- 1 tablespoon grated shallot
- 1 tablespoon lemon juice
- ⅛ to ¼ teaspoon hot sauce

In a small bowl stir together the mayonnaise, pickle relish, olives, capers, shallot, lemon juice, and hot sauce. Cover and chill for at least 2 hours before serving.

YIELD: 1¼ CUPS

White Sauce

THIN

This sauce looks like the thickness of coffee cream. It can be used in creamed vegetables and soups.

- 1 tablespoon butter
- ½ to 1 tablespoon all-purpose flour
- ¼ teaspoon salt
- ⅛ teaspoon pepper
- 1 cup milk

MEDIUM

This sauce is similar to thick cream and is usually used in creamed and scalloped dishes.

- 2 tablespoons butter
- 2 tablespoons all-purpose flour
- ¼ teaspoon salt
- ⅛ teaspoon pepper
- 1 cup milk

THICK

This sauce is similar to a batter and is generally used for croquettes and soufflés.

- ¼ cup (½ stick) butter
- ¼ cup all-purpose flour
- ¼ teaspoon salt
- ⅛ teaspoon pepper
- 1 cup milk

In a heavy saucepan on low heat melt the butter. Blend in the flour, salt and pepper, stirring constantly. Cook over low heat, continuing to stir until the mixture is smooth and bubbly. Remove from the heat. Stir in the milk. Return to the heat and bring to a boil while stirring constantly. Boil for 1 minute.

> Hint: For a cheese sauce, use the medium sauce and add ¼ teaspoon dry mustard with the seasonings. After adding the milk, stir in ½ cup grated sharp cheddar cheese and stir until it is melted.

YIELD: 1 CUP

Giblet Gravy

A southern favorite for roast turkey and always seen on the table at a southern holiday meal.

2 cups chicken broth
1 hard-cooked egg, coarsely chopped
¼ cup coarsely chopped chicken or turkey giblets
1 to 2 teaspoons cornstarch
1 tablespoon cold water

In a medium-size saucepan on medium heat combine the chicken broth, egg, and the chicken or turkey giblets. Bring to a boil. Dissolve 1 to 2 teaspoons cornstarch in the cold water. Gradually stir the cornstarch mix into the gravy to the desired thickness.

YIELD: ABOUT 2 CUPS

Pan or Cream Gravy

This gravy is made in the skillet after frying chicken, pork chops, or other meats.

6 tablespoons drippings
6 tablespoons all-purpose flour
1½ cups sweet milk
Salt and pepper

Remove the meat from the skillet, leaving about 6 tablespoons drippings. Turn the heat to medium. Stir the flour into the drippings and cook until lightly browned, stirring constantly. Slowly stir in the milk. Continue cooking the gravy over low heat until it is smooth and thick, stirring occasionally. Add salt and pepper to taste.

YIELD: ABOUT 1½ CUPS

Roux

Alice Edgerly, Billie's former mother-in-law, got this recipe from her mother-in-law who was from Louisiana of Cajun-French descent. Alice taught Billie how to make this roux. Only two ingredients make a roux. The slowly cooked blend contributes a rich depth of flavor to Creole and Cajun cookery and is the heart of every real gumbo. Plan to spend 30 to 40 minutes whisking the precious thickener. The smoky, nutty flavor of a roux cannot be rushed. If the heat is too high, the roux will burn and it will have to be thrown away.

1½ cups vegetable oil
2 cups all-purpose flour

Over medium heat in a large cast iron skillet heat the oil. Gradually whisk in the flour, and cook, whisking constantly, until the flour is a dark mahogany color, about 30 minutes.

Hint: The roux can be used in a recipe immediately. Or allow to cool and then store it in an airtight container for up to 2 weeks.

YIELD: ABOUT 3½ CUPS

Sausage Gravy

This gravy is "to die for" served over buttermilk biscuits or grits.

8	ounces pork sausage
¼	cup all-purpose flour
2⅓	cups milk
½	teaspoon salt
½	teaspoon pepper

In a large skillet over medium heat cook the sausage, stirring, until it crumbles and is no longer pink. Remove the sausage. Drain on paper towels. Reserve 1 tablespoon of drippings in the skillet. Whisk the flour into the hot drippings until it is smooth. Cook, whisking constantly, for 1 minute. Gradually whisk in the milk, and cook, whisking constantly, 5 to 7 minutes or until thickened. Stir in the sausage, salt, and pepper.

YIELD: 2 CUPS

Tomato Gravy

This is delicious gravy to serve over meatloaf.

2	tablespoons butter or margarine
2	tablespoons all-purpose flour
⅓	cup beef broth
1	(8-ounce) can tomato sauce
¼	teaspoon salt
¼	teaspoon pepper

In a small saucepan on medium-low heat melt the butter. Whisk in the flour and cook, whisking constantly, for 1 minute. Gradually whisk in the broth and the tomato sauce. Reduce the heat to low and simmer until thickened. Whisk in the salt and pepper. Pour into a gravy boat and serve hot.

YIELD: ABOUT 1 CUP

Breads

Homemade breads were the culinary mortar of Southern life. Bread was a must for each meal every day and bread making was considered a vital skill for any cook. The smell of biscuits baking in the morning would signal that the day had begun and the smell of fresh baked bread would draw anyone in for dinner. In this chapter we have included recipes that will give you an opportunity to recapture the luscious comforting smells and tastes in your own kitchen of the old-time homemade breads.

Banana-Nut Bread

This is a delicious bread with afternoon tea or morning coffee. It is often used at church as a treat for guests.

½   cup solid vegetable shortening
1   cup granulated sugar
2   eggs
1   teaspoon lemon juice
1   cup mashed overripe bananas
2   cups all-purpose flour
1   tablespoon baking powder
½   teaspoon salt
1   cup chopped pecans (optional)

Preheat the oven to 350°. Grease a bread loaf pan. In a small bowl cream the shortening and the sugar together. In a separate bowl beat the eggs until they are light and fluffy. Add the lemon juice and the mashed bananas. Blend the egg mixture with the shortening mixture. Sift the flour, baking powder, and salt together. Mix quickly into the banana mixture. Add the pecans, if desired. Pour the mixture into the prepared loaf pan. Bake for 1 hour and 15 minutes or until a toothpick inserted in the middle comes out clean.

Hint: Add ¾ cup semisweet chocolate chips for a sweeter touch.

YIELD: 1 LOAF

Bran Raisin Bread

2   cups boiling water
2   cups raisins
4   teaspoons baking soda
3   cups all-purpose flour
2   cups crushed bran cereal
2   cups granulated sugar
½   teaspoon salt
2   eggs, lightly beaten
½   cup vegetable oil

Preheat the oven to 350°. In a medium-size mixing bowl pour the boiling water over the raisins and baking soda. Set aside to allow the raisins to cool. Stir together the flour, cereal, sugar, and salt. In a small mixing bowl slightly beat together the eggs and oil with a fork and stir into the dry mixture. Stir this mixture into the raisin mixture. Pour equal amounts of the batter into three greased bread pans and bake for 50 to 60 minutes.

Hint: To prevent fruit or nuts sinking to the bottom of a bread or cake batter, shake them in a zip-lock bag with a small amount of flour, lightly dusting them before adding them to the batter.

YIELD: 3 LOAVES

Joyce Dina
Gainesville, Florida

Fritters

Fritters are fruits or vegetables that have been dipped in batter and fried until they are a golden brown outside and tender inside. Fritters can also be chopped or grated foods mixed into a thick batter and fried in balls. Fritter batters can also be used as a coating for fried meats and fried seafood.

THICK BATTER

1	cup all-purpose flour
1	teaspoon baking powder
1	teaspoon salt
2	large eggs
½	cup milk
1	teaspoon vegetable oil

THIN BATTER

1	cup all-purpose flour
1	teaspoon baking powder
½	teaspoon salt
1	large egg
1	cup milk
¼	cup vegetable oil

In a medium-size mixing bowl sift together the flour, baking powder, and salt. In a small bowl mix the eggs, milk, and oil. Add the wet mixture to the dry ingredients to make a batter. Prepare the foods to be fried. If the food is frozen, thaw completely before frying.

Fill a skillet about 1 inch deep with vegetable oil or a deep-fat fryer to about one-third full of cooking oil—just deep enough to allow the food to float. Heat the oil to 375°.

Dry the food being used thoroughly on paper towels. Before dipping the food in the batter, coat with flour. Using tongs or a fork, dip the floured food into the batter, letting the excess drop off. Use a thin batter if you want to retain the shape of the food. Fold chopped or grated food into a thick batter. Fry the dipped food until it is a golden brown. The length of frying time will depend on the thickness of the food and the type of batter used. Food dipped in the thick batter will take about 1 minute longer. Drain on paper towels. Serve hot.

Meat and seafood fritters can be served as an appetizer or main dish. Serve fruit and vegetable fritters as a meat accompaniment. Fruit fritters can also be served as a dessert with a sauce or confectioners' sugar.

Hint: For apple or pineapple fritters, make the thick batter and add 1 large chopped apple or 1 cup drained crushed pineapple to the batter. Drop by the one-fourth cupful (or less) into the hot oil and fry. Drain on paper towels. Roll in confectioners' sugar. For corn fritters, make the thick batter and add 1 cup drained canned corn to the batter. Drop by the one-fourth cupful (or less) into the hot oil. Fry and drain on paper towels.

YIELD: 12 TO 15 FRITTERS

Cheddar Corn Bread

2   (8.5-ounces) boxes corn bread/muffin mix

2   eggs, beaten

½   cup milk

½   cup plain yogurt

1   (14¾-ounce) can cream-style corn

½   cup shredded cheddar cheese

Preheat the oven to 400°. In a bowl combine the corn bread mix, eggs, milk, and yogurt until blended. Stir in the corn and cheese. Pour into a greased 9 x 13-inch baking dish. Bake 18 to 22 minutes or until a toothpick inserted near the center comes out clean. Cut into squares. Serve warm.

YIELD: 12 SERVINGS

Crackling Bread

The skins and residue left from the rendering of pork fat at hog-killing times make cracklings. Ask a southerner whose memory goes back far enough to know about crackling bread crumbled up in buttermilk, and watch his eyes light up. Crackling bread has been served at the Blue Willow Inn on various occasions.

2   cups cornmeal

1   teaspoon baking powder

½   teaspoon salt

     Boiling water

⅔   cup cracklings

Preheat the oven to 425°. In a medium-size mixing bowl sift together the cornmeal, baking powder, and salt. Pour into this mixture enough boiling water to make a stiff batter. Add the cracklings. Mold into pones (oval shapes). Place the pones on a baking sheet and bake until light brown.

Serve with tall glasses of very cold buttermilk, and with instructions that the hot crackling bread is to be broken into the milk and eaten with an iced tea spoon.

Hint: Crackling bread can be cooked in an iron skillet or in muffin tins.

YIELD: 6 TO 8 SERVINGS

Gift of the Magi Bread

This is a unique bread to serve at Christmas.

½   cup (1 stick) butter or margarine, softened

1   cup granulated sugar

2   eggs

1   teaspoon vanilla extract

2   cups all-purpose flour

1   teaspoon baking soda

½   teaspoon salt

1   cup ripe mashed bananas (about 2 medium)

1   (11-ounce) can mandarin oranges, drained

1   cup flaked coconut

1   cup chocolate chips

½ cup plus 3 tablespoons sliced almonds

½ cup maraschino cherries

½ cup chopped dates or raisins

Preheat the oven to 350° degrees. In a large mixing bowl cream the butter and sugar. Beat in the eggs and vanilla. Add the flour, baking soda, and salt alternately with the bananas. Stir in the oranges, coconut, chocolate chips, ½ cup almonds, cherries, and dates or raisins.

Pour into two greased loaf pans. Sprinkle the remaining 3 tablespoons almonds on top of the bread. Bake for 45 to 50 minutes or until a toothpick inserted in the center comes out clean. After removing from the oven, cool for 10 minutes before removing the loaves from the pans to a wire rack to cool completely.

YIELD: 2 LOAVES

Vivian Beasley
Monroe, Georgia

When bread is baking, a small dish of water in the oven will help keep the crust from hardening.

Gingerbread

Serving this recipe with lemon sauce (recipe on page 134) transforms it from a good snack bread into a wonderful warm and light dessert.

¾ cup brown sugar

¾ cup molasses

¾ cup (1½ sticks) butter, melted

2 eggs, well beaten

2½ cups all-purpose flour

½ teaspoon baking powder

½ teaspoon salt

2 teaspoons baking soda

2½ teaspoons ground ginger

1½ teaspoons ground cinnamon

⅓ teaspoon cloves

1 cup boiling water

Preheat the oven to 350°. In a large mixing bowl combine the brown sugar, molasses, and butter. In a small mixing bowl beat the eggs and add them to the sugar mixture. In a medium-size mixing bowl sift together the flour, baking powder, salt, baking soda, ginger, cinnamon, and cloves; mix well. In a small saucepan on high heat bring the water to a rolling boil. Add the water to the batter and mix well.

Bake in a 9 x 13-inch floured pan at for 35 minutes or until a toothpick inserted in the middle comes out clean. After removing from the oven, set aside to cool.

YIELD: 24 SERVINGS

Grandma's Strawberry Nut Loaf

My grandmother, Elizabeth Fischer, made this recipe for her Mother's Club meetings. They always had great refreshments along with the fellowship. This recipe creates a tender, moist bread that is always a treat with tea.

½   cup (1 stick) butter or margarine
¾   cup granulated sugar
½   teaspoon vanilla extract
2   eggs
1½ cups all-purpose flour
½   teaspoon salt
⅜   teaspoon cream of tartar
¼   teaspoon baking soda
½   cup strawberry preserves
¼   cup sour cream
¼   cup finely chopped nuts

Preheat the oven to 350°. Grease and line with waxed paper an 8 x 4 x 2-inch loaf pan. In a large mixing bowl cream the butter, sugar, and vanilla. Add the eggs one at a time, beating well after each addition. In a medium-size bowl sift together the flour, salt, cream of tartar, and baking soda. In a small mixing bowl combine the strawberry preserves and the sour cream and mix well. Alternately add the strawberry mixture and the dry ingredients to the creamed mixture. Mix thoroughly after each addition until all ingredients are blended. Pour the mixture into the lined loaf pan. Trim the waxed paper around the edges (otherwise, it will smoke in the oven). Bake for 50 minutes.

YIELD: 1 LOAF

Judy Suggs
York, South Carolina
First Place Winner—Breads
Blue Willow Inn Restaurant Recipe Contest—2004

Granny Julia's Sausage Bread

1   loaf frozen bread dough
1   pound smoked sausage, finely chopped
1   pound bulk sausage
5   ounces cheddar cheese, shredded
5   ounces Romano cheese, shredded
5   ounces Mozzarella cheese, shredded
1   (4.2-ounce) jar ripe olives, chopped
4   ounces stuffed olives, chopped
1   green onion, diced
7   tablespoons butter, melted

Preheat the oven to 350°. Roll out the loaf of bread dough. In a large mixing bowl combine the smoked sausage, bulk sausage, cheddar cheese, Romano cheese, mozzarella cheese, ripe olives, stuffed olives, and green onion. Spread the sausage mixture on the rolled-out dough. Roll the filling up in the bread loaf as tightly as possible, tucking in the ends to seal. Place the loaf, sealed side down, on a greased baking sheet. Brush the top of the dough with the melted butter. Bake for 25 to 30 minutes.

YIELD: 1 LOAF

Melissa Hoganson
Port St. Lucie, Florida

Green Tomato Bread

8	to 10 medium green tomatoes, coarsely chopped
⅔	cup raisins
⅔	cup boiling water
⅔	cup vegetable shortening
2½	cups granulated sugar
3	eggs
3½	cups all-purpose flour
2	teaspoons baking soda
1½	teaspoons salt
½	teaspoon baking powder
1	teaspoon ground cinnamon
1	teaspoon cloves

Place the tomatoes in a blender and blend until smooth. Use enough tomatoes to make 2 cups of pulp. In a small bowl soak the raisins in the boiling water and set aside to cool. In a large mixing bowl, cream the shortening and the sugar until it is fluffy. Add the eggs, tomato pulp, and raisins with the soaking water. Beat well. In a small bowl combine the flour, baking soda, salt, baking powder,

cinnamon, and cloves. Mix well. Add this mixture to the tomato mixture. Stir well. Divide the batter between two oiled loaf pans. Bake for approximately 60 to 70 minutes.

YIELD: 2 LOAVES

Hushpuppies

These are a wonderful treat served with fried fish—especially catfish. They can even be cooked in the same oil you use to fry the fish. This gives them a little more crunch. There are several stories concerning the origin of hushpuppies. One is that when the men were out hunting and fishing for a few days and the dogs got hungry, they would mix up a cornmeal batter and fry it in the cooking grease on the campfire. This fried dough would be thrown to the dogs saying, "Hush, puppy!" The name stuck.

2	cups plain cornmeal
2	teaspoons baking powder
½	teaspoon salt
1½	cups sweet milk
½	cup grated or finely chopped onion
	Shortening for frying

In a medium-size mixing bowl combine the cornmeal, baking powder, and salt. Add the milk and then the onion. Blend the batter thoroughly. In a skillet or deep-fat fryer heat the shortening until it is hot but not smoking. Drop the batter by the heaping tablespoonful into the hot oil. Fry until golden brown.

YIELD: 12 TO 15 HUSHPUPPIES

Red and Green Confetti Corn Bread

This is a wonderful moist cornbread, very colorful, very healthy, and good to serve anytime. It is especially decorative at Christmas.

2   (8½-ounce) boxes corn muffin mix
1   (14½-ounce) can cream-style corn
2   eggs
½   cup milk
¼   cup drained pimientos
1   (10-ounce) package frozen chopped broccoli
1   cup shredded cheddar cheese

Preheat the oven to 350° degrees. Lightly coat a 9 x 13-inch baking pan with nonstick spray. In a large mixing bowl mix the corn muffin mix, corn, eggs, milk, pimientos, broccoli, and cheese. Pour the mixture into the pan and bake for 20 to 25 minutes or longer until the top is golden and a tester comes out clean.

Hint: For a spicier bread you can substitute a 4½-ounce can green chiles for the broccoli.

YIELD: ABOUT 24 SERVINGS

Nancy Guerine
Kennesaw, Georgia

Sally Lunn Bread

Sally Lunn, a pride of southern cooks, is said to be named after a young lady who in the 18th century sold the warm, crumbly bread in the streets of England. Recipes for Sally Lunn Bread show up in old Southern cookbooks dating back to the time of the Jamestown colonists.

1   cup whole milk
½   cup shortening, butter, or margarine
¼   cup water
2   plus 1⅓ plus ⅔ cups all-purpose flour
3   eggs
⅓   cup granulated sugar
2   teaspoons salt
2   (¼-ounce) packages active dry yeast

In a medium saucepan over medium heat combine the milk, shortening, and water until very warm (about 120°). The shortening does not need to melt. In a large mixing bowl blend 1⅓ cups flour, the sugar, salt, and dry yeast. Blend the warm liquid into the flour mixture. Beat with an electric mixer at medium speed for about 2 minutes, scraping the sides of the bowl occasionally. Gradually add the ⅔ cup flour and the eggs and beat at high speed for 2 minutes. Add the remaining 2 cups flour and mix well. The batter will be thick but not stiff.

Cover and allow the dough to rise in a warm, draft-free place (about 85° degrees) until it is double in bulk (about 1 hour and 15 minutes). Beat the dough down with a spatula or at the lowest speed of the electric mixer. Turn it into a greased 10-inch tube or Bundt pan. Cover and let the dough rise in a warm, draft-free place until increased in bulk by one-third to one-half, about 30 minutes. Preheat the oven to 350° and bake for 40 to 50 minutes. Run a knife around the center and outer edges of the bread and turn onto a plate to cool.

YIELD: 1 LOAF

Skillet Corn Bread

Some southern foods just aren't the same when they are cooked in something other than cast iron. In the South cast iron skillets and pots are handed down from mother to daughter. Every good cook must have a seasoned cast iron skillet because there is no better way to prepare corn bread. If you have a new skillet, the following is the best way to season the cast iron.

First, scrub the skillet with a steel wool soap pad. Then wash it with dishwashing soap and hot water. Thoroughly dry it and then spread a layer of vegetable shortening on the inside (including the underside of the lid if the skillet has a lid). Preheat the oven to 250°. Bake the prepared skillet for 15 minutes. Remove the skillet from the oven. Wipe out the shortening. Return the skillet to the oven and bake for 2 more hours. Remove the skillet from the oven and set it aside to cool at room temperature. Repeat this process two or three times. Once the cast iron is seasoned, never use soap to clean it—and never put it in a dishwasher.

2	to 3 teaspoons bacon drippings
2	cups buttermilk
1	large egg
1¾	cups white cornmeal
1	teaspoon baking powder
1	teaspoon baking soda
1	teaspoon salt

Preheat the oven to 450°. Coat the bottom and sides of a 10-inch cast-iron skillet with the bacon drippings. Heat the skillet in the oven.

While the skillet is heating, in a medium-size bowl whisk the buttermilk and egg together. Add the cornmeal, stirring well. Whisk in the baking powder, soda, and salt. Pour the batter into the hot skillet. Bake the bread for 15 minutes or until it is a golden brown. Remove from the oven and immediately place the cornbread upside-down onto a plate. Serve immediately while it is still hot for a luscious fresh-from-the-oven flavor.

YIELD: 6 TO 8 SERVINGS

Heat a knife blade in hot water, and dry it off quickly before slicing fresh bread. This makes the job much easier.

Sourdough Bread

Make a starter for bread and keep it available in the refrigerator for the best in bread baking.

STARTER

2	(¼-ounce) packages active dry yeast
1	plus ½ cup warm water
⅔	cup granulated sugar
3	tablespoons instant potato flakes

FEED

¾	cup granulated sugar
3	tablespoons instant potatoes
1	cup warm water

BREAD

⅓	to ½ cup granulated sugar
1	cup starter
1	to 1½ cups warm water
½	cup vegetable oil
1	teaspoon salt
6	cups bread flour

For the **starter:** In a small mixing bowl dissolve the yeast in ½ cup warm water. Stir in the remaining 1 cup warm water, sugar, and potato flakes. Allow the mixture to sit all day at room temperature. Refrigerate for 2 to 5 days. Remove from the refrigerator and feed.

For the **feed:** In a small mixing bowl mix together the sugar, instant potatoes, and water. Add this mixture to the starter. Let the new mixture sit out of the refrigerator for 8 to 10 hours. This does not rise, only bubbles. Take out 1 cup of the starter for baking bread and return the remaining starter to the refrigerator. Keep in the refrigerator for 3 to 5 days and feed again. If not baking bread, discard or give away 1 cup of the starter. The container holding the starter should be open slightly. If the top is left tightly on for a period of time, the starter will eventually explode.

For the **bread:** In a large mixing bowl mix the sugar, starter, warm water, oil, salt, and flour. Place in a large greased bowl and coat the sides and top of the bread dough with oil. Cover lightly and allow it to stand overnight at room temperature. Punch down the dough and knead a little. Divide the dough into three parts and knead each on a floured board 8 to 10 times. Put into greased and floured loaf pans. Brush with oil or butter. Cover lightly and let rise 4 to 5 hours (all day is fine). The dough rises very slowly. When ready to bake, preheat the oven to 350°. Place the dough on the bottom rack of the oven and bake for 25 to 30 minutes. If shaped into rolls rather than loafs, bake at 350° for about 10 minutes.

YIELD: 3 LOAVES OR 3 DOZEN ROLLS

Jeannette Allen
Loganville, Georgia

Southern Spoon Bread

This recipe was originally published in a 1938 cookbook called "Katch's Kitchen" by the Department of Applied Education of the Woman's Club in West Palm Beach, Florida.

2	cups cold cooked grits
½	cup plain cornmeal
2	cups milk
2	eggs
½	teaspoon salt
2	tablespoons butter
½	teaspoon baking powder

Preheat the oven to 375°. In a medium saucepan on medium heat, scald the cornmeal in the milk and set aside to cool. In a large mixing bowl lightly beat the eggs about 1 minute. Add the cold grits and the salt. Add the cooled cornmeal mixture, the butter, and baking powder. Pour in a buttered pudding dish and bake for 35 to 40 minutes or until brown.

YIELD: 6 TO 8 SERVINGS

Georgianna Alexander
Snellville, Georgia

Spoon Bread

The name is somewhat deceptive, for spoon bread is more like a cornmeal soufflé than any known piece of breadstuff. Etiquette demands you eat it with a fork, but it gets its name from the fact that it is served from the pan with a large spoon.

4	eggs, separated
2	cups milk
3	tablespoons butter
1	cup plain cornmeal
1	teaspoon baking powder
½	teaspoon salt
½	teaspoon cream of tartar

In a mixing bowl beat the egg yolks with an electric mixer at high speed until thick and light. In a saucepan over medium heat, combine the milk and butter. When hot, stir in the cornmeal, baking powder, and salt. When the batter thickens, remove from the heat, and gradually beat in the egg yolks. Preheat the oven to 375°. In a medium bowl, beat the egg whites with the cream of tartar until they are stiff. Gently fold the egg whites into the batter, and pour into a greased 2-quart baking dish. Bake for 35 minutes, or until a toothpick inserted in the center comes out clean. Serve immediately with butter.

YIELD: 8 SERVINGS

Sweet Potato Bread

3   large sweet potatoes
4   tablespoons vanilla extract
1½ cups all-purpose flour
4   eggs
2   tablespoons ground cinnamon
1½ teaspoons ground nutmeg
2   cups granulated sugar
1   cup milk

Wash and peel the potatoes. Cover with water and boil until cooked through. Drain off the water and mash the potatoes, using a whisk or potato masher. Preheat the oven to 350°. Combine the mashed sweet potatoes with the vanilla, flour, eggs, cinnamon, nutmeg, sugar, and milk. Mix well. Place in a large loaf pan, and bake for 20 to 25 minutes.

YIELD: 1 LOAF

Zucchini-Parmesan Appetizer Bread

3   cups grated zucchini
1   cup Bisquick
½   cup finely chopped onion
½   cup grated Parmesan cheese
2   tablespoons dried parsley
½   teaspoon seasoned salt
½   teaspoon dried oregano

4   eggs, lightly beaten
1   garlic clove, finely chopped
½   cup vegetable oil

Preheat the oven to 350°. Grease a 9 x 13-inch baking pan. In a large mixing bowl lightly mix with an electric mixer the zucchini, Bisquick, onion, Parmesan cheese, parsley, seasoned salt, oregano, eggs, garlic, and oil. Do not overbeat. Spread the mixture in the greased baking pan and bake for 25 minutes or until a toothpick inserted comes out clean. Cut into squares and serve.

YIELD: ABOUT 24 SERVINGS

Joanne Jenkins
Covington, Georgia

Angel Biscuits

These biscuits are served by southern ladies for luncheons and for Sunday dinner. They are heavenly with fried chicken.

4   cups all-purpose flour
¼   cup granulated sugar
3   teaspoons baking powder
1   teaspoon baking soda
1   teaspoon salt
½   cup shortening
1   (¼-ounce) package active dry yeast
2   teaspoons warm water
2   cups buttermilk

Preheat the oven to 475°. In a medium-size mixing bowl sift together the flour, sugar, baking powder, baking soda, and salt. Cut in the shortening. In a small bowl soften the yeast in the warm water and stir until dissolved. Mix with the buttermilk and combine this mixture with the dry ingredients. Mix until a dough ball forms. Place the dough on a lightly floured surface and roll out to ¼-inch thickness. Cut the dough with a biscuit cutter. Place the biscuits on a buttered baking pan and bake for 10 to 12 minutes or until golden brown.

YIELD: 12 TO 15 BISCUITS

Blue Willow Buttermilk Biscuits

2	cups self-rising flour
	Dash of salt
½	teaspoon granulated sugar
3	tablespoons shortening
½	cup buttermilk
½	cup sweet milk
1	tablespoon water
1	plus 1 tablespoons butter, melted

Preheat the oven to 475°. In a medium-size mixing bowl sift together the flour, salt, and sugar. Cut in the shortening until the mixture is coarse. Add the buttermilk, sweet milk, water, and 1 tablespoon butter. Mix lightly until well mixed. Do not overmix. Turn the dough onto a lightly floured surface and knead it two or three times. Knead several more times only if using the biscuits for sandwich biscuits.

With floured hands pat out the dough to about ½-inch thickness. Cut the dough with a biscuit cutter. Do not twist the cutter. Bake for 10 to 12 minutes or until golden brown. After removing from the oven, brush the biscuits with the remaining 1 tablespoon melted butter.

YIELD: 10 TO 12 BISCUITS

Cheesy Drop Biscuits

2	cups self-rising flour*
1	cup (2 sticks) butter or margarine, melted
1	(8-ounce) container sour cream
1	cup (4 ounces) shredded cheddar cheese
1	cup toasted chopped pecans (optional)

Preheat the oven to 350°. In a large mixing bowl combine the flour, butter, sour cream, and cheese until blended. Add pecans if desired. Drop by the heaping tablespoonful onto a lightly greased baking sheet (or line with parchment paper). Bake for 20 to 25 minutes or until golden brown. Cool for 5 minutes before removing from pan.

*Hint: Create your own self-rising flour by combining 1½ teaspoons baking powder, ½ teaspoon salt, and 2 cups all-purpose flour.

YIELD: 2 DOZEN

Jean Elder
Covington, Georgia

Sausage Biscuits

1   (¼-ounce) package active dry yeast
¼   cup warm water
¾   pound bulk sausage
2⅔ cups all-purpose flour
2   tablespoons granulated sugar
1   teaspoon baking powder
½   teaspoon baking soda
½   teaspoon salt
½   cup shortening
1   cup buttermilk
    Melted butter

Preheat the oven to 425°. Dissolve the yeast in the warm water and let it stand for 5 minutes.

In a medium-size skillet on medium-high heat crumble and cook the sausage. Remove from the heat, drain, and set aside to cool. In a large mixing bowl combine the flour, sugar, baking powder, baking soda, and salt. Cut the shortening into the dry mixture. Stir in the buttermilk and yeast mixture. Stir in the completely cooled sausage. Turn the dough out on a lightly floured board. Knead the mixture three or four times. Roll out the dough to about ½-inch thickness and cut the biscuits. Place in a greased baking pan and brush the tops with the melted butter. Bake the biscuits for 10 minutes or until lightly browned.

YIELD: 2½ DOZEN

Marilynn Walker
Loganville, Georgia

Sweet Potato Biscuits

These biscuits are a great companion to any pork dish. Chopped pecans can be added to this recipe for a delicious treat.

2   cups all-purpose flour
1   teaspoon salt
1   teaspoon baking soda
1   tablespoon granulated sugar
⅓   cup shortening
1   cup cooked and mashed sweet potatoes
¾   cup buttermilk

Preheat the oven to 450°. In a medium-size mixing bowl sift the flour, salt, baking soda, and sugar together. Cut in the shortening. Add the sweet potatoes. Stir in enough buttermilk to make the dough stiff; use more than called for if necessary.

Turn the dough onto a floured board and knead it lightly. Roll out to ½-inch thickness and cut with a floured cutter. Put the biscuits on a cookie sheet and bake until golden brown.

YIELD: 12 TO 15 BISCUITS

The secret of good muffins is in the mixing. Combine all the dry ingredients in a bowl, and form a well in the center of the mixture. Add the liquid all at once and stir only enough to moisten the dry ingredients. The mixture will be lumpy, but further mixing will make the muffins tough.

Apple Muffins

2	cups granulated sugar
1½	cups vegetable oil
3	eggs
3	cups all-purpose flour
1	teaspoon salt
1	teaspoon baking soda
1	teaspoon baking powder
1	teaspoon ground cinnamon
1	teaspoon ground nutmeg
2	teaspoons vanilla extract
1	(8-ounce) box chopped dates
1	cup chopped pecans
1	cup flaked or shredded coconut
3	cups diced apples

Preheat oven to 350°. In a large mixing bowl cream the sugar and oil. Add the eggs one at a time. In a second large mixing bowl sift the flour and then add the salt, baking soda, baking powder, cinnamon, and nutmeg. Add these dry ingredients to the sugar mixture. Add the vanilla extract, dates, pecans, coconut, and apples. (Be sure to add the apples last.) Fill 24 greased muffin cups ⅔ full of batter. Bake about 15 to 20 minutes or until brown.

YIELD: ABOUT 2 DOZEN

Dorothy Pace

Bran Muffins

These muffins are often served at the Blue Willow Inn Restaurant.

1	cup boiling water
1	cup 100% bran flakes cereal
½	cup shortening
1	cup granulated sugar
½	cup packed dark brown sugar
¼	cup molasses
¼	cup honey
3	eggs
2½	cups sifted all-purpose flour
2½	teaspoons baking soda
1	teaspoon salt
2	cups buttermilk
2	cups All-Bran cereal
1	cup raisins
1	cup chopped nuts (optional)

Preheat the oven to 400°. Pour the boiling water over the bran flakes and allow to cool. Cream the shortening, granulated sugar, brown sugar, molasses, and honey together. Add the eggs, one at a time, beating after each addition. Add the flour, baking soda, salt, and buttermilk. Mix well. Add the all-bran cereal, raisins, and nuts if desired. Stir only until well mixed. Pour the batter into lightly greased muffin tins or muffin cups. Bake for 20 minutes. Batter will hold well in the refrigerator for 3 to 4 weeks in a closed container.

YIELD: 3 DOZEN MUFFINS

Corn Bread or Corn Muffins

This traditional bread is served with most southern meals. Muffins are especially good with soups and vegetables or even with just a touch of butter. To give these a different flavor, add a half cup of real bacon bits.

2	cups self-rising cornmeal
1	egg
½	cup buttermilk
1	tablespoon, granulated sugar
¼	cup (½ stick) butter or margarine, softened

Preheat the oven to 350°. In a large mixing bowl combine the cornmeal, egg, buttermilk, sugar, and butter. Mix with a whisk. Do *not* beat.

For **corn bread:** Pour the batter into a 9 x 12-inch pan coated with shortening or nonstick spray. A prepared iron skillet can be used.

For **muffins:** Pour into 12 to 15 greased or paper-lined muffin cups.

For **sticks:** Pour into a corn-stick pan coated with shortening or a nonstick spray.

Bake for 15 to 18 minutes or until golden brown. Remove from the oven and brush with melted butter. Cut the corn bread into squares (or remove the muffins or sticks from the pan.) Serve hot.

YIELD: ABOUT 24 SERVINGS

Journey Cakes

Field workers and travelers would often put several of these cakes in their pockets for a simple meal to have on the road or while working.

2 cups cold cooked rice
2 large eggs, lightly beaten
2 cups milk
1½ cups rice flour
1½ tablespoons butter, melted
2 teaspoons salt
Peanut oil

In a large bowl stir together the rice, eggs, milk, flour, butter, and salt. In a heavy (cast iron) skillet pour the oil to a depth of ¼ inch. Heat the oil to 350°. Drop the batter by the ¼ cupful into the hot oil and fry in batches for about 2 minutes on each side or until golden brown. Drain on wire racks over paper towels. Serve immediately or pack them for traveling.

YIELD: 20 CAKES

Knee Caps

2 (¼-ounce) packages active dry yeast
¼ cup warm water
2 cups scalded whole milk
½ cup shortening
½ cup granulated sugar
¾ teaspoon salt
2 eggs
6½ cups sifted all-purpose flour
6 cups vegetable oil
Confectioners' sugar
Raspberry jelly for filling
Whipped topping

In a small mixing bowl stir the yeast into the warm water and let it stand until bubbly. In a small saucepan on low heat scald the milk and allow it to cool until just warm. In a large mixing bowl cream the shortening, granulated sugar, and salt together. Add the eggs. Stir in the yeast mixture and the scalded milk. Add the flour and knead the dough until it is smooth and elastic. Place the dough into a large, greased mixing bowl and allow it to rise in a warm place until it has doubled in bulk.

Roll the dough out to ½-inch thickness on a floured board or canvas. Cut the dough with a 2½-inch-round cookie or biscuit cutter. Cover the rounds with a towel and allow them to rise for 30 minutes. With the bottom of a glass or bottle, about 1 to 1½-inches in diameter, press an indentation in the center of each risen Knee Cap.

Pour the vegetable oil into an electric skillet or deep fryer and heat to 400°. Drop the Knee Caps (indented side down) into the hot oil. Fry them to a golden brown on both sides. Drain them on paper towels and dust them with the confectioner's sugar. Fill the holes in the Knee Caps with raspberry jelly (or your favorite jelly or jam) and top with the whipped topping.

YIELD: 3 DOZEN

Alma K Smith
Foley, Alabama

Blueberry Muffins

1   egg
½   cup milk
¼   cup vegetable oil
1½   cups all-purpose flour
½   cup granulated sugar
2   teaspoons baking powder
½   teaspoon salt
1   cup fresh blueberries or ¾ cup frozen
     blueberries, thawed and drained

Preheat the oven to 400°. In a large mixing bowl combine the egg, milk, oil, flour, sugar, baking powder, salt, and blueberries. Mix lightly. Pour into greased muffin cups and bake for 20 to 25 minutes.

YIELD: 1 DOZEN

Buttery Biscuit Rolls

1   cup (2 sticks) butter or margarine
1   cup sour cream
2   cups self-rising flour

Preheat the oven to 350°. In a large saucepan over medium heat, melt the butter, whisking until completely melted. Add the sour cream and flour. Mix lightly. Spoon the batter into miniature muffin cups (do not grease), filling each one to the top. Bake for 15 minutes. Serve immediately. To freeze, remove the rolls from the oven several minutes early. Cool completely before freezing.

To serve, thaw the rolls, and bake at 350° for a few minutes until a golden brown.

Hint: Adding 1 tablespoon of dried herbs such as basil, rosemary, or 2 tablespoons of fresh chopped herbs to the batter makes a tasty addition to your meal.

YIELD: ABOUT 2 DOZEN

Cinnamon Breakfast Rolls

ROLLS
1   (18.25-ounce) package French vanilla
     cake mix
5¼   cups all-purpose flour
2   (¼-ounce) envelopes active dry yeast
1   teaspoon salt
2½   cups warm water
½   cup granulated sugar
2   teaspoons ground cinnamon
¼   plus ¼ cup (1 stick) butter or
     margarine, melted
¼   plus ¼ cup raisins
¼   plus ¼ plus ¼ cup chopped pecans

GLAZE
1   cup confectioners' sugar
1½   tablespoons milk
½   teaspoon vanilla extract

For the rolls: In a large mixing bowl stir together the cake mix, flour, dry yeast, salt, and warm water. Cover and allow this mixture to rise in a warm place free from drafts for 1 hour. In a small bowl combine the granulated sugar and cinnamon. Turn the dough out onto a well-floured surface and divide it in half. Roll one portion into an 12 x 18-inch rectangle. Brush this dough with ¼ cup melted butter. Sprinkle with half the sugar and cinnamon mixture (about ¼ cup), ¼ cup raisins, and ¼ cup chopped pecans. Roll the dough starting at the long end. Cut crosswise into 16 (1-inch-thick) slices. Place the rolls on a lightly greased 9 x 13-inch pan.

Repeat this procedure with the remaining dough rectangle. Cover and chill the rolls in the refrigerator for 8 hours. Remove from the refrigerator and let the rolls stand for 30 minutes. Preheat the oven to 350°. Bake them for 20 to 25 minutes or until golden brown. Remove them from the oven and allow them to cool slightly.

For the **glaze:** In a small bowl stir together the confectioners' sugar, milk, and vanilla. Drizzle this mixture over the rolls. Sprinkle with the remaining ¼ cup chopped pecans.

YIELD: 32 ROLLS

Gramma's Rolls

This is my most requested recipe when we go to visit relatives for the holidays. My family expects me to make my famous rolls for Thanksgiving Dinner and cinnamon rolls for Christmas morning. It is quite the tradition. This recipe can be used to make dinner rolls, crescent rolls, or cinnamon rolls. The rolls have a richer flavor and better texture when a baking stone is used.

½	cup warm water
2	tablespoons active dry yeast
2	tablespoons plus ¾ cup sugar
1	cup boiling water
½	cup (1 stick) margarine
½	cup butter-flavored shortening
2	teaspoons salt
3	eggs, beaten
7½	cups all-purpose flour
1	cup cold water

In a small mixing bowl combine the warm water, yeast and 2 tablespoons of the sugar and let it rest for 5 minutes. In a medium-size mixing bowl pour the boiling water over the margarine, shortening, the remaining ¾ cup sugar, and the salt. Stir well. In a large mixing bowl, using 2 cups at a time, alternate the ingredients as follows: Pour in 2 cups of flour, then the yeast mixture and mix. Add 2 cups of flour, then the beaten eggs and mix. Add 2 cups flour, then the cold water and mix. Add the remaining 1½ cups flour and mix very well; the dough will be very sticky. Cover and refrigerate for 5 hours or overnight.

When ready to serve, preheat the oven to 350°. Shape the dough into rolls. Place on a nonstick baking sheet and bake for about 15 to 20 minutes.

YIELD: 3 DOZEN

Diane Bevan
Camp Hill, Pennsylvania

Beignets

"Beignet" is French for "fritter" and warm beignets are a luscious taste of a special part of the South. They offer a sweet invitation to Southern Louisiana, and no trip to New Orleans is complete without a beignet. Try them with honey or syrup as a Saturday morning breakfast treat.

1	(¼-ounce) envelope active dry yeast
3	tablespoons warm water
¾	cup milk
¼	cup granulated sugar
¼	cup shortening
1	teaspoon salt
1	large egg, lightly beaten
2	plus 1 cups all-purpose flour
10	to 12 cups vegetable oil
	Confectioners' sugar

In a large bowl dissolve the yeast in the warm water. Allow this mixture to stand for 5 minutes. In a small saucepan over medium heat warm the milk, but do not allow it to boil. Stir in the sugar, shortening, and salt. Remove from the heat and cool to lukewarm. Add the milk mixture, egg, and 2 cups flour to the yeast mixture. Stir well. Gradually stir in enough of the remaining 1 cup flour to make a soft dough.

Turn the dough onto a floured surface. Roll the dough into a 12 x 10-inch rectangle. Cut the dough into 2-inch squares. Place on a floured surface; cover and allow to rise in a warm place free from drafts for 30 minutes or until the dough has doubled in bulk.

Pour the oil into a Dutch oven or fryer to a depth of 2 to 3 inches. Heat the oil to 375°. Fry the beignets in batches about 1 minute on each side or until golden brown. Drain on paper towels. Sprinkle with the confectioners' sugar while they are still hot.

Hint: Beignets can be cut into fun shapes with a cookie cutter. Children love to help do this. The easiest method to coat the beignets with confectioners' sugar is to put the sugar in a zip-lock bag, put the hot drained beignets in the bag, and shake.

YIELD: 2½ DOZEN

Crêpes

Crêpes are very thin pancakes and can be filled with meats, vegetables, fruits, ice cream, puddings, or numerous other fillings of your choice. Make a wonderful dessert filling the crêpes with strawberries and sweetened cream cheese. Fold the sides of the crêpe over and top with strawberries and whipped topping.

3	large eggs
¼	teaspoon salt
2	cups all-purpose flour
2	cups milk
¼	cup (½ stick) butter, melted, or vegetable oil

In a medium-size mixing bowl combine the eggs and salt. With a mixer gradually add the flour alternately with the milk, beating until smooth. Beat in the melted butter or oil. (If using for a dessert, add 1 or 2 tablespoons of granulated sugar to the batter. If the batter seems too thick, add 1 or 2 tablespoons of milk or water.)

After combining the ingredients, let the mixture stand for 1 hour before cooking. Refrigerate the batter if allowed to stand longer. Letting it stand allows the flour to expand and some of the bubbles to collapse.

Lightly oil the bottom of a crêpe pan or small skillet, and then pour in 2 or 3 tablespoons of batter. Swirl the pan so that the batter covers the bottom in a very thin layer. Cook over medium-high heat until the bottom of the crêpe is browned. Carefully turn with a spatula and brown the other side for a few seconds. Stack on a plate or tray.

YIELD: 30 TO 35 CREPES

Yvonne McMillan
Red Springs, North Carolina

Pancakes

1   large egg
1¼   cups buttermilk
1¼   cups all-purpose flour
2   tablespoons shortening, softened
1   teaspoon granulated sugar
1   teaspoon baking powder
½   teaspoon baking soda
½   teaspoon salt
    Butter and syrup for serving

Slowly heat a griddle while preparing the batter. To test the heat, sprinkle a few drops of water on the griddle; if it bubbles the heat is right. Grease the griddle with butter or nonstick cooking spray.

In a medium-size mixing bowl beat the egg. Beat in the buttermilk, flour, shortening, sugar, baking powder, baking soda, and salt. Continue to beat until the batter is smooth. Pour about ¼ cup batter in a small pool onto the griddle. Turn the pancake as soon as it is puffed and full of bubbles, but before the bubbles break. Brown the pancake on the other side. Serve hot with butter and syrup.

Hint: For variety with pancakes add ½ cup blueberries (or other fruits) or nuts to the batter. Omit the sugar and add ½ to 1½ cups chopped ham or crumbled bacon. For a different pancake add ½ cup canned, drained, whole kernel corn. Billie Sexton of Loganville, Georgia, adds ½ pound cut okra to hers for a vegetable pancake.

YIELD: 16 (4-INCH) PANCAKES

Hot Cross Buns

A delicious bun that is wonderful served for Easter morning breakfast or brunch.

BUNS

2	(¼-ounce) envelopes active dry yeast
½	cup warm water
1	cup warm milk
½	cup (1 stick) butter, softened
½	cup granulated sugar
½	teaspoon salt
3	large eggs
1½	teaspoons vanilla extract
5	cups all-purpose flour
1½	teaspoons ground cinnamon
1	cup raisins

SUGAR GLAZE

1	cup confectioners' sugar
1½	tablespoons milk
½	teaspoon vanilla extract

For the **buns**: in a large mixing bowl combine the yeast and warm water. Let the mixture stand for 5 minutes. Add the warm milk, butter, granulated sugar, salt, eggs, and vanilla extract. Using an electric mixer, beat at medium speed until blended.

In a small bowl combine the flour and cinnamon. Gradually add this to the yeast mixture, beating at medium speed for 2 minutes. Stir in the raisins. Place the dough in a well-greased bowl, turning to grease the top. Cover the bowl and allow the dough to rise in a warm place free from drafts for 2 hours or until doubled in bulk. Punch the dough down. Cover and let rise again for 30 minutes.

Turn the dough out onto a well-floured surface. Roll it to a ½-inch thickness. Cut rolls with a 2-inch round cutter. Place in a lightly greased 10 x 15-inch jellyroll pan. Cover and let rise in a warm place for 45 minutes or until doubled in bulk.

Preheat the oven to 350°. Bake the rolls, uncovered, for 20 to 25 minutes or until lightly browned.

While the rolls are baking, prepare the **sugar glaze**. In a small mixing bowl whisk together the confectioners' sugar, milk, and vanilla extract until smooth. Remove the rolls from the oven and allow them to cool for 10 minutes. Pipe each roll with the sugar glaze in an "X" shape.

YIELD: 4 DOZEN BUNS

Preheat your cookie sheet, muffin tins, or cake pans when baking. You get better results.

Colonel Bill

The Blue Willow Inn Restaurant, Social Circle, Georgia

Colonel Bill Kuhn and
Miranda Wilson, greeters at the
Blue Willow Inn Restaurant

A summer luncheon with fried chicken and the trimmings. Makes you want to go home to Grandma's!

[top] Ohhh! the ambrosia
looks delicious.

[right] Dominick Stella, Blue
Willow chef and general manager.
Proof you can turn a Yankee
Southern.

Pot Roast (page 220)
—a good Sunday main dish.

Green Tomatoes, when fried are sweet, tart, and full of flavor. Malinda McGuire is slicing green tomatoes. The Blue Willow Inn uses thirty to forty 20-pound cases weekly.

Southern vegetables are used fresh daily at Blue Willow.

Ann Lowe has been our head cook since 1991.

Southern beans

Blue Willow Buttermilk Biscuits (page 151) and Corn Bread
Muffins (page 154) are always served at the Blue Willow Inn, and
they are always as delicious as they look here.

Stuffed bell peppers are a great way to use leftover meatloaf.

Green beans and new red potatoes.

Chicken Divine (page 236) is a good family dish and goes well at a covered dish function.

Fresh Collard Greens (page 175) are God's gift to the South!

Strawberry Shortcake (page 308) for a crowd

William Dale enjoying a slice of watermelon outside the Blue Willow Inn

Fresh water catfish (page 250) is a Southern staple and fried is the only way to go.

Yeast Rolls

These rolls melt in your mouth and butter is their best friend.

1	cup water
¼	cup shortening
¼	cup butter plus melted butter for brushing
⅓	cup granulated sugar
1	(¼-ounce) envelope active dry yeast
1	egg
1	teaspoon salt
3⅔	cups all-purpose flour

In a small saucepan bring the water to a rolling boil over high heat. In a large mixing bowl pour the boiling water over the shortening and the ¼ cup butter. When the shortening and butter have melted, add the sugar and allow the mixture to cool to lukewarm. Add the yeast and stir until dissolved. Add the egg and salt.

Sift the flour into the liquid about ¾ cup at a time until all the flour has been mixed into the batter. Add enough additional flour to make a soft dough. Set the batter aside to rise until doubled. This will take about 1 hour.

Punch the dough down and form it into rolls. Let it rise again until it has almost doubled. This should take about ½ hour.

Preheat the oven to 350°. Bake the rolls for 10 minutes on an ungreased baking pan. When you take the rolls from the oven, brush them with the additional melted butter and serve immediately.

YIELD: 24 ROLLS

French Toast

2	eggs, beaten
¼	teaspoon salt
½	cup milk
	Butter
6	slices day-old bread
	Confectioners' sugar for serving
	Syrup, jelly, honey, or strawberries for serving

Heat a griddle while preparing the batter. To test for cooking temperature, sprinkle with a few drops of water. The heat is right if the water bubbles or bounces around.

In a shallow bowl beat the eggs and stir in the salt and milk. Melt butter on the hot griddle to grease it. Dip the stale bread into the mixture and place on the griddle. Cook until both sides of the bread are browned. Serve hot. Sprinkle with confectioners' sugar and serve with syrup, jelly, honey, or strawberries.

YIELD: 6 PIECES OF FRENCH TOAST

Waffles

Waffles, like pancakes, can be made in numerous varieties. Check the hint for pancakes on page 159 for additions to waffles.

2	large eggs
2	cups buttermilk
1	teaspoon baking soda
2	cups all-purpose flour
2	teaspoons baking powder
½	teaspoon salt
6	tablespoons shortening, softened
	Butter, syrup, honey, fruits for serving

While preparing the batter, heat the waffle iron, using the automatic heat control set at whatever temperature the manufacturer suggests for waffles. If needed, spray with nonstick cooking spray.

In a medium bowl beat the eggs well. Beat in the buttermilk, baking soda, flour, baking powder, salt, and shortening until smooth. This makes a thin batter. Pour the batter from a measuring cup or pitcher onto the center of the hot waffle iron. If the batter thickens on standing, spread it to cover the surface of the iron. Do not keep the iron open any longer than necessary. Bake the waffle until the steaming stops or the light on the iron indicates it is done. Lift the waffle from the iron carefully with a fork. Serve hot with butter and syrup, honey, fruits, or various other spreads.

YIELD: 8 WAFFLES

Instead of shortening, use cooking or salad oil in waffles and hot cakes.

Side Dishes

In the South side dishes were served in large numbers, it was not uncommon to have as many as ten sides served at one meal. These might include vegetables, salads, pickles, fruit dishes, and others to tempt the palate of a hungry family.

Acorn Squash

2	acorn squash
⅔	cup cracker crumbs
½	cup butter, melted
3	teaspoons light brown sugar
½	teaspoon salt
¼	teaspoon nutmeg

Preheat the oven to 350°. Cut the squash in half and remove the seeds. Place on a large baking sheet. In a medium-size mixing bowl combine the cracker crumbs, butter, sugar, salt, and nutmeg. Mix thoroughly. Spoon equal amounts of this mixture into the cavities of the squash halves. Bake for 50 to 60 minutes until tender and brown.

Hint: Add 1 pound ground beef or 1 pound ground sausage to the filling in this dish for a wonderful main course. The squash is also good topped with Stove Top Stuffing.

YIELD: 4 SERVINGS

Asparagus Casserole

This is a tasty casserole for a buffet or luncheon.

3	cups asparagus from cans, not drained (if frozen, add water)
1	(10¾-ounce) can condensed cream of mushroom soup
1	cup grated sharp cheddar cheese
1¼	cups Ritz cracker crumbs

3	eggs, well beaten
2	tablespoons chopped pimientos
	Salt and pepper
2	tablespoons butter, melted

Preheat the oven to 350°. In a bowl mix the asparagus with juice, mushroom soup, cheese, cracker crumbs, eggs, pimientos, and salt and pepper to taste. Pour into a 9 x 13-inch casserole dish. Pour the butter over the top. Bake uncovered for 30 minutes or until lightly browned.

YIELD: 6 TO 8 SERVINGS

Asparagus Vegetable Casserole

WHITE SAUCE

4	tablespoons margarine, melted
4	tablespoons all-purpose flour
2	cups milk
	Salt and pepper

CASSEROLE

2	cups white sauce
2½	cups drained green peas
1	(14½-ounce) can asparagus pieces, drained
1	(8-ounce) can sliced water chestnuts, drained
1	(3-ounce) can mushroom stems and pieces
4	hard-cooked eggs, sliced
	Breadcrumbs
3	tablespoons margarine

For the **white sauce**, in a saucepan over low heat combine the margarine, flour, milk, and salt and pepper to taste. Mix well and cook to medium thickness, stirring to prevent sticking.

Preheat the oven to 325°. In a large casserole dish alternate layers of the peas, asparagus, water chestnuts, mushrooms, eggs, and white sauce, ending with the white sauce to cover the top of the casserole. Sprinkle with the breadcrumbs and dot with the margarine. Season with salt and pepper to taste. Bake for 30 to 40 minutes.

YIELD: 6 TO 8 SERVINGS

Nada McDowell

Covington, Georgia

Baked Apples

6	Granny Smith apples or other tart apples
½	cup butter, melted
¼	cup light brown sugar
½	teaspoon ground cinnamon
½	teaspoon nutmeg
¼	cup chopped pecans

Preheat the oven to 350°. Wash and partially core the apples from the top, leaving a cavity that can be filled with the butter/sugar mixture. Place the apples with tops up in a large baking dish.

For the filling, in a small mixing bowl combine the butter, brown sugar, cinnamon, nutmeg, and pecans and mix. Pour the filling into the cavities of the apples. Bake for 30 to 35 minutes until tender, or microwave the apples on high for 10 to 15 minutes.

YIELD: 6 SERVINGS

Barbecued Green Beans

1	pound bacon
2	tablespoons bacon grease
½	cup chopped onion
¾	cup ketchup
½	cup packed brown sugar
3	teaspoons Worcestershire sauce
¾	teaspoon salt
4	cups well-drained green beans

In a large skillet on medium heat brown the bacon until crisp. Break it into small pieces. Reserve about 2 tablespoons of the bacon drippings and sauté the onion in the drippings. In a mixing bowl mix the ketchup, brown sugar, Worcestershire sauce, and salt. Stir in the bacon and onion. Place the green beans in a large mixing bowl. Pour the sauce mixture over the green beans and mix lightly. Pour into a slow cooker and cook on high for 3 to 4 hours or on low for 6 to 8 hours.

YIELD: 20 SERVINGS

Shirley Smith Bowyer

Foley, Alabama

Baked Beans

These hearty baked beans are a real treat when served with barbeque or hamburgers. They're a real crowd pleaser.

1	pound ground beef
1	pound mild sausage links, sliced
1	large onion, chopped
1	large green bell pepper, chopped
1	to 2 teaspoons French's Chili-O mix (to taste)
¼	cup ketchup
¼	cup granulated sugar
4	teaspoons prepared mustard
¼	cup molasses
¼	cup packed dark brown sugar
2	(28-ounce) cans pork and beans, undrained
1	(14-ounce) can dark red kidney beans, undrained
1	(14-ounce) can light red kidney beans, undrained

In a large skillet on medium heat brown the ground beef. When the beef begins to come apart and is partially brown, add the sausage, onion, and bell pepper. Cook until brown. Pour off the excess grease. Turn the heat down to low. Add the chili mix and stir well. Add the ketchup, granulated sugar, mustard, molasses, brown sugar, and the liquid from the beans. Mix well. Cook, stirring often, for 2 to 3 minutes. Add the beans and continue to stir. Turn the heat to high and continue stirring to prevent the beans from sticking. Heat the mixture until bubbly. Turn the heat to low and simmer for 45 minutes. Preheat the oven to 350°. Pour the beans into a baking dish and bake for 45 minutes.

Hint: The beans can be topped with strips of bacon prior to baking.

YIELD: 8 TO 10 SERVINGS

Baked Vidalia Onions

In Vidalia, Georgia, the Vidalia onion capital, they claim that the onions are so sweet and mellow that you can eat them like an apple. Baking will soften them and burnish their natural sweetness even further. When they are combined with cheese and mayonnaise and served warm, they become a delicious and "to-die-for" cracker dip. On another note, when visiting the South you might like to be in Vidalia the first weekend in May for the Vidalia Onion Run. You will enjoy the race and the onions, and you will surely take a bag home.

6	medium Vidalia onions
¼	cup water
½	cup crushed croutons
	Salt and pepper
½	cup (1 stick) butter, melted
½	cup shredded cheddar cheese

Preheat the oven to 350°. Peel the onions. Make two cuts diagonally across the top of each onion, cutting one-half to two-thirds through the onion. Place in a medium-size baking dish with the water. Sprinkle the onions with the croutons and the salt and pepper to taste. Pour a small amount of the butter over each onion, using all the butter. Bake uncovered for 25 to 30 minutes (or in the microwave on high for 12 to 15 minutes) until tender. Remove from the oven and top with the cheddar cheese. Return to the oven to melt the cheese.

Hint: Vidalia onions are naturally the best and sweetest onion for this recipe; but if they are not available, Texas sweets or Washington State sweets will also work—just not as tasty.

YIELD: 6 SERVINGS

Black-Eyed Peas

½   plus 1 gallon water
2   cups dry black-eyed peas
2   tablespoons bacon grease
4   ounces fatback
4   ounces ham hock or ham
     Salt and pepper

In a large pan cover the peas with ½ gallon water to clean. Rinse well and drain. Rinse again and discard the peas that float to the top of the water. In a large stockpot combine the remaining 1 gallon water with the black-eyed peas. Add the bacon grease, fatback, ham hock or ham, and salt and pepper to taste to the pot. Turn the heat to high and bring the mixture to a boil. Turn the heat down to low and simmer, stirring often, for 1 hour.

Hint: The peas have a tendency to stick and scorch the pot if the water is allowed to cook down too low. Simply add more water during cooking to avoid scorching.

YIELD: 6 TO 8 SERVINGS

Baked Corn Chex and Cheese

My sister gave this recipe to me in the 1970s. She passed away eight years ago, so it is a very special reminder of her. We serve it with fried chicken. She said she got the recipe from a cereal box.

2   tablespoons butter
¼   cup chopped green pepper
½   cup chopped onion
2   eggs
2   cups milk
1   teaspoon salt
½   teaspoon granulated sugar
⅛   teaspoon pepper
1   cup shredded cheddar cheese
1   (15¾-ounce) can corn, drained
1   plus 1 cups coarsely crushed corn Chex

Preheat the oven to 325°. In a large skillet melt the butter over low heat. After the butter has melted, increase the heat to medium and sauté the green pepper and onion in the butter. Beat together the eggs, milk, salt, sugar, and pepper. Stir in the cheese, corn, sautéed peppers and onions, and 1 cup of the crushed Chex. Pour the mixture into a buttered, 2-quart casserole dish and top with the remaining 1 cup crushed Chex. Bake uncovered for 50 minutes or until set.

YIELD: 6 TO 8 SERVINGS

Joyce Dina
Gainesville, Florida

Baked Pineapple Casserole

Louis had to pull a lot of strings, beg, and plead to get this recipe from Pastor Harvey's wife, Billie. If you haven't yet read the history of the mansion, Louis and Billie purchased it from the Harveys and it became the Blue Willow Inn Restaurant.

1   (28-ounce) can crushed pineapple, not drained
1¼ cups granulated sugar
2½ cups Ritz cracker crumbs
½   cup (1 stick) butter, melted
2   plus ¼ cups grated cheddar cheese
½   cup chopped pecans (optional)

Preheat the oven to 350°. In a small saucepan over low heat combine the pineapple and juice with the sugar. Heat until the sugar is dissolved. Remove from the heat. In a casserole or baking dish layer the pineapple mixture, cracker crumbs, butter, and 2 cups of the cheese. Repeat the layers until you have three to four layers. Sprinkle the remaining ¼ cup cheese over the top of the casserole. Bake uncovered for approximately 20 to 25 minutes until bubbly and golden brown.

YIELD: 8 TO 10 SERVINGS

Blender Soufflé

This recipe came to us from Frances Ann Straight of Social Circle. It can be made at the last minute or a day ahead. It never fails.

1   (8-ounce) package grated sharp cheddar cheese, divided in half
5   plus 5 slices buttered bread, crusts removed
2   plus 2 eggs
1   plus 1 cups milk
1   teaspoon salt
½   teaspoon dry mustard

Preheat the oven to 350°. In a blender combine half the cheese, 5 slices of the bread, 2 of the eggs, and 1 cup of the milk. Blend at high speed until all ingredients are thoroughly mixed. Remove from the blender and place in a medium-size mixing bowl. In the blender put the remaining half package of cheese, the remaining 5 slices bread, the remaining 2 eggs, the remaining 1 cup milk, salt, and dry mustard. Turn the blender on high and mix thoroughly. Remove from the blender and combine with the first blended mixture. Mix both batches together well. Pour into a greased 1½-quart casserole dish and bake uncovered for 1 hour.

YIELD: 6 TO 8 SERVINGS

Blue Willow Corn Pudding

Throughout the warm months of the year in the South, you find corn on the cob eaten off well-set tables as well as picnic blankets. In the cooler months, you can count on corn breads, spoon bread made with cornmeal, corn bread dressing to go with pork chops or turkey, and some kind of creamed corn pudding. The recipe that follows is one of the all-time greats for corn pudding.

4	eggs, beaten
½	cup (1 stick) butter, melted
1	cup heavy cream
1	teaspoon salt
⅓	cup granulated sugar
½	cup all-purpose flour
	Pinch of cayenne pepper
2	(15-ounce) cans creamed corn
2	(10-ounce) packages semi-thawed frozen corn niblets

Preheat the oven to 350°. In a large bowl mix together the eggs, butter, cream, salt, sugar, flour, and cayenne pepper. Gently mix in the creamed corn. Add the corn niblets to the mixture, taking care not to crush the kernels. Pour the mixture into an ungreased 9 x 13-inch Pyrex or china baking dish. Bake for 1 hour or until the top is golden and the custard is set.

YIELD: 8 SERVINGS

Blue Willow Inn's Mac & Cheese

Macaroni and cheese is another Blue Willow tradition and is found on the menu every day. It is one of our customers' favorite dishes.

1	(8-ounce) package macaroni noodles
1	teaspoon vegetable oil or shortening
¾	plus ¼ cup grated cheddar cheese
½	cup Cheez Whiz
¾	cup milk
2	eggs, beaten
1	tablespoon mayonnaise
½	teaspoon prepared mustard
	Salt and pepper

Preheat the oven to 350°. In a saucepan on medium heat cook the macaroni according to package instructions, adding the oil or shortening to the water. Do not overcook. Drain the macaroni. In a large bowl combine the macaroni, ¾ cup of the cheddar cheese, Cheez Whiz, milk, eggs, mayonnaise, prepared mustard, and salt and pepper to taste. Bake in an ungreased, 9 x 12-inch casserole dish for 25 to 30 minutes. Remove from the oven and top with the remaining ¼ cup cheese. Return the casserole to the oven to melt the cheese.

YIELD: 8 TO 10 SERVINGS

Blue Willow Inn's Famous Fried Green Tomatoes

The Blue Willow Inn's Fried Green Tomatoes are legendary, having put the newly opened restaurant on the map shortly after a visit from famed columnist Lewis Grizzard in 1992. Following his visit, Grizzard authored a column in which he raved about the Blue Willow Inn Restaurant and the food it served—especially the Fried Green Tomatoes. Following the national publicity the restaurant received from Grizzards' column, Fried Green Tomatoes became a delicious Blue Willow tradition, and they are always served at every meal with a side of Tomato Chutney (recipe on page 127).

3	green tomatoes
1½	cups buttermilk
2	eggs, lightly beaten
½	plus ½ teaspoon salt
½	plus ½ teaspoon black pepper
1	tablespoon plus 1½ cups self-rising flour
2	cups vegetable oil

Wash and slice the tomatoes into ¼-inch slices. In a medium-size bowl mix the buttermilk and eggs. Add ½ teaspoon of the salt, ½ teaspoon of the pepper, and 1 tablespoon of the flour. Mix well. Place the tomato slices in the buttermilk and egg mixture. Set aside to rest. Preheat the oil in a heavy skillet or electric fryer to 350°. In a medium-size bowl mix the remaining 1½ cups flour, ½ teaspoon salt, and ½ teaspoon pepper. Remove the tomato slices from the buttermilk/egg mixture and toss them, one at a time, in the flour mixture, coating them thoroughly. Carefully place the tomato slices in the heated oil and fry until golden brown. Turn them two or three times. Be careful not to crowd the tomatoes during frying. Do not allow them to overlap or they will stick together. Cook until crisp. Drain on paper towels. Serve immediately.

YIELD: 6 SERVINGS

Broccoli Casserole

2	(10-ounce) packages frozen broccoli
1	(10¾-ounce) can condensed cream of mushroom soup
1	cup mayonnaise
1	egg
¾	plus ¼ cup grated cheddar cheese
	Salt and pepper
½	cup Ritz cracker crumbs

Preheat the oven to 350°. Butter a casserole dish. Cook and drain the broccoli following the package instructions. In a medium-size bowl combine the broccoli, soup, mayonnaise, egg, ¾ cup of the cheddar cheese and the salt and pepper to taste. Pour into the buttered casserole dish. Top with the cracker crumbs and bake for 30 minutes or until bubbly. Remove from the oven. Top with the remaining ¼ cup cheese and return the casserole to the oven until the cheese is melted.

YIELD: 8 TO 10 SERVINGS

Brussels Sprouts in Sour Cream

2   (10-ounce) packages frozen Brussels sprouts
2   tablespoons margarine
½   cup chopped onion
1   tablespoon all-purpose flour
1   tablespoon packed light brown sugar
1   teaspoon salt
½   teaspoon dry mustard
½   cup milk
1   cup sour cream

Cook the Brussels sprouts according to package directions. Drain and keep them warm. In a large skillet on medium heat melt the margarine. Cook the onion in the margarine until tender. Stir in the flour, sugar, salt, and mustard. Stir in the milk and cook until thickened and bubbly. Stir in the sour cream. Add the sprouts and stir gently. Heat through, but do not boil.

YIELD: 6 TO 8 SERVINGS

Dot Marks
Savannah, Georgia

Boiled Okra

1   pound stemmed fresh okra or 1 (10-ounce) package frozen okra
2   cups water
    Salt and pepper

In a stockpot over medium heat cover the okra with the water. Season the okra to taste with salt and pepper. Simmer for 18 to 20 minutes until tender.

YIELD: APPROXIMATELY 4 SERVINGS

Candied Yams

6   large sweet potatoes
2   cups granulated sugar
2   tablespoons vanilla extract
1   cup (2 sticks) butter or margarine

Preheat the oven to 350°. Wash and peel the sweet potatoes. Cut into 1½-inch rounds. Place in a large casserole or baking dish and top with a mixture of the sugar, vanilla, and butter. Bake uncovered for 1 hour.

YIELD: 8 TO 10 SERVINGS

Cabbage Casserole

This recipe comes to us from Sybil Allen. Billie found this dish at a church covered-dish dinner. She was unsure as to what it was and decided to stand by the table until the owner of the dish came by to pick it up. Billie asked Sybil, "What is this wonderful dish?" Sybil simply replied, "Oh, that's just an ole cabbage casserole." This popular side item is served almost every Thursday at the Blue Willow Inn with liver and onions.

1	large head cabbage, chopped
1	teaspoon salt
8	bacon strips
1	medium onion, chopped
1	medium green bell pepper, chopped
3	slices bread, toasted and crumbled
1	stick butter, melted
1	(10¾-ounce) can condensed cream of mushroom soup
¾	cup grated cheddar cheese
½	cup milk

Preheat the oven to 350°. In a large saucepan on medium heat cook the chopped cabbage for 8 minutes in salted water. In a skillet on medium heat fry the bacon until crisp. Drain, reserving the bacon drippings, and chop the bacon into small pieces. Sauté the onion and the bell pepper in the bacon grease. Remove from the skillet.

Toss the bread in the melted butter. In a large mixing bowl combine the cabbage, onion, bell pepper, soup, grated cheese, and milk. Crumble the bacon into the cabbage mixture and mix thoroughly. Pour the mixture into a casserole dish. Top with the breadcrumbs. Bake for 35 minutes.

YIELD: 8 TO 10 SERVINGS

Carrots au Gratin

3	cups diced carrots
	Salt
6	crushed soda crackers
1	teaspoon onion salt
¼	cup chopped green bell pepper
⅓	to ¼ teaspoon black pepper
2	tablespoons butter, melted
½	cup grated sharp cheddar cheese

Preheat the oven to 425°. In a medium-size saucepan on medium heat cook the carrots in ½-inch boiling salted water for 10 minutes. In a mixing bowl combine the crackers, onion salt, bell peppers, and black pepper. Grease a 1-quart baking dish. In the baking dish alternate layers of the carrots and layers of the crumb mixture, ending with the crumb mixture. If there is any liquid left from cooking the carrots, spoon it over the top of the casserole. Pour the melted butter over the top and sprinkle with the cheese. Bake for 15 to 20 minutes or until the cheese melts.

YIELD: 6 SERVINGS

Nada McDowell
Covington, Georgia

Carrot Casserole

This is a very tasty dish.

1	tablespoon grated onion
½	cup mayonnaise
1	teaspoon horseradish
2	cups cooked and sliced fresh carrots
¾	cup crumbled Ritz crackers
1	tablespoon margarine

Preheat the oven to 350°. In a medium-size mixing bowl combine the onion, mayonnaise, and horseradish. Stir in the carrots. Turn into a lightly greased casserole dish. Cover with the cracker crumbs. Dot with the margarine. Bake for 15 to 20 minutes.

YIELD: 4 TO 6 SERVINGS

Cauliflower-Cheese Casserole

My husband is not crazy about cauliflower. But when he enjoyed this at a covered dish social, I knew I had to get the recipe. I have been making this for about twenty-five years.

	Salted water
1	large head cauliflower
1	plus 2 tablespoons butter
1	small red bell pepper, chopped
1	small green bell pepper, chopped
1	garlic clove, mashed
2	tablespoons cornstarch
1½	cups milk
1	teaspoon salt
¼	teaspoon pepper
1	cup shredded Jack cheese
2	tablespoons dry breadcrumbs
1	tablespoon butter, melted

Preheat the oven to 350°. In a large saucepan bring enough water to a boil to cover the cauliflower. Separate the cauliflower into florets and drop them into the boiling salted water. Cook for 5 minutes or until tender-crisp. Drain. Arrange the florets in a well-buttered, 2-quart baking dish. In a medium-size skillet over low heat melt 1 tablespoon butter. Sauté the red and green pepper and garlic in the butter. Sprinkle the mixture over the cauliflower. In a small mixing bowl stir the cornstarch into the milk. Add the remaining 2 tablespoons butter to the skillet. Stir in the cornstarch mixture. Cook, stirring until the mixture thickens. Add the salt, pepper, and cheese. Stir until the cheese is blended. Pour the mixture over the vegetables. In a small mixing bowl mix the breadcrumbs and melted butter. Sprinkle the breadcrumbs on top of the casserole. Bake for 30 minutes.

YIELD: 6 TO 8 SERVINGS

Joyce Dina
Gainesville, Florida

Carrots Vichy

This recipe comes to us from Sally Sieweke, the manager of the Blue Willow Inn Gift Shop. Her mother's dearest friend, Sally Carey, gave her this recipe. Sally's real name is Sarah, but she has always been called Sally in honor of this friend.

10	medium carrots
⅔	cup chicken broth
1	tablespoon granulated sugar
2	tablespoons butter
	Pinch of salt
2	tablespoons chopped fresh parsley

In a medium-size saucepan on medium-low heat combine the carrots, chicken broth, sugar, butter, and salt. Cover and simmer until the broth cooks away. Turn the heat to low and shake until the carrots are glazed. Sprinkle with the parsley before serving.

YIELD: 6 TO 8 SERVINGS

Cheese Apples

Tasty, tasty, tasty.

1½	cups granulated sugar
1	cup all-purpose flour
1½	sticks butter, diced
12	ounces Velveeta cheese, diced
2	(15-ounce) cans apples

Preheat the oven to 375°. Spray a 2-quart casserole dish with nonstick spray. In a small mixing bowl mix the sugar and flour. In a medium saucepan on low heat melt the butter and cheese, stirring to prevent sticking. Place the apples in the casserole dish. Pour the sugar-flour mixture over the apples. Stir in the cheese and butter mixture. Bake for 30 to 45 minutes.

YIELD: 15 SERVINGS

Melissa Hoganson
Port St. Lucie, Florida

Cinnamon Acorn Squash Rings

2	tablespoons firmly packed brown sugar
2	tablespoons milk
1	egg, lightly beaten
¾	cup soft breadcrumbs
¼	cup cornmeal
2	teaspoons ground cinnamon
1	medium acorn squash, cut crosswise into ½-inch slices and seeded
4	tablespoons butter, melted

Preheat the oven to 400°. In a medium bowl mix the sugar, milk, and egg. In a second medium bowl mix the breadcrumbs, cornmeal, and cinnamon. Dip the squash slices into the egg mixture and then coat them with the breadcrumb mixture. Place the squash in an ungreased baking pan. Drizzle with the melted butter. Bake uncovered for 30 to 35 minutes or until tender.

YIELD: 4 SERVINGS

Cheese Casserole

This recipe is good as a meatless main course or as a side dish with meat or seafood. One of our employees who is not a cheese lover thought this was d-d-delicious.

1 pound Velveeta cheese

8 ounces grated sharp cheddar cheese

8 ounces cottage cheese

½ cup (1 stick) butter, melted

4 eggs

1 tablespoon all-purpose flour

Preheat the oven to 350°. Cut the Velveeta into 2-inch-square pieces and place in a greased, 1-quart casserole dish. Sprinkle the grated cheddar over the Velveeta. In a small mixing bowl combine the cottage cheese, butter, eggs, and flour. Pour over the other cheeses. Bake for 30 minutes.

Hint: The ingredients may be combined the day before serving and refrigerated. Bake just before serving.

YIELD: 15 SERVINGS

Shirley Smith Bowyer

Foley, Alabama

Collard Greens

Whether you love them or hate them, collard greens are God's gift to the South.

1 bunch fresh collard greens

2 tablespoons bacon grease

1 tablespoon granulated sugar

6 ounces fatback or ham hock

½ teaspoon salt

¼ teaspoon black pepper

¼ teaspoon baking soda

1 quart water

Pull the leaves of the collards from the stems. Discard the stems (small stems may be cooked with leaves). Coarsely chop or tear the collards. Wash thoroughly in cold water and drain. In a large saucepan combine the collard greens, bacon grease, sugar, fatback or ham hock, salt, pepper, baking soda, and water. Bring to a boil. Cook at a slow boil for 2 hours or until tender.

YIELD: 6 TO 8 SERVINGS

Cooked Cabbage

1 medium head cabbage

1 quart water

2 plus 2 tablespoons butter

Salt and pepper

Remove the outside leaves from the cabbage. Cut in half and cut out the core. Cut the cabbage into bite-size sections. Place the chopped cabbage in a medium-size stockpot and cover with the water. Add 2 tablespoons of the butter and season with salt and pepper to taste. Cook until tender, but do not overcook. Drain the cabbage. Melt the remaining 2 tablespoons butter and pour the butter over the cabbage. Serve hot.

YIELD: 4 TO 6 SERVINGS

Corn

Corn is an incredibly important part of Southern cooking, from grits in the morning to pecan pie made from corn syrup for dessert. Whether you cook it fresh, frozen, or canned, corn is served in most southern households on a regular basis. Your quickest recipe is canned corn, your tastiest would be fresh corn cut from the cob, and frozen corn can be almost as good as fresh if you purchase the best quality available and follow the easy steps below.

1   (10-ounce) package frozen or 1 (15¾-ounce) canned or 1 pound fresh corn
    Butter
    Salt and pepper
1   to 2 teaspoons granulated sugar

When preparing frozen or fresh corn, cover the desired amount of corn with water and season with the desired amount of butter, salt, pepper, and sugar. Bring to a boil and boil for 7 to 8 minutes, being careful not to overcook because that will make it tough.

When preparing canned corn, remember that the corn is already precooked. For best results, drain the liquid from the can and replace it with an equal amount of tap water. Then add a small amount of butter, salt, pepper, and sugar.

YIELD: 4 TO 6 SERVINGS

Corn Casserole

This recipe comes to us from Janet Huckabee, First Lady of the State of Arkansas. She said she usually serves this casserole for family gatherings such as Thanksgiving dinner. She also said that she included this recipe in her family Christmas cards a few years ago and that it is truly one of her favorites.

½   cup (1 stick) butter
½   medium red bell pepper, chopped
½   medium green bell pepper, chopped
½   medium onion, chopped
2   eggs
1   (7.5-ounce) Jiffy corn muffin mix
1   (15-ounce) can creamed corn
1   (15-ounce) can whole corn, drained
1   (8-ounce) container sour cream
    Milk
2   cups shredded cheddar cheese
    Paprika

Preheat the oven to 325°. In a small skillet on medium heat melt the butter and sauté the bell peppers and onion. In a medium-size mixing bowl mix together the eggs, corn muffin mix, creamed corn, and whole corn. Add the onion and peppers. Pour into a 2-quart casserole dish. Mix the sour cream with a little milk and spread it on top. Add the cheese and sprinkle with the paprika. Bake for 45 minutes.

YIELD: 8 TO 10 SERVINGS

Corn Pudding

I have been using this recipe for forty years. I have used it at home and carried it to potluck suppers, to folks who were ill, and to church dinners. Everyone was always pleased and wanted the recipe. I prepare it every holiday, and once when I didn't, my family wanted to know, "Where is the corn pudding?"

3	tablespoons margarine
1	(15-ounce) can whole kernel corn, drained
3	eggs
½	cup granulated sugar
3	tablespoons self-rising flour
2	cups milk

Preheat the oven to 400°. Melt the margarine in a 2-quart casserole dish. In a medium-size mixing bowl combine the corn, eggs, sugar, flour, and milk. Mix well. Pour into the prepared casserole dish. Bake for 40 to 45 minutes or until the pudding is set.

YIELD: 4 TO 6 SERVINGS

Juanita Gasaway
Monroe, Georgia

Corn Bread Dressing

When you make corn bread of any kind, don't worry about the leftovers. They are the foundation of this great side dish. This is the traditional dressing (or stuffing, as it is known farther north) of the South and is always served with giblet gravy and roasted turkey or baked chicken. It's a classic below the Mason-Dixon line.

½	cup chopped onion
¼	cup chopped celery
¼	cup butter or margarine
4	cups corn bread crumbs
2	cups biscuit crumbs
4	eggs, lightly beaten
2	hard-cooked eggs
½	cup chopped chicken or turkey giblets
1	teaspoon sage
	Salt and pepper
2	cups chicken broth

Preheat the oven to 350°. Sauté the onion and celery in the butter in a small skillet. In a large mixing bowl combine the onion, celery, corn bread crumbs, biscuit crumbs, beaten eggs, hard-cooked eggs, chopped chicken or turkey giblets, sage, and salt and pepper to taste. Mix well. Add the chicken broth and mix well. Pour into a greased baking or casserole dish. Bake for 35 to 40 minutes or until golden brown.

YIELD: 8 TO 10 SERVINGS

Cornwallis Yams

3   medium sweet potatoes, cooked and mashed
½   cup granulated sugar
¼   teaspoon salt
¼   teaspoon ground cinnamon
¼   teaspoon nutmeg
¼   cup (½ stick) butter
1   egg, beaten
½   cup crushed pineapple
¾   cup milk
    Flaked coconut

Preheat the oven to 350°. In a large mixing bowl combine the sweet potatoes, sugar, salt, cinnamon, nutmeg, butter, egg, pineapple, and milk. Mix well. Pour this mixture into a greased baking dish. Bake for 35 minutes. Remove from the oven and sprinkle the coconut over the top of the casserole. Return to the oven and bake for another 10 minutes.

YIELD: 6 SERVINGS

Creamed Corn

1   (15-ounce) can creamed corn
1   cup frozen or fresh whole kernel or shoepeg corn
2   eggs

1   tablespoon self-rising flour
1   tablespoon bacon grease
4   strips bacon, fried crisp and coarsely chopped
    Salt and pepper

Preheat the oven to 350°. Combine the creamed corn, whole kernel or shoepeg corn, eggs, self-rising flour, bacon grease, bacon, and salt and pepper to taste and mix well. Do not beat. Cook in an ungreased 9 x 13-inch casserole dish for 30 to 40 minutes.

YIELD: 4 TO 6 SERVINGS

Creamed Peas

2   tablespoons all-purpose flour
2   tablespoons butter, melted
1   (15-ounce) can early June peas, not drained
½   cup milk
    Salt and pepper

In a medium-size saucepan combine the flour and butter. Pour half the liquid from the peas into the saucepan and add the milk. Over medium heat bring the mixture to a slow boil, being careful not to scorch the milk. Simmer until the liquid is the consistency of gravy. Add the peas and salt and pepper to taste. Simmer for 5 to 8 minutes.

YIELD: 4 TO 6 SERVINGS

Creamed Potatoes or Mashed Potatoes

6	medium potatoes
1½	(6 cups) quarts water
	Salt and pepper
¼	cup milk
⅓	cup butter, melted
1	tablespoon mayonnaise (optional)

Peel and dice the potatoes. In a medium-size saucepan bring the water to a boil. Add the potatoes and season with salt and pepper to taste. Boil until tender, about 15 to 20 minutes. Pour off the water and add the milk, butter, and mayonnaise if using. With a potato masher or hand-held electric mixer cream the potatoes. If the potatoes are too stiff, add a little more milk and butter to get the consistency you like.

Hint: For a variation, you can add more milk and butter to make the potatoes very creamy and then add a can of English peas for creamed peas and potatoes.

YIELD: 4 TO 6 SERVINGS

Deviled Eggs

What holiday meal, luncheon, or Sunday dinner would be complete without the traditional Southern deviled eggs? Every Southern hostess knows the importance of preparing deviled eggs, and protocol dictates that a true southern lady owns several deviled egg dishes to properly display this southern favorite. The plates can range from plain—even plastic for picnics or other outdoor events—to crystal for special occasions.

7	eggs
2	tablespoons mayonnaise
½	teaspoon prepared mustard
1	tablespoon sweet pickle relish
	Salt and pepper
	Paprika (optional)
	Black or green olives for garnish (optional)
	Fresh parsley for garnish (optional)

In a medium-size saucepan over medium heat cover the eggs with water and bring to a rolling boil. Boil for 3 minutes. Turn the heat off and allow the eggs to sit for 5 minutes. Run cold water over the eggs and peel. Cut each of 6 eggs in half lengthwise and remove the yolks from the cut eggs. In a medium-size mixing bowl combine the egg yolks, the one remaining whole egg, mayonnaise, mustard, pickle relish, and salt and pepper to taste. Mix well with a fork to mash the egg yolks and the one egg white. Either pipe or spoon the egg filling into the egg cavities. If desired, sprinkle each egg with a small amount of paprika before garnishing. Garnish each egg with a green or black olive half and parsley sprig. Serve in a deviled-egg dish.

YIELD: 6 SERVINGS

Deviled Ham Stuffed Eggs

This is an old recipe often served for Sunday supper.

1   dozen hard-cooked eggs
    Salt and pepper
1   (4.25-ounce) can deviled ham
    Dash of grated onion
    White Sauce (recipe on page 136)
    Breadcrumbs

Cut the eggs in half and separate the yolks from the egg whites. Mash the yolks. Preheat the oven to 350°. Salt and pepper the yolks and then mix them with the deviled ham. Add the grated onion. Stuff the egg whites with this mixture. Place the eggs in a baking dish and cover with the white cream sauce and breadcrumbs. Bake for 20 minutes to heat through and brown the breadcrumbs.

YIELD: 15 SERVINGS

Dried Fruit Pilaf

This is a delicious side dish with poultry or pork. The sweet flavor will make each bite a delight to the palate. With the chicken added, it becomes a delight for a ladies' luncheon or one-course meal for the family.

2   teaspoons vegetable oil
2   tablespoons packed light brown sugar
2   tablespoons soy sauce
½   teaspoon crushed red pepper
1   (14.5-ounce) can chicken broth
2¼ cups water
2   cups long-grain white rice
½   teaspoon ground cinnamon
¼   teaspoon ground cardamom or ground ginger
½   teaspoon ground coriander
½   cup red raisins
½   cup white raisins
½   cup thinly sliced green onions
½   cup minced fresh parsley

Heat the oil in a Dutch oven or large deep skillet with a lid over medium heat. Add the brown sugar, soy sauce, and crushed red pepper. Stir and cook until a glaze is formed. Pour the chicken broth and water into the skillet. Add the rice, cinnamon, cardamom, and coriander. Cover and bring to a boil. Reduce the heat to low and simmer until the rice is tender and the liquid is absorbed, about 20 minutes. Remove from the heat. Stir in the raisins, green onions, onions, and parsley. Cover and let stand for 5 minutes.

Hints: Alter this recipe by adding various dried fruits as desired to change the flavor. For a one-dish meal you can add cubes of chicken breast. Just put the chicken in the oil first and let it cook for about 5 minutes or until browned. Reduce the heat to medium and add the brown sugar, soy sauce, and red pepper. Glaze the chicken for about 2 minutes and continue with the recipe.

YIELD: 8 TO 10 SERVINGS

Eggplant and Tomatoes

1   small eggplant
1   medium onion, chopped
1   tablespoon vegetable oil
2   cups diced canned tomatoes
1   tablespoon granulated sugar
    Salt and pepper

Peel and cube the eggplant. In a medium-size skillet on medium heat sauté the onion in the oil. Add the eggplant, tomatoes, sugar, and salt and pepper to taste. Reduce the heat to low and simmer until the eggplant and tomatoes are tender, 10 to 15 minutes.

YIELD: 6 TO 8 SERVINGS

Dot Marks
Savannah, Georgia

Eggplant Casserole

A co-teacher, Mary Sue Thomson, from Avondale High School in DeKalb County shared this recipe with me more than thirty years ago. I have made this casserole at least once every summer since then. My husband, Robert, always plants eggplants each summer even though he never eats them. The marjoram is the key to its delicious flavor.

1   large eggplant
½   cup water

1   cup cottage cheese
2   plus 1 slices bread, torn into small pieces
½   medium onion, sliced
1   medium green bell pepper, chopped
1   whole pimiento, chopped
1   egg
½   teaspoon salt
    Dash of pepper
    Dash of marjoram
2   tablespoons butter
    Dash of paprika

Preheat the oven to 350°. Peel and cube the eggplant. In a covered saucepan over medium high heat cook the eggplant in the water for 15 minutes. Add the cottage cheese, 2 slices of the bread, the onion, green pepper, pimiento, egg, salt, pepper, and marjoram. Mix well. Pour the mixture into a buttered 1½-quart casserole dish. Top with the remaining torn bread. Dot with the butter. Sprinkle with the paprika. Bake for 45 minutes.

Note: This recipe may be assembled ahead of time and baked when ready to serve.

YIELD: 4 TO 6 SERVINGS

Rose Lewis
Covington, Georgia

Eggs Golden

This is great for a Christmas breakfast. My husband, Bill, always had the job of peeling and chopping the eggs.

1	dozen hard-cooked eggs
12	slices toast or English muffins
	Medium-thick white sauce

WHITE SAUCE

4	tablespoons butter
4	tablespoons all-purpose flour
3	cups milk
	Salt and pepper

Peel the eggs and separate the yolks from the whites. In a small bowl finely chop the whites. In a separate bowl mash the yolks with a fork.

For the **white sauce**, in a small saucepan on medium heat melt the butter. Add the flour and stir until moistened. Slowly add the milk, stirring constantly. Add the salt and pepper to taste. Bring to a slow boil until the sauce reaches the desired thickness. Add the egg whites. Serve over the toast or English muffins. Top with the egg yolks. Garnish with parsley.

YIELD: 10 TO 12 SERVINGS

Sophia DeMoss
Social Circle, Georgia

Farmer's Garden Stew

Since summer brings all of our fresh garden vegetables, I've learned to make use of all of them with the following simple, but delicious, recipe. I used to dread people's handing me all their excess squash and zucchini, but now I buy lots of it at our Farmers Market. Although this recipe calls for eggplant, if I do not have any I use whatever is in the fridge. I have used squash, zucchini, and eggplant. This is one of our favorite summertime meals.

3	tablespoons olive oil
1	teaspoon salt
1	medium onion, chopped
2	or 3 garlic cloves, minced
1	medium eggplant, chopped into 1-inch cubes
2	small zucchini (or yellow squash or both), chopped
1	medium bell pepper (any color), chopped
3	medium tomatoes, chopped
½	teaspoon dried thyme
1	teaspoon black pepper
2	ears corn (kernels removed)
	Parmesan cheese (optional)

In a heavy, wide pan or a wok on high heat, combine the oil and salt. Add the onion and garlic. Add the eggplant and stir. Add the zucchini and/or yellow squash and stir. Add the bell pepper and stir. Add the tomatoes and continue to stir. Add the thyme and black pepper. Turn the heat to low and simmer for 30 minutes or until all vegetables are tender. Add the corn about 10 to 15 minutes before the stew finishes cooking. Garnish with Parmesan cheese if desired.

Hint: Serve this over egg noodles and garnish with sliced black olives.

YIELD: 10 TO 12 SERVINGS

Marilyn Miller

Somerset, Kentucky

Fried Cabbage

4	slices bacon
1	large head cabbage, coarsely chopped
1	teaspoon salt
1	teaspoon pepper

In a large skillet on medium heat cook the bacon until it is crisp. Remove the bacon and drain on paper towels. Reserve 1 tablespoon of the drippings in the skillet. Crumble the bacon. Add the cabbage to the hot drippings in the skillet. Sprinkle with the salt and pepper. Sauté the cabbage over medium-high heat for 10 to 12 minutes or until tender. Sprinkle with the bacon to serve.

YIELD: 4 TO 6 SERVINGS

Fried Corn

This is a heavenly way to serve corn fresh from the garden. Add freshly picked tomatoes and cornbread with a glass of sweet tea and you will surely think that "all is well with the world."

12	ears fresh corn
8	slices bacon
4	tablespoons butter
2	to 4 teaspoons granulated sugar
2	teaspoons salt
¼	teaspoon black pepper

Cut the corn kernels from the ears and place them in a bowl. Scrape the corn milk and remaining pulp from each ear and add to the kernels. Cook the bacon in a heavy skillet until crisp. Remove the bacon and all but 2 tablespoons of bacon grease. Add the corn mixture, butter, sugar, salt, and pepper to the skillet. Cook over medium to low heat until the corn is tender and the mixture thickens. Stir often to prevent sticking. Serve in a vegetable bowl with crumbled bacon on top.

YIELD: 8 SERVINGS

Spray a grater with cooking spray before grating cheese, as this will prevent it from sticking to the grater.

Fried Okra

A favorite in the South.

2 pounds fresh okra
2½ cups water
2 cups vegetable oil
1 cup all-purpose flour
1 cup plain cornmeal
Salt and pepper

Wash and cut the okra, discarding the ends. Pour the water into a mixing bowl. Place the cut okra in the water to moisten. Preheat the vegetable oil in a large heavy skillet on medium heat. In a large mixing bowl, combine the flour, cornmeal, and salt and pepper to taste and mix. Remove the okra from the water and toss in the flour mixture. Place each piece of okra separately in the heated oil. Cook until golden brown. When done, remove from the oil and drain on paper towels.

Yield: 8 to 10 servings

Fried Onion Rings

A great topping for green bean casserole and also a great complement to steaks or just to munch a bunch. Vidalia onions make luscious onion rings.

Vegetable oil
1 cup buttermilk
2 eggs, beaten
Salt and pepper
1 tablespoon plus 2 cups self-rising flour
1 large onion, sliced

Preheat the vegetable oil in a large, deep frying pan to 325° degrees. In a mixing bowl combine the buttermilk, eggs, salt and pepper to taste, and 1 tablespoon flour. Mix well. Separate the onion slices into rings and place the onion rings in the buttermilk/egg mixture. In a mixing bowl place the remaining 2 cups flour. Dredge the onion rings in the flour. Place the battered rings in the frying pan and cook 8 to 10 minutes until golden brown, turning twice. Drain on paper towels.

Yield: 1 serving for onion lovers or 2 to 6 for others

Fried Red Tomatoes and Creamed Gravy

My mother's family lived on the Eastern shores of southern Delaware and southern Maryland. One of her favorite recipes from her family was Fried Red Tomatoes and Creamed Gravy. This is now one of my family's favorites too, though we do not use the creamed gravy.

1	pound bacon
8	to 10 large, firm red tomatoes
	Salt and pepper
	All-purpose flour
	Granulated sugar
	Whole milk

In a large cast-iron skillet fry the bacon until very well done. Remove the bacon. Drain on paper towels and set aside in a warm oven. Strain the bacon grease and return it to the skillet. Cut off the tops and bottoms of the tomatoes and slice them into ½-inch slices. Salt and pepper one side of the tomatoes generously and dredge with flour.

Heat the skillet on medium heat and add the strained bacon grease. Place the seasoned side of the tomato slices in the grease and cook over medium heat until brown. Salt and pepper the exposed side of the tomato slices. On each slice sprinkle a scant teaspoon of sugar and shake on enough flour to cover the tops of the slices. Turn, lower the heat, and cook until brown and tender. Remove the tomatoes to a large, hot platter and place bacon around the platter edges.

For the creamed gravy, add a small amount of flour into the skillet on low heat and blend thoroughly. Add some milk, stirring constantly until the gravy is brown and the right consistency. Pour into a small gravy boat and serve with the tomatoes and bacon.

YIELD: 8 TO 10 SERVINGS

Mrs. Bernice Wilson
Lawrenceville, Georgia

Fried Squash

6	medium yellow gooseneck or zucchini squash
2	cups water
2	cups vegetable oil
1	cup buttermilk
½	teaspoon salt
	Dash of pepper
1	egg, beaten
1	tablespoon plus 1½ cups self-rising flour

Wash and slice the squash and discard the ends. Put the water in a mixing bowl and place the sliced squash in water. In a large, heavy skillet heat the oil. In a medium-size mixing bowl combine the buttermilk, salt, pepper, egg, and 1 tablespoon of the flour. Mix well. Remove the squash from the water and soak in the buttermilk mixture. In a second mixing bowl place the remaining 1½ cups flour. Remove the squash from the buttermilk and toss the slices in the flour, coating each piece well (when the batter begins to set, stir gently). Place each piece of squash in the heated oil. Cook until golden brown and drain on paper towels to serve.

YIELD: 6 TO 8 SERVINGS

Glazed Carrots

1½ pounds carrots
½   cup packed light brown sugar
½   teaspoon salt
2   teaspoons butter
¼   cup orange marmalade
1   tablespoon Grand Marnier (optional)

Wash, peel, and cut the carrots into 1-inch pieces. Place in a medium-size saucepan and cover with water. Cook over high heat until tender and almost done. Pour off half the water. In a mixing bowl combine the sugar, salt, butter, orange marmalade, and Grand Marnier. Pour over the carrots and stir gently. Bring back to a slow boil and cook for 4 to 5 minutes longer, stirring frequently to prevent sticking.

YIELD: 6 TO 8 SERVINGS

Georgia Okra

I always had a big birthday supper for my daughter, Deanna, whose birthday is August 13, and for my mother, Jolene, whose birthday was August 20. I made large meals and used fresh vegetables from the garden. I never thought I could eat boiled okra, but if you do not overcook it, this dish is not slimy, and I had several to ask for the leftovers if there were any.

4   cups chopped Vidalia onions
1   tablespoon butter

4   cups fresh or canned chopped tomatoes
4   cups chopped okra
⅔   cup granulated sugar
2   teaspoons salt
    Dash of pepper

In a large saucepan on medium heat cook the onions and the butter for about 10 minutes in as little water as possible. Add the tomatoes and cook for about 10 more minutes. Add the okra on top and cook for another 10 minutes. Do not stir while cooking. You can pull a knife through the mixture making sure the layers stay intact. Add the sugar, salt, and pepper and mix thoroughly.

YIELD: 8 TO 10 SERVINGS

Governor Mark Sanford's Favorite Butter Bean Casserole

Jenny Sanford, First Lady of the State of South Carolina, sent this recipe to us. As you can see from the title this is one of her husband's favorites.

2   (16-ounce) packages frozen butter (lima) beans (or fresh), cooked
1   (28-ounce) can diced tomatoes (or 3 cups diced fresh tomatoes)
1   small onion, chopped
1   small green bell pepper, chopped
½   plus ½ cup grated sharp cheddar cheese

Preheat the oven to 350°. In a large mixing bowl combine the butter beans, tomatoes, onion, pepper, and ½ cup cheese. Mix well. Place these ingredients in a greased, 3-quart casserole dish. Top with the remaining ½ cup cheese. Bake for 30 to 35 minutes or until warm and bubbly.

Hint: This is best when it is made with fresh butter beans and fresh tomatoes.

YIELD: 8 SERVINGS

Green Bean and Corn Casserole

1   (15-ounce) can French-style green beans
1   (15-ounce) can white shoepeg corn
1   (8-ounce) container sour cream
1   (10¾-ounce) can cream of celery soup
    Grated cheddar cheese
    Ritz crackers, crushed
    Sliced almonds
1   stick butter, melted

Preheat the oven to 350°. Drain the beans and corn. Place the beans and then the corn in a greased 2-quart casserole dish. In a small mixing bowl combine the sour cream and soup. Mix thoroughly. Pour this mixture over the vegetables. Cover the top of the casserole with cheese. Cover this with the Ritz crackers. Sprinkle almonds on top and pour the melted butter over the casserole. Bake for 30 minutes or until bubbly.

YIELD: 6 TO 8 SERVINGS

Carolyn Kitchen
Hard Labor Creek, Georgia

Green Rice

Sally Sieweke, manager of the Blue Willow Inn Gift Shop, gave this recipe to us. Sally says this recipe was served during a birthday celebration for her and several friends when she was attending Wheaton College. She says it is delicious with beef fondue.

3   cups hot cooked rice
½   pound chopped Velveeta cheese (room temperature)
2   eggs
1   cup milk
1   small green bell pepper, finely chopped
1   small garlic clove, minced
8   green onions, sliced (use green tops also)
1   bunch fresh parsley, chopped (use top 2 inches)
    Salt and pepper
1   tablespoon vegetable oil

Preheat the oven to 350°. In a medium-size mixing bowl mix the hot rice with the cheese and stir until the cheese melts. In a blender or food processor mix the eggs, milk, bell pepper, garlic, green onion, and parsley together. Stir this into the rice and cheese mixture. Add the salt and pepper to taste and the vegetable oil. Pour into a greased, 3-quart baking dish and bake, covered, for 1 hour. Remove the cover the last 10 minutes so the top will brown.

YIELD: 6 TO 8 SERVINGS

Green Bean Casserole

2   (15-ounce) cans French-cut green
    beans, drained
1   (10¾-ounce) can condensed cream of
    mushroom soup
½   cup grated cheddar cheese
    Salt and pepper
    Canned or fresh fried onion rings to
    taste

Preheat the oven to 350°. Drain the green beans. In a mixing bowl combine the green beans, soup, cheese, and salt and pepper to taste. Mix well. Pour into a 9 x 12-inch casserole or baking dish. Bake for 35 to 40 minutes until bubbly. Top with onion rings.

Hint: If using fresh fried onion rings, cut onion into thin slices and fry extra crispy following the Fried Onion Ring recipe on page 184 and maybe fry a few extra for the cook.

YIELD: 6 TO 8 SERVINGS

Green Beans

1⅔ cups water
4   ounces fatback
4   ounces cooked ham or ham hock
2   tablespoons bacon grease
¼   teaspoon brown sugar
    Salt and pepper
1   (28-ounce) can Italian cut green beans

In a medium-size stockpot on medium heat combine the water, fatback, cooked ham or ham hock, bacon grease, brown sugar, and salt and pepper to taste. Bring to a boil. Drain the green beans and add the beans to the boiling stockpot. Return the green beans to a boil and allow to slowly boil for 20 to 25 minutes to season.

YIELD: 4 TO 6 SERVINGS

Green Pea Casserole

1   (15-ounce) can peas, drained
1   (10¾-ounce) can condensed cream of
    celery soup
1   (2.5-ounce) package slivered almonds
1   (2.8-ounce) can onion rings, divided
1   (2-ounce) jar pimientos
1   (12-ounce) can evaporated milk

Preheat the oven to 350°. Grease a 1½-quart casserole dish with margarine. In a medium-size mixing bowl combine the peas, soup, almonds, ½ can of the onion rings, pimientos, and evaporated milk. Pour into the casserole dish and bake for 15 minutes. Add the remaining ½ can onion rings to the top of the casserole and bake for another 5 minutes until bubbly.

YIELD: 6 TO 8 SERVINGS

Green Tomato Pie

4   cups green tomatoes, sliced
    Boiling water

1½   cups sugar

2   tablespoons all-purpose flour

1   teaspoon ground cinnamon

¼   teaspoon nutmeg

1   tablespoon lemon juice (optional)

2   tablespoons butter

2   (9-inch) piecrusts

Preheat the oven to 425°. In a medium-size bowl cover the tomato slices with boiling water. Let stand 10 minutes. Drain on paper towels. In a mixing bowl combine the sugar, flour, cinnamon, and nutmeg. Place 1 piecrust in a 9-inch pie plate and trim the edges. Spread ½ cup of the sugar mixture in the pie shell. Arrange the well-drained tomato slices on top. Sprinkle with the lemon juice. Top with the remaining sugar mixture. Dot with the butter. Cover with the remaining piecrust. Make a few slits in the crust and flute the edges. Bake for 15 minutes and then lower the temperature to 375°. Bake an additional 30 minutes.

YIELD: 12 SERVINGS

Grits Casserole

This is a savory side dish for almost any hot lunch or supper. Grits Casserole is served every Friday and Saturday night at the Blue Willow Inn on the seafood/Southern buffet.

4   cups water

1   teaspoon salt

¼   teaspoon black pepper

1   teaspoon garlic powder (optional)

1   cup quick-cooking grits

2   tablespoons butter or margarine

1   plus ½ cups grated cheddar cheese

4   eggs, beaten

½   cup milk

In a large saucepan on high heat bring the water to a boil. Add the salt and pepper and the garlic powder if desired. Gradually stir in the grits. Lower the heat to medium and simmer, stirring occasionally, for 5 to 7 minutes. Remove from the heat and stir in the butter and 1 cup cheese. Preheat the oven to 350°. In a small bowl mix the eggs with the milk and add to the grits. Stir well. Pour the grits into a greased 2-quart casserole dish. Top the casserole with the remaining ½ cup cheese. Bake for 1 hour.

YIELD: 8 TO 10 SERVINGS

Harvard Beets

1   tablespoon cornstarch

½   cup apple cider vinegar

½   cup granulated sugar

½   teaspoon salt

1   (15¾-ounce) can sliced beets, drained

In a small mixing bowl dissolve the cornstarch in a small amount of the vinegar. In a medium-size saucepan on medium heat combine the dissolved cornstarch, remaining vinegar, sugar, and salt. Cook until the mixture is clear. Add the beets to the saucepan and cook over low heat for 20 to 25 minutes,

YIELD: 4 TO 6 SERVINGS

Holiday Mashed Potatoes

3   pounds potatoes, peeled, cooked, and hot
1   (8-ounce) package softened cream cheese
½   cup (1 stick) butter, softened
½   cup sour cream
2   eggs, lightly beaten
¼   onion, finely chopped
½   cup milk
    Salt and pepper

Preheat the oven to 350°. In a large mixing bowl mash the hot potatoes. When the lumps are removed, add the cream cheese in small pieces and then the softened butter. Beat well until the cream cheese and butter are both melted and mixed into the mashed potatoes. Mix in the sour cream. In another bowl, combine the eggs, onion, and milk and stir. Add the milk mixture to the potato mixture and mix well. Add salt and pepper to taste. Beat well until light and fluffy. Place in a greased round casserole dish and refrigerate several hours or overnight. The potatoes can be frozen at this point and later baked after thawing. Bake for 45 minutes or until lightly browned on top.

YIELD: 8 TO 12 SERVINGS

Marilyn Goucher
Oxford, Georgia

Hoppin' John

This dish is a New Year's Day tradition in most southern households and is believed to bring good luck and pocket change for the coming year. When served with collard greens, it is said you will have plenty of dollar bills also. The dish originally was brought over from Africa and has been a part of Southern cooking tradition for more than 300 years. A part of the tradition is that you are supposed to hop around the table before eating the dish when it is served.

1   (16-ounce) package dried black-eyed peas
2   large ham hocks (¾ pound each)
2   tablespoons bacon drippings
4   cups water
1   large onion, cut into 6 or 8 wedges
1   teaspoon salt
1   teaspoon pepper
½   teaspoon dried crushed red pepper
½   teaspoon dried thyme
2   bay leaves
1   teaspoon minced garlic
1   chicken bouillon cube
    Hot cooked white rice

In a Dutch oven on medium-high heat bring the black-eyed peas and water to cover to a boil. Remove from the heat and let stand for 1 hour. Drain the peas. Remove the skin from the ham hocks. Chop the meat from the ham hocks and reserve the bones. In a large skillet over medium-high heat sauté the meat in the bacon drippings for 3 minutes or until slightly brown. In the Dutch oven on medium heat combine the peas, meat, bones, 4 cups water, onion, salt, pepper, red pepper, thyme, bay leaves, garlic, and bouillon cube. Bring to a boil. Reduce the heat to low and simmer for approximately 1 to 1½ hours, gently stirring occasionally. Cook until the peas are tender. Remove the ham bones and discard. Serve over the hot rice.

YIELD: 8 TO 10 SERVINGS

Hot Curried Fruit

This is a simple side dish that goes nicely with pork and is often used on special occasions and/or holiday meals to complement pork main entrées. You will always find this on the Blue Willow buffet at Thanksgiving.

1	(8-ounce) can sliced peaches in juice
1	(8-ounce) can sliced pears in juice
8	ounces apples, sliced
6	ounces apricots, sliced
6	ounces cherries, stemmed and pitted
⅓	cup butter
¾	cup packed light brown sugar
2	teaspoons curry powder

Partially drain the peaches and pears, reserving half the liquid. In a stockpot on medium heat stir together the peaches, pears, reserved liquid, apples, apricots, cherries, butter, sugar, and curry powder. Bring to a boil, reduce the heat to low, and allow to simmer for 30 to 40 minutes. Remove from the heat and allow to cool. Refrigerate overnight.

YIELD: 10 TO 12 SERVINGS

Jill's Asparagus

1½	pounds asparagus
2	tablespoons olive oil
2	tablespoons butter
1	teaspoon garlic salt
½	teaspoon pepper
¼	cup Parmesan cheese

Rinse the asparagus and trim the bottoms. In a medium-size nonstick skillet on medium heat add the olive oil and butter. Sauté the asparagus, adding the garlic salt and pepper, for 5 to 10 minutes until nearly tender. Add the cheese and cook for 3 minutes. Serve immediately.

YIELD: 4 TO 6 SERVINGS

Jill Nicholson
Loganville, Georgia

Pour all leftover vegetables and water in which they are cooked into a freezer container. When full, add tomato juice and seasonings to create a "free" soup.

Lee's Baked Garlic Cheese Grits

This is a favorite used often for guests.

1	cup coarse grits
1	plus ½ sticks butter
1	medium onion, chopped
1	teaspoon salt
½	to ⅔ pound Velveeta cheese (can use sharp cheddar)
2	garlic cloves, chopped
4	eggs
	Milk
⅔	to 1 cup cornflakes

Preheat the oven to 350°. In a medium-size saucepan prepare the grits according to the package directions. In another medium saucepan over low heat melt 1 stick butter. Add the onion, salt, cheese, garlic, eggs, and enough milk to make 1 cup liquid. Stir as the cheese melts and everything blends together. When the liquid is smooth, add it to the grits and mix. Pour into a buttered casserole dish. In a small saucepan over low heat melt the remaining ½ stick butter. Stir in the cornflakes. Pour this mixture on top of the casserole. Bake for 30 minutes. Serve hot.

YIELD 6 TO 8 SERVINGS

Lee Seiler
Covington, Georgia

Macaroni and Cheese and Corn Bake

This is a simple and easy dish for those rushed days.

1	(15-ounce) can whole kernel corn, undrained
1	(15-ounce) can cream-style corn
1	cup uncooked macaroni
1	cup cubed Velveeta cheese

Preheat the oven to 350°. In a medium-size mixing bowl combine the whole kernel corn, cream-style corn, macaroni, and cheese. Mix well. Pour into a 2-quart baking dish and bake uncovered until tender.

YIELD: 6 TO 8 SERVINGS

Ginny Johnston
Covington, Georgia

Mashed Potato Cakes

Don't throw out those leftover mashed or creamed potatoes. Here's a great recipe that lets you get the most from those leftovers.

¼	cup chopped onion
3	tablespoons bacon grease
¼	cup chopped bacon (optional)

4 cups leftover creamed potatoes (see recipe on page 179)

1 cup all-purpose flour

6 eggs

Vegetable oil

In a small skillet on medium heat sauté the onion in the bacon grease until soft. Add the chopped bacon if desired and cook. In a mixing bowl combine the onion, bacon grease, chopped bacon if desired, creamed potatoes, flour, and eggs. Mix well but do not beat.

In a heavy skillet on medium heat pour enough oil to thoroughly cover the bottom of the skillet. Form the potato mixture into patties ¾-inch thick and 2½ to 3 inches in diameter. Place the patties in the hot oil and cook each side until golden brown.

Add oil as needed while cooking the patties.

YIELD: 8 POTATO CAKES

Minted Peas

1 (10-ounce) package frozen green peas

2 tablespoons water

1 tablespoon green crème de menthe

1 tablespoon margarine

In a saucepan on medium heat cook the peas for 3 to 5 minutes. Stir in the crème de menthe and margarine.

YIELD: 4 TO 6 SERVINGS

Dot Marks
Savannah, Georgia

Mincemeat Stuffing

1 (16-ounce) loaf crusty French bread

3 tablespoons butter or margarine

1 large onion, chopped

2 celery ribs, chopped

2 cups prepared mincemeat

½ cup chopped pecans, toasted

⅓ cup dry white wine

3 tablespoons chopped fresh sage or 1 teaspoon dried

1 teaspoon salt

½ teaspoon pepper

2 large eggs, lightly beaten

Preheat the oven to 350°. Cut the bread into 1-inch cubes. Place the cubes in a large mixing bowl. In a large skillet on medium heat melt the butter. Add the onion and celery and sauté for 5 to 7 minutes or until the onion is tender. Add the onion mixture to the bread cubes. Stir in the mincemeat, pecans, white wine, sage, salt, pepper, and eggs. Stir until well mixed. Pour the mixture into a lightly greased 2-quart baking dish. Bake for 35 to 40 minutes or until the stuffing is set in the center.

YIELD: 6 TO 8 SERVINGS

Mom's Sweet Potato Casserole

My mom has fixed this Sweet Potato Casserole for Thanksgiving dinner for as many years as I can remember. I LOVE IT! Ever since I got married 15 years ago, I always volunteer to bring the Sweet Potato Casserole to share with both sides of the family. The topping is unique since it's not the traditional marshmallow topping. It does not contain any spices, but the flavor is creamy and delicious.

CASSEROLE

3	cups cooked sweet potatoes
½	cup granulated sugar
2	eggs, beaten
½	teaspoon salt
¼	cup (½ stick) butter, melted
½	cup milk
½	to 1 teaspoon vanilla extract

TOPPING

½	cup brown sugar
⅓	cup all-purpose flour
1	cup chopped pecans
⅓	stick butter or margarine, at room temperature

Preheat the oven to 325°. For the casserole, in a mixing bowl mash the sweet potatoes. Add the sugar, eggs, salt, butter, milk, and vanilla. Mix well, using an electric beater. Put in a shallow 1½-quart baking dish.

For the topping, in a bowl combine the brown sugar, flour, pecans, and butter. Mix well until blended. Spread over the top of the sweet potatoes. Bake for 30 minutes.

YIELD: 4 TO 6 SERVINGS

Joanna Dykes
Snellville, Georgia

Morgan & Seth's Wacky Beans

These beans were created one day when I needed a side dish for some barbequed ribs. I wanted a twist on the plain baked beans most people serve. They have a unique sweet-hot taste that everyone seemed to enjoy, and I have received several requests to make them for family dinners and barbeques. They are even better the second day.

1	small onion, diced
1	pound ground beef
2	(15-ounce) cans drained pork and beans
1	cup firmly packed brown sugar
1	cup ketchup
½	cup prepared mustard
1	tablespoon hot mustard powder
¼	cup honey mustard
¼	cup A1 sauce
¼	cup Heinz 57 sauce
	Dash of hot sauce (10 drops)
½	tablespoon freshly ground peppercorns

In a large skillet on medium heat mix and brown the onion and ground beef. Add the beans, brown sugar, ketchup, prepared mustard, hot mustard powder, and honey mustard. Stir and bring to a boil over medium heat. Add the A1 sauce, Heinz 57 sauce, hot sauce, and peppercorns. Reduce the heat to low, cover, and let simmer for 30 minutes.

YIELD: 15 SERVINGS

Stacey Hicks

Cleveland, Tennessee

Okra and Tomatoes

Serve this over rice with some corn bread for a great dish.

2   slices bacon
1   medium onion, chopped
1   (14.5-ounce) can whole tomatoes, cut coarsely
1   (10-ounce) package frozen or fresh okra
    Salt and pepper

In a heavy skillet on medium heat fry the bacon slices. Remove from the skillet. Drain on a paper towel. Sauté the onion in the bacon grease. Add the tomatoes and the okra. Crumble the bacon into the mixture. Season with the salt and pepper to taste. Cook for 15 to 20 minutes or until done.

YIELD: 4 TO 6 SERVINGS

Onion Pie

This recipe is a favorite of Kitty Jacobs, who is retired as an Atlanta tour guide. Kitty has been a frequent guest at Blue Willow Inn. She and the Van Dykes became friends and she continues to visit from time to time.

1   cup fine saltine cracker crumbs
4   plus 2 tablespoons margarine, melted
2   cups thinly sliced onions (2 medium onions)
¾   cup milk
2   eggs, lightly beaten
¾   teaspoon salt
    Dash of pepper
¼   cup shredded sharp cheddar cheese
    Dash of paprika

Preheat the oven to 350°. In a small bowl mix the cracker crumbs with 4 tablespoons of the melted margarine. Press the crumbs into the bottom and sides of an 8-inch pie plate. In a small skillet on medium heat cook the onions in the remaining 2 tablespoons margarine, stirring to separate the rings. Cook until the onions are tender but not brown. Place the onions in the pie shell. In a small bowl combine the milk, eggs, salt, and pepper. Pour this mixture over the onions. Sprinkle with the cheese and paprika. Bake for 30 minutes or until a knife inserted halfway between the center and the edge of the pie comes out clean. Serve hot.

YIELD: 6 TO 8 SERVINGS

Pinto Beans

1   pound dry pinto beans
     Water
4   ounces fatback and/or ham
1   teaspoon bacon grease
     Salt and pepper

Place the dry beans in a medium-size pot and cover with water. Allow the beans to soak for 1 hour. Discard all the beans that float to the top. Rinse the beans three times with cold water. Put the beans in a stockpot over medium heat and cover with water, at least 2 inches above the beans. Add the fatback or ham, bacon grease, and salt and pepper to taste. Cook the beans, stirring often, for 1½ to 2 hours. Always make sure the beans are covered with water, adding water if necessary. Cook the beans until the juices are thick and the beans are tender.

YIELD: 6 TO 8 SERVINGS

Potatoes au Gratin

3   to 4 medium potatoes
¼   plus ¼ cup (1 stick) butter
2   tablespoons all-purpose flour
1   cup milk
2   tablespoons Cheez Whiz
½   cup grated cheddar cheese
1   small onion, sliced
     Salt and pepper

Wash, peel, and slice the potatoes into ¼-inch rounds. In a medium-size stockpot over medium heat cover the potatoes with water and cook until just tender, being careful not to overcook them. In a small saucepan combine ¼ cup of the butter with the flour and milk. Cook over medium heat until the mixture begins to thicken. Add the Cheez Whiz and cheddar cheese to the saucepan and stir until the cheese is melted and well mixed. In a small skillet sauté the onion in the remaining ¼ cup butter and add it to the cheese mixture. Add the salt and pepper to taste. Preheat the oven to 350°. Place the potatoes in a 9 x 13 inch casserole dish and pour the cheese mixture over the potatoes. Cook uncovered for 25 to 30 minutes.

YIELD: 10 TO 12 SERVINGS

Potato Soufflé

This recipe was obtained from a dear friend and great cook from Dublin, Georgia, in the late 1980s. We have enjoyed it at many of our Christmas holiday parties with ham or taken to covered-dish dinners at church. It is a wonderful dish that should be prepared the night before and refrigerated overnight to enhance the flavor. It presents well and suggests much time and effort, but really does not require too much. It doesn't last long because everybody loves it.

8   to 10 medium potatoes, peeled
1   (8-ounce) package softened cream cheese
1   (8-ounce) carton sour cream
½   cup (1 stick) butter or margarine, melted
1   garlic clove, minced

2   teaspoons salt
¼   cup chopped chives
     Paprika for garnish

In a large saucepan over medium heat cook the potatoes in water until tender. Drain the potatoes and mash. In a mixing bowl beat the cream cheese with a mixer until smooth. Add the potatoes, sour cream, butter, garlic, salt, and chives. Beat just until combined. Spoon the mixture into a lightly buttered 2-quart casserole. Sprinkle with the paprika. Cover and refrigerate 6 to 8 hours or overnight.

When ready to cook, preheat the oven to 350°. Remove the potatoes from the refrigerator 15 minutes before baking. Uncover and bake for 30 minutes or until thoroughly heated.

YIELD: 10 TO 12 SERVINGS

Gena McLendon
Conyers, Georgia

Red New Potatoes

2   pounds small red new potatoes
¼   plus ¼ cup (1 stick) butter
½   teaspoon salt
     Chopped fresh parsley

Wash the potatoes. Place in a stockpot over medium heat with enough water to cover plus one cup. Add ¼ cup of the butter and the salt. Bring the potatoes to a boil and allow to boil for 16 to 18 minutes or until tender when pierced with a fork. Remove the potatoes from the water and place in a serving bowl. Melt the remaining ¼ cup butter and pour it over the potatoes. Sprinkle with chopped parsley.

YIELD: 4 TO 6 SERVINGS

Roasted New Potatoes

8   small red new potatoes
¼   cup butter, melted
½   teaspoon garlic salt
¼   cup chopped parsley
     Salt and pepper

Preheat the oven to 350°. Wash the potatoes, cut in half, and place them on an ungreased baking sheet. Brush each potato with melted butter and sprinkle the garlic salt, parsley, and salt and pepper to taste on top of each potato. Cook uncovered for 20 to 25 minutes until the potatoes begin to turn light brown.

YIELD: 8 SERVINGS

Rutabagas

3   to 4 rutabagas
3   to 4 cups water
¼   cup butter
     Salt and pepper

Peel and dice the rutabagas into bite-size pieces. In a stockpot over medium heat place the rutabagas and cover them with the water. Add the butter and the salt and pepper to taste. Bring to a boil. Cook for 1 to 1½ hours until tender.

YIELD: 4 TO 6 SERVINGS

Savannah Red Rice

4   cups rice
6   slices bacon
1   medium onion, chopped
1   small red bell pepper
1   (28-ounce) can tomatoes, undrained
1   (14-ounce) jar ketchup
2   ounces bacon grease
1   teaspoon Worcestershire sauce
1   teaspoon salt
     Dash of black pepper
     Tabasco sauce

Preheat the oven to 350°. Cook the rice according to the package instructions. Drain the rice. In a large skillet on medium high heat fry the bacon until it is crisp. Chop the bacon. Sauté the onion and bell pepper in the bacon grease. In a medium-size mixing bowl combine the rice, bacon, onion, bell pepper, tomatoes, ketchup, bacon grease, Worcestershire sauce, salt, pepper, and Tabasco to taste. Mix well and pour into a casserole dish. Bake for 40 to 50 minutes or until bubbly.

YIELD: 15 TO 20 SERVINGS

Scalloped Potatoes

3   to 4 medium potatoes
¼   plus ¼ cup (1 stick) butter
2   tablespoons flour
1   cup milk
1   small onion, sliced
     Salt and pepper

Preheat the oven to 350°. Wash, peel, and slice the potatoes into ¼-inch rounds. In a medium-size stockpot over medium heat cover the potatoes with water and cook until just tender. Do not overcook. In a small saucepan over medium heat combine ¼ cup of the butter with the flour and milk. Cook over medium heat until the mixture begins to thicken. Sauté the onion in the remaining ¼ cup butter. Add to the milk mixture. Add the salt and pepper to taste. Place the potatoes in a 2-quart casserole dish and pour the sauce mixture over the potatoes. Bake uncovered for 25 to 30 minutes.

YIELD: 6 TO 8 SERVINGS

Sherried Fruit

1   (15-ounce) can peach halves, drained
1   (15-ounce) can pear halves, drained
1   (20-ounce) can pineapple chunks, drained
1   (15.5-ounce) jar apple rings, drained
½   cup packed brown sugar

½   cup (1 stick) margarine, softened
1   teaspoon cornstarch
½   cup dry sherry

In a casserole dish layer the peaches, pears, pineapple, and apple rings, with the apple rings on top. In a small saucepan on medium heat mix the brown sugar and margarine. Bring to a boil, stirring constantly. Remove from the heat and add the cornstarch and sherry and mix. Pour this mixture over the layered fruit and marinate overnight. When ready to serve, preheat the oven to 350° and bake for 30 minutes.

YIELD: APPROXIMATELY 2½ PINTS

Nada McDowell
Covington, Georgia

Skillet Tomatoes and Zucchini

2   tablespoons butter or margarine
2   small zucchini, sliced
1   medium onion, sliced
2   medium tomatoes, sliced
½   teaspoon garlic salt
¼   teaspoon chopped fresh basil
    Dash of pepper
1   cup shredded mozzarella cheese
1   cup seasoned croutons

In a large skillet on medium heat melt the butter or margarine. Add the zucchini and onion and sauté until tender.

Add the tomatoes, garlic salt, basil, and pepper. Cover and cook until the tomatoes are tender. Remove from the heat and sprinkle with the cheese and croutons. Cover and allow the dish to stand for 2 to 3 minutes until the cheese melts.

YIELD: 6 TO 8 SERVINGS

Slow-Cooker Macaroni and Cheese

1   (16-ounce) box macaroni
1   teaspoon salt
1   teaspoon vegetable oil
1   (8-ounce) carton sour cream
¼   cup (½ stick) margarine
1   egg
2   (8-ounce) packages shredded four-cheese blend
    Pepper

Cook the macaroni according to package directions with the salt and oil. Remove from the heat and drain. In a slow cooker combine the sour cream, margarine, egg, shredded cheese, and pepper to taste. Stir the cooked macaroni into this mixture. Cook for 1 hour on high.

Hint: Should you need a longer cooking time while at church or running errands, set the controls to low.

YIELD: 8 TO 10 SERVINGS

Debra Stanhope
Port Wentworth, Georgia

Skillet Squash

8	yellow squash
1	cup water
½	plus ¼ cup (1½ sticks) butter, melted
4	tablespoons bacon grease
1	small onion, thinly sliced
4	slices bacon, fried crisp and chopped
	Salt and pepper

Wash and slice the squash. In a large skillet combine the water, ½ cup of the butter, bacon grease, and onion and cook over medium-high heat until the onion is tender. Add the squash, bacon, and salt and pepper to taste. Cook until desired tenderness. Drain. Pour the remaining ¼ cup butter over the squash and serve.

YIELD: 6 SERVINGS

Sophia's Green Beans in Blankets

Billie's and Louis' longtime friend and next-door neighbor, Sophia DeMoss, provided this tasty twist on green beans.

1	pound bacon
1	(15-ounce) can whole green beans, drained
1	(16-ounce) bottle Catalina salad dressing

Preheat the oven to 350°. Cut the bacon slices in half and wrap 4 to 5 beans with a piece of bacon. Continue until all the beans are wrapped in bacon. Place the cut side of the bacon down in a Pyrex baking dish. Pour the Catalina dressing over the beans and bake for 45 minutes or until the bacon is done. Drain the grease from the baking dish and serve in the dish or transfer to another dish.

YIELD: 4 SERVINGS

Sophia's Squash Casserole

This is a favorite requested for all potluck suppers.

3	cups cooked and drained squash
2	eggs, beaten
1	cup milk
¾	stick butter, melted
1	teaspoon salt
1	teaspoon pepper
12	saltine crackers, crumbled
1	cup chopped onion
½	plus ½ cup grated cheddar cheese

Preheat the oven to 375°. In a mixing bowl combine the squash, eggs, milk, butter, salt, pepper, crackers, onion, and ½ cup grated cheese. Pour into a casserole dish. Cover with the remaining ½ cup grated cheese. Bake for 45 minutes. Serve warm.

YIELD: 6 TO 8 SERVINGS

Spiced Mixed Fruit

1   cup granulated sugar
1   cup water
1   cup dry white wine
2   whole cloves
1   (2-inch) cinnamon stick plus 1 for garnish
½   teaspoon vanilla extract
6   navel oranges
3   grapefruits
3   bananas

In a saucepan over medium heat combine the sugar, water, white wine, cloves, and 1 cinnamon stick. Bring to a boil. Reduce the heat to low and simmer, stirring occasionally, for 15 minutes. Stir in the vanilla. Remove from the heat and cool the syrup. Discard the cloves and cinnamon stick.

Peel and section the oranges and grapefruits. Place in a large bowl. Gently stir in the syrup. Chill the mixture if desired. Slice the bananas and stir in just before serving. Garnish with the remaining cinnamon stick if desired.

YIELD: 6 TO 8 SERVINGS

Squash Casserole

3   pounds squash, sliced
1   medium onion, chopped
2   tablespoons bacon grease
½   teaspoon salt
1   (10-ounce) can condensed cream of chicken soup
1   cup sour cream
½   cup (1 stick) butter
3   eggs, lightly beaten
¼   cup chopped bacon
¼   plus ¼ cup grated cheddar cheese
1½   plus ½ cups Ritz cracker crumbs

Preheat the oven to 350°. In a medium saucepan over medium heat cook the squash until done, but firm. Sauté the onion in the bacon grease. In a mixing bowl combine the onion and bacon grease, salt, soup, sour cream, butter, eggs, bacon and ¼ cup cheese. Mix together. Add the squash and 1½ cups cracker crumbs. Mix gently. Do not mash the squash. Pour into a 9 x 12-inch casserole or baking dish. Bake for 25 to 30 minutes. Remove from the oven and top with the remaining ½ cup cracker crumbs and ¼ cup cheese. Return to the oven to brown the cracker crumbs and melt the cheese.

YIELD: 8 TO 10 SERVINGS

Squash Dressing

A now-deceased friend gave this recipe to me. It is very delicious and I serve it at church and family gatherings.

2 cups cooked and drained sliced squash

2 cups crumbled corn bread

1 (10¾-ounce) can condensed cream of chicken soup

½ cup chopped onion

½ cup (1 stick) butter, melted

3 eggs

Sage

Preheat the oven to 350°. Grease a 3-quart casserole dish. In a large mixing bowl combine the squash, cornbread, soup, onions, butter, eggs, and sage to taste. Mix well. Pour into the casserole dish and bake for 35 to 40 minutes.

YIELD: 10 TO 12 SERVINGS

Mary Landress
Loganville, Georgia
First Place Winner, Vegetables and Side Dishes
Blue Willow Inn Restaurant Recipe Contest, 2004

Stewed Apples

Stewed apples are used not only as a side dish, but also are commonly served with ice cream or as a filling for apple pie. They are also wonderful in the mornings with oatmeal.

3 to 4 large Granny Smith apples

1½ cups water

¼ cup packed brown sugar

2 tablespoons all-purpose flour

¼ teaspoon salt

½ teaspoon ground cinnamon

¼ teaspoon nutmeg

Wash, core, peel, and slice the apples. In a medium-size saucepan over low heat combine the apples, water, brown sugar, flour, salt, cinnamon, and nutmeg and cook for 30 to 40 minutes. Simmer until the apples are tender, but not too soft.

YIELD: 6 SERVINGS

Stewed Tomatoes

1 (16-ounce) can whole tomatoes, undrained

2 slices bacon, cooked and chopped

1 tablespoon bacon grease

¼ teaspoon granulated sugar (optional)
Salt and pepper

3 to 4 slices white bread

In a medium-size saucepan on medium heat put the tomatoes with their juice. Mash the tomatoes with a fork. Add the bacon, bacon grease, sugar, and salt and pepper to taste. Bring the mixture to a boil. Tear the bread into strips, add to the tomatoes, and stir. Remove from the heat and serve over rice or creamed potatoes (see page 179).

YIELD: 4 TO 6 SERVINGS

Stuffed Eggplant

1   large eggplant
4   plus 2 tablespoons margarine
½   cup minced onion
1   (4-ounce) can sliced mushrooms, drained
1   plus ½ cups grated cheddar cheese
1   cup soft breadcrumbs
     Salt and pepper

Preheat the oven to 375°. Cut the eggplant in half lengthwise. Scoop out the interior, leaving a ¼-inch shell. Place the shells in a baking dish. Dice the scooped out portion of the eggplant. In a medium-size skillet on medium heat melt 4 tablespoons margarine and sauté the eggplant in the margarine until it is tender, stirring occasionally. In a small skillet on medium heat melt the remaining 2 tablespoons margarine. Add the onion and cook for 2 minutes. Add the mushrooms and cook for 5 minutes. In a medium-size mixing bowl combine the eggplant, mushrooms, and onions, 1 cup cheese, breadcrumbs, and salt and pepper to taste. Mix well. Divide the filling between the two eggplant shells. Sprinkle with the remaining ½ cup cheese. Bake for 15 to 20 minutes. To serve, cut each shell in half or thirds.

YIELD: 4 TO 6 SERVINGS

Stuffed Zucchini Squash

6   yellow gooseneck squash
2   large (10-inch) zucchini squash
2   tablespoons bacon grease
2   tablespoons butter, melted
½   cup chopped onion
4   slices crisped-cooked bacon
¾   plus ¼ cup grated cheddar cheese
¾   plus ¼ cup Ritz cracker crumbs
¼   teaspoon salt
     Pepper

Preheat the oven to 350°. Wash and slice the yellow squash, discarding the ends. In a saucepan over medium heat place the sliced yellow squash and cover with water. Bring to a boil and cook until tender, 4 to 5 minutes. Remove from the heat and drain.

Wash the zucchini squash and cut in half lengthwise. Scoop out the centers of the zucchini squash from end to end using a knife or spoon and place the flesh in a small bowl. Make sure to leave the ends of the squash intact.

In a small skillet heat the bacon grease and butter. Sauté the onion in the skillet until tender. In a mixing bowl combine the meat from the zucchini squash, the cooked yellow squash, bacon, ¾ cup cheese, ¾ cup cracker crumbs, onion, salt, and pepper to taste. Mix, but do not beat. Spoon the mixture into the zucchini shells. Place in a casserole dish with ¼-inch water and bake uncovered for 40 to 50 minutes. Top with the remaining ¼ cup cracker crumbs and ¼ cup cheese. Return to the oven to melt the cheese. Cut each stuffed zucchini into three sections and serve.

YIELD: 6 SERVINGS

Sweet Potato Puffs

2	pounds sweet potatoes or yams
¾	teaspoon salt
1½	tablespoons granulated sugar
¾	teaspoon ground cinnamon*
2	tablespoons butter
2	eggs, separated
1	cup all-purpose flour
	Milk
1½	cups breadcrumbs**

Preheat the oven to 400°. Wash and scrub the potatoes (grease the potatoes prior to baking as this makes peeling easier). Bake for 45 minutes or until tender. After baking, peel the potatoes and discard the skins and the objectionable dark potato pulp. In a large mixing bowl mash the potatoes. Add the salt, sugar, cinnamon, butter, and the egg yolks. Blend the mixture well. Cover and chill. After the mixture has chilled, form it into three-quarter-inch balls and roll the balls in flour. Chill the puffs. Whip the egg whites and add enough milk to equal 1 cup liquid. Dip the floured puffs into the milk and then roll them in the crumbs. Fry at 375° until golden brown. Drain on paper towels.

Hints: The potatoes may be baked one day and finished the next day. A ½ cup pecan pieces add a nice texture and taste.

*Grated rind of a lemon or orange or ½ teaspoon vanilla extract may replace the ground cinnamon.

**Shredded almonds, coconut, or cornflakes may replace all or part of the bread crumbs. A pecan meal and breadcrumbs combination also makes for an interesting and crispy fried puff.

YIELD: 6 SERVINGS

Sweet Potato Soufflé

3	cups cooked fresh sweet potatoes
3	eggs
½	cup (1 stick) butter, melted
½	cup milk
¼	cup packed light brown sugar
½	cup granulated sugar
¼	teaspoon vanilla extract
	Dash of nutmeg
¼	cup raisins (optional)
	Miniature marshmallows
	Pecan Topping (recipe on page 355)

Preheat the oven to 350°. Mash the sweet potatoes with a whisk or potato masher. In a large mixing bowl combine the sweet potatoes, eggs, butter, milk, brown sugar, granulated sugar, vanilla, nutmeg, and raisins if desired, and mix well. Pour into a 9 x 12-inch casserole dish and bake for 25 to 30 minutes. Top with the miniature marshmallows and the pecan topping for sweet potatoes if desired. Return to the oven to melt and brown the marshmallows.

YIELD: 8 TO 10 SERVINGS

Tomato-Corn Casserole

4   peeled and sliced tomatoes
1   (15-ounce) can creamed corn, drained
2   shallots or green onions, chopped
    Salt and pepper
1   tablespoon butter
2   slices crisp-cooked bacon

TOPPING

3   tablespoons mayonnaise
4   tablespoons soft breadcrumbs
1   teaspoon Worcestershire sauce
    Cayenne pepper
1   egg white, stiffly beaten
    Chopped parsley

Preheat the oven to 325°. In a greased 2-quart casserole, layer the tomato slices, corn, and shallots. Add the salt and pepper to taste. Dot with the butter. Add the bacon. In a small mixing bowl combine the mayonnaise, breadcrumbs, Worcestershire sauce, cayenne pepper, egg white, and parsley. Mix well. Spread the mixture over the casserole. Bake for 25 minutes.

YIELD: 6 TO 8 SERVINGS

Joan L. McMillan
Social Circle, Georgia

Sugar Snap Peas with Bacon Dressing

3   slices bacon, diced
1   (10-ounce) package sugar snap peas
2   tablespoons water
2   teaspoons finely chopped onion
¼   teaspoon celery seed
    Salt

In a saucepan on medium heat fry the diced bacon. Add the peas, water, onion, celery seed, and salt to taste. Bring to a boil. Reduce the heat to low. Cover and simmer for 5 to 7 minutes.

YIELD: 6 TO 8 SERVINGS

Turnip Greens

No southern dinner table is complete without turnip greens or collards. Louis believes that collards are "God's gift to the South." Billie begs to differ and thinks it is turnip greens. Billie is wrong, according to Louis. Turnip greens are best when served with Tomato Chutney (recipe on page 127)

1	large bunch fresh (or frozen) turnip greens
2	to 3 quarts water
4	tablespoons bacon grease
6	ounces fatback or ham
½	teaspoon salt
½	teaspoon granulated sugar (optional)
	Pepper
	Turnips (optional)

Separate the stems of the turnip greens from the leaves and throw the stems away. Wash the leaves in cold water. In a large stockpot on medium heat combine the water, bacon grease, fatback or ham, salt, sugar if desired, and pepper to taste. Bring to a boil and add the turnip greens. Boil over medium heat for 1½ hours until tender. If desired, wash and dice the turnips, add to the boiling water, and cook with the turnip greens.

YIELD: 8 TO 10 SERVINGS

Twice-Baked Potatoes

Next-door neighbors Bill and Sophia DeMoss introduced Louis and Billie to this recipe back in the seventies. It is often served at the restaurant and when it is, the kitchen struggles to keep up with the demand.

4	baking potatoes
¼	cup sour cream
⅓	stick butter
¼	plus ¼ cup grated cheddar cheese
¼	cup milk
	Salt and pepper

Preheat the oven to 350°. Bake the potatoes in their skins until tender. Cool for 20 minutes or until cool enough to handle. Cut the potatoes in half lengthwise, scoop out the insides, and put them in a large mixing bowl. Mash the potatoes with a fork and add the sour cream, butter, ¼ cup cheese, and a little milk. Mix well. Season to taste with the salt and pepper. Scoop the potato mixture back into the skins and place on a cookie sheet. Top with the remaining ¼ cup grated cheese. Bake until the cheese melts, 12 to 15 minutes. Serve hot.

YIELD: 8 SERVINGS

Vegetable Casserole

My mother used to get up at 5:00 a.m. to cook her special meals—turkey and dressing with gravy, rolls, salads, cakes, pies, green beans, corn, and other goodies. One year I talked her into cutting down on all the cooking. I asked her to let me bring a vegetable casserole so she would not have to cook the green beans and the corn. After that first meal with the vegetable casserole, I was to bring it for every dinner we had afterward. I have been asked over and over for this recipe.

1   (14½-ounce) can French-style green beans, drained
1   (11-ounce) can Mexicorn, drained
1   (5-ounce) can water chestnuts, drained
1   (8-ounce) carton sour cream
1   (10¾-ounce) can condensed cream of chicken soup
1   large Vidalia onion, diced
1¼ sleeves crushed Ritz crackers
1¼ sticks margarine, melted

Preheat the oven to 325°. In a large mixing bowl combine the green beans, Mexicorn, water chestnuts, sour cream, soup, and onion. Mix well. Place in a 9 x 13-inch casserole. In a small mixing bowl combine the crackers and margarine. Spread on top of the casserole. Bake for 30 to 40 minutes or until bubbly.

YIELD: 8 TO 10 SERVINGS

Juanita Muse
Calhoun, Georgia

Vegetable Pilaf

1   tablespoon vegetable oil
3   cups coarsely chopped fresh broccoli
3   medium carrots, julienned
1   large onion, chopped
1½   cups sliced fresh mushrooms
3   garlic cloves, minced
¾   teaspoon dried thyme
¾   teaspoon dried basil
¾   teaspoon salt
¼   teaspoon pepper
5   cups cooked brown rice (1½ cups uncooked, prepared in chicken broth)
½   cup toasted pecans
     Freshly grated Parmesan cheese (optional)

In a large pan heat the oil until hot. Add the broccoli, carrots, and onion. Cook and stir for 5 to 7 minutes or until the broccoli and carrots are soft and the onion is beginning to brown. Add the mushrooms, garlic, thyme, basil, salt, and pepper. Cook and stir for 2 to 3 minutes or until the mushrooms are tender. Add the rice and pecans. Cook for 1 to 2 minutes, stirring until well blended and thoroughly heated. Just before serving, sprinkle with cheese if desired.

Hint: To toast the pecans, place them on a baking sheet and bake at 350° for 5 to 7 minutes or until the nuts are just beginning to darken and become fragrant.

YIELD: 10 TO 12 SERVINGS

Betty Stephens
Monroe, Georgia

Vidalia Onion Casserole

2   tablespoons butter, melted
2   tablespoons all-purpose flour
1   (5⅓-ounce) can evaporated milk
1   cup chicken broth
3½   cups sliced Vidalia onions
½   teaspoon salt
⅔   cup toasted slivered almonds
1   cup breadcrumbs or croutons
½   cup grated cheddar cheese

Preheat the oven to 375°. In a medium-size saucepan over medium heat combine the butter, flour, evaporated milk, and chicken broth. Cook, stirring constantly, until thick and smooth. Add the onions, salt, and almonds. Pour the mixture into a buttered 1½-quart casserole dish. Cover with the crumbs and grated cheese and bake for 30 minutes.

Hint: If Southern sweet Vidalia onions are not available, Texas Sweets or Washington State Sweets will work as well.

YIELD: 6 TO 8 SERVINGS

POPULAR SOUTHERN SAYING

She clouded up and rained all over my parade.

Vidalia Onion Pie

Great for brunch. I first tried this dish when my three children were teenagers. It instantly became a family favorite. The children, who are all grown, request this dish when they come to visit. It's even good when reheated in the microwave.

8   slices bacon
1   large thinly sliced Vidalia onion
3   tablespoons all-purpose flour
2   eggs, beaten
1   cup milk
     Salt and pepper
¼   cup grated Swiss cheese
¼   cup grated Parmesan cheese
1   (9-inch) unbaked pie shell

Preheat the oven to 350°. Fry the bacon and sauté the onion in the bacon drippings. In a mixing bowl crumble the bacon and mix with the sautéed onion. Sprinkle the flour over the mixture. In a small mixing bowl beat the eggs and add the milk. Season with the salt and pepper to taste. Sprinkle the cheeses over the bottom of the pie shell. Spread the bacon mixture evenly over the cheeses. Cover with the milk mixture. Bake for 1 hour.

YIELD: 4 TO 5 SERVINGS

Ellen Hester
Monroe, Georgia

Vidalia Onion Shortcake

I first had this dish at a funeral in Mount Pleasant, South Carolina. I thought this casserole was one of the best things I had ever eaten. I finally got the recipe by way of Susan Freeman of Birmingham, Alabama. I have gotten many wonderful recipes at Southern funerals. I think "Southern Funeral Food" is in a class by itself.

1	large Vidalia onion, peeled and sliced
¼	cup (½ stick) butter or margarine
1	cup sour cream
¼	teaspoon salt
½	plus ½ cup grated sharp cheddar cheese
1	(7½-ounce) package corn muffin mix
1	egg, beaten
⅓	cup milk
1	(15-ounce) can cream-style corn
2	drops Tabasco (or more)

Preheat the oven to 400°. In a medium-size skillet on medium heat sauté the sliced onion in the butter. Cool. Add the sour cream, salt, and ½ cup cheese. In a medium-size mixing bowl combine the muffin mix, egg, milk, corn, and Tabasco. Pour into a greased, 8-inch-square pan. Spread the onion mixture over the batter. Sprinkle the remaining ½ cup cheese over the top. Bake for 25 to 30 minutes. Serve warm.

YIELD: 12 TO 16 SERVINGS

Barbara Sams
Social Circle, Georgia

Yams Louie

4	large sweet potatoes
½	cup (1 stick) butter
¼	cup granulated sugar
¼	cup packed brown sugar
⅓	cup orange marmalade
⅓	cup crushed pineapple
1	teaspoon vanilla extract
1	teaspoon cornstarch
¼	cup chopped pecans

Preheat the oven to 350°. Wash and peel the sweet potatoes. In a medium-size stockpot on medium heat cook the potatoes covered with water until done, but still firm (about 20 minutes). Set aside to cool. Cut into 1-inch rounds. Place the potato rounds on a sheet pan. In a small saucepan on medium heat combine the butter, granulated sugar, brown sugar, orange marmalade, crushed pineapple, and vanilla. Bring to a slow boil.

Dissolve the cornstarch in small amount of cold water and add it to the saucepan. Stir until thick and smooth. Add the pecans. Pour the mixture over the potatoes and bake uncovered for 25 to 30 minutes until the potatoes are tender.

YIELD: 16 TO 18 SERVINGS

Yellow Squash and Tomatoes

2	to 3 tablespoons margarine
2	large onions, halved then sliced
2	pounds yellow squash, sliced 1 inch thick
2	(16-ounce) cans whole tomatoes, chopped and drained
½	cup juice from canned tomatoes
½	to 1 teaspoon dried oregano, crumbled
⅛	teaspoon garlic powder
	Salt and pepper

In a large skillet on medium heat melt the margarine. Sauté the onions in the margarine until soft. Add the squash, chopped tomatoes, tomato juice, oregano, garlic powder, and salt and pepper to taste. Stir gently. Cook until the squash is just tender, stirring occasionally.

Hint: Two pounds of fresh tomatoes may be used. Be sure to peel, core, and chop. For another variation 1 cup corn can be added. Be sure to drain the corn.

YIELD: 8 TO 10 SERVINGS

Dot Marks
Savannah, Georgia

Main Dishes

True to Southern dining style, the main dishes of the Old South didn't feature many of the tender cuts of meat common to us today. In the Old South grass fed animals and hunting were the norm. Wild game such as venison, turkey, goose, and others were served at the table. Meats were often marinated or served with gravies and sauces. Farmers still raise hogs, sheep, goats, and cattle for meat. Today's main dishes can range from a single meat dish to a casserole with meat and vegetables to a hearty soup or stew.

Beef Hash

This is a good way to use leftover roast beef.

- 2   tablespoons butter
- 1   cup cubed leftover beef
- 1   medium onion, finely chopped
- 2   cups boiling water
- 1   cup cubed uncooked potatoes
      Salt and pepper

In a medium-size skillet on medium heat melt the butter. Add the beef and onion and cook in the butter. Add the boiling water and the potatoes. Add the salt and pepper to taste. Turn the heat to medium-low and cover the skillet, allowing the ingredients to cook slowly until all are tender. The hash should have plenty of gravy; more hot water may be needed and a small amount of flour may be added for thickening if needed. Serve on toast.

YIELD: 3 TO 4 SERVINGS

Beef Stroganoff

- ¼   cup (½ stick) butter
- ¼   cup cooking sherry
- 1   medium onion, chopped
- 3   pounds cubed sirloin tip roast or ground beef
- ¾   cup sliced fresh mushrooms, or 2 (8-ounce) jars sliced mushrooms
- 1   (10¾-ounce) can condensed cream of mushroom soup

- 1   cup sour cream
      Salt and pepper

In a large heavy skillet on medium heat melt the butter. Add the sherry, onion, and beef. Sauté the beef and onion until tender and done. Add the mushrooms and continue to cook for 2 to 3 minutes. Stir in the soup, sour cream, and salt and pepper to taste. Turn the heat to low. Cover the skillet and simmer, stirring occasionally, for 15 to 20 minutes. Serve over cooked noodles.

YIELD: 6 TO 8 SERVINGS

Betty Whitman's Hamburger Casserole

- 1   cup uncooked macaroni
- 1   pound ground beef
- 3   tablespoons ketchup
- 3   tablespoons dry onion soup mix
- ¼   teaspoon salt
- 1   (8-ounce) can tomato sauce
- ½   cup grated cheddar cheese

Cook the macaroni according to package directions. Drain. In a large skillet on medium heat brown the ground beef. After the beef has browned, add the ketchup, onion soup mix, salt, tomato sauce, and the drained macaroni. Turn the heat to low and simmer for 30 minutes. Preheat the oven to 350°. Pour the ground beef mixture into a casserole dish and sprinkle with the cheese. Bake for 10 to 15 minutes until the cheese browns.

Hint: Add a can of mixed vegetables or a can of vegetable soup for a different dish that makes a meal.

YIELD: 4 TO 6 SERVINGS

Jimmy Clack
Cordele, Georgia

Bob's Blue Ribbon Favorite, "Rileyhouse Beef Stew"

Patsy Riley, first lady of the state of Alabama, said, "When I asked Bob for his favorite dish for a cookbook, he gave me a fast answer—'I don't know.'" "You mean you just like so many things you can't decide?" she asked. "No, it's been so long since you cooked, I can't remember."

½	cup vegetable oil
2	pounds sirloin tips
½	cup steak sauce (Dale's) or Worcestershire sauce
1	(1.63-ounce) package stew seasoning (French's)
6	cups water
1	(15-ounce) can tomato sauce
1	(14½-ounce) can stewed tomatoes
10	small potatoes
½	(16-ounce) package baby carrots
¼	cup granulated sugar
3	tablespoons butter
10	small whole onions

In a large skillet on medium, heat the oil and brown the beef tips in the hot oil until each side is browned. Add the steak sauce or Worcestershire sauce. Simmer for 15 minutes. Add the stew seasoning and water. Stir. Add the tomato sauce, stewed tomatoes, potatoes, carrots, sugar, butter, and onions. Cook on low heat for 1 hour or longer. More water may be added if you want a soup-like stew. I usually serve this with corn on the cob and corn bread.

YIELD: 6 TO 8 SERVINGS

Chipped Beef with White Gravy

This is a very quick recipe to use for Sunday night supper, or it can be served on Saturday morning with grits and eggs.

¼	cup (½ stick) butter
1½	tablespoons all-purpose flour
1½	cups milk
	Salt and pepper
2	pounds cooked roast beef, very thinly sliced
	Toasted sliced white bread

Preheat the oven to 350°. In a saucepan on low heat combine the butter and flour. Stir and mix to a thick texture. Stir in the milk and salt and pepper to taste. Bring to a simmer, stirring often. Place the sliced beef in a 9 x 13-inch casserole dish. Pour the white gravy over the beef. Cover and bake for 15 to 20 minutes. Serve over crisp toast.

Hint: This recipe can be used for chipped ham by simply substituting very thinly sliced ham for the roast beef.

YIELD: 6 SERVINGS

Country-Fried Steak

This dish has been a favorite at the Blue Willow Inn since its opening. As a child, Louis grew up having country-fried steak (or as Texans call it, chicken fried steak) at least once a week. It is great with mashed potatoes or rice.

¼	cup vegetable oil
½	medium onion, sliced
½	cup all-purpose flour
	Salt and pepper
6	(4-ounce) portions cubed beefsteaks
1	(10¾-ounce) can condensed cream of mushroom soup
½	cup water

Cover the bottom of a large heavy skillet with cooking oil. Turn the heat to medium and sauté the onion until it is tender. Remove from the skillet. In a small mixing bowl combine the flour with the salt and pepper to taste. Using a meat mallet, tenderize the cubed beefsteaks. Dredge the steaks in the flour mixture and place them in the skillet in the heated oil. Fry each side of the steaks for 4 to 5 minutes. Remove them from the skillet. Add the soup and the water to the steak drippings. Add more salt and pepper if desired. Continue to cook over medium heat, stirring often.

There are two methods to finish cooking the country-fried steak:

1. Return the steaks to the gravy. Place the onions on top. Turn the heat to low. Cover and cook for 15 to 18 minutes.

2. Preheat the oven to 350°. Place the cooked steaks in a casserole dish. Pour the gravy over the steaks. Cover with the onions. Bake, covered, for 15 to 20 minutes.

YIELD: 6 SERVINGS

Easy Oven Stew

2	pounds stew beef
2	tablespoons all-purpose flour
1	teaspoon paprika
2	tablespoons vegetable oil
4	small onions, chopped
4	small carrots, chopped
4	small potatoes, diced
1	cup sliced celery
1	teaspoon salt
	Dash of pepper
1	(14-ounce) can tomato sauce
2	cups water

Preheat the oven to 400°. Place the beef in a 3-quart casserole dish. Sprinkle with the flour and paprika. Toss with the oil. Bake uncovered for 30 minutes, stirring once while baking. Add the onions, carrots, potatoes, celery, salt, and pepper. Pour the tomato sauce and water over the vegetables. Reduce the heat to 350°. Bake for 1¾ hours.

YIELD: 6 TO 8 SERVINGS

Nellie Baines
Jersey, Georgia

Ground Chuck Casserole

1   (12-ounce) package egg noodles
1   large onion, chopped
2   tablespoons bacon drippings
2   pounds ground chuck
1   (15-ounce) can sweet peas, not drained
1   (10¾-ounce) can condensed cream of mushroom soup, undiluted
1   (10¾-ounce) can condensed cream of tomato soup, undiluted
1   teaspoon salt
4   ounces grated sharp cheddar cheese

Prepare the noodles as directed on the package. Preheat the oven to 350°. In a large pan on medium heat lightly brown the onion in the bacon drippings. In a frying pan on medium-high heat cook the ground chuck until no longer pink. Add the chuck to the onion. Add the peas with their juice, the condensed soups, and salt. Drain the prepared noodles and add to the mixture. Stir lightly and pour into a casserole dish. Top with the cheese and bake for about 30 minutes or until bubbly.

YIELD: 10 SERVINGS

Sue O'Kelley
Loganville, Georgia

Hamburger Stroganoff

1   pound ground beef
1   medium onion, chopped (about ½ cup)
¼   cup (½ stick) butter or margarine
2   tablespoons all-purpose flour
1   teaspoon salt
1   teaspoon garlic salt or 1 garlic clove, minced
¼   teaspoon pepper
1   (8-ounce) can mushrooms, drained
1   (10¾-ounce) can cream of chicken soup
1   cup sour cream
2   cups hot cooked noodles
    Snipped parsley

In a large skillet on medium-high heat cook and stir the ground beef and onion in the butter until the onion is tender. Turn the heat to medium. Stir in the flour, salt, garlic salt, pepper, and mushrooms. Cook for 5 minutes, stirring constantly. Remove from the heat. Stir in the soup. Turn the heat to low and simmer, uncovered, for 10 minutes. Stir in the sour cream. Heat through. Pour over the noodles, and sprinkle with the snipped parsley to serve.

Hawkins Swiss Steak

My dad, who passed away many years ago, created this recipe when he cooked for the officers in the Marine Corps. He served this dish with a big tossed salad, French fries, and fresh bread. It is an absolutely wonderful dish. He prepared this for the family all of my life. It was always a treat and can be made to stretch farther just by adding more steak. Dad never really gave us the recipe, but I watched him prepare it many times and even fixed it for him on one occasion. Each time I prepare it I am reminded of its origin. Good memories.

3   to 4 pounds round steak (a good cut is important)
½   plus ½ cup all-purpose flour
     Salt and pepper
     Olive oil
½   cup water
¼   teaspoon garlic salt
1½   tablespoons Worcestershire sauce
1   (10-ounce) bottle Heinz Chili Sauce (no substitute)
½   cup ketchup

Cut the round steak into serving-size pieces, 5 to 6 ounces each. In a small bowl combine ½ cup flour and the salt and pepper to taste. With a tenderizer, pound this mixture into the steak. Cover the bottom of a large iron skillet with olive oil and place it over medium-high heat. Brown the meat well on both sides. In a large bowl mix the remaining ½ cup flour with the ½ cup water. This will be pasty. To this mixture add the garlic salt, Worcestershire sauce, Heinz Chili Sauce, and ketchup. Fill the Chili Sauce bottle with water and add to the mixture. Pour this mixture over the meat. Turn the heat to medium and cook for 2 to 2½ hours. Stir occasionally to prevent sticking. The gravy will thicken as the meat cooks.

YIELD: 8 to 10 servings

Frances Hawkins Fuller
McDavid, Florida

Lasagna

We know lasagna is not a Southern dish, but this recipe from Joanna Lewis, one of the servers at Blue Willow Inn, is one of Billie's favorite dishes. Joanna bakes lasagna for Billie on her birthday, for Christmas, and for Boss's Day. This is a wonderful dish.

3   garlic cloves, minced
¼   cup olive oil
2   (12-ounce) cans tomato paste
1   (12-ounce) can tomato purée
5   cups water
3   teaspoons dried sweet basil, or 3 fresh sweet basil leaves, chopped
2   teaspoons dried oregano
2   tablespoons dried parsley flakes
1   teaspoon garlic powder
½   teaspoon salt
½   plus 2 teaspoons black pepper
1½   pounds ground beef
1   pound bulk Italian sausage

1   (8-ounce) package grated Parmesan cheese, divided

2   (16-ounce) packages ricotta cheese

½   cup chopped fresh parsley

1   pound lasagna noodles, cooked for 8 to 10 minutes, divided

2   (12-ounce) packages grated mozzarella cheese, divided

1   (16-ounce) container cottage cheese, divided

In a large Dutch oven on medium heat brown the garlic in the olive oil. Add the tomato paste and tomato purée. Stir. Add the water, sweet basil, oregano, parsley flakes, garlic powder, salt, and ½ teaspoon of the black pepper. In a skillet on medium heat sauté the ground beef and sausage until partially cooked. Pour off the grease. Add the meat and ¼ cup of the Parmesan cheese to the sauce. Mix well. Bring to a boil, turn the heat to low, and simmer for 2½ to 3 hours or until the sauce is thick. In a bowl mix the ricotta cheese, parsley, and the remaining 2 teaspoons black pepper.

Preheat the oven to 350°. In a 9 x 13-inch baking pan spoon enough of the sauce to cover the bottom of the pan. Put a layer of lasagna noodles lengthwise on top of the sauce, overlapping slightly. Spread more sauce over the noodles. Sprinkle some of the mozzarella cheese over the sauce. Spoon some ricotta mixture and some cottage cheese over the mozzarella. Sprinkle with some Parmesan cheese. Arrange the next layer of lasagna noodles across the width of the pan. Repeat the order of sauce and cheeses. This should make three or four layers of lasagna in the baking dish. Bake for 45 to 55 minutes. Allow the lasagna to cool for 10 to 20 minutes before serving.

YIELD: 10 TO 12 SERVINGS

Liver and Onions

This old Southern recipe is served at the Blue Willow Inn every Thursday for lunch and supper. It seems that few people cook liver at home anymore because there is always one member of the family who can't stand it. Louis makes sure we provide it for the large contingent of liver lovers who miss one of the South's traditional meals and count on this recipe once every week.

¼   to ⅓ cup vegetable oil

1   medium onion, sliced

½   cup all-purpose flour
    Salt and pepper

1   to 2 pounds beef liver

In a heavy skillet on medium heat add the oil and sauté the sliced onions until tender and slightly brown. Remove the onions from the skillet.

Pour the flour into a flat pan and mix the salt and pepper to taste into the flour. Coat each side of the liver pieces with the flour. Make sure there is enough oil in the skillet to cover the bottom, add oil if necessary, and heat the oil. Place the liver in the hot oil. When the red juices are flowing from the top, turn the liver over. Add a little more oil, if necessary. Cook for 2 to 3 minutes and turn, cooking 2 to 3 minutes longer. Do not overcook because the liver will be tough. When done, remove the liver from the heat and smother with the sautéed onions.

YIELD: 4 TO 5 SERVINGS

Lynn's Sausage Casserole

2   pounds hot bulk sausage
      Vegetable oil
4   or 5 green onions (tops and all), chopped
1   large green bell pepper, chopped
1   cup chopped celery, including leaves
2   (1-ounce) packages dry chicken noodle soup mix
4½   cups boiling water
1   cup uncooked rice
1   (8-ounce) can water chestnuts, diced

In a skillet on medium-high heat slightly brown the sausage. Remove from the heat and drain off the grease. In the skillet in a small amount of vegetable oil brown the onions, pepper, and celery. In a saucepan on medium-high heat cook the soup in the boiling water for 7 minutes. Add the rice and blend. Add the water chestnuts, vegetables, and sausage. Preheat the oven to 350°. Pour the sausage mixture into a 3-quart casserole dish. Cover and bake for 45 minutes to 1 hour. Freeze any leftovers, or divide and freeze as is.

YIELD: 6 SERVINGS

Lynn Grace
Grayson, Georgia

Meatloaf

One of the favorite dishes served at the Blue Willow Inn. You'll find it almost every Thursday and sometimes even on a Sunday.

1½   pounds ground beef
3   eggs
½   plus ½ cup ketchup, divided
1   cup cornflakes
3   leftover biscuits or 5 to 6 slices white bread
¼   cup chopped green bell pepper
¼   cup chopped onion
1   tablespoon Worcestershire sauce
      Salt and pepper

Preheat the oven to 350°. In a large mixing bowl combine the ground beef, eggs, ½ cup of the ketchup, cornflakes, biscuits or bread, bell pepper, onion, Worcestershire sauce, and salt and pepper to taste. Mix the ingredients well and pour the mixture out onto a sheet pan. Work the ingredients several times as if kneading bread and then mold it into a loaf. Place the mixture in a loaf pan and bake for 30 to 40 minutes or until done. Remove from the oven and top with the remaining ½ cup ketchup.

YIELD: 5 TO 6 SERVINGS

President Ronald Reagan's Favorite Beef Stew

Just as the rest of the country did, the South also adopted President Reagan, so his favorite recipe is included.

4	teaspoons vegetable oil
2	large onions, sliced
1	garlic clove, split
⅓	cup all-purpose flour
2	teaspoons salt
	Pepper
4	pounds lean beef stew meat
2	teaspoons dill weed
1	cup Burgundy wine
1	(10¾-ounce) can beef consommé
1	(10-ounce) package frozen artichoke hearts
1	(8-ounce) can mushrooms, drained
2	(8-ounce) packages refrigerated biscuits
½	cup (1 stick) butter, melted
16	ounces grated Parmesan cheese

Heat the oil in a large skillet on medium heat. Sauté the onions and garlic. Remove them from the skillet. In a small bowl mix the flour, salt, and pepper to taste. Dredge the meat in the flour mixture and brown it well in the hot oil. Return the onion mixture to the skillet. Add the dill weed, wine, and consommé. Cover tightly, reduce the heat to low, and simmer about 2 hours or until the meat is tender. Cook the artichokes for 1 minute less than the package directions indicate. Drain. Add the artichokes to the meat. Add the mushrooms. Mix gently. Taste for seasoning. Preheat the oven to 400°. Pour the mixture into a 2½-quart casserole. Crown with the biscuits. Brush the biscuits evenly with the butter. Sprinkle with the grated cheese. Bake for 15 to 20 minutes.

YIELD: 10 TO 12 SERVINGS

Roast Beef

Leftover roast beef is wonderful to use in the chipped beef recipe on page 213 or the beef hash recipe on page 212.

1	(6 to 8-pound) top round beef roast
½	teaspoon garlic salt
½	teaspoon black pepper
1	cup water
	Flour

Preheat the oven to 425°. Place the roast in a roasting pan fat side up. Season the roast with the garlic salt and pepper. Pour the water into the bottom of the pan. Cook for 15 minutes and reduce the heat to 350°. Continue to cook for 1½ to 2 hours or until the roast is done. For medium roast beef, the center should be pink but not red.

For gravy, in a skillet on medium heat pour the drippings from the roasting pan and stir in a small amount of flour. Cook until the flour is brown. If the gravy is too thick, add a small amount of water. After it has thickened, let it simmer 3 to 4 minutes, stirring occasionally. The gravy can be poured over sliced roast beef or served on the side.

YIELD: 14 TO 16 SERVINGS

Pot Roast

A meal in itself. Serve this with a salad, and dinner is complete.

1	(6 to 8-pound) beef rump roast
¼	teaspoon garlic salt
3	large potatoes, peeled and cut into 1-inch pieces
4	carrots, peeled and cut into ¼-inch thick pieces
3	celery ribs, cut into 4 or 5 pieces per rib
1	medium onion, sliced
2	cups water
	Salt and pepper
	All-purpose flour

Preheat the oven to 350°. Sprinkle the roast with the garlic salt. In a large mixing bowl combine the potatoes, carrots, celery, and onion. Place the roast in the center of a roasting pan. Spread the mixed vegetables around the roast. Add the water to the pan. Sprinkle salt and pepper to taste over the vegetables and roast. Cover and cook for 45 to 55 minutes. Remove the cover and cook another 15 minutes.

For gravy, combine the drippings from the pot roast with ¼ to ½ cup of water in a small skillet over medium heat. Add 2 to 3 tablespoons flour to thicken. Simmer to thicken, stirring occasionally. If too thick, add more water. If not thick enough, add a small amount of flour. The gravy can be poured over the pot roast or served as a side dish.

YIELD: 10 TO 12 SERVINGS

Steak Rolls with Sour Cream Sauce

1	pound tenderized round steak
¼	cup all-purpose flour
¼	teaspoon salt
⅛	teaspoon pepper
2	tablespoons shortening
3	tablespoons finely chopped mushrooms
3	tablespoons chopped onion
1	(8-ounce) can refrigerated crescent dinner rolls

SOUR CREAM SAUCE

1	cup sour cream
1	tablespoon butter
½	teaspoon parsley flakes
¼	teaspoon salt

Cut the steak into four rectangular pieces. In a small bowl combine the flour, salt, and pepper. Dredge the steak pieces in the flour mixture. Put the shortening in a large skillet on medium-high heat and brown the steak pieces on both sides. Remove the meat from the skillet and drain on paper towels. Sauté the mushrooms and onion in the pan drippings. Remove from the pan. Preheat the oven to 400°. Place 1½ tablespoons of the mushroom mixture on one end of each of the browned steak pieces. Fold the steak pieces over, covering the mushroom mixture. Unroll the crescent roll dough, leaving two triangles joined to form four rectangles. Press at the perforation to seal. Place the steak piece in the center of a dough rectangle. Fold up the sides and the ends of the dough, tightly sealing the edges. Place the rolled rectangles seam side down on a cookie sheet. Bake for 10 to 12 minutes until golden brown.

For the **sour cream sauce**, combine the sour cream, butter, parsley flakes, and salt in a saucepan on low heat. Heat thoroughly, stirring occasionally to prevent sticking, but do not boil. Pour the sauce over the steak rolls.

YIELD: 4 SERVINGS

Swiss Steak

6	tablespoons all-purpose flour
1	teaspoon salt
½	teaspoon ground black pepper
2	pounds flank steak or sirloin steak
¼	cup vegetable oil
2	(28-ounce) cans whole tomatoes, chopped
¼	teaspoon garlic salt
1	medium onion, sliced

In a small mixing bowl combine the flour, salt, and black pepper. With a meat mallet, pound this mixture into the steak until about 1½ inches thick. Heat the oil in an iron skillet on medium heat. Fry the steak in the skillet, turning until it is brown on both sides. Add the tomatoes, garlic salt, and onion. Turn the heat to low. Cover and simmer on the stovetop for 2 to 2½ hours.

YIELD: 6 SERVINGS

Asparagus with Ham

4	slices thin white bread
2	egg whites
⅓	cup mayonnaise
2	(15-ounce) cans asparagus spears, drained
½	cup (1 stick) butter
	Salt
4	thick slices cooked ham

Toast the bread slices. Beat the egg whites until they are stiff and fold in the mayonnaise. With a little water in a saucepan on medium heat, warm the asparagus with the butter and salt. Drain the asparagus spears. Preheat the oven to 400°. Lay the pieces of toasted bread on a cookie sheet. Place 1 piece of ham on each piece of bread. Place 3 to 4 asparagus spears on the ham. Spread the egg mixture on top. Place the toasted bread in the oven and cook until the topping turns brown. Remove from the oven and serve hot.

YIELD: 4 SERVINGS

Baked Pork Chops

This is a simple and quick dish for those on the go.

6   center-cut pork chops
1   (10¾-ounce) can cream of mushroom
     soup
⅔   cup water
     Pepper
     Garlic salt

Preheat the oven to 350°. Lightly grease a 9 x 13-inch casserole dish. Place the pork chops in the casserole dish. Combine the soup and water. Cover and cook for 30 to 40 minutes or until done. Add the pepper and garlic salt to taste.

YIELD: 6 SERVINGS

Baked Pork Chops and Rice

6   pork chops
¼   cup vegetable oil
1   cup uncooked rice
3   cups hot water
1   teaspoon salt
1   teaspoon pepper
1   large onion, chopped
1   (10¾-ounce) can condensed cream of
      mushroom soup
1   large green bell pepper, sliced into
      rings

Preheat the oven to 350°. Trim the fat off the pork chops. In a large skillet on medium heat, heat the oil and brown the pork chops on both sides in the hot oil. In a 9 x 13-inch baking dish mix the rice, water, salt, pepper, onion, and undiluted soup. Add the green pepper rings to the top of the mixture. Place the pork chops on top. Cover with foil and bake for 45 minutes to 1 hour.

YIELD: 6 SERVINGS

Casserole of Chops

This casserole is a meal in itself and is another great one for those on the go.

4   pork chops
      All-purpose flour
      Vegetable oil
1½   cups cubed potatoes
1   cup sliced carrots
1   cup canned peas
¼   cup diced celery
3   tablespoons chopped onion
      Salt and pepper
¼   cup hot water
2   tablespoons minced fresh parsley

Trim the fat from the chops. Place the flour in a bowl and dredge the pork chops in the flour. Fill a large skillet with ¼ inch of oil. Heat the oil on medium-high and brown the chops, turning to brown both sides. Remove from the skillet and drain on paper towels.

Preheat the oven to 350°. Place the potatoes, carrots,

peas, celery, and onions in a 2-quart casserole dish. Add the salt and pepper to taste and the hot water. Place the browned chops on top of the vegetables. Sprinkle with the parsley. Cover and bake for 1 hour.

Hint: Canned vegetables may be substituted for fresh vegetables, but just be sure to reduce the cooking time.

YIELD: 4 SERVINGS

Cheesy Ham Potato Casserole

| 2 | pounds cooked ham |
| 6 | medium potatoes or 12 red new potatoes, cooked with skin on |

CHEESE SAUCE

1½	plus ½ cups milk
½	cup Cheez Whiz
½	cup grated cheddar cheese
½	teaspoon salt
	Dash of black pepper
¼	cup all-purpose flour

Cut the ham and potatoes into ¾-inch cubes. If using new red potatoes, cut in half. Place the ham and potatoes in a 9 x 13-inch casserole dish.

Prepare the **cheese sauce** by mixing 1½ cups of the milk with the Cheez Whiz, cheddar cheese, salt, and pepper in a heavy saucepan. Cook over low heat, stirring constantly until the cheese melts and the sauce simmers. In a small mixing bowl stir the remaining ½ cup milk into the flour until smooth. Stir this mixture into the cheese mixture

and cook until it thickens. Simmer for 20 minutes, stirring constantly.

Preheat the oven to 350°. Pour the cheese sauce over the ham and potatoes to cover. Bake uncovered for 20 to 25 minutes or until the cheese begins to brown.

YIELD: 10 TO 12 SERVINGS

Christmas Breakfast Casserole

This wonderful casserole recipe was given to us by Sandi McClain, former manager of the Blue Willow Inn gift shop, and it is easy to prepare for Christmas breakfast. It is made the night before and placed in the refrigerator to await Christmas morn. This makes for an easy meal in preparation for the formal Christmas dinner that is to come.

8	to 10 slices white bread, crusts trimmed
2	cups milk
6	eggs, beaten
1	pound sharp cheddar cheese, shredded
1	pound hot pork sausage, cooked, crumbled, and drained
1	teaspoon dry mustard

Line a greased 9 x 13-inch baking pan with the bread. In a large bowl combine the milk, eggs, cheese, sausage, and mustard and mix well. Spoon this mixture over the bread. Cover and refrigerate 6 to 8 hours or overnight. When ready to bake, preheat the oven to 350°. Bake for 45 minutes.

YIELD: 8 TO 10 SERVINGS

Company Breakfast Strata

12   slices whole wheat bread

12   ounces extra sharp cheddar cheese, sliced or grated

1   (10-ounce) package frozen chopped broccoli, cooked and drained

2   cups cooked and diced ham

SAUCE

6   eggs, lightly beaten

3½   cups milk

1   tablespoon bottled minced onion

½   teaspoon salt

¼   teaspoon dry mustard

Remove and discard the crusts from the bread. Using a biscuit cutter cut a round piece from each slice of bread, saving the "round" for the last layer of the casserole. In a 9 x 13-inch baking dish layer the casserole as follows: bread scraps, cheese, broccoli, ham, and bread rounds.

For the **sauce**, combine the eggs, milk, onion, salt, and dry mustard in a medium-size bowl. Pour the sauce over the casserole. Cover and refrigerate for at least 6 hours. When ready to bake, preheat the oven to 325°. Bake for 55 minutes or until the top is lightly brown and the casserole is almost firm. Let the casserole stand for 10 minutes before serving.

Hint: This casserole can be made a day ahead and refrigerated until ready to bake.

YIELD: 12 TO 15 SERVINGS

Marilyn Goucher
Oxford, Georgia

Fried Fatback (also known as Streak O'Lean)

This dish is as luxuriously porky as food can be. Also known as "streak o'lean" (lean it ain't), just don't let your doctor know you are indulging in this not-too-healthy, but deliciously tasty, dish.

½   to 1 pound fatback or streak o'lean

2   tablespoons all-purpose flour

1¼   cups milk
       Salt and pepper

Cut the fatback into ¼-inch slices. Soak in water for 30 to 40 minutes. Shake off the excess water. In a cast-iron skillet on medium heat fry the fatback, turning to cook on both sides until it is golden brown and crisp. Remove the meat from the skillet.

To make the gravy, reserve 2 tablespoons of the drippings in the skillet after removing the meat. Add the flour to the drippings, stirring with a fork or whisk until smooth. Stir in the milk a little at a time and cook, stirring constantly, until the desired thickness is reached. Add the salt and pepper to taste. Pour over the fatback and enjoy.

YIELD: 4 TO 6 SERVINGS

Fried Ham with Redeye Gravy

In the Old South almost everyone raised his own hogs. On the coldest day in the fall the hogs would be slaughtered. The meat would be hickory smoked, sugared, or salt-cured. The coffee for the redeye gravy would have been

made from the beans that were hand-ground fresh each morning. One explanation of how the gravy got its name is that black coffee and ham drippings never totally mix, and if you pour the coffee into the ham drippings nice and easy, it will spread out in the hot fat and resemble a very bloodshot eye. Ham and redeye gravy is wonderful with fresh biscuits and grits.

2	cups hot strong-brewed coffee
¼	cup firmly packed brown sugar
4	center-cut country ham slices (¼-pound each)

In a bowl stir the coffee and sugar together. In a large cast-iron skillet on medium heat fry the ham slices until they are brown on both sides. Remove the ham to a platter, reserving the drippings in the skillet. Add the coffee mixture to the hot drippings. Stir to loosen the particles from the bottom of the skillet. Bring to a boil and allow the mixture to boil, stirring occasionally, until the liquid is reduced by about half. Pour the redeye gravy over the ham to serve.

YIELD: 4 SERVINGS

Fried Pork Chops

6	(5 to 6-ounce) center-cut pork chops
1	to 1½ cups all-purpose flour
	Salt and pepper
¼	cup vegetable oil

Wash the pork chops in water. On a dish combine the flour and salt and pepper to taste. Dredge the pork chops in the flour mixture. Pour enough cooking oil in a large, heavy skillet to cover the bottom, and turn the heat to medium. Place the pork chops in the skillet. Do not crowd. Cook until the red juices are showing on the top side. Turn them over and add a little more oil, if necessary, to prevent sticking. Cook for 8 to 10 minutes or until golden brown.

To make gravy after cooking the pork chops, add ¼ cup water and 3 tablespoons flour to the drippings. Cook over medium to high heat while stirring to bring to the consistency of gravy. If too thick, add a little more water. If too thin, add a little more flour. Turn the heat to medium and cook for 10 to 15 minutes.

Hint: The gravy can be served as a side dish with the pork chops, or the pork chops can be returned to the skillet and covered with the gravy.

YIELD: 6 SERVINGS

Fresh Ham

1	(8 to 10-pound) fresh ham
1	cup water
	Salt and pepper

Preheat the oven to 375°. Place the ham on a roasting pan with the fat side down. Pour the water into the pan. Add the salt and pepper to taste. Cook the ham uncovered for 2½ to 3 hours until fully done. Slice and serve.

YIELD: ABOUT 25 SERVINGS

Grilled Ham

Grilled ham is a great meat served in hot biscuits. And that combination is wonderful when served with grits and eggs. This can be the beginning of a delicious sandwich too.

Vegetable oil
Desired amount of cooked ham, sliced (½-inch slices)

Coat the bottom of a heavy skillet with a small amount of oil. Place the ham in the skillet and turn the heat to medium. Cook the ham until it is brown on one side; turn it over and brown on the other side. If the ham begins to stick, add a small amount of oil. Serve with grits and eggs.

YIELD: DEPENDS ON THE AMOUNT OF HAM

Ham and Cheese Pie

This is a delicious dish to serve at a brunch or ladies' luncheon. It is wonderful with the addition of a few slices of melon on the plate. This dish is perfect to serve during the holidays since it can be prepared ahead of time. While it is baking, you can visit with family or friends.

1	plus 1 cups shredded cheddar cheese
1	(9-inch) uncooked deep-dish piecrust
¾	plus ¾ cup cooked ham, chopped
⅓	cup all-purpose flour
¼	teaspoon pepper

1	cup milk
4	eggs

Preheat the oven to 350°. Sprinkle 1 cup of the cheese in the bottom of the pastry shell. Sprinkle ¾ cup of the ham on top of the cheese. Repeat the layers with the remaining 1 cup cheese and ¾ cup ham. In a medium-size bowl combine the flour and pepper. Gradually stir in the milk. Add the eggs, one at a time, beating the mixture well after each egg. Pour the egg mixture over the ham and cheese. Bake for 55 to 60 minutes.

YIELD: 6 TO 10 SERVINGS

Hawaiian Grilled Ham

¼	cup pineapple juice
¼	cup firmly packed light brown sugar
¼	cup (½ stick) butter
6	(5 or 6-ounce) slices cooked ham
6	pineapple rings, fresh or canned
6	maraschino cherries, whole with stems

In a small saucepan on medium heat combine the pineapple juice, brown sugar, and butter. Stir often until the sugar dissolves and the mixture thickens. Place the ham slices side by side in a heavy skillet and turn to medium heat. Coat each piece of ham with some of the sugar glaze. Cook until the glaze begins to bubble in the skillet. Turn the ham slices over and place a pineapple ring and cherry on top of each slice. Pour the remaining glaze over the ham. Cook for another 3 to 4 minutes. Remove from the heat and serve.

YIELD: 6 SERVINGS

Ham & Broccoli Noodle Casserole

Meat-based casseroles are deeply Southern—they are beautiful, unusual, complex, and tasty.

½	cup mayonnaise
2	cups broccoli florets, fresh or frozen
1	plus ½ cup grated sharp cheddar cheese
1	cup chopped cooked ham
1½	cups macaroni or corkscrew noodles, cooked and drained
2	tablespoons finely chopped green bell pepper
¼	cup milk
½	cup seasoned croutons

Preheat the oven to 350°. In a medium bowl mix together the mayonnaise, broccoli, 1 cup of the cheese, the ham, macaroni, bell pepper, and milk. Spoon the mixture into a 9 x 13-inch casserole dish. Sprinkle with the remaining ½ cup cheese and the croutons. Bake for 25 to 30 minutes until bubbly.

YIELD: 10 TO 12 SERVINGS

Hawaiian Pineapple Ham Steaks

I remember my mother making this dish when I was young and living in Buckhead before there were nightclubs, curfews, and road races. She was from the Boston area and this was a family recipe that became comfort food to me. With ingredients kept in your freezer and pantry, it can be made ahead, and then crowned as a culinary wonder. This dish is also a real "lip-smacking" pleaser at potlucks and family gatherings.

2	(1-pound) ham steaks, approximately ¼-inch thick
1	(8-ounce) can crushed pineapple, divided
1	(8-ounce) can pineapple chunks
½	cup packed dark brown sugar, divided
6	cloves
2	tablespoons butter

Preheat the oven to 350°. Cut each ham steak into two portions. Drain the juice from the crushed pineapple and the pineapple chunks, reserving the juice. Sprinkle 2 tablespoons of the reserved juice on the bottom of a 9 x 9-inch baking pan. Sprinkle with 2 tablespoons of the crushed pineapple and 2 tablespoons of the brown sugar. Cover this layer with ham steaks.

Repeat the layering until all the ham has been used, finishing with the remaining crushed pineapple and 4 to 6 teaspoons brown sugar. Sprinkle the cloves and pineapple chunks over the top layer. Then add enough of the reserved pineapple juice to come halfway up the ham. The ham will provide more juice during the cooking process. Dot the top with butter. (At this point, if you are not ready to cook, the dish can stand in the refrigerator for several hours.) Bake for 45 minutes.

YIELD: 2 TO 4 SERVINGS

Richard Sears
Atlanta, Georgia

Pineapple Ham

3½   cups cooked ham, cut into bite-size
      pieces
3   pounds cooked sweet potatoes, peeled
      and sliced
1   (15¼-ounce) can sliced pineapple,
      drained
¾   cup chopped pecans
½   cup raisins
¾   cup butter-flavored pancake syrup

Preheat the oven to 350°. Arrange the ham and potatoes alternately in a 3-quart baking dish. Cut the pineapple slices in half and arrange on top of the ham and potatoes. Sprinkle the pecans and raisins on top. Cover and bake for 15 minutes. Remove from the oven and pour the syrup on top. Return to the oven and bake, uncovered, for another 15 minutes or until bubbly and brown.

YIELD: 8 TO 10 SERVINGS

Pork Roast

1   (3 to 4-pound) Boston butt pork roast
½   teaspoon garlic salt
1   teaspoon black pepper
1   cup water

Preheat the oven to 375°. Place the pork roast in a roasting pan fat side down. Sprinkle with the garlic salt and pepper. Pour the water into the roasting pan. Cook 1½ to 2 hours or until done. The pork should be cooked completely through and not show any pink.

To make gravy, place the drippings from the cooked roast in a skillet over medium heat. Add enough flour to thicken. To stretch the gravy if the drippings are not sufficient, add a small amount of water or wine. Season the gravy with additional garlic salt and pepper. This is a rich gravy and a little goes a long way. It is good served over baked sweet potatoes with butter.

YIELD: 8 TO 12 SERVINGS

Pork Tenderloin

This recipe comes from Elton Wright, Blue Willow Inn's former business manager. It is a favorite of his and is a good example of how sweet and succulent pork can be.

1   (3-pound) pork tenderloin, cut in half
2   tablespoons yellow mustard
2   teaspoons dried thyme
1   teaspoon ground ginger
1   teaspoon salt
½   teaspoon minced garlic
½   teaspoon black pepper
½   cup port wine
¼   cup soy sauce
2   tablespoons vegetable oil
¼   cup currant jelly

Place the halved tenderloin in a rimmed pan barely big enough to hold it. In a small bowl mix together the mustard, thyme, ginger, salt, garlic, and black pepper. Spread the mixture over the tenderloin. In a mixing cup blend the port wine and soy sauce and pour over the tenderloin. Cover the tenderloin and refrigerate for 24 hours. Remove the tenderloin from the marinade, reserving the marinade. Heat the vegetable oil in a heavy skillet. Brown both sides of the tenderloin in the oil, beginning with the fat side.

Preheat the oven to 375°. Remove the tenderloin from the skillet, reserving the drippings, and place it on a roasting pan coated with nonstick vegetable oil. Combine the marinade with the reserved drippings and pour over the meat. Cook the meat, covered, for about 5 minutes per pound. Uncover and cook for an additional 7 minutes per pound until done. Combine the drippings from the roasting pan with the currant jelly. Serve as a condiment for the meat.

YIELD: 8 TO 10 SERVINGS

Roast Pork
with Spiced Cherry Sauce

1   (3 to 4-pound) boneless pork loin roast, rolled

1   teaspoon salt

1   teaspoon black pepper

1   teaspoon dried sage

1   (15-ounce) can pitted sour or tart red cherries

12   whole cloves

1   (3-inch) stick cinnamon

1½   cups granulated sugar

¼   cup white vinegar

¼   cup cornstarch

1   tablespoon lemon juice

1   tablespoon butter, melted

3   to 4 drops red food coloring (optional)

Preheat the oven to 325°. Sprinkle the roast with the salt, pepper, and sage. Place the roast fat side up on the rack of a shallow roasting pan. Bake for 1½ to 2 hours (30 to 35 minutes per pound).

Drain the cherries, reserving the liquid. Add enough water to the cherry liquid to equal ¾ cup. Tie the cloves and cinnamon in a cheesecloth bag. In a small saucepan on medium heat combine ½ cup of the cherry liquid with the spice bag. Bring to a boil. Reduce the heat to low and simmer, uncovered, for 10 minutes. Remove the spice bag. In a small mixing bowl combine the cornstarch and the remaining ¼ cup cherry liquid. Stir into the hot cherry liquid. Turn the heat to medium and cook for 1 minute, stirring constantly, until the mixture is thickened and bubbly. Stir in the cherries, lemon juice, butter, and food coloring if using. Serve over the roast pork.

YIELD: ABOUT 16 SERVINGS

Roast Pork Creole

¼   teaspoon salt

¼   teaspoon crushed red pepper

¼   teaspoon instant minced garlic

1   (3½-pound) pork loin

CREOLE SAUCE

½   cup chopped celery

½   cup chopped bell pepper

1   large onion, chopped

1   small garlic clove, chopped

1   tablespoon vegetable oil

1   tablespoon prepared mustard

9   (8-ounce) can tomato sauce

1   bay leaf

Preheat the oven to 325°. In a small bowl mix the salt, pepper, and garlic. Rub this mixture onto the pork loin. Place the pork loin in a roasting pan. Bake for 2 hours.

To prepare the **Creole sauce**, sauté the celery, bell pepper, onion, and garlic in the oil in a large skillet on medium heat until the vegetables are tender. Add the mustard, tomato sauce, and the bay leaf. Reduce the heat to low and simmer for 15 minutes.

After 2 hours of baking the pork loin, pour the hot Creole sauce over and around the meat. Continue to bake for approximately 40 minutes or until the roast is tender and is done. Remove the bay leaf. Slice and serve with the sauce.

YIELD: 10 SERVINGS

Sausage and Egg Casserole

This dish is a nice breakfast or brunch entrée that even the men will enjoy.

1   pound mild bulk sausage

1   pound hot bulk sausage

18   eggs

3   cups croutons, unseasoned, or toasted breadcrumbs

4   cups grated sharp cheddar cheese

6   cups milk

1   tablespoon salt

1   tablespoon prepared mustard

2   tablespoons Worcestershire sauce

1   (10¾-ounce) can condensed cream of mushroom soup

In a heavy skillet on medium heat cook the sausage. Drain thoroughly. In a large mixing bowl stir the eggs to break the yolks. Add the sausage, croutons, cheese, milk, salt, mustard, Worcestershire sauce, and mushroom soup. Stir, but do not beat. Cover and place in the refrigerator overnight to enhance the flavors.

When ready to serve, remove from the refrigerator. Preheat the oven to 350°. Pour the ingredients into a 3-quart casserole dish and cook for 45 to 50 minutes until firm.

YIELD: 16 SERVINGS

Jeannie Rushing
Warrenton, Georgia

Sausage and Gravy

Sausage and gravy is also known as Hoover gravy from the days of the Depression. This dish is a natural companion for hot biscuits and grits.

1   **pound pork sausage, cut into rounds**
1   **tablespoon all-purpose flour**
¾   **cup milk**
¼   **cup water**
      Salt and pepper

In an iron skillet over medium heat cook the sausage, turning once. Pour off all but 2 tablespoons of sausage drippings and any pieces of sausage from the skillet. Add the flour and stir with a fork or wire whisk until it has browned. Slowly stir in the milk and water. Cook until the desired thickness is reached. Season with the salt and pepper to taste. Serve the gravy in a gravy boat along with the cooked sausage.

YIELD: 4 TO 6 SERVINGS

Sugar-Cured Ham

Sugar-cured hams are fully cooked, and although it is not necessary to heat the ham when serving this meat as a main course, doing so brings out the full flavor of the ham.

1   **(15 to 18-pound) sugar-cured ham**

Preheat the oven to 350°. Place the ham on a roasting pan and cook for 1 to 1½ hours depending on the size of the ham. Serve hot.

Hint: When you've finished eating the ham, make sure you save the ham bone to season greens or beans. Old Southern cooks would almost kill for ham bones.

YIELD: ABOUT 3 SERVINGS PER POUND

Sausage Casserole

This was one of my mom's favorite recipes to bake when I was a child. I always looked forward to it because it contained sausage. I have baked this recipe for my family many, many times over the fifteen years that I have been married, and I look forward to passing it along in the future to my children and their spouses.

1   **pound bulk pork sausage**
1   **(10¾-ounce) can consommé**
1   **cup uncooked rice**
¼   **cup finely chopped onion**
      Salt and pepper
1   **cup water**

In a skillet on medium heat brown the sausage. Drain. Preheat the oven to 375°. In a mixing bowl combine the consommé, rice, onion, salt and pepper to taste, and water. Place in a 2-quart casserole dish. Cover with the sausage. Cover with foil. Bake for 45 minutes or until the liquid is absorbed.

YIELD: 6 TO 8 SERVINGS

Joanna Dykes
Snellville, Georgia

Shredded Potato & Ham Pie

4   eggs, lightly beaten
1   cup frozen mixed peas and carrots
1   cup chopped cooked ham
1   plus ¼ cups shredded cheddar cheese
½   cup milk
¼   cup chopped onion
2   medium potatoes, peeled and shredded
    Salt and pepper

Preheat the oven to 350°. In a large bowl combine the eggs, peas and carrots, ham, and 1 cup of the cheese. In a medium-size bowl combine the milk, onion, potatoes, the remaining ¼ cup cheese, and salt and pepper to taste. Press this potato mixture into the bottom and up the sides of an ungreased, 9-inch pie plate or 1½-quart baking dish. Pour the ham filling into the potato-lined pie plate. Bake for 45 to 50 minutes or until the center is set.

YIELD: 8 TO 10 SERVINGS

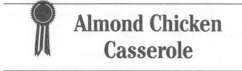

Almond Chicken Casserole

½   cup chopped onion
½   cup chopped celery
1   (8-ounce) can sliced water chestnuts, drained
1   (10¾-ounce) can condensed cream of mushroom soup
⅔   cup mayonnaise
2   cups coarsle chopped cooked chicken

TOPPING

1   (8-ounce) can crescent rolls
⅔   cup shredded Swiss cheese
½   cup slivered almonds
3   tablespoons butter

Preheat the oven to 375°. Put the onion and celery into a bowl and microwave on high for 2 minutes. In a medium-size saucepan on medium heat combine the onion, celery, water chestnuts, chicken soup, and mayonnaise. Cook this mixture until bubbly all the way through. This will blend the flavors. Add the chicken. Pour into a 9 x 13-inch casserole dish.

For the **topping**, unfold the crescent rolls and place on top of the casserole. Sprinkle with the cheese and then with the almonds. Melt the butter and drizzle on top. Bake for 25 minutes.

YIELD: 10 TO 12 SERVINGS

Nancy Morris
Covington, Georgia

First Place Winner, Meats and Main Dishes
Blue Willow Inn Restaurant Recipe Contest, 2004

Apricot Baked Chicken

1   whole chicken, cut into 8 pieces
1   (18-ounce) jar apricot preserves
1   (16-ounce) bottle Catalina French dressing
1   (1-ounce) package onion soup mix

Preheat the oven to 350°. Place the chicken pieces on a foiled-lined pan. In a small bowl mix the preserves, dressing, and soup mix. Pour this mixture over the chicken. Bake for 1 to 1½ hours.

YIELD: 4 SERVINGS

Lois Dalton
Covington, Georgia

Asparagus Chicken Casserole

Patsy Riley, the first lady of the state of Alabama, sends this recipe. There is never enough left of this casserole to have leftovers. This has been in my file for more than thirty years. Mary Frances Pruet gave it to me in 1965, the year our son Rob was born.

4   bone-in chicken breasts
2   to 3 cups cooked white rice
1   (15-ounce) can asparagus spears, undrained
    Medium white sauce

1½   cups cheddar cheese
1   cup slivered almonds
½   stick butter, melted

Boil the chicken until tender. I add a few dashes of garlic salt and a pat of butter to the water. Drain after cooking. When cool, pull the meat from the bones. Preheat the oven to 350°. Place the rice in a 9 x 13-inch casserole. Drain the asparagus, reserving the liquid. Place the asparagus and chicken pieces on top of the rice. Prepare a medium white sauce (page 136) using equal parts milk and reserved asparagus liquid. Pour the sauce over the rice, chicken, and asparagus. Top with the cheese and almonds. Pour the butter over the cheese and almonds and bake for 40 minutes or until the mixture bubbles and the almonds are golden brown.

YIELD: 6 TO 8 SERVINGS

Baked Chicken

1   whole chicken, cut into eight pieces
¼   cup butter, melted
    Salt and pepper

Preheat the oven to 350°. Remove the excess fat from the chicken and wash the pieces. Place the chicken pieces skin side up on a lightly buttered baking pan. Baste with the melted butter and season with the salt and pepper to taste. Bake uncovered for 45 to 50 minutes until golden brown.

YIELD: 4 SERVINGS

Blue Willow Chicken Casserole

This casserole appears regularly in the buffet room at the Blue Willow Inn. It was a gift to Billie from Becky Young, the wife of Kenneth Young, former pastor of the Monroe, Georgia, Church of God. Its multiple ingredients are bound together and infused with the flavors of canned soup. It is more distinctly Dixie due to the inclusion of crumbled Ritz crackers.

1	cup sour cream
1	(10¾-ounce) can condensed cream of chicken soup
1	(10¾-ounce) can condensed cream of mushroom soup
1	cup chicken broth
8	chicken breasts, cooked and boned
2	sleeves Ritz crackers, crumbled
1½	sticks butter, melted

Preheat the oven to 350°. In a medium-size mixing bowl blend together the sour cream, chicken soup, mushroom soup, and chicken broth. Place the chicken breasts in a 9 x 13-inch baking dish. Pour the soup mixture over the chicken. Top with the Ritz cracker crumbs and drizzle the butter over the crumbs. Bake for 35 to 40 minutes until the crackers are browned.

YIELD: 8 SERVINGS

Chicken and Rice

1	whole baking chicken with giblets
½	cup chopped celery
2	tablespoons butter
¼	cup sliced mushrooms
4	cups cooked rice
1	(10¾-ounce) can condensed cream of chicken soup
2	hard-cooked eggs, diced
¼	cup milk

Wash the chicken. In a stockpot on medium high heat, cover the chicken, including the giblets, with water and cook until done. Remove it from the broth, reserving ½ cup of the broth. Cool the chicken in cold water. Remove the bones, fat, and skin. Tear the chicken into bite-size pieces. Coarsely chop the giblets.

Preheat the oven to 350°. In a small skillet on medium heat sauté the celery in the butter. When the celery is almost tender, add the mushrooms and sauté. Combine the chicken, celery and mushrooms, cooked rice, the reserved chicken broth, chicken soup, eggs, and milk. Mix well. Pour the ingredients into a 9 x 13-inch baking dish and bake for 30 to 40 minutes.

Hint: The mixture should be almost too moist when placed in the oven, otherwise it will be too dry. For a better flavor, cook the rice in the chicken broth after you have boiled the chicken.

YIELD: 14 TO 16 SERVINGS

Chicken and Rice Casserole

"God giveth us all things richly to enjoy."

1   (10¾-ounce) can condensed cream of onion soup

1   (10¾-ounce) can condensed cream of celery soup

1   (10¾-ounce) can condensed cream of chicken soup

1½   soup cans milk

1   cup uncooked rice

8   chicken breast halves (or 1 whole chicken cut up)

3   ounces grated Parmesan cheese

1   small package slivered almonds

Preheat the oven to 275°. Butter a 9 x 13-inch baking dish generously. In a medium-size mixing bowl mix the onion soup, celery soup, chicken soup, and milk well. Pour half of this mixture into a small bowl. Add the rice to the bowl and stir to mix. Pour the rice and soup mixture into the baking dish. Place the chicken skin side up on top of the rice mixture. Pour the remaining half of the soup mixture over the chicken. Sprinkle with the cheese and almonds. Bake uncovered for 3 hours. The baking dish will be full but because of the slow baking, it will not overflow.

YIELD: 8 SERVINGS

Patsy Joiner
Snellville, Georgia

Chicken Casserole

1   (4 to 6-pound) chicken

1   (1-ounce) envelope onion soup mix

3   (10¾-ounce) cans chicken broth

1   (8-ounce) package Pepperidge Farm Stuffing Mix

1   (10¾-ounce) can condensed cream of chicken soup

Boil the chicken until it is tender. Cool the chicken and remove from the bones. Cut the chicken into bite-size pieces. Preheat the oven to 350°. In a large mixing bowl combine the soup mix and chicken broth. Spray a 9 x 13-inch pan with nonstick vegetable spray. Spread the stuffing mix on the bottom of the pan. Place the chicken pieces on the stuffing mix. Pour the broth mixture over the chicken. Bake for 45 minutes. Do not overbake.

YIELD: 8 TO 12 SERVINGS

POPULAR SOUTHERN SAYING

Well, butter my butt and call me a biscuit!

Chicken and Dressing Casserole

This casserole is just right when you are craving chicken and dressing, but do not want to go to the trouble of roasting a chicken and making dressing. It is great served with cranberry sauce. I don't recall where the recipe originated, but it has been in our family for twenty-five years or more. My mother-in-law, Cornelia, who cooked for her family until she was ninety-six years old, often prepared it for Sunday dinner. In 1994, when she was ninety years old, she was featured in a major newspaper in the Atlanta area as one of Georgia's cooks.

1	whole chicken
½	cup (1 stick) margarine
1	medium onion, chopped
1	(7-ounce) package dry dressing mix
1	(10¾-ounce) can condensed cream of chicken soup
1	(10¾-ounce) can condensed cream of celery soup

Boil the chicken and set aside to cool, reserving the broth. Remove the chicken from the bones. Preheat the oven to 350°. In a large skillet on medium heat melt the margarine. Sauté the onion in the margarine. Stir in the dressing mix. In a bowl combine the cream of chicken soup, cream of celery soup, and 1 cup of the reserved chicken broth. In a 3-quart casserole dish layer the ingredients in the following order: chicken, dressing mix, soup mixture, chicken, dressing mix, soup mixture. Top with the remaining dressing mix. Bake for 35 minutes.

YIELD: 12 SERVINGS

Rose Lewis
Covington, Georgia

Chicken Divine

This makes a wonderful party dish. It serves a number of guests and you would need only a salad or relish to complete the meal. It is a great way to use any leftover chicken, or turkey for that matter.

2	(10¾-ounce) cans condensed cream of chicken soup
¾	cup mayonnaise
⅔	cup milk
2½	plus ⅓ cups grated cheddar cheese
3	tablespoons concentrated lemon juice
1	tablespoon curry powder
3	pounds broccoli, cooked
3	pounds skinless, boneless chicken, cooked
2	cups crumbled Ritz crackers

Preheat the oven to 350°. In a large bowl combine the soup, mayonnaise, milk, 2½ cups of the cheese, lemon juice, and curry powder. Mix well but do not beat. Layer a casserole or baking pan with the broccoli, then the chicken. Spread the sauce mixture over the chicken. Add the cracker crumbs. Bake for 30 to 40 minutes. Remove from the oven and top with the remaining ⅓ cup cheese. Return to the oven only long enough for the cheese to melt.

YIELD: 10 TO 15 SERVINGS

Chicken Fry-Bake

This is an original recipe created many years ago by my mother, who now is almost ninety-two years old. Everyone who has tried it loves it. We serve it with rice, green beans, and a pear salad.

1½	cups all-purpose flour
	Salt and pepper
5	(8-ounce) split chicken breasts
	Vegetable oil
1	(10¾-ounce) can condensed cream of celery soup
½	soup can water
¼	cup minced onion
1	cup grated cheddar cheese

In a small bowl combine the flour and salt and pepper to taste. Lightly coat the chicken breasts in this mixture. In a large skillet on medium-high heat add 1 inch of oil and fry the chicken to a light golden brown. Preheat the oven to 300°. Place the chicken skin side up in a 9 x 13-inch baking dish. In a medium-size mixing bowl combine the soup, water, onion, and cheese. Pour this mixture over the chicken. Cover with foil and bake for 1½ hours.

YIELD: 10 SERVINGS

Sue Staples
Monroe, Georgia

Chicken Macaroni

4	cups diced cooked chicken
1	(8-ounce) package elbow macaroni, uncooked
2	cups grated cheddar cheese
2	(10¾-ounce) cans condensed cream of mushroom soup
½	cup milk
¼	cup diced green bell pepper
4	hard-cooked eggs, coarsely chopped
1	teaspoon salt
	Dash of pepper
1	(5-ounce) can sliced water chestnuts, drained
1	small minced onion

In a large mixing bowl combine the chicken, macaroni, cheese, soup, milk, bell pepper, eggs, salt, pepper, water chestnuts, and onion. Pour this mixture into a 9 x 13-inch casserole dish. Cover and set in the refrigerator 6 to 8 hours or overnight. Remove from the refrigerator 15 minutes before baking. Preheat the oven to 350°. Bake for 1 hour.

Hint: Turkey, tuna, shrimp, or crab can be substituted for the chicken.

YIELD: 8 TO 10 SERVINGS

Chicken Noodle Delight

This dish has become a family favorite and is a great dish to serve to guests.

1   (16-ounce) container sour cream
2   (10¾-ounce) cans condensed cream of chicken soup
4   cooked chicken breasts, diced
1   (16-ounce) package wide egg noodles, cooked
    Salt and pepper
2   sleeves Ritz crackers, crushed
1   stick butter, melted

Preheat the oven to 350°. In a large bowl mix the sour cream and soup. Add the diced chicken and cooked noodles. Add the salt and pepper to taste. Place in a greased 9 x 13-inch baking pan. Top with the crackers and butter. Cook for 30 minutes until hot and bubbly.

Hint: Fresh mushrooms or other vegetables can be added to this casserole if desired.

YIELD: 10 TO 12 SERVINGS

Chicken Pecan Pasta

6   (5 to 7-ounce) skinless, boneless chicken breasts
    Vegetable oil
¾   cup chopped onion
2   garlic cloves, minced
2   cups sliced fresh mushrooms
¼   cup (½ stick) butter (not margarine)
2   tablespoons all-purpose flour
2   tablespoons plus 1¾ cups half-and-half
2   tablespoons instant chicken bouillon granules dissolved in water according to package directions
¾   cup grated fresh Parmesan cheese
4   ounces softened cream cheese
1   (8-ounce) package angel hair pasta, cut into 3-inch pieces before cooking
1   cup chopped toasted pecans

In a large skillet on medium heat sauté the chicken breasts in vegetable oil or bake them in the oven at 350° until just done. Do not overcook. Allow the chicken to cool and then cut into pieces. In a large skillet on medium-low heat cook the onion, garlic, and mushrooms in the butter. In a small bowl blend the flour with 2 tablespoons of the half-and-half. Add this mixture to the vegetables. Add the remaining 1¾ cups half-and-half and the bouillon. Cook this mixture, stirring occasionally, until it is thick. Add the Parmesan cheese, cream cheese, and chicken. Cook the pasta al dente. Add the pasta to the chicken mixture and spoon into a 3-quart casserole dish. Preheat the oven to 350°. Cook the casserole until heated through. Sprinkle the chopped pecans on top just before serving.

YIELD: 6 SERVINGS

Chicken Pie
with Sweet Potato Crust

SWEET POTATO CRUST

1	cup sifted all-purpose flour
1	teaspoon baking powder
½	teaspoon salt
1	cup cold, mashed sweet potatoes
⅓	cup butter, melted
1	egg, well-beaten

CHICKEN PIE

3	cups cooked and diced chicken
1	cup cooked and diced carrots
1	medium onion, chopped
1	tablespoon chopped fresh parsley
1	cup evaporated milk
1	cup chicken broth
2	tablespoons all-purpose flour
1	teaspoon salt
⅛	teaspoon pepper

For the **Sweet Potato Crust**, sift the flour, baking powder, and salt together in a medium-size bowl. Work the mashed sweet potatoes, butter, and egg into the flour mixture. This should form a dough-like mixture. Roll out on a floured board to a ¼-inch thickness.

Preheat the oven to 350°. For the **chicken pie**, in a 2-quart casserole dish arrange the chicken, carrots, onion, and parsley. In a saucepan on low heat combine the milk and chicken broth. Slowly add the flour and blend well with a whisk. Continue to cook, stirring constantly, until the mixture thickens. Add the salt and pepper. Pour this mixture over the chicken and vegetables in the casserole dish. Cover with the sweet potato crust. Crimp the edges and make slits in the top. Bake for 45 to 55 minutes.

YIELD: 6 TO 8 SERVINGS

Chicken Pot Pie

1	(15-ounce) can early June peas, drained
1½	cups shredded cooked chicken
½	cup cooked, diced potatoes
½	cup cooked, chopped celery
½	cup sliced carrots
¾	cup chicken broth
1	(10¾-ounce) can condensed cream of chicken soup
	Salt and pepper
	Pastry crust

PASTRY CRUST

1	cup all-purpose flour
½	teaspoon salt
⅓	cup shortening
3	tablespoons cold water

Preheat the oven to 350°. In a large mixing bowl mix the peas, chicken, potatoes, celery, carrots, chicken broth, soup, and the salt and pepper to taste. Pour the chicken mixture into a lightly greased 9 x 13-inch casserole dish. Top with the pastry crust. Cut slits in the pastry so the steam can escape. Cook for 30 to 40 minutes or until the top is a golden brown and the pie is bubbly.

For the **pastry crust**, combine the flour and salt in a medium-size mixing bowl. Cut in the shortening with a pastry blender until the mixture resembles coarse meal. Sprinkle cold water on the surface and stir with a fork until all the dry ingredients are moistened. Shape into a ball. Place in the refrigerator to chill. Roll the pastry out to fit the top of the casserole dish to about ¼-inch thickness.

YIELD: 6 TO 8 SERVINGS

Chicken Tetrazzini

Though named for the internationally famous, Victorian-era, Italian coloratura soprano Luisa Tetrazzini, this dish reassures eaters around the globe. It combines those two mainstays of comfort food—chicken and noodles. In the South, two others are added— creamed soup and Cheez Whiz.

1	(8-ounce) package vermicelli (spaghetti) noodles
1	quart chicken broth
¼	cup coarsely chopped green peppers
¼	cup coarsely chopped onions
½	cup sliced mushrooms
1	heaping tablespoon pimientos
¼	cup chopped black olives
3	tablespoons butter
⅛	tablespoon garlic powder
1½	cups chopped cooked chicken
½	cup milk

¼   cup Cheez Whiz

1   (10¾-ounce) can condensed cream of chicken soup

½   plus ¼ cup grated cheddar cheese

Cook the vermicelli noodles in the chicken broth according to package directions. Drain. Preheat the oven to 350°. In a small skillet on medium-low heat sauté the peppers, onions, mushrooms, pimientos, and black olives in the butter. In a large mixing bowl combine the noodles, sautéed vegetables, garlic powder, chicken, milk, Cheez Whiz, soup, and ½ cup of the grated cheese. Mix well. Pour the ingredients into a 10 x 13-inch casserole dish. Bake for 30 to 40 minutes until bubbly. Top with the remaining ¼ cup grated cheese and return to the oven just long enough to melt the cheese.

Hint: Upon completion of cooking, the dish should be moist, not dry.

YIELD: 12 SERVINGS

POPULAR SOUTHERN SAYING

This is gooder'n grits. (Good, really good!)

Chicken Spectacular

This is an easy dish that looks impressive and tastes like a lot of effort was required.

3   cups chopped cooked white chicken meat

1   small chopped onion

¾   cup mayonnaise

1   (6-ounce) package Uncle Ben's wild and white rice, prepared

1   (2-ounce) jar pimientos, drained

1   (10¾-ounce) can condensed cream of celery or cream of chicken soup

1   (15-ounce) can French-style green beans, drained

1   (8-ounce) can water chestnuts, drained and diced

1   cup grated cheddar cheese
Salt and pepper

1   cup crushed cheddar crackers

Preheat the oven to 350°. In a large mixing bowl mix the chicken, onion, mayonnaise, rice, pimientos, soup, green beans, water chestnuts, cheese, and salt and pepper to taste. Place in a 9 x 13-inch baking dish. Sprinkle with the crackers. Bake for 30 minutes.

YIELD: 10 SERVINGS

Cherie Powell
Newborn, Georgia

Fried Chicken Livers

Vegetable oil
2 cups water
Chicken livers
1 to 2 cups all-purpose flour
Salt and pepper

In a large, deep skillet heat enough oil on medium-high heat to cover the bottom of the skillet about ¼ inch deep. Wash the chicken livers, place them in a medium-size bowl, and cover them with the water. In a small mixing bowl combine the flour and the salt and pepper to taste. Remove the chicken livers from the water, one at a time, shaking the excess water from the liver. Dredge the livers in the flour mixture and place them one at a time in the hot oil. Gently stir frequently while cooking. Cook for 4 to 6 minutes or until the livers are a golden brown, turning once. When the livers are done, remove them from the oil and drain on paper towels.

Hint: Chicken livers tend to pop grease when cooked. If you have a skillet screen, place it over the pan to prevent popping grease from burning you.

YIELD: DEPENDS ON THE NUMBER OF LIVERS COOKED

Grilled Lemon Pepper Chicken

This is an easy and delicious recipe that our former manager of the Blue Willow gift shop, Sandi McClain, gave us. Sandi also decorated Blue Willow's Magnolia Hall Catering Facility, and at a ladies' luncheon and fashion show there the recipe was a big hit and has been served often since.

6 (4-ounce) skinless boneless chicken breasts
¾ cup all-purpose flour
½ cup (1 stick) butter
Lemon pepper
½ tablespoon lemon juice

Rinse the chicken breasts and pound them two to three times with a meat mallet. Dredge the chicken in the flour. In a large, heavy skillet melt the butter. Place the chicken breasts in the skillet and sprinkle generously with lemon pepper. Cook over medium heat for 6 minutes. Turn the chicken to the other side and sprinkle again with the lemon pepper. Cook for 6 minutes. When the chicken has cooked on both sides, turn the skillet down to low heat and add the lemon juice. Cook for an additional 5 minutes.

YIELD: 6 SERVINGS

Martha Washington's Turkey Potpie

From the City Tavern Cookbook *(© 1999 by Walter Staib, Running Press Book Publishing, Philidelphia & London). The City Tavern is Louis and Billie's favorite restaurant in Pennsylvania and the Martha Washington's Turkey Potpie is indescribably delicious—it truly is a "to die for" item.*

½ cup vegetable oil
3 sprigs fresh thyme, chopped (about 1 tablespoon), divided

½   bunch fresh parsley, chopped (about 3 tablespoons), divided

1   medium shallot, chopped, divided

4   garlic cloves, chopped, divided

1   whole turkey (8 to 10 pounds)

1   large white onion, diced

4   celery ribs, diced

2   large carrots, diced

1   cup dry white wine

4   cups (1 quart) chicken stock

1   cup shelled fresh peas

1   cup sliced button mushrooms

1   cup chopped red skinned potatoes

2   cups heavy cream
    Salt and freshly ground black pepper

½   cup (1 stick) unsalted butter, softened

½   cup all-purpose flour

3   pounds purchased puff pastry

1   egg, lightly beaten with 1 teaspoon water

In a small bowl mix together the oil and 1½ teaspoons each of the thyme, parsley, shallot, and garlic. Reserve the remaining herbs for later use. Rub the oil seasoning mixture all over the turkey. Place the turkey on a tray, cover with plastic wrap, and refrigerate overnight. Preheat the oven to 450°. Place the turkey on a rack in a large roasting pan. Reduce the oven to 350° and roast the turkey for about 2½ hours or until a meat thermometer inserted into the thigh reads 185°.

Remove the turkey from the oven and let cool thoroughly. Remove the skin and the meat from the bones. Cut the turkey meat into 1-inch pieces and reserve. Discard the skin and bones. Preheat the oven to 350°. Discard the pan drippings in the roasting pan and place the pan on the stovetop. Add the onion, celery, and carrots and sauté over medium heat for 3 minutes until tender. Add the wine to deglaze the pan, loosening any browned bits on the bottom of the pan with a wooden spoon. Add the chicken stock, peas, mushrooms, and potatoes. Bring to a boil over medium heat. Add the heavy cream and the reserved thyme, parsley, shallot, and garlic. Season with salt and pepper to taste.

Bring to a boil over high heat and add the turkey meat. Bring back to a boil. Reduce the heat and simmer about 5 minutes until the ingredients are fully cooked. In a small bowl combine the butter and flour into a paste. Slowly stir the butter-flour mixture into the turkey mixture until it is combined and the mixture is thickened. Ladle the turkey mixture into a large ovenproof dish or eight (14 to 16-ounce) individual casserole dishes. Cover with the puff pastry, allowing a 1-inch overhang. Crimp the pastry to the edge of the dish.

Reheat the oven to 350°. Using a fork, gently prick the pastry to allow steam to escape, being careful not to break the dough. Gently brush the egg mixture over the surface of the puff pastry. Bake for 12 to 15 minutes until the pastry edges are brown.

YIELD: 8 SERVINGS

Mama's Fried Chicken

This recipe comes to us from Patsy Riley, first lady of the state of Alabama. She says she is dedicating the recipe to her three daughters. It promises to "catch a man." If he doesn't take this bait, he's not worth having. Good luck, girls.

8   (6 to 8-ounce) skinless, boneless chicken breasts or strips
2   eggs
1   quart (4 cups) buttermilk
6   cups self-rising flour
1   bottle vegetable oil
     Salt

Wash the chicken. In a large bowl beat the eggs. Add the buttermilk and blend. Add the chicken to the milk mixture and marinate for 30 minutes. Roll the chicken one piece at a time in the flour. Pour the oil in a large skillet and place on medium heat. Fry in the hot oil until the chicken is golden brown. Salt to taste.

Hint: Mrs. Riley uses a Fry Daddy; she finds it works best.

YIELD: 8 SERVINGS

Poppy Seed Chicken

8   skinless, boneless chicken breasts
10   ounces sour cream
2   (10¾-ounce) cans condensed cream of chicken soup
2   (10¾-ounce) cans condensed cream of mushroom soup
2   sleeves Townhouse crackers, crumbled
3   sticks butter, melted
3   tablespoons poppy seeds

Preheat the oven to 400°. Boil and cube the chicken. In a bowl combine the sour cream, chicken soup, and mushroom soup. Mix well. Add the chicken and mix. Pour this mixture into a 3 to 4-quart casserole dish. In another bowl mix the crumbled crackers and butter. Spread this mixture over the top of the casserole. Sprinkle the poppy seeds on top. Cover with foil (to keep the crackers from burning) and bake for 25 minutes. Remove the foil and bake another 15 to 20 minutes or until the chicken mixture bubbles around the edges. Serve over rice.

YIELD: 8 TO 10 SERVINGS

Jo Ann Abreo
Social Circle, Georgia

Oven-Fried Chicken

My mother was a wonderful cook and I'm blessed to have many of her old recipes. She's been gone for many years, but I've picked up her cooking habits, which, not surprisingly, were quite similar to those of my maternal grandmother and are now being imitated by my grown children. Perhaps there's hope that home cooking will not become a lost art. The following is a recipe that I'm copying from Mother's own handwriting, but when I pass it on, I explain that I use choice pieces of chicken such as breasts, legs and thighs. This chicken looks and tastes like it has been fried in a skillet—brown and crispy.

2 tablespoons butter

¾ cup all-purpose flour

1 tablespoon parsley flakes

2 teaspoons paprika

1 teaspoon salt

1 teaspoon thyme or oregano

1 whole chicken cut into pieces

Preheat the oven to 425°. Melt the butter in a 9 x 13-inch baking dish. In a medium bowl mix the flour with the parsley flakes, paprika, salt, and thyme. Dredge the chicken pieces in this mixture. Place in the prepared baking dish. Bake for about 35 minutes. Turn and cook for about 15 minutes or so until fork tender.

YIELD: 4 TO 6 SERVINGS

Marilyn Miller

Somerset, Kentucky

Orange-Pecan Glazed Chicken and Wild Rice

Mother's Day is an extra special occasion at the Blue Willow Inn, and this is one dish that is always available on the Mother's Day buffet. Billie says it's a good dish for any special occasion or holiday meal and the women love it.

1 (6-ounce) package Uncle Ben's Long Grain & Wild Rice

Chicken broth as needed

1 (4 to 5-pound) chicken, cut into 8 pieces

3 plus 1 tablespoons (½ stick) butter, melted

Salt and pepper

½ cup orange marmalade

¼ cup frozen orange juice concentrate

1 teaspoon cornstarch

½ cup chopped pecans

Cook the rice according to the package directions, using chicken broth instead of water. Preheat the oven to 350°. Place the chicken pieces on a baking pan. Baste with 3 tablespoons of the butter and season to taste with the salt and pepper. Bake the chicken for 25 to 30 minutes. In a saucepan on medium heat combine the remaining 1 tablespoon butter, marmalade, and orange juice concentrate. Bring to a boil. In a small bowl or cup dissolve the cornstarch in a small amount of water. Slowly stir in enough of the cornstarch mixture to thicken the butter mixture. Add the pecans. Place the cooked rice in 9 x 13-inch casserole dish. Arrange the baked chicken pieces on top of the rice. Pour the orange-pecan glaze over the chicken. Return to the oven and cook for 12 to 15 minutes or until the glaze begins to brown.

Hint: Cornish game hens can be substituted for the chicken in this festive recipe. Simply cut in half lengthwise or cook them whole.

YIELD: 6 TO 8 SERVINGS

Pecan-Encrusted Chicken

1   cup finely grated pecans plus 3 or 4 pecan halves

1   plus 1 cups all-purpose flour

1   egg

2   cups water

3   (8-ounce) boneless, skinless chicken breasts

     Vegetable oil

3¾   tablespoons butter

2   ounces bourbon

4   ounces honey

In a small bowl mix the grated pecans with 1 cup of the flour. In a small bowl, beat the egg and mix in the 2 cups water. Place the remaining 1 cup flour in a bowl and lightly dredge the chicken breasts in the flour. Dip the chicken in the egg wash and then thoroughly cover with the pecan mixture. In a large skillet on medium-high heat put enough cooking oil to cover the bottom of the skillet. After the oil is heated, fry the pecan-covered chicken until it is a golden brown. Remove from the heat and place in a serving dish or on a serving platter. In a small saucepan on medium heat melt the butter and add the pecan halves. When the saucepan is hot, add the bourbon. After the bourbon comes to a rapid boil, add the honey. Turn the heat to low and continue to cook until the sauce is smooth and pourable. Pour over the chicken breasts.

YIELD: 6 SERVINGS

Roast Turkey

The traditional holiday turkey of the South is served with Corn Bread Dressing and Giblet Gravy (page 137). After Thanksgiving, it is a Southern tradition to use the chilled leftover turkey to make a wonderful turkey sandwich—white bread, plenty of mayonnaise, and cold turkey.

1   (12 to 14-pound) tom turkey

¼   cup butter, melted

1   teaspoon salt

½   teaspoon pepper

1   cup water

Preheat the oven to 350°. Remove the giblets and the neck from the cavity and save for the giblet gravy. Rinse the turkey with cold water. Place in a large roasting pan. In a small mixing bowl combine the butter, salt, and pepper. Pour this mixture over the turkey. Pour 1 cup water in the base of the roasting pan. Bake the turkey for 3 to 4 hours or until fully cooked. Reserve the pan drippings for giblet gravy.

Hint: Since most turkeys today are sold frozen, allow turkey to thaw 2 to 3 days in the refrigerator before cooking.

YIELD: 10 TO 12 SERVINGS

Southern Fried Chicken

Since Louis is a fried chicken fanatic, he was somewhat fussy about the recipe he developed for the fried chicken at Blue Willow Inn. It is a simple recipe, but it works. It is a grand and true Southern fried chicken, nearly greaseless, but with a well-spiced crust that has a luscious texture, shattering at first bite and infusing the meat with flavor. It is one dish that is always served on the hot buffet for every meal at the Blue Willow Inn and referred to as "to-die-for fried chicken" by Savannah Magazine.

1	whole chicken, cut into 8 pieces
1	quart (4 cups) water
1½	cups all-purpose flour
½	teaspoon salt
½	teaspoon black pepper
	Vegetable oil

Wash the chicken thoroughly and remove the excess fat. Place the chicken in a large bowl and cover it with the water. Allow the chicken to sit in the water for 3 to 4 minutes. In a bowl mix the flour, salt, and pepper. Remove the chicken from the water, shaking off only part of the water since the chicken should remain moist. Dredge the chicken in the flour mixture. In a large, deep, heavy skillet, on medium-high heat, add enough oil to cover the chicken. Place the chicken in the hot oil, and cook uncovered. Make sure the hot oil covers the chicken. Do not crowd the chicken pieces in the oil. Turn once to cook and brown the other side. When the chicken pieces are golden brown, remove them from the oil and drain on paper towels.

YIELD: 4 TO 8 SERVINGS

Stuffed Chicken Breast

Peggy Hawkins, our events manger at Magnolia Hall for various events, uses this recipe. It is time consuming to make, but is always well received.

4	(8-ounce) chicken breasts, boned
4	cups herb stuffing mix
4	to 5 tablespoons water
3	tablespoons finely chopped onion
¼	cup (½ stick) butter, melted
¼	teaspoon salt
¼	teaspoon pepper
½	teaspoon poultry seasoning
2	tablespoons butter
½	teaspoon dried sage
½	teaspoon dried thyme
1	(10¾-ounce) can condensed cream of mushroom soup

Preheat the oven to 350°. Lay each breast flat. In a medium-size mixing bowl thoroughly combine the stuffing mix, water, onion, melted butter, salt, pepper, poultry seasoning, butter, sage, and thyme. Divide this mixture into four equal parts. Roll into balls. Place one ball of the stuffing mixture in the center of each chicken breast. Fold the sides around it and hold them in place with a toothpick. Place the chicken breasts toothpick side down in a greased 9 x 13-inch casserole dish. Cover with the soup. Cook for 1 hour. Cover with foil if the casserole gets too brown.

YIELD: 4 SERVINGS

Baked Flounder

4   (6 to 8-ounce) flounder fillets
¼   cup butter, melted
      Salt
½   teaspoon lemon pepper
      Sliced lemon
      Sliced almonds (optional)
      Fresh parsley sprig (optional)

Preheat the oven to 350°. Lightly butter the inside of a baking pan. Place the flounder fillets in the pan. Using a pastry brush, baste the flounder with the butter. Sprinkle with salt to taste and the lemon pepper. Bake for 12 to 15 minutes, depending on the thickness of the fillets. Remove from the oven and garnish with the lemon slices and almonds and parsley if using.

> Hint: For Baked Flounder Amandine, lightly toast slivered almonds and sprinkle them on top of the fillets before baking. Turbot fillets can be easily substituted for flounder.

YIELD: 4 SERVINGS

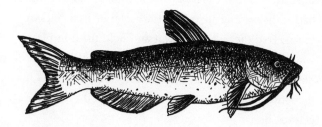

Catfish Stew

Billie's foster father, Marvin Exley, inspired the Van Dykes' recipe for catfish stew. Mr. Exley had a shack on Ebenezer Creek near Savannah and whenever the family visited, he made his stew from catfish caught there.

1   pound bacon
1½   pounds catfish fillets
1½   cups chopped onions
4   cups diced potatoes
2   (16-ounce) cans tomatoes
⅓   cup tomato paste
2   tablespoons Worcestershire sauce
      Salt and pepper

Fry the bacon until crispy and chop it into small pieces. Cut the catfish fillets into bite-size pieces. Remove the bacon and fry the fish and onions in the bacon grease until the fish are done and the onions are tender. In a large pot combine the potatoes, tomatoes, tomato paste, Worcestershire sauce, and salt and pepper to taste and bring to a boil. Cover the pot, reduce the heat, and simmer until the potatoes are tender. Add the fish, onions, bacon, and bacon grease to the mixture. Cover and simmer for another 20 minutes.

YIELD: 12 TO 14 SERVINGS

Crab Cakes

These are very tasty served with the Dijon sauce on page 133.

2	tablespoons butter or margarine
1	small onion, minced
3	celery ribs, diced
1	pound fresh lump crabmeat, drained
2	tablespoons minced fresh parsley
1	teaspoon minced fresh thyme
¼	teaspoon salt
¼	teaspoon pepper
1½	cups soft breadcrumbs
2	large eggs, lightly beaten
¼	cup vegetable oil

In a large skillet on medium heat melt the butter. Add the onion and sauté for 3 minutes. Stir in the celery. Turn the heat to low. Cover and cook for 5 minutes. Remove from the heat and set aside to cool. In a medium-size mixing bowl combine the crabmeat, onion mixture, parsley, thyme, salt, and pepper. Gently stir together. Stir in the breadcrumbs and eggs. Shape the crabmeat mixture into twenty-five 1½-inch patties. Place in a container and chill for at least 30 minutes. Heat the oil in a large skillet on medium-high heat. Cook the crab cakes in the hot oil for about 3 minutes on each side or until golden brown. Drain on paper towels.

YIELD: 6 TO 8 CRAB CAKES

Crab Casserole

1	cup mayonnaise
1	cup milk
3	cups toasted breadcrumbs
1	small onion, chopped
	Dash of Worcestershire sauce
	Dash of soy sauce
	Dash of Tabasco
	Dash of lemon juice
	Salt and pepper
	Paprika
	Parsley
1	pound crabmeat

In a large mixing bowl thoroughly combine the mayonnaise, milk, breadcrumbs, onion, Worcestershire sauce, soy sauce, Tabasco, lemon juice, and the salt, pepper, paprika, and parsley to taste. Add the crabmeat and mix thoroughly. Cover and refrigerate for several hours. Remove from the refrigerator 30 minutes prior to baking. Preheat the oven to 350°. Bake for 30 minutes.

YIELD: 6 TO 8 SERVINGS

Nada McDowell
Covington, Georgia

Crabmeat Casserole

12 ounces imitation crabmeat (Sea Legs brand)

1 (8-ounce) can sliced water chestnuts, drained

½ cup chopped onion

1 small green bell pepper, chopped

2 cups coarsely chopped celery

1 cup mayonnaise

4 hard-cooked eggs, sliced

½ teaspoon salt

½ teaspoon paprika

½ cup buttered breadcrumbs

Preheat the oven to 350°. In a large bowl combine the crabmeat, water chestnuts, onion, bell pepper, celery, mayonnaise, eggs, salt, and paprika. Mix lightly. Pour into a 9 x 13-inch casserole dish. Sprinkle the top with the breadcrumbs. Bake for 30 minutes or until golden brown and bubbly.

YIELD: 8 TO 10 SERVINGS

Fried Catfish

Fried catfish is best when served with slaw, French fries, hush puppies, grits, and a tall glass of sweetened iced tea.

6 (4 to 8-ounce) catfish fillets

1 gallon (16 cups) cold, salted water
Vegetable oil

2 cups plain cornmeal

½ teaspoon salt

Place the fish in a bowl of the salted water and allow them to sit for 10 to 15 minutes. Remove the fish from the water and blot off the excess water. Heat enough cooking oil in a large heavy skillet on medium-high heat to cover the fish. In a flat dish mix the cornmeal and salt to taste. Dredge the fish in the cornmeal. Place the fish in the oil and cook on each side for 6 to 10 minutes depending on the size of the catfish. Drain on paper towels.

YIELD: 6 SERVINGS

Mildred's Imperial Crab

My mother's family lived on the eastern shores of southern Delaware and southern Maryland. My mother loved to serve her mother's Imperial Crab recipe at special dinner parties for her family and friends. This entrée was always delicious and received many compliments every time she served this dish. Many members of her family are still serving Imperial Crab in their homes and still receiving rave reviews.

1 hard-cooked egg, minced and mashed into a paste

1 egg, lightly beaten

3 slices day-old white bread, finely crumbled

3 tablespoons minced pimiento

3 tablespoons minced green bell pepper, parboiled for 5 minutes

2 tablespoons minced fresh parsley

4 tablespoons Worcestershire sauce

4 tablespoons mayonnaise

2 tablespoons butter, melted

Salt and pepper

2 pounds back-fin crabmeat

6 glass crab shells

Paprika

Preheat the oven to 350°. In a large mixing bowl thoroughly combine the hard-cooked egg, beaten egg, bread, pimiento, bell pepper, parsley, Worcestershire sauce, mayonnaise, butter, and salt and pepper to taste. Gently fold in the crabmeat. Grease the crab shells with additional butter. Place the crab mixture in the shells and mound it high. Put a dollop of mayonnaise on the tops of the mounds. Sprinkle the tops with paprika. Bake for 30 minutes or until slightly brown on the tops.

YIELD: 6 SERVINGS

Bernice Wilson
Lawrenceville, Georgia

Pine-Bark Stew

Pine-Bark Stew is said to have originated when two French priests visited South Carolina and observed how the women ingeniously set up nets in the rivers to snag whatever fish were available and then added available vegetables and herbs to the pot. A piece of pine bark is said to have fallen in the stew, which the priests declared the best they had ever tasted. Thereafter, all stew had a bit of pine bark added to it. Today's version, just as appealing, omits the pine bark.

¾ cup diced celery

½ cup diced onion

½ cup diced green bell pepper

1¾ cups diced potatoes

3 quarts chicken stock

1½ teaspoons dried thyme

¾ teaspoon white pepper

¾ teaspoon salt

½ cup (1 stick) margarine, melted

¾ cup flour

12 ounces fish

8 ounces shrimp

8 ounces crab

1 cup scallops, chopped

8 ounces oysters

¾ cup sherry

In a large stockpot on medium heat simmer the celery, onion, bell pepper, potatoes, thyme, pepper, and salt in the chicken stock until the vegetables are done. Combine the melted margarine with the flour. Mix into the vegetables to thicken and simmer for 5 minutes. Add the fish, shrimp, crab, scallops, and oysters. Simmer for 10 minutes. Remove from the heat and stir in the sherry.

YIELD: ABOUT 20 SERVINGS

Salmon Croquettes

1   (14.75-ounce) can salmon packed in water
2   eggs
1   heaping tablespoon chopped onion
¼   cup all-purpose flour
     Cooking oil

In a medium-size mixing bowl combine the salmon, eggs, onion, and flour. Mix well. Roll the salmon mixture into balls about the size of golf balls. If the mixture seems too loose, add more flour and mix well. Pat into rounds about ½-inch thick. In a heavy skillet pour enough cooking oil to cover the bottom of the skillet. Cook the salmon patties on medium heat for 7 to 8 minutes on each side, adding oil when necessary to cover the bottom of the skillet. After the patties are done, remove them from the skillet and drain on paper towels.

YIELD: 3 SERVINGS

Savannah Shrimp and Rice

Savannah, Georgia, is where both Billie and Louis Van Dyke grew up and where they learned to eat and to cook. For the Friday night buffet at the Blue Willow Inn seafood is the order of the day. This deluxe dish is one of Billie's specialty recipes acquired from a neighbor years ago while living on Burnside Island in Savannah, Georgia.

1   small onion, chopped
1   small green bell pepper, chopped
1   tablespoon butter
2   pounds rice, cooked
1   pound shrimp, cooked, peeled and deveined
1   (10¾-ounce) can condensed cream of mushroom soup
¼   teaspoon curry powder
     Salt and pepper
½   cup grated cheddar cheese

Preheat the oven to 350°. In a small skillet on medium heat sauté the onion and the bell pepper in the butter. In a mixing bowl combine the onion and pepper with the rice, shrimp, mushroom soup, curry powder, and salt and pepper to taste. Mix well. Pour the shrimp mixture into a 9 x 13-inch baking dish. Bake for 25 to 30 minutes until bubbly. Remove from the oven and immediately sprinkle the cheese on top. Serve hot.

YIELD: 8 SERVINGS

Scalloped Oysters

1   pint oysters
2   cups cracker crumbs
½   cup (1 stick) butter, melted
1   teaspoon Worcestershire sauce
¼   teaspoon salt
½   cup milk

Preheat the oven to 350°. Layer the oysters and cracker crumbs in an ungreased 1½-quart baking dish beginning with oysters and ending with cracker crumbs. Dot each layer with the butter. Sprinkle the oysters with the Worcestershire sauce and salt. Pour the milk over the casserole and bake for 40 minutes.

YIELD: 4 TO 6 SERVINGS

Seafood Gumbo

Serve this delicious seafood coastal-classic gumbo over a bed of hot rice.

3 tablespoons butter
1 cup chopped celery
1 cup chopped onion
1 chopped green bell pepper
1 pound fresh or frozen okra
3 quarts water
2 (14.5-ounce) cans tomatoes
1 (12-ounce) can tomato sauce
   Salt and pepper
   Tabasco
2 pounds shelled and cleaned shrimp
1 pound crabmeat
1 pint raw oysters
   Cooked rice

In a large heavy skillet on medium heat melt the butter and sauté the celery, onion, and bell pepper until the onion is soft. Add the okra and continue to cook and stir until the okra is tender. In a 6-quart stockpot combine the water, tomatoes, tomato sauce, the salt and pepper to taste, and the Tabasco sauce to taste. Cook on medium heat for 30 minutes. Add the sautéed vegetables to the pot and continue to cook on low heat for two hours, stirring occasionally. Add the shrimp and cook for 15 more minutes. Add the crabmeat and oysters and cook for another 15 minutes. Serve over hot rice.

Hint: For a thicker gumbo, dissolve 1 to 2 teaspoons cornstarch in 1 tablespoon water. Add to the pot and stir to thicken.

YIELD: ABOUT 5 QUARTS

Seafood au Gratin

1½ plus ½ cups milk

½   cup Cheez Whiz

½   cup grated cheddar cheese

½   teaspoon salt

    Dash of black pepper

¼   cup all-purpose flour

1½ cups cooked and peeled shrimp

1   (8-ounce) can lump crabmeat

8   ounces cooked flounder or turbot

In a medium-size heavy saucepan on low heat mix 1½ cups of the milk with the Cheez Whiz, cheddar cheese, salt, and pepper. Cook, stirring constantly, until the cheese melts and the sauce simmers. In a small mixing bowl combine the flour with the remaining ½ cup milk. Stir until smooth. Stir this into the cheese mixture and continue to cook until it thickens. Simmer for 20 minutes, stirring constantly. Preheat the oven to 350°. In a mixing bowl combine the shrimp, crabmeat, and flounder. Stir to break apart the fish and the crabmeat. Transfer the seafood into a 2-quart casserole dish or au gratin dishes. Pour the cheese sauce over the seafood to cover. Bake for 20 to 25 minutes until the cheese begins to brown.

YIELD: 6 TO 8 SERVINGS

Shrimp & Wild Rice Casserole

My sister-in-law tried this recipe about fifteen years ago and told me that it was a hit at her dinner party. She was so right. This is the recipe I count on when I want to prepare something special. I have never served it without having to give the recipe to someone who enjoyed it. It is easy to prepare early in the day and refrigerate until time to bake. If I prepare it ahead, I do not add the shrimp until the rice mixture has heated. This prevents the shrimp from overcooking.

CREAM SAUCE

2   tablespoons butter

2   tablespoons flour

½   teaspoon salt

2   cups chicken broth

CASSEROLE

¼   cup thinly sliced onion

¼   cup thinly sliced green bell pepper

½   pound mushrooms, sliced

½   cup (1 stick) butter

1   tablespoon Worcestershire sauce

4   drops Tabasco

2   (6-ounce) boxes Uncle Ben's Wild Rice, cooked

2   cups thin cream sauce

1½ pounds shrimp, cooked

To prepare the **cream sauce**, in a small saucepan over medium heat melt the butter. Add the flour and salt, stirring as it begins to make a paste. Gradually add the chicken broth and allow the mixture to thicken.

Preheat the oven to 300°. For the **casserole**, in a large pan on medium heat sauté the onion, green pepper, and mushrooms in the butter. Add the Worcestershire sauce and Tabasco. Add the rice and cream sauce. Allow this mixture to heat through. Remove from the heat. Add the shrimp. Pour the mixture into a 3-quart casserole dish and bake for 30 to 45 minutes.

YIELD: 10 TO 12 SERVINGS

Ellen Hester
Monroe, Georgia

Southern Fried Oysters

1   cup self-rising cornmeal
1   cup self-rising flour
¼   teaspoon red hot pepper (optional)
2   eggs
2   tablespoons milk
24   ounces fresh select oysters, drained
      Vegetable oil

In a bowl combine cornmeal, flour, and red pepper if using, and mix well. In a separate bowl combine the eggs and milk, beating well with a fork. In a large deep skillet or fryer heat the oil to 375° degrees. Dip the oysters in the egg mixture and dredge them in the flour mixture. Drop the oysters in the oil one at a time and fry for 2 to 3 minutes until golden brown.

YIELD: 4 TO 6 SERVINGS

Tuna Casserole

Although this dish is not particularly Southern, and you probably won't find it on the buffet at the Blue Willow Inn, it is one of Louis' favorites and maybe yours too.

1   (6-ounce) can solid white tuna packed in water
1   (9-ounce) package seashell noodles, cooked and drained
1   (10¾-ounce) can condensed cream of mushroom soup
½   plus ½ cup grated cheddar cheese
½   teaspoon salt
25   Ritz crackers, crumbled

Preheat the oven to 350°. In a medium-size mixing bowl mix the tuna, noodles, soup, ½ cup of the cheese, and the salt together. Pour these ingredients into a 1½- quart casserole dish and bake for 30 minutes. Top with the cracker crumbs and the remaining ½ cup cheese. Return the casserole to the oven just long enough for the cheese topping to melt.

YIELD: 4 TO 6 SERVINGS

Fried Young Rabbit

1   young rabbit, cleaned and cut up
1   quart (4 cups) water
1½   cups all-purpose flour
½   teaspoon salt
½   teaspoon black pepper
     Vegetable oil

Thoroughly wash the rabbit pieces and place in a large bowl. Cover the rabbit with the water. Allow it to sit in the water for 3 to 4 minutes. In a bowl mix the flour, salt, and pepper. Remove the rabbit from the water, shaking off some of the water, keeping it moist. Dredge the rabbit in the flour mixture. Into a large, deep heavy skillet on medium-high heat, add enough oil to cover the rabbit pieces. Place the rabbit in the hot oil and cook uncovered. Make sure the hot oil covers the rabbit and do not crowd the pieces in the oil. Turn once to cook and brown the other side. When the rabbit pieces are golden brown, remove them from the oil and drain on paper towels.

YIELD: 4 TO 8 SERVINGS

Fried Squirrel

1   egg, beaten
½   cup milk
3   large squirrels, cleaned and cut up
     All-purpose flour
     Salt and Pepper
¼   cup vegetable oil

GRAVY

½   cup all-purpose flour
1½   cups sweet milk
     Salt and pepper

In a large mixing bowl combine the beaten egg and milk. Place the squirrel pieces in this mixture to soak for about 20 minutes. In a medium-size bowl combine the flour and salt and pepper to taste. Heat the vegetable oil in a large skillet on medium-high heat. Dredge the squirrel pieces in the flour mixture and place in the heated oil. Fry the squirrel until done. Remove from the pan, reserving the pan dripping for the gravy. Place on a serving platter.

For the **gravy**, stir the flour into the reserved pan drippings. Cook, stirring continuously over low heat, until the flour mixture is a golden brown. Slowly add the milk, stirring continuously. Add the salt and pepper to taste. Allow this mixture to cook, stirring occasionally, until it is thick and smooth. Pour over the squirrel.

YIELD: 6 SERVINGS

John Lowe's Quail

This recipe comes to us from John Lowe. John and his mother were very dear and faithful customers in the early days of Blue Willow Inn. Every so often there are customers who endear themselves to the entire staff, and we can truly make this statement concerning John and his mother. Serve with angel biscuits, cream gravy, baked sweet potatoes, plum or cherry preserves, and a green salad for a meal to be remembered.

6   quail breasts, split in half
2   cups buttermilk
2   cups all-purpose flour
    Thyme
    Black pepper
½   cup (1 stick) butter
3   medium apples, sliced

CREAMY GRAVY

1½ cups spring water
4   tablespoons white all-purpose flour
5   tablespoons drippings from quail recipe

Preheat the oven to 350°. Soak the quail breasts in the buttermilk. In a small bowl season the flour to taste with the thyme and black pepper. Put the soaked quail pieces in a sealed container with 2 cups of the seasoned flour and shake the pieces. Melt the butter in a skillet and brown the quail breasts (215°). (Reserve the drippings for the gravy.) Place the browned quail breasts on top of the apple slices in an uncovered, lightly greased baking pan. Bake for 30 minutes.

For the **creamy gravy**, put the spring water and flour in a container with a tight top so that it can be shaken vigorously. Shake until the mixture is foamy and then shake again just before pouring it into the skillet with the drippings. Turn the heat on medium-high and continually stir the mixture with a straight edge spatula until it has boiled about 1½ minutes or the desired thickness is attained. Pour over the quail just before serving.

Hint: To make real brown gravy, brown the flour in the oven before mixing.

YIELD: 4 TO 6 SERVINGS (2 TO 3 SPLIT BREASTS PER SERVING)

Roast Leg of Lamb with Mint Sauce

MINT SAUCE

¼   cup water
1   tablespoon granulated sugar
¼   cup finely chopped fresh mint
½   cup malt vinegar

LAMB

2   tablespoons salt
1   tablespoon black pepper
1   tablespoon finely chopped fresh rosemary (or 2 teaspoon dried)
2   garlic cloves, crushed
4   to 5 pound leg of lamb

Make the **mint sauce** first. In a saucepan over high heat combine the water and sugar and bring to a boil, stirring until the sugar completely dissolves. Remove from the heat and stir in the mint leaves and vinegar. Adjust the sugar to your taste. Let the mint sauce sit at room temperature for 2 to 3 hours.

Preheat the oven to 500°. For the **lamb**, combine the salt, pepper, rosemary, and garlic and stir to form a paste. Using a small knife, cut slits in the lamb and fill with the garlic paste. Transfer the lamb to a rack in a roasting pan. Roast for 15 minutes. Reduce the oven temperature to 375° and roast for 1 hour longer (about 20 minutes per pound). Transfer the lamb to a heated platter and allow it to rest for at least 15 minutes before slicing. Stir the mint sauce and serve in a sauceboat along with the lamb.

YIELD: 15 TO 20 SERVINGS

Sautéed Quail

8	quail breasts halves
¾	cup plus 1 tablespoon all-purpose flour
	Salt and pepper
½	cup (1 stick) butter
½	cup chicken broth
¼	cup chopped parsley for garnish

Coat the quail with ¾ cup of the flour and sprinkle with the salt and pepper to taste. Melt the butter in a frying pan over medium heat. Place the quail in the frying pan and brown well, turning often. Add the chicken broth. Cover the pan and cook the quail about 15 minutes. Put the quail on a hot platter. Add the remaining 1 tablespoon flour to the pan juices and cook until thickened. Pour the gravy over the quail and sprinkle with the parsley.

Hint: A little white wine can be added along with the chicken broth.

YIELD: 3 TO 4 SERVINGS

Stuffed Wild Goose

1	(4 to 4½-pound) dressed wild goose
½	teaspoon salt
⅛	teaspoon pepper
6	slices bacon
¼	cup chopped green bell pepper
1	cup sliced green onions
¼	cup chopped celery
2	(8-ounce) packages herb stuffing mix
2½	cups water
2	tablespoons butter, melted
1	egg, lightly beaten

Preheat the oven to 350°. Remove the giblets and neck from the goose. Rinse the goose in cold water and pat it dry. Sprinkle the inside cavity of the goose with the salt and pepper. In a large skillet on medium-high heat, cook the bacon until it is crisp. Remove the bacon and reserve the drippings. Sauté the bell pepper, green onions, and celery in the drippings until they are tender. In a medium-size bowl combine the stuffing mix, water, butter, egg, and the pepper, onion, and celery mixture. Stir well. Spoon this mixture into the goose cavity. Close the cavity with skewers and truss the goose. Place the goose on a roasting pan, breast side up. Bake for 1 to 2 hours until done.

YIELD: 4 TO 6 SERVINGS

Venison Stew

1½ pounds venison steak
2   tablespoons all-purpose flour
    Salt and pepper
2   tablespoons vegetable oil
½   cup chopped onion
½   cup chopped celery
2   (28-ounce) cans diced tomatoes, not drained
1   teaspoon granulated sugar
½   teaspoon dried rosemary
½   teaspoon dried basil
1   teaspoon salt
½   teaspoon pepper
2   medium carrots, diced
2   medium potatoes, diced

Cut the venison into ½-inch cubes. In a small bowl combine the flour with salt and pepper to taste. Coat the venison with the flour mixture. In a Dutch oven on medium-high heat brown the venison in the hot oil. Add the onion and celery and cook until tender. Add the tomatoes, sugar, rosemary, basil, salt, and pepper. Reduce the heat to low, cover, and simmer for 30 minutes. Remove the cover and add the carrots. Cook uncovered for 30 minutes. Add the potatoes and cook for another 30 minutes or until the vegetables and venison are tender.

YIELD: 6 TO 8 SERVINGS

Desserts & Sweets

Some things never change. Dessert has always played an important role on the Southern table. Sunday dinners would often have sideboards laden with cakes, pies, puddings, cobblers, and pastries. Ask the average man what he prefers for dessert and he will answer, "Pie." Pie is often called the American dessert—and it is usually apple!

Aunt France's Brownie Recipe

¾   cup all-purpose flour

½   teaspoon baking powder

¼   teaspoon salt

1   cup granulated sugar

2   eggs, lightly beaten

⅓   cup butter, melted

2   squares semisweet chocolate, melted

½   cup chopped pecans

1   teaspoon vanilla or almond flavoring

Preheat the oven to 350°. Sift together the flour, baking powder, salt, and sugar. Add the eggs, butter, and chocolate. Add the pecans and vanilla or almond flavoring. Stir with a wooden spoon until the ingredients are mixed, but do not overmix. Pour into a greased 8 x 8-inch baking pan. Bake for 20 minutes. Turn off the heat before the brownies are done and let them settle a few minutes before removing them from the oven. Set aside to cool completely before cutting.

YIELD: 16 SERVINGS

Babe's Brownie Stuff

My family members are native Georgians and my immediate family members are Atlanta natives. We enjoy our "little bite of something sweet" at the end of a meal. My grandmother, who well into her 80s still fixed that big noon meal, always said, "I'm so full, but I could use a little bite of something sweet." My mother came up with

this recipe about 40 years ago and dished up and served it in pretty individual cut-glass dishes. This recipe surely fits the bill for that "little bite."

1   (21-ounce) package brownie mix

1½   cups chopped pecans or walnuts

1   half-gallon vanilla ice cream (Blue Bell or Mayfield)

Bake the brownie mix according to package directions, adding the chopped nuts to the batter. While the brownies are baking, empty the entire carton of ice cream into a 9 x 13-inch (or slightly larger) glass or metal pan. Cut the ice cream into pieces so it begins to soften. When the brownies are ready and still hot, dump the baked brownies on the ice cream in the dish. Mix the brownies and ice cream together, leaving some of the brownies in small pieces, but still well incorporated into the ice cream. This mixture will be slightly soupy and chunky. Cover the dish with foil and freeze until firm. Scoop out as you would ice cream into serving bowls.

YIELD: 24 SERVINGS

Carole Turner
Acworth, Georgia

Banana Bars

½   cup (1 stick) margarine, softened

2   cups granulated sugar

3   eggs

3   ripe bananas, mashed

1 teaspoon vanilla extract

2 cups all-purpose flour

1 teaspoon baking soda

Pinch of salt

1½ teaspoons ground cinnamon

½ cup chopped pecans

FROSTING

½ cup (1 stick) margarine, softened

1 (8-ounce) package cream cheese, softened

4 cups confectioners' sugar

2 teaspoons vanilla extract

½ cup chopped pecans

Preheat the oven to 350°. In a large bowl beat the margarine and granulated sugar together. In a small bowl combine the eggs, bananas, and vanilla. Beat this into the margarine mixture. In a small bowl combine the flour, baking soda, salt, and cinnamon. Thoroughly blend this into the banana mixture. Add the pecans. Mix well. Pour the batter into a greased 10 x 15-inch baking pan. Bake for 25 to 30 minutes or until a toothpick inserted in the center comes out clean. Set aside to cool.

For the **frosting**, mix together the margarine, cream cheese, confectioners' sugar, vanilla, and pecans in a medium-size bowl. Spread this over the cooled cake. Cut into bars to serve.

YIELD: 36 BARS

Blue Willow Squares

The special dishes of Blue Willow Inn, like so much of American cooking, are a combination of dishes made from scratch as well as canned or boxed goods in a mix-and-match fashion. Blue Willow Squares, a variation on what many home cooks know as Park Avenue Squares, start with an off-the-shelf cake mix, but become something totally different. This dreamy, moist square is yummy for the tummy.

1 (18.25-ounce) package yellow cake mix

½ cup (1 stick) butter or margarine, softened

1 cup chopped pecans

2 plus 1 eggs

1 (8-ounce) package cream cheese, softened

1 (16-ounce) box confectioners' sugar

Preheat the oven to 350°. In a large mixing bowl combine the cake mix, butter, pecans, and 1 egg by hand with a spoon. Mix well. Press the dough by hand into an ungreased 8 x 11-inch baking pan. (Use ice water to chill your hands for easier handling.) In a mixing bowl lightly beat the 2 remaining eggs. Add the softened cream cheese and beat well. Add the confectioners' sugar and blend. The mixture should be slightly lumpy. Spoon this over the cake mixture and spread evenly. Bake for 35 to 40 minutes or until golden brown. Remove from the oven and set aside to cool for 1 hour. Cut into squares for serving.

YIELD: ABOUT 20 SERVINGS

Buttermilk Brownies

1   cup (2 sticks) butter or margarine
⅓   cup cocoa powder
1   cup water
2   cups sifted all-purpose flour
2   cups granulated sugar
1   teaspoon baking soda
½   teaspoon salt
2   eggs, lightly beaten
½   cup buttermilk
1½   teaspoons vanilla extract

FROSTING

¼   cup (½ stick) butter
3   tablespoons cocoa powder
3   tablespoons buttermilk
2¼   cups sifted confectioners' sugar
½   cup chopped walnuts or pecans
½   teaspoon vanilla extract

Preheat the oven to 375°. In a saucepan on medium heat combine the butter, cocoa powder, and water. Bring this mixture to a boil, stirring constantly. Remove from the heat. In a large bowl sift together the flour, granulated sugar, baking soda, and salt. Stir in the eggs, buttermilk, and vanilla. Add the cocoa mixture. Mix until blended. Pour into a greased 10 x 15-inch baking pan. Bake for 30 to 45 minutes, checking after 30 minutes to see if the brownies are done.

For the **frosting**, mix the butter, cocoa powder, and buttermilk in a saucepan on medium heat. Cook and stir until boiling. Remove from the heat and beat in the confectioners' sugar, nuts, and vanilla.

When the brownies are done, remove from the oven and immediately pour the frosting over the brownies. Spread evenly. Cool and cut into bars.

YIELD: 60 BARS

Betty Hartzog
Loganville, Georgia

Chewies

Alice Edgerly, Billie's first mother-in-law, always made Chewies and served ambrosia with them on such special occasions as Thanksgiving and Christmas. This has since become a family tradition for the Van Dyke's also.

½   cup (1 stick) butter or margarine
1   pound packed light brown sugar
3   eggs
2   cups self-rising flour
1   teaspoon vanilla extract
2   cups chopped pecans or walnuts

Preheat the oven to 325°. In a small saucepan on low heat melt the butter. In a large mixing bowl combine the butter and brown sugar. Stir for 10 minutes. Do NOT over-stir or under stir. Add the eggs one at a time and beat well after each addition. Blend in the flour and the vanilla. Beat well. Add the nuts and mix. Pour the batter into a greased 9 x 13-inch pan and bake for 30 to 45 minutes until brown. When ready to serve, cut into squares.

YIELD: 24 SERVINGS

Cream Cheese Peanut Bars

2 plus 1 eggs

1 (18.25-ounce) box butter cake mix (Duncan Hines)

½ cup (1 stick) butter, melted

1 (16-ounce) box confectioners' sugar

1 (8-ounce) package cream cheese

½ cup creamy peanut butter

1 teaspoon vanilla extract

1 cup finely chopped pecans

Preheat the oven to 300°. Spray a 9 x 13-inch pan with a nonstick spray. In a large bowl beat 1 egg. Add the cake mix and the butter. Mix well. Press this mixture into the baking pan. In a large bowl beat the remaining 2 eggs and confectioners' sugar together. Add the cream cheese and mix well. Add the peanut butter and vanilla. Mix well. Pour this mixture over the cake base. Sprinkle with the pecans. Bake for 50 to 60 minutes or until golden brown. Remove from the oven and set aside to cool. Cut into bars before serving.

YIELD: 24 BARS

Chocolate Scotcheroos

This is a dessert that I carried to our family dinners. The youngsters always preferred it to many other desserts, and it is the first thing my daughter, Deanna, wanted to learn to prepare.

1 cup granulated sugar

1 cup light corn syrup

1 cup peanut butter

6 cups Rice Krispies cereal

6 ounces butterscotch morsels

3 ounces semisweet chocolate morsels

4 ounces peanut butter morsels

In a 3-quart saucepan on medium heat combine the sugar and corn syrup. Cook, stirring constantly, until the mixture begins to bubble. Remove from the heat and stir in the peanut butter. Mix well. Add the rice cereal and stir until it is well coated with the peanut butter mixture. Press this mixture into a greased 9 x 13-inch pan.

In a saucepan over low heat, stirring constantly, melt and mix together the butterscotch, chocolate, and peanut butter morsels. Spread this mixture evenly over the rice mixture. Place in the refrigerator and chill until firm. Remove from the refrigerator about 10 minutes before serving.

YIELD: 24 SERVINGS

Juanita Muse
Calhoun, Georgia

Crème de Menthe Squares

Sandi McClain, former manager of the Blue Willow Inn gift shop, bakes these wonderful mint squares during the holidays, and she makes one batch especially for Louis as a part of his Christmas gift.

½	plus ½ cup (2 sticks) softened butter
1	cup granulated sugar
4	eggs, beaten
1	cup all-purpose flour
½	teaspoon salt
1	(16-ounce) can chocolate syrup
1	teaspoon vanilla extract
2	cups confectioners' sugar
2	tablespoons green crème de menthe
1	cup chocolate chips, melted
6	tablespoons butter, melted

Preheat the oven to 350°. For the first layer, beat ½ cup of the butter with the granulated sugar in a medium bowl. Add the beaten eggs and mix. Add the flour, salt, chocolate syrup, and vanilla. Blend well. Pour the mixture into a greased 9 x 13-inch pan. Bake for 20 to 25 minutes. Remove from the oven and set aside to cool.

For the second layer, in a medium bowl combine the confectioner's sugar, the remaining ½ cup butter, and the crème de menthe. Spread this mixture over the first layer.

For the third layer, combine the chocolate chips and the melted butter in a medium bowl. Let the chocolate mixture cool. Spread it on top of the other layers. Allow the layers to cool long enough to become firm before cutting them into squares.

YIELD: 24 SERVINGS

Date Balls

½	cup (1 stick) margarine
1	cup packed light brown sugar
1	(8-ounce) box dates
2	tablespoons hot water
2	cups Rice Krispies cereal
1	cup chopped pecans
1	(7-ounce) can coconut
	Confectioners' sugar for coating

In a saucepan on medium heat combine the margarine, brown sugar, dates, and hot water. Cook, stirring continuously, for about 6 minutes, allowing the margarine to melt and the brown sugar to dissolve and blend with the dates. Remove from the heat and add the rice cereal, pecans, and coconut. Mix well. Allow to cool slightly. Shape into balls. Roll in the confectioners' sugar.

YIELD: 40 BALLS

Lois Dalton
Covington, Georgia

Deluxe Chocolate Marshmallow Bars

¾   cup (1½ sticks) butter or margarine

1½ cups granulated sugar

3   eggs

1   teaspoon vanilla extract

1⅓ cups all-purpose flour

½   teaspoon baking powder

½   teaspoon salt

3   tablespoons cocoa powder

½   cup chopped nuts (optional)

4   cups miniature marshmallows

TOPPING

1⅓ cups (8 ounces) chocolate chips

3   tablespoons butter or margarine

1   cup peanut butter

2   cups crisp rice cereal

Preheat the oven to 350°. In a mixing bowl beat the butter and sugar. Add the eggs and vanilla. Beat until fluffy. In a bowl combine the flour, baking powder, salt, and cocoa powder. Add to the creamed mixture. Stir in the nuts if using. Spread in a greased jelly-roll pan. Bake for 15 to 18 minutes. Sprinkle the marshmallows evenly over the cake. Return to the oven for 2 to 3 minutes. Using a knife dipped in warm water, spread the melted marshmallows evenly over the cake. Set aside to cool.

For the topping, combine the chocolate chips, butter, and peanut butter in a small saucepan on low heat. Cook, stirring constantly, until the chocolate and peanut butter are melted and well blended. Remove from the heat and stir in the cereal. Spread over the bars. Chill.

YIELD: 3 DOZEN

Easy Lemon Squares

1   (18.25-ounce) box lemon cake mix

½   cup (1 stick) butter, melted

3   plus 1 eggs

1   (16-ounce) can lemon frosting

1   (8-ounce) package cream cheese, softened

Preheat the oven to 325°. In a large bowl combine well the cake mix, butter, and 1 egg. Spread this mixture in a 9 x 13-inch pan. In a small bowl mix the lemon frosting and cream cheese together. Reserve approximately 1¼ cups of this mixture. Add the remaining 3 eggs to the remaining frosting/cream cheese mixture. Mix thoroughly. Pour this topping over the cake batter. Bake until the cake is light brown and begins to turn loose from the pan. Remove from the oven and set aside to cool. Ice with the reserved 1¼ cups frosting.

YIELD: 24 SERVINGS

Frosted Creams

This is an old, old recipe that has been handed down in my family. It is much more delicate and lightly flavored than gingerbread.

1	cup shortening
1	cup granulated sugar
2	eggs
2	teaspoons baking soda
¼	teaspoon ground cinnamon
¼	teaspoon ground nutmeg
3¾	cups all-purpose flour
	Pinch of salt
1	cup milk
1	cup molasses
1	(16-ounce) can lemon or vanilla frosting

Preheat the oven to 350°. In a large mixing bowl with an electric mixer beat the shortening and sugar. Add the eggs one at a time. In a bowl combine the baking soda, cinnamon, nutmeg, flour, and salt. Alternately add this dry mixture and the milk to the egg mixture. Add the molasses and stir well. Pour the ingredients into a 9 x 13-inch pan and bake 25 to 30 minutes or until a toothpick inserted in the middle comes out clean. Ice the cake with the lemon or vanilla frosting.

YIELD: 32 BARS

Jeanne Smith
Covington, Georgia

Frozen Lemon Squares

A ribbon festival of luxurious ingredients shot through with the zest of lemon, these squares are best served ten minutes out of the freezer so they are still icy cold but blossoming with flavor as they begin to thaw.

¼	cup (½ stick) butter or margarine
1¼	cups graham cracker crumbs
¼	cup granulated sugar
3	egg yolks
1	(14-ounce) can sweetened condensed milk
½	cup lemon juice from concentrate
	Refrigerated whipped topping, thawed
	Lemon zest for garnish

In a large bowl combine the butter, graham cracker crumbs, and sugar. Press this mixture into the bottom of an 8 or 9-inch-square pan. In a medium bowl beat the egg yolks. Stir in the sweetened condensed milk and the lemon juice. Pour into the prepared crust. Top with the whipped topping. Freeze the pie for 4 to 6 hours or until firm. Let it stand for 10 minutes before cutting into squares. Garnish with the lemon zest.

YIELD: 6 TO 8 SERVINGS

Fudge Cuts

These are delicious with coffee or hot tea. Not too sweet or fudgy, just good and chocolatey. Wonderful addition to a brunch or morning coffee.

2	ounces unsweetened chocolate
½	cup (1 stick) butter
½	plus ¼ cup chopped walnuts
1	cup granulated sugar
2	eggs, well beaten
1	teaspoon vanilla flavoring
½	cup sifted all-purpose flour
⅛	teaspoon salt

Preheat the oven to 400°. Grease a 9 x 13-inch baking dish. In the top of a double boiler melt the chocolate and butter. Stir in ½ cup of the nuts. Add the sugar, beaten eggs, and vanilla. Mix well. Add the flour and salt, stirring until smooth. Spread the mixture evenly in the pan. Sprinkle with the remaining ¼ cup of nuts. Bake 15 to 18 minutes. Turn the oven off and leave inside the oven for about another 5 minutes. Cool and cut into squares.

Hint: Check while cooking as some ovens bake faster. Fudge cuts are best when they are moist.

YIELD: 24 SERVINGS

Kitty Jacobs
Atlanta, Georgia

Grandmother Alice's Brownies

Our children's grandmother always prepared this special treat at Christmas. After Alice passed on, our son, Chip, continued this tradition and Christmas just wouldn't be the same without her brownies.

¾	cup (1½ sticks) butter or margarine
1½	ounces unsweetened chocolate
4	eggs
2	cups granulated sugar
1½	cups self-rising flour
1	teaspoon vanilla flavoring
2½	cups chopped pecans

ICING

1	ounce butter (approximately ½-inch of a stick)
½	ounce unsweetened chocolate
½	cup instant coffee granules
¼	cup hot water
½	(8-ounces) box 10X confectioners' sugar
1	teaspoon vanilla extract

Preheat the oven to 325°. In a small saucepan on low heat melt the butter and the chocolate together, stirring occasionally. In a large mixing bowl beat the eggs. Add the granulated sugar and mix well. Add the flour and mix well. Add the vanilla and mix well. Add the pecans and mix well. Pour the dough into a greased 9 x 13-inch pan. Bake for 20 to 30 minutes.

For the icing, melt the butter and the chocolate in a saucepan on low heat, stirring occasionally. In a medium-size mixing bowl combine the coffee and hot water. Add the confectioners' sugar 1 tablespoonful at a time, mixing after each addition. The mixture should be thick. Add the chocolate mixture. Stir in the vanilla. Spread the icing over the hot brownies.

YIELD: 24 SERVINGS

Grasshoppers

Melanie A. Blunt, first lady of the state of Missouri, sent this recipe to us. It is a luscious combination of chocolate and peppermint. This recipe comes from Sassafras, The Ozarks Cookbook, *compiled by the Junior League of Springfield, of which Mrs. Blunt is a member.*

4	eggs
2	cups granulated sugar
1	cup cocoa powder
1	cup all-purpose flour
1	teaspoon peppermint extract
1	cup (2 sticks) butter, melted

FROSTING

3½	cups (1 pound) confectioners' sugar
½	cup butter
3	drops green food coloring
½	teaspoon peppermint extract
1	to 2 tablespoons milk
3	ounces unsweetened chocolate
3	tablespoons butter

Preheat the oven to 350°. Grease and flour an 11 x 17-inch pan. In a large mixing bowl beat the eggs and sugar until thick. Add the cocoa powder, flour, and peppermint extract. Stir in the butter. Pour into the prepared pan. Bake at 350° for 15 to 20 minutes, being careful not to overbake. Set aside to cool.

For the **frosting**, beat together the confectioners' sugar, butter, food coloring, and peppermint extract in a medium-size mixing bowl. Add enough milk to make a spreading consistency. Spread over the cooled cake. In a double boiler on medium heat, or in the microwave, melt the chocolate and butter. Carefully brush over the frosted cake. Refrigerate to harden. Cut into 1 x 2-inch bars.

YIELD: 7 TO 8 DOZEN

Lemon Squares

1	cup (2 sticks) butter, softened
2	cups all-purpose flour
½	cup confectioners' sugar plus extra for sprinkling

FILLING

4	eggs
2	cups granulated sugar
4	tablespoons lemon juice
4	tablespoons all-purpose flour
½	teaspoon baking powder

Preheat the oven to 350°. In a medium-size bowl combine the butter, flour, and confectioners' sugar. Mix well. Press this pastry mixture into the bottom of a 9 x 13-inch baking pan. Bake for 15 minutes.

For the **filling**, preheat the oven to 350°. In a mixing bowl beat the eggs well. Add the sugar and lemon juice. Fold in the flour and baking powder. Mix well. Pour onto the pastry and bake for an additional 25 minutes.

Remove from the oven and sprinkle with confectioners' sugar while warm. Allow to cool and cut into squares.

YIELD: 24 SQUARES

Betty Hartzog
Loganville, Georgia

Louis' Brownies

This is a delicious chewy brownie that is especially well suited for large groups.

2   (26 or 28-ounce) packages brownie mix
    Eggs
    Vegetable oil
¾   cup chocolate icing
1   cup chopped pecans
¼   cup granulated sugar plus some for coating pan
    All vegetable shortening

Preheat the oven to 350°. In a large mixing bowl prepare the brownie mix according to package directions, *except* use 1 less egg than called for in the preparation and use ½ cup less oil. Add the chocolate icing, pecans, and sugar. Mix gently. Do not beat. Grease two baking pans with the shortening and coat with sugar. Pour and spread the brownie mix into the baking pans. Bake for 15 to 17 minutes.

Hint: Remove the brownies from the oven while the center of the brownies is still loose. Be careful. If this recipe is cooked until the centers are firm, the end result will be hard and crisp brownies that are overcooked.

YIELD: 6 TO 7 DOZEN BROWNIES

Pineapple Squares

I have been using this recipe since 1974. A dear friend who was a wonderful baker gave it to me.

2   cups (4 sticks) butter
4   cups all-purpose flour
1   cup sour cream
1   teaspoon vanilla extract
3   cups crushed pineapple
3   tablespoons cornstarch
1   cup granulated sugar
    Confectioners' sugar

In a medium-size bowl cut the butter into the flour with a pastry blender. Add the sour cream and vanilla. Mix well. Refrigerate at least 2 hours. In a saucepan on medium heat cook the pineapple, cornstarch, and granulated sugar, stirring constantly, until it is thick and clear.

Preheat the oven to 325°. Remove the dough from the refrigerator. Roll out the dough and place half of it on an ungreased cookie sheet. Spread the pineapple filling over the dough. Cover with the remaining dough. Bake for 55 minutes or until golden. Sprinkle with the confectioners' sugar. Cut into squares. Refrigerate any leftover squares.

YIELD: 24 SQUARES

Strawberry Pretzel Delight

2   cups stick pretzels, broken
3   tablespoons granulated sugar
¾   cup (1½ sticks) butter, melted
1   (8-ounce) package cream cheese, softened
1   (16-ounce) container whipped topping
1   cup confectioners' sugar
2   (3-ounce) boxes strawberry gelatin
2   cups boiling water
2   (10-ounce) packages frozen strawberries

Preheat the oven to 400°. In a large bowl mix the pretzels, granulated sugar, and butter. Pour the mixture into a 9 x 13-inch pan and bake for 8 minutes. Set aside to cool.

In a medium-size bowl with an electric mixer beat the cream cheese, whipped topping, and confectioners' sugar. Pour this over the cooled pretzel crust.

In a medium bowl dissolve the gelatin in the boiling water. Stir until the gelatin is dissolved completely. Add the frozen strawberries and stir until the berries are no longer frozen. Pour the strawberries over the cream cheese mixture and refrigerate for 2 hours or until firm.

YIELD: 24 SERVINGS

Ann Chlapowski
Tallahassee, Florida

Triple Chocolate Clusters

2   (4-ounce) white chocolate bars
1   cup milk chocolate morsels
1   cup (6-ounces) semisweet chocolate morsels
1½   cups chopped pecans
1½   cups broken pretzels

In a heavy saucepan over low heat melt the white chocolate, milk chocolate, and semisweet chocolate, stirring constantly. Stir in the pecans and pretzels. Remove from the heat and drop by the tablespoonful onto lightly greased wax paper. Cool until hardened. Store in an airtight container in the refrigerator up to one month.

Note: These clusters are very rich. You may want to drop by the teaspoonful rather than by the tablespoonful.

YIELD: ABOUT 100

Triple-Layer Brownies

½   cup dry roasted peanuts, chopped
1   cup quick or old-fashioned oats
½   cup packed brown sugar
⅓   cup all-purpose flour
¼   teaspoon baking soda
½   cup butter or margarine, melted

1   (19 to 21-ounce) package fudge brownie mix (plus required ingredients)

¾   cup semisweet chocolate morsels

½   cup creamy peanut butter

Additional chopped peanuts (optional)

Preheat the oven to 350°. Spray a 9 x 13-inch pan with nonstick cooking spray. In a small bowl combine the peanuts, oats, brown sugar, flour, and baking soda. Add the butter and mix well. Press this mixture onto the bottom of the pan. Bake for 8 minutes. Remove from the oven.

Prepare the brownie mix according to the package directions. Gently spoon the batter over the partially baked oat crust. Carefully spread to the edges. Bake according to the package directions for the brownies (28 to 30 minutes). Remove from the oven and cool completely.

In a microwavable bowl combine the chocolate morsels and peanut butter. Microwave, uncovered, on high for 1 minute. Stir until smooth. Spread the chocolate mixture evenly over the cooled brownies. Sprinkle with additional chopped peanuts if desired. Cut into bars. Store in a tightly covered container in the refrigerator.

YIELD: 32 BARS

Lynn Grace
Grayson, Georgia

Amy's Orange Pineapple Layer Cake

1   (18.25-ounce) box Pillsbury yellow cake mix with pudding

1   (11-ounce) can mandarin oranges, not drained

4   eggs

⅓   cup vegetable oil

FROSTING

1   (16-ounce) container whipped topping

1   (20-ounce) can crushed pineapple, not drained

1   (5.9-ounce) box instant vanilla pudding

Preheat the oven to 350°. Grease two round cake pans. In a large mixing bowl with a wire whisk mix together the cake mix, oranges, eggs, and oil. Pour into the cake pans and bake for 25 minutes. Set aside to cool completely.

For the frosting, fold together the whipped topping, crushed pineapple, and pudding mix in a medium-size mixing bowl. Frost the cake with this mixture and refrigerate. This cake must be kept refrigerated.

YIELD: 1 (2-LAYER) CAKE

Amy Corasaniti
Monroe, Georgia

Apple Walnut Cake

1⅔ cups granulated sugar
2   eggs
½   cup vegetable oil
2   teaspoons vanilla extract
2   cups all-purpose flour
2   teaspoons baking soda
1½ teaspoons ground cinnamon
1   teaspoon salt
½   teaspoon ground nutmeg
4   cups chopped apples, not peeled
1   cup chopped walnuts

FROSTING

2   (3-ounce) packages cream cheese, softened
3   tablespoons butter or margarine, softened
1   teaspoon vanilla extract
1½ cups confectioners' sugar

Preheat the oven to 350°. In a mixing bowl beat the granulated sugar and the eggs. Add the oil and vanilla. Mix well. In a small bowl combine the flour, baking soda, cinnamon, salt, and nutmeg. Gradually add this to the sugar mixture. Mix well. Stir in the apples and walnuts. Pour into a greased and floured 9 x 13-inch baking pan. Bake for 50 to 55 minutes or until the cake tests done. Cool on a wire rack.

For the frosting, in a mixing bowl beat the cream cheese, butter, and vanilla together. Gradually add the confectioners' sugar until the frosting is light. Frost the cake after it has cooled.

YIELD: 16 TO 20 SERVINGS

Banana Split Cake

This is one of Louis' favorite cakes. My husband, Dr. Roger Bailey, and I have been friends of the Van Dykes for a number of years. I have made this cake for Louis for various occasions, including his and Billie's thirty-fifth anniversary celebration.

2   cups graham cracker crumbs
1   stick margarine, melted

FILLING

3   eggs
1   cup (2 sticks) margarine, softened
1   (16-ounce) box confectioners' sugar
3   to 4 large bananas
2   (20-ounce) cans well-drained crushed pineapple
1   (16-ounce) container whipped topping
1   cup chopped walnuts or pecans
    Maraschino cherries (optional)
    Chocolate syrup (optional)

In a small mixing bowl combine the graham cracker crumbs with the melted margarine until the crumbs are well coated and the mixture sticks together. Press the crumbs into a 9 x 13-inch baking dish to form a crust.

For the filling, beat the eggs, margarine, and sugar in a large mixing bowl for at least 20 minutes. Pour over the crust. Thinly slice the bananas and spread over the filling. Pour the drained pineapple over the bananas. Spoon the whipped topping evenly over the pineapple. Sprinkle the chopped nuts evenly over the whipped topping. If desired, garnish with maraschino cherries and chocolate syrup. Refrigerate 6 to 8 hours or overnight.

YIELD: 24 SERVINGS

Bobbi Bailey
Monroe, Georgia

Birthday Cake

This is the cake recipe that Louis' mother, Anne Van Dyke, used every year to make birthday cakes for the family. The celebration always included a cookout—hot dogs when the children were small, hamburgers as they got older, and steaks when more prosperous.

½	cup (1 stick) butter, softened
1½	cups granulated sugar
1	teaspoon vanilla extract
¼	teaspoon almond extract
3	cups sifted cake flour
3	teaspoons baking powder
¾	teaspoon salt
½	cup milk
½	cup water
3	egg whites

Preheat the oven to 375°. In a large mixing bowl beat the butter thoroughly. Add the sugar and continue to cream until fluffy. Add the vanilla and almond flavorings. In a bowl sift together the cake flour, baking powder, and salt. In another bowl combine the milk and water. Add about one-third of the dry mixture and one-third of the liquid mixture to the butter mixture. Continue to alternate, adding these mixtures to the butter mixture. In a bowl beat the egg whites until they are stiff but not dry. Fold the beaten egg whites into the batter. Pour the batter into two greased 9-inch cake pans and bake for about 20 minutes. Turn the layers out onto a wire rack. Allow to cool completely before frosting.

YIELD: 1 (9-INCH) TWO-LAYER CAKE

Burnt Sugar Cake

BURNT SUGAR SYRUP

⅔   cup granulated sugar

⅔   cup boiling water

CAKE

1½   cups granulated sugar

½   cup butter

1   teaspoon vanilla extract

2   eggs

2½   cups sifted cake flour

3   teaspoon baking powder

½   teaspoon salt

¾   cup cold water

3   tablespoons burnt sugar syrup

BURNT SUGAR FROSTING

2   egg whites

1¼   cups granulated sugar

3   to 4 tablespoons burnt sugar syrup

¼   cup cold water

Dash of salt

1   teaspoon vanilla extract

FILLING

1½   cups chopped dates

⅓   cup granulated sugar

1   cup water

¼   teaspoon salt

¼   cup burnt sugar frosting

¼   cup English walnuts

For the **burnt sugar syrup**, in a small heavy skillet on medium-high heat caramelize (melt) the granulated sugar, stirring constantly. When the sugar is dark brown and forms a syrup, remove it from the heat. Slowly add the boiling water and stir until the sugar dissolves. Return to the heat and boil until reduced to ½ cup. Set aside to cool.

To make the **cake**, preheat the oven to 375°. In a large mixing bowl with an electric mixer beat the sugar and butter. Add the vanilla extract. Add the eggs one at a time, beating 1 minute after each egg. Sift together the cake flour, baking powder, and salt. Add the sifted ingredients and the water alternately to the butter mixture. Add 3 tablespoons of the burnt sugar syrup. Beat 4 minutes at medium speed. Bake in two 9-inch parchment-lined pans for 20 minutes. After removing from the oven, cool for 10 minutes in the pans.

For the **burnt sugar frosting**, combine the egg whites, sugar, 3 to 4 tablespoons of the burnt sugar syrup, cold water, and salt in a mixing bowl. Beat the ingredients for 1 minute with an electric or rotary beater. Pour into the top of a double boiler over boiling water. Cook, beating constantly, until peaks form, about 7 minutes. Remove from the heat. Add the vanilla and beat for 2 minutes. Reserve ¼ cup for the filling.

For the **filling**, in a saucepan on medium heat combine the dates, sugar, water, and salt. Bring the mixture to a boil. Cook gently, stirring continuously for 4 minutes or until thick. Remove from the heat. Set aside to cool at room temperature. Fold in ¼ cup of the frosting and the walnuts. Spread evenly between the cooled layers. Frost the cake before serving.

YIELD: 1 (9-INCH) TWO-LAYER CAKE

Blueberry-Banana-Pecan-Nut Cake

This is a wonderful brunch item. When blueberries are in season, this is served at the Blue Willow Inn Restaurant on a large platter with blueberry sauce in a small bowl in the middle for topping the cake.

1	cup fresh or frozen blueberries
1½	cups (3 sticks) butter, softened
1½	cups granulated sugar
4	eggs
3	large ripe bananas, mashed
1	(14-ounce) container sour cream
2	cups all-purpose flour
1	teaspoon baking soda
1	teaspoon baking powder
¼	teaspoon salt
1	cup chopped pecans

Preheat the oven to 375°. Rinse and drain the blueberries. In a mixing bowl beat the butter and sugar. Add the eggs one at a time, mixing well with each addition. Add the bananas and sour cream. Mix well. In a bowl combine the flour, baking soda, baking powder, and salt. Add this a little at the time to the butter mixture. Mix well. Fold the blueberries and the pecans into the batter. If using frozen blueberries, dust them with a small amount of flour before adding the batter. Pour the batter into two greased and floured 9-inch loaf pans. Bake for 45 to 55 minutes or until a toothpick inserted in the middle comes out clean. Set out to cool. Top with warm blueberry sauce (recipe on page 130) immediately before serving.

YIELD: 2 LOAVES

Bishop's Cake

First lady of Texas, Anita Perry, sent this recipe from the kitchen at the governor's mansion.

1	cup (2 sticks) unsalted butter
2	cups granulated sugar
2	cups unbleached flour
1	tablespoon fresh lemon juice
1	teaspoon vanilla extract
5	eggs

Preheat the oven to 350°. Grease and flour a 10-inch Bundt pan. In a mixing bowl beat the butter and sugar until fluffy. Sift the flour and add it to the butter mixture. Stir just enough to blend. Add the lemon juice and vanilla; stir well. Add the eggs, one at a time, mixing well after each addition. Pour the batter into the prepared Bundt pan. Bake for 30 minutes, loosely cover the pan with aluminum foil, then bake 45 minutes longer or until a cake tester inserted into the center of the cake comes out clean. After the cake has cooked for 30 minutes. When the cake is done, cool in the pan on a cake rack for 10 minutes. Remove from the pan and cool completely.

YIELD: 1 CAKE

Brown Sugar Pound Cake

1   (16-ounce) box light brown sugar
1   cup granulated sugar
1   cup shortening
½   cup (1 stick) margarine
5   large eggs
1   cup self-rising flour
2   cups all-purpose flour
1   cup milk
2   teaspoons vanilla extract
½   teaspoon maple flavoring
¾   cup chopped pecans

Preheat the oven to 325°. In a mixing bowl beat the brown sugar, granulated sugar, shortening, and margarine. Add the eggs one at a time. Mix well after each addition. Alternately add the flour and milk. Add the vanilla, maple flavoring, and pecans. Bake in a greased and floured 10-inch tube pan for 1½ hours.

YIELD: 1 CAKE

Cameo Cake with White Chocolate Frosting

This is a beautiful cake and worth the special effort.

3   plus ½ cups all-purpose flour
1   cup chopped toasted pecans
2¼   cups granulated sugar
1½   teaspoons baking soda
½   teaspoon salt
1   cup (2 sticks) unsalted butter (no substitutes)
¾   cup water
4   ounces white chocolate squares, coarsely chopped
1½   cups buttermilk
4   large eggs, lightly beaten
1½   teaspoons vanilla extract

FROSTING

4   ounces white chocolate squares, coarsely chopped
1   (8-ounce) plus 1 (3-ounce) packages cream cheese, softened
5   tablespoons unsalted butter or margarine, cut up
3   cups confectioners' sugar, sifted
1½   teaspoons vanilla extract
     Chopped toasted pecans for garnish (optional)

Preheat the oven to 350°. Grease and lightly flour three 9-inch round cake pans. Line the bottoms with wax paper. In a small bowl combine ½ cup of the flour with the pecans. In a large bowl combine the remaining 3 cups flour, the granulated sugar, baking soda, and salt. In a saucepan on medium heat bring the butter and water to a boil, stirring occasionally, until the butter melts. Remove from the heat and stir in the white chocolate until it is melted. Stir in the buttermilk, eggs, and vanilla until blended. Gradually whisk the white chocolate mixture into the dry ingredients until the mixture is smooth. Fold in the pecan mixture. Pour into the prepared pans.

Bake for 30 to 35 minutes or until a toothpick inserted in the center of the cakes comes out clean. Remove from the oven and cool in the pans on wire racks for 10 minutes. Remove from the pans and place the cakes on the racks to cool completely.

For the **frosting**, microwave the white chocolate in a small microwavable bowl on high for 1½ minutes until it is almost melted. Stir until it is smooth. Cool slightly for 10 minutes. While the chocolate is cooling, in a large mixing bowl with an electric mixer beat the cream cheese and butter until light and fluffy. Beat in the melted chocolate. Gradually add the confectioners' sugar and the vanilla. Beat, scraping down the sides of the bowl with a rubber spatula, until the frosting is completely smooth. Refrigerate for 1 hour until the frosting is firm and spreadable. Frost between the layers and on the top and sides of the cake. Garnish with the chopped pecans. Cover the cake loosely and refrigerate 6 to 8 hours or overnight.

YIELD: 1 (9-INCH) THREE-LAYER CAKE

Celestial Snow Cake

This is a quick, yet beautifully presented, cake. It makes a special birthday cake or a Christmas dessert. A very special friend gave the recipe to me more than 25 years ago. Compared to many other cake recipes, it is unique.

CAKE

1	(18.25-ounce) box butter yellow cake mix
¾	cup vegetable oil
4	eggs
1	(11-ounce) can mandarin orange segments with juice
1	cup chopped pecans

FROSTING

1	cup confectioners' sugar
1	(8-ounce) can crushed pineapple with juice
1	(8-ounce) container whipped topping
1	(8-ounce) carton sour cream

Preheat the oven to 350°. Lightly grease and flour three 8-inch or two 9-inch cake pans. In a large mixing bowl combine the cake mix, vegetable oil, eggs, orange segments and juice, and pecans. With an electric mixer blend the ingredients until moistened, and then beat on medium-high speed 4 minutes. Pour into the cake pans and bake for 25 to 30 minutes. Let the cakes cool completely before icing.

For the frosting, combine the sugar, pineapple with juice, whipped topping, and sour cream in a large mixing bowl. Immediately spread on the layers, top, and sides of the cake. Refrigerate immediately.

YIELD: 1 CAKE

Caramel Cake

This traditionally Southern cake is delicious to the last bite.

CAKE

2	cups granulated sugar
1½	cups vegetable shortening
5	large eggs
3	cups all-purpose soft-wheat flour (White Lily)
¼	teaspoon salt
½	teaspoon baking powder
1¼	cups milk
1	teaspoon vanilla extract
	Pecan halves

CARAMEL

3	plus ¼ cups granulated sugar
¼	cup boiling water
½	cup (1 stick) butter
¼	teaspoon baking soda
1	teaspoon vanilla extract
1	cup milk

Preheat the oven to 325°. For the **cake**, grease and lightly flour four 9-inch cake pans. Cut a piece of wax paper to fit the bottom of each of the pans and grease and flour them. In a large mixing bowl, mix the sugar and shortening together, beating with an electric mixer until light and fluffy. Add the eggs one at a time, beating after each addition. In another bowl sift together the flour, salt, and baking powder three times. Alternately, add about one-fourth at a time of the flour mixture and one-fourth of the milk to the shortening mixture. Beat after each addition. Add the vanilla and beat until the mixture is smooth. Pour the batter into the cake pans and bake for 35 minutes or until a toothpick inserted in the middle comes out clean. Remove to a wire rack to cool. After the cakes have cooled, remove from the pans and peel off the paper.

For the **caramel**, melt ¼ cup of the sugar in an iron skillet on medium-high heat until it is a golden brown. Add the boiling water and cook until the caramel mixture is well blended and no lumps remain. In a large saucepan on medium heat bring the remaining 3 cups sugar, the butter, baking soda, vanilla, and milk to a boil. Add a little of the milk mixture to dissolve and remove all the caramel from the skillet. Then pour the caramel into the boiling milk mixture. Boil rapidly, stirring constantly, to the soft-ball stage (240°). Remove the pan from the heat and place it in a bowl of ice cold water to stop the cooking. Beat until the icing is very thick and creamy. Cool and spread between the cake layers and on the top and sides of the cake. Decorate the top and sides with pecan halves.

YIELD: 1 (9-INCH) FOUR-LAYER CAKE

Cheesecake

A special friend shared this recipe with me more than twenty-five years ago. It always gets lots of compliments and is delicious served plain or with whipped cream, fresh fruit, or a fruit pie filling.

4   large eggs

3   (8-ounce) packages cream cheese, softened

1   cup granulated sugar

3   tablespoons cornstarch

2   graham cracker pie shells

TOPPING

1   pint sour cream

½   cup granulated sugar

1   teaspoon vanilla extract

Preheat the oven to 350°. In a large bowl with an electric mixer on medium to high speed blend the eggs, cream cheese, sugar, and cornstarch together until they are smooth. Pour this mixture into the two pie shells and bake for 30 minutes or until the centers of the cakes are almost firm. Cool completely.

For the **topping**, preheat the oven to 375°. In a large bowl combine the sour cream, sugar, and vanilla. Blend together well. Spread on top of the cheesecakes. Bake for 10 to 15 minutes. Cool and cover. Refrigerate or freeze.

YIELD: 2 CHEESECAKES

Chocolate Cherry Cake

This recipe is from Nellie Baines, now retired as one of the managers at the Blue Willow Inn Restaurant. Several times a year Nell would bake this cake for her fellow employees and there was never a crumb left. We often use this cake at various cooking demonstrations and people clamor for our cookbook after seeing and tasting this cake.

CAKE

1   (16-ounce) can cherry pie filling

1   (18.25-ounce) package fudge cake mix

1   teaspoon almond extract

2   eggs, beaten

FROSTING

1   cup granulated sugar

5   tablespoons butter

½   cup milk

1   teaspoon almond extract

1   (6-ounce) package semisweet chocolate chips

Preheat the oven to 350°. For the **cake**, drain the cherry pie filling into a large mixing bowl. Set the cherries aside. Add the cake mix, almond extract, and eggs to the drained cherry juice. Mix well. Fold in the cherries. Pour the batter into a greased and floured 9 x 13-inch baking pan or casserole dish. Bake for 30 to 35 minutes.

For the **frosting**, combine the sugar, butter, and milk in a small saucepan on medium heat. Bring this mixture to a boil and boil for 1 minute, stirring constantly. Remove from the heat and add the almond extract and chocolate chips. Beat with an electric mixer until smooth. Cool and spread over cake.

YIELD: 24 SERVINGS

Nell's Carrot Cake

This is another recipe from Nell Baines. Everyone loves Nell's cakes. They are "cooked- just- right" culinary delights. They are one of those "fight-over-the-last-piece" items.

CAKE

2	cups all-purpose flour
2	teaspoons baking soda
½	teaspoon salt
2	teaspoons ground cinnamon
½	teaspoon ground nutmeg
¼	teaspoon ground ginger
1	cup granulated sugar
1	cup firmly packed brown sugar
1	cup buttermilk
¾	cup vegetable oil
4	large eggs
1½	teaspoons vanilla extract
1	(1-pound) bag carrots, peeled and grated
1	(8-ounce) can crushed pineapple, drained
1	cup chopped pecans
1	cup flaked coconut
½	cup raisins

CREAM CHEESE FROSTING

½	cup (1 stick) butter at room temperature
1	(8-ounce) package cream cheese at room temperature
1	(16-ounce) box confectioners' sugar
1	teaspoon vanilla extract

Preheat the oven to 350°. For the **cake**, grease and flour three 9-inch cake pans. Line the bottoms with wax paper. Grease and flour the wax paper. In a large bowl sift together the flour, baking soda, salt, cinnamon, nutmeg, and ginger. In another large bowl mix the granulated sugar and the brown sugar. Stir the buttermilk, vegetable oil, eggs, and vanilla into the sugar mixture. Mix well. Pour the flour mixture into the sugar mixture. Add the carrots, pineapple, pecans, coconut, and raisins. Stir these just until well blended. Pour the batter equally into the three cake pans. Bake for 30 minutes or until a wooden toothpick inserted in the center comes out clean. Cool the cake layers in the pans for 10 minutes. Loosen the layers from the edges of the pans and invert onto wire racks. Peel off the wax paper. Cool completely.

For the **frosting**, in a large mixing bowl beat the butter and cream cheese together until light and fluffy. Add the confectioners' sugar and vanilla, mixing well to a smooth consistency.

YIELD: 1 (3-LAYER) CAKE

Chocolate Pound Cake

1	cup (2 sticks) butter or margarine
½	cup shortening
3	cups granulated sugar
5	eggs
3	cups all-purpose flour
½	teaspoon baking powder

½ cup cocoa powder

½ teaspoon salt

¼ cup milk

¼ cup sour cream

1 teaspoon vanilla extract

Preheat the oven to 325°. In a mixing bowl beat the butter, shortening, and sugar. Add the eggs one at a time. Beat for 1 minute after each egg. In another bowl sift the flour, baking powder, cocoa powder, and salt together three times. Add this to the butter mixture alternately with the milk and sour cream. Add the vanilla and beat for 1 minute. Pour into a greased tube pan. Bake for 1 hour at 325°. Reduce the heat to 300° and bake for 15 minutes more. Remove from the oven and cool for 1 hour before removing from the pan.

YIELD: 1 CAKE

Coca-Cola Cake with Broiled Peanut Butter Frosting

We want to thank Jane and Michael Stern of Gourmet *magazine and co-authors of* The Blue Willow Inn Cookbook *for giving us this recipe. It is a deliciously moist cake that is gobbled up by everyone who tries it. You can substitute Pepsi for the Coca-Cola, but do not under any circumstances use a diet version of either beverage.*

2 cups all-purpose flour

2 cups granulated sugar

1 cup (2 sticks) butter, melted

2 tablespoons unsweetened cocoa powder

1 cup Coca-Cola with fizz

½ cup buttermilk

2 eggs, beaten

1 teaspoon baking soda

1 teaspoon vanilla extract

1½ cups miniature marshmallows

BROILED PEANUT BUTTER FROSTING

6 tablespoons butter

1 cup dark brown sugar

⅔ cup smooth peanut butter

¼ cup milk

⅔ cup chopped peanuts

Preheat the oven to 350° degrees. Grease and flour a 9 x 13 x 2-inch sheet cake pan. In a large bowl combine the flour and sugar. In another bowl combine the butter, cocoa powder, and Coke. Pour this over the flour and sugar mixture. Stir until it is well blended. Add the buttermilk, eggs, baking soda, and vanilla. Mix well. Stir in the marshmallows. Pour into the prepared pan. Bake for 40 minutes. Remove the cake from the oven and frost it while still barely warm.

For the **broiled peanut butter frosting**, in a medium-size mixing bowl beat the butter, brown sugar, and peanut butter together. Beat in the milk. Fold in the peanuts. Spread over the cake. Heat the oven broiler and place the frosted cake under the broiler about 4-inches from the heat source. Broil just a few seconds or until the topping starts to bubble. Watch constantly and be careful not to scorch the frosting.

YIELD: 1 LARGE SHEET CAKE

Country Lane Cake

1	cup shortening
2	cups granulated sugar
½	teaspoon salt
7	egg whites
4	cups all-purpose flour
1⅓	cups milk
4	teaspoons baking powder
2	teaspoons vanilla extract

FROSTING

1	cup (2 sticks) butter
1⅓	cups granulated sugar
7	egg yolks
1	heaping cup chopped pecans
1	heaping cup raisins
1	heaping cup coconut
1	teaspoon vanilla extract

Preheat the oven to 400°. In a large mixing bowl with an electric mixer beat the shortening, sugar, and salt. Add the egg whites (do not beat them). Blend well, beating the mixture until smooth. Alternately add in the flour and milk. Sift the baking power into the last bit of the flour before it is added. Blend well after each addition. Add the vanilla extract. Bake in three well-greased 9-inch cake pans for 20 minutes. Remove from the oven and cool.

For the frosting, in the top of a double boiler combine the butter, sugar, and egg yolks. Cook this mixture over boiling water until it is thickened to custard consistency.

Add the pecans, raisins, coconut, and vanilla extract. Spread the frosting between the cake layers and ice the top and sides.

YIELD: 1 (3-LAYER) CAKE

Karol Trammel
Monroe, Georgia

Death by Chocolate

This is a favorite dessert recipe of Kathleen Babineaux Blanco, governor of Louisiana. She says she hopes everyone enjoys it as much as she does.

2	(18.25-ounce) boxes devil's food cake mix
¼	plus ¼ cup Kahlúa
3	(3-ounce) boxes Jell-O no-bake chocolate silk dessert
3	(16-ounce) containers lite whipped topping
1	plus 1 (8-ounce) bags Heath Bar Crumbles

Bake the two cakes as directed on the box. After removing the cakes from the oven, break up the cakes or poke holes in them. Pour ¼ cup Kahlúa over each cake. In a large, clear trifle dish (6 to 8 inches deep) place the pieces of one of the broken cakes in the bottom. Prepare the silk dessert mixes according to the package directions, using fat-free milk. Pour half of the silk pie mixture over the first chocolate cake to form a layer. Spread half the whipped topping in a layer over the chocolate. Sprinkle 1 bag Heath Bar Crumbles over the whipped topping layer. Add the second crumbled cake, the remaining silk pie mix, the remaining whipped topping, and the remaining bag of Heath Bar Crumbles. Keep covered in the refrigerator until ready to serve.

YIELD: 1 LARGE TRIFLE

Dutch Chocolate Cake

Glenna Fletcher, first lady of the state of Kentucky, sent us this luscious cake recipe.

CAKE

1	cup sifted cocoa powder
2	cups boiling water
2	cups sifted all-purpose flour
2	teaspoons baking soda
¾	teaspoon salt
½	teaspoon baking powder
1	cup (2 sticks) butter, softened
2½	cups granulated sugar
4	eggs
1½	teaspoons vanilla extract

FILLING

1	cup butter, softened
1	cup confectioners' sugar
½	cup sifted cocoa powder
2	eggs

FROSTING

2	cups heavy whipping cream
¾	cup sifted confectioners' sugar
1	teaspoon vanilla extract

Preheat the oven to 350°. For the **cake**, in a small bowl mix the cocoa powder and boiling water together until the cocoa is completely dissolved in the water. Set aside to cool completely. In a large mixing bowl sift together the flour, baking soda, salt, and baking powder. In another bowl, with an electric mixer on high speed, beat together the butter, granulated sugar, eggs, and vanilla until it is light and fluffy, approximately 5 minutes. At low speed on the mixer alternately beat in the dry ingredients and the cocoa powder mixture. Divide the batter evenly into three 9-inch pans. Bake for 30 minutes or until a toothpick comes out clean; cool completely and fill and frost.

For the **filling**, in a large mixing bowl with an electric mixer on high beat the butter, confectioners' sugar, cocoa powder, and eggs together until light and smooth. Spread between the cake layers when they are cooled.

For the **frosting**, in a large mixing bowl with an electric mixer on high combine the cream, confectioners' sugar, and vanilla. Beat until the mixture is stiff enough to spread. Frost the sides and top of the filled cake. Refrigerate at least 1 hour before serving. Keep the cake refrigerated. The flavor improves if allowed to sit for 1 day.

YIELD: 1 (3-LAYER) CAKE

Dirt Cake

Using Dirt Cake served in flowerpots with either plastic flowers or gummy worms decorating the tops makes a wonderfully fun addition to a children's party.

1	(20-ounce) bag Oreo cookies, crushed
¼	cup butter
1	cup confectioners' sugar
1	(8-ounce) package softened cream cheese
3⅓	cups whole milk
2	(3½-ounce) packages French vanilla instant pudding
1	(8-ounce) package frozen whipped topping, thawed

Using a rolling pin, crush the cookies in a large plastic sealed bag. In a medium-size mixing bowl beat the butter, confectioners' sugar, and cream cheese. In another bowl beat the milk, instant pudding, and thawed whipped topping. Combine the two mixtures. In small, clean flowerpots alternate layers of the cookie crumbs and the pudding mixture, beginning and ending with the cookie crumbs. Chill or freeze. You can decorate your "cakes" with plastic flowers or gummy worms.

> Hint: This dessert can be made in a glass bowl, adding a layer of 1 (16-ounce) can cherry pie filling and topping with refrigerated whipped topping. Whole Oreo cookies can be used to garnish the top. It makes a luscious dessert.

YIELD: 24 SERVINGS

Eight-Layer Butter Cake

Seena Wilkes from Surrency, Georgia, gave us this recipe. She often makes this cake for her family and friends on birthdays and other special occasions.

1	(18.25-ounce) box butter cake mix
	Nonstick baking spray

FROSTING

1	cup (2 sticks) margarine
2	cups granulated sugar
½	cup canned evaporated milk
⅓	cup cocoa powder
½	teaspoon vanilla extract
5	marshmallows

Preheat the oven to 350°. Follow the directions on the box to mix the cake. After mixing, spray eight 8-inch cake pans with a nonstick baking spray and divide the batter equally among the eight pans. Cook the layers, four pans at a time, until golden brown. Remove from the oven and cool completely before icing.

For the **frosting**, in a saucepan on medium heat melt the margarine. Stir in the sugar, milk, and cocoa powder. Boil for 2 minutes. Remove from the heat and add the vanilla and marshmallows. Beat until the icing is creamy enough to spread. Spread the icing on each layer of the cake as you stack them on top of one another.

YIELD: 1 (8-LAYER) CAKE

Feud Cake

Years ago at a Mississippi state fair the ladies got into a big fight over which cake was to get the blue ribbon. This is the recipe that won, and it now called the Feud Cake.

CAKE

6	large eggs, separated
1½	cups granulated sugar
2½	tablespoons all-purpose flour
1	teaspoon baking powder
3	cups pecan meal

FROSTING

1	pint whipping cream
1	teaspoon vanilla extract
1	cup confectioners' sugar

Preheat the oven to 350°. For the **cake**, line three 8-inch cake pans with wax paper. Grease and flour the pans. In a large bowl beat the egg yolks with an electric mixer and gradually add the granulated sugar. Blend in the flour and add the baking powder. Add the pecan meal. In another bowl with an electric mixer beat the egg whites until they are stiff. Fold the egg whites into the batter. Divide the batter equally among the three prepared cake pans. Bake for 30 minutes or until a toothpick inserted in the center comes out clean. Remove from the oven and cool.

For the **frosting**, in a large bowl beat the whipping cream until it is stiff. Add the vanilla extract. Add the confectioners' sugar, continuing to beat until the mixture is smooth. Spread between the cake layers and on the sides and top. Garnish with more pecan meal or chopped pecans.

YIELD: 1 (3-LAYER) CAKE

Betty Hartzog
Loganville, Georgia

Fresh Apple Cake

This recipe is a favorite of Elton and Jean Wright of Social Circle. Elton is a friend and employee of the Van Dykes. He is the "head chef" at home, a role for which his wife is very grateful.

2	cups granulated sugar
½	cup vegetable oil
3	eggs
3	cups all-purpose flour
1	teaspoon salt
1	teaspoon baking soda
1½	teaspoons vanilla extract
3	cups peeled and diced firm Granny Smith apples
¾	cup flaked coconut
1	cup black walnut or pecan pieces

Preheat the oven to 325°. In a large mixing bowl combine the sugar and oil. Add the eggs and beat well. In another bowl combine the flour, salt, and baking soda. Add this to the oil mixture. Mix well. Stir in the vanilla, apples, coconut, and nuts. Pour the batter into a 9-inch greased pound-cake or tube pan. Bake for 80 to 90 minutes. Cool to serve.

YIELD: 1 CAKE

Fresh Coconut Cake from Scratch

Louis and Billie have proclaimed this "the best cake ever." Every coconut lover will surely agree. It is moist, fluffy, and sweet. It is truly a tall, layered classic —utterly beautiful. Topped with 7-Minute Icing and sprinkled with tender shreds of coconut, it is suitable for Sunday supper, holiday meals, birthdays, and wedding anniversaries.

CAKE

1	cup (2 sticks) butter, softened
2	cups granulated sugar
4	eggs, beaten
3	cups all-purpose flour
2	teaspoons baking powder
¼	teaspoon baking soda
¼	teaspoon salt
1	cup milk
1	teaspoon vanilla extract
½	teaspoon lemon juice

7-MINUTE ICING

3	egg whites
1⅔	cups granulated sugar
¼	cup white corn syrup
¼	cup coconut milk (or water)
	Dash of salt
1	teaspoon vanilla extract or lemon juice
3	to 4 cups freshly grated coconut

Preheat the oven to 350°. For the **cake**, in a large mixing bowl beat the butter and sugar. Add the beaten eggs (egg whites are optional). In another bowl sift together the flour, baking powder, baking soda, and salt. Add the flour mixture and the milk alternately to the butter mixture. (At the Blue Willow Inn, we start and end with the flour.) Mix thoroughly after each addition. Add the vanilla or lemon juice. Mix thoroughly. This recipe makes three thick 9-inch layers or four thinner 9-inch layers. Bake the cake for 20 to 25 minutes or until a toothpick inserted into the center comes out clean. While the cake is baking, make the icing.

For the **7-Minute Icing**, in the top of a double boiler over simmering water cook the egg whites, sugar, corn syrup, coconut milk and salt for 7 minutes, beating with a hand mixer until peaks begin to drop off a spoon. Remove from the heat and add the vanilla. Spread the icing between the layers, on the sides, and on the top. Sprinkle freshly grated coconut between the layers and all over the sides and the top.

YIELD: 1 CAKE

Sweetened iced tea is the champagne of the South, a little too strong, a little too sweet.

Black-eyed Susans growing on the grounds at Blue Willow

Dining outside is a good idea on cool summer days.

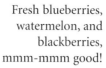

Fresh blueberries,
watermelon, and
blackberries,
mmm-mmm good!

Fresh Georgia peaches

Eleanor Stanhope and Paul and Nancy Posner enjoying lunch in Blue Willow's Lewis Grizzard dining room.

[top] Billie and Louis Van Dyke with Susie

[right] Gourmet Potato Salad (page 112) and Deviled Eggs (page 179). No Southern meal is complete without deviled eggs.

The Blue Willow Inn's Famous Fried Green Tomatoes (page 170) and Tomato Chutney (page 127). The Van Dyke's recipe is considered the best in the South.

Malinda McGuire, one of the antebellum girls at The Blue Willow Inn

Fresh, shelled butter beans and crowder peas are favorites during the summer.

Blue Willow Inn's Mac & Cheese (page 169) complements almost any meal.

Georgia peanuts (also called goobers) are great boiled or roasted.

Baked Sugar Cured Ham (page 231), fresh cooked butter beans, and Candied Yams (page 171) make a good Southern Sunday menu.

Skillet Squash (page 200) is a tasty way to prepare fresh squash.

Roasted turkey with stuffing, cranberry relish (page 127), fresh corn on the cob and creamed potatoes (page 179) with gravy—Very Southern.

Meatloaf (page 218) with caulifower, broccoli, and carrots is a delight for dinner at anytime.

[top] Seafood Au gratin (page 254) is a great company dish.

[right] Blue Willow Squares (page 263) and Louis' Brownies (page 271) are "so good you'll want to slap your mama"—but don't!

Red Hat Society ladies enjoying a meal at the Blue Willow Restaurant

Julian's Pecan Pie (page 334)

Peach Cobbler (page 346) is served daily at The Blue Willow Inn.

You'll have a fight for the last serving of Blueberry Salad (page 102).

Fresh Apple Cake (page 287), Lemon Meringue Pie (page 336), and Strawberry Cake (page 307)—You'll think you're in heaven.

Green Velvet Cake

My college roommate, Pam, gave this recipe to me. It was originally a Red Velvet Cake, but she changed it to green to represent our sorority colors since red was the rival sorority's color. Since college, however, it has become my Christmas cake because each year when we return to Louisiana for Christmas, I am not allowed in the door unless I have the cake with me. We think this would be a fun dessert for St. Patrick's Day.

CAKE

2   cups granulated sugar

1½   cups vegetable oil

2   eggs

2½   cups all-purpose flour

1   teaspoon salt

1   teaspoon baking soda

2   teaspoons cocoa powder

½   (1-ounce) bottle green food coloring

1   teaspoon white vinegar

1   cup buttermilk

1   teaspoon vanilla extract

FROSTING

1   (8-ounce) package cream cheese, softened

½   cup (1 stick) butter, softened

1   (16-ounce) box confectioners' sugar

1   cup chopped pecans

1   teaspoon vanilla extract

Preheat the oven to 350°. For the **cake**, in a large mixing bowl with an electric mixer beat the sugar and oil. Add the eggs and beat well. In another bowl sift the flour, salt, and baking soda together. In a small bowl mix the cocoa powder and the green food coloring. Add the vinegar to this and mix well. Add this mixture to the sugar mixture. Alternately add the flour mixture and the buttermilk to the cocoa mixture. Mix well after each addition. Add the vanilla and beat well. Pour the batter into three greased and floured 8-inch cake pans. Bake for 35 minutes. Remove from the heat and set aside to cool.

For the **frosting**, make sure the cream cheese and butter are at room temperature. In a mixing bowl with an electric mixer beat together the cream cheese and butter until fluffy. Add the confectioners' sugar, pecans, and vanilla. Mix well. Spread the frosting between the layers and over the cake.

YIELD: 1 (3-LAYER) CAKE

Deborah Butler
Decatur, Georgia

Fruit Cake

1	pound pitted dates, chopped
1	pound chopped pecans
¼	pound red candied cherries, chopped
¼	pound green candied cherries, chopped
½	pound candied pineapple, sliced and chopped
1	cup granulated sugar
1	cup all-purpose flour
2	teaspoons baking powder
1	teaspoon ground cinnamon
½	teaspoon salt
4	large eggs, beaten
1	teaspoon vanilla extract

Preheat the oven to 250°. In a large mixing bowl combine the dates, pecans, red cherries, green cherries, and pineapple. In a second large mixing bowl combine the sugar, flour, baking powder, cinnamon, and salt. Mix well. Add the fruit mix to the dry mixture, stirring well. Stir in the eggs and vanilla. Spoon the batter into a greased, parchment-paper-lined tube pan. Bake for 2 hours or until a wooden pick inserted in the center comes out clean. Allow the cake to cool completely in the pan. Remove the cake from the pan and remove the paper. This cake can be baked in two greased and paper-lined 8-inch loaf pans for 1 hour and 20 minutes. Test with a wooden pick for doneness.

YIELD: 1 CAKE

Hummingbird Cake

This cake is truly the sweetest import from the South, and although the true origin of the cake is a mystery, the first published recipe for Hummingbird Cake was in the February 1978 issue of Southern Living *magazine. Louis won the booby prize for his Hummingbird Cake—he forgot the baking soda. His prize was a cookbook about how to bake cakes. I made this cake for Larry Munson, the voice of the Georgia Bulldogs, leaving out the coconut. He had never heard of it. He thought the name was crazy, and he wasn't sure about even tasting it. He liked it so much that three days later, he called to get the recipe for his sister in Minneapolis. She had never heard of it either and wanted to try it because Larry had raved so much about it.*

CAKE

3	cups all-purpose flour
1	teaspoon baking soda
½	teaspoon salt
2	cups granulated sugar
2	teaspoons ground cinnamon
3	eggs, lightly beaten
1	cup vegetable oil
½	cup buttermilk
1½	teaspoons vanilla extract
1	(8-ounce) can crushed pineapple, not drained
1	cup chopped pecans
2	cups mashed ripe bananas (about 5 or 6)
1	cup coconut (optional)

CREAM CHEESE FROSTING

½ cup (1 stick) butter, softened

1 (8-ounce) package cream cheese, softened

1 (16-ounce) package confectioners' sugar

1 teaspoon vanilla extract

1 cup chopped pecans

Preheat the oven to 350°. For the **cake**, in a large bowl combine the flour, baking soda, salt, sugar, and cinnamon. Add the eggs, oil, and buttermilk, stirring until the dry ingredients are moistened. Do *not* beat. Stir in the vanilla, pineapple, pecans, bananas, and coconut if using. Pour the batter into three greased and floured 9-inch round cake pans. Bake for 25 to 35 minutes or until a wooden pick inserted in the center comes out clean. Cool in pans for 15 minutes. Remove from the pans and cool completely on wire racks.

For the **frosting**, in a large mixing bowl with an electric mixer beat the butter and cream cheese. Gradually add the confectioners' sugar. Beat until the mixture is light and fluffy. Stir in the vanilla. Stir in the pecans. Spread between the layers and on the sides and top of the cake.

YIELD: 1 (3-LAYER) CAKE

Teresa Bish
Watkinsville, Georgia

Hershey's Syrup Cake

CAKE

½ cup (1 stick) margarine

1 cup granulated sugar

4 eggs

1 (16-ounce) can chocolate syrup

1 teaspoon vanilla extract

1 cup all-purpose flour, sifted

¼ teaspoon salt

FROSTING

1 tablespoon cocoa powder

1 cup granulated sugar

½ cup chopped pecans

¼ cup margarine

¼ cup milk

1 teaspoon vanilla extract

Preheat the oven to 325° degrees. For the **cake**, grease and flour an 11 x 13-inch pan. In a large mixing bowl beat the margarine and sugar thoroughly. Add the eggs one at a time, beating after each addition. Mix in the Hershey's syrup, vanilla, sifted flour, and salt. Pour into the baking pan and bake for 30 to 35 minutes.

For the **frosting**, while the cake is still warm, bring the cocoa powder, sugar, margarine, and milk to a boil. Boil for a little more than a minute. Boiling too long will give the frosting a sugary consistency. Remove from the heat and add the vanilla and chopped nuts. Beat with a wire whisk until the frosting is of spreading consistency and spread it on the cake.

YIELD: ABOUT 30 SERVINGS

Kathy Walden
Monroe, Georgia

Ice Cream Cake

Kitty Jacobs gave this recipe to us. She has retired from a local tour company and remains a friend of the Van Dykes.

1	angel food cake
1	(3-ounce) package strawberry gelatin
1	(3-ounce) package lime gelatin
1	(3-ounce) package orange gelatin
1	(16-ounce) package frozen strawberries
½	gallon vanilla ice cream
1	(15-ounce) can blueberries
1	(11-ounce) can mandarin oranges

Pull the cake apart into bite-size pieces and divide them among three separate bowls. Pour a package of gelatin into each bowl of cake pieces. Mix well with your fingers. In a springform pan, mold the strawberry cake mixture evenly around the pan. Spread the frozen strawberries over the strawberry cake and smooth one-third (a little more that 2½ cups) of the ice cream evenly over the strawberries. Spread the lime cake over the ice cream and cover it with the blueberries. Cover this with one-third of the ice cream. Spread the orange gelatin cake and the mandarin oranges next. Cover this with the remaining one-third of the ice cream. Freeze the cake. To serve, remove the side of the pan and slice the cake.

YIELD: 1 CAKE

Italian Cream Cake

This is another wonderful cake recipe from Nell Baines, a former manager at the Blue Willow Inn.

CAKE

½	cup shortening
½	cup (1 stick) butter, softened
2	cups granulated sugar
5	eggs, separated
2	cups all-purpose flour
1	teaspoon baking soda
1	cup buttermilk
1	teaspoon vanilla extract
1	cup chopped pecans
1	(7-ounce) can flaked coconut

CREAM CHEESE FROSTING

1	(8-ounce) package of cream cheese, softened
¼	cup butter, softened
1	teaspoon vanilla extract
1	(1-pound) pound box confectioners' sugar, sifted

Preheat the oven to 350°. For the **cake**, grease and flour three 9-inch cake pans. In a large bowl with an electric mixer on medium to high beat the shortening, butter, and granulated sugar until light and fluffy. Add the egg yolks and mix well. In another bowl sift the flour and the baking soda together. Alternately add the flour mixture and the buttermilk to the creamed mixture. Mix well after each addition. Stir in the vanilla, pecans, and coconut. In another bowl beat the egg whites until stiff. Fold these into the batter. Divide the batter equally among the three prepared cake pans. Bake for 30 minutes. The cake is done when a toothpick inserted in the center comes out clean. Remove from the oven and set aside to cool. When cool, remove from the pans and frost with the cream cheese frosting.

For the **cream cheese frosting**, in a large bowl with an electric mixer on medium to high speed beat together the cream cheese, butter, and vanilla. Add the confectioners' sugar gradually, continuing to beat until all is well blended and smooth. Spread the frosting between each layer and on the sides and top of the cake.

YIELD: 1 (9-INCH) THREE-LAYER CAKE

To keep fruit or nuts from sinking to the bottom of a bread or cake batter, shake them in a bag with a small amount of flour to lightly dust them before adding them to the batter.

1-2-3-4 Cake

This fundamental sugar-butter-egg pound cake was the first cake Billie ever baked. She never has really let us know how successful her trial run was.

1	cup (2 sticks) **butter, softened**
2	cups granulated **sugar**
4	eggs
3	cups all-purpose flour
1	tablespoon baking powder
¼	teaspoon salt
1	cup milk
1	teaspoon vanilla extract

Preheat the oven to 350°. In a large bowl beat the butter and sugar until it is light and fluffy. Add the eggs, one at a time, beating well after each addition. In a separate bowl sift together the flour, baking powder, and salt. Add the dry ingredients to the batter alternately with the milk, beating well after each addition. Add the vanilla and pour the batter into a greased and floured tube pan. Bake for 1 hour or until the cake pulls away from the sides of the pan. Turn the cake out onto a cooling rack.

YIELD: 1 TUBE CAKE

Lane Cake

Every southern lady serves this wonderful cake at special occasions—a family reunion, an Easter Sunday dinner, or when a special guest comes for supper. All those great occasions are enjoyed around the table.

1	cup (2 sticks) butter or margarine, softened
1	cup granulated sugar
3¼	cups cake flour, sifted
2	teaspoons baking powder
	Pinch of salt
1	cup milk
2	teaspoons vanilla extract
8	egg whites, stiffly beaten

FILLING

8	egg yolks
1	cup granulated sugar
½	cup (1 stick) butter or margarine
1	cup golden raisins, finely chopped
⅓	cup bourbon or brandy
1	teaspoon vanilla extract

FROSTING

½	cup granulated sugar
¼	cup light corn syrup
2	teaspoons water
⅛	teaspoon salt
2	egg whites
½	teaspoon vanilla

Preheat the oven to 375°. In a large bowl beat the butter. Gradually add the sugar, beating with an electric mixer until light and fluffy. In another bowl combine the cake flour, baking powder, and salt. Stir well. Add the flour mixture to the butter mixture alternately with the milk. Beat well after each addition. Stir in the vanilla. Fold in the egg whites. Pour the batter into three greased and floured 9-inch cake pans. Bake for 20 minutes or until the cake tests done. Cool in the pans for 10 minutes. Remove the cakes from the pans and let them cool completely. Spread the filling between the layers and spread the top and sides of the cake with the frosting.

For the **filling**, combine the egg yolks, sugar, and butter in a 2-quart saucepan. Cook over medium heat, stirring constantly until the mixture is thickened, about 20 minutes. Remove from the heat and stir in the raisins, bourbon, and vanilla. Let the filling cool before spreading on the cake.

For the **frosting**, combine the sugar, corn syrup, water, and salt in a heavy saucepan. Cook over medium heat, stirring constantly until the mixture is clear. Continue cooking until the syrup reaches 245°. In a bowl beat the egg whites until soft peaks form and continue to beat the egg whites while slowly adding the syrup mixture. Add the vanilla. Continue beating until stiff peaks form and the frosting is thick enough to spread.

YIELD: 1 (3-LAYER) CAKE

Lemon Meringue Cake

This cake makes a nice presentation at any special occasion. I always make it for our Fourth of July family get-together. It is very light and summery.

1	(18.25-ounce) package Pillsbury Plus Lemon Cake Mix
1	cup water
⅓	cup vegetable oil
3	eggs

FILLING

1	cup granulated sugar
3	tablespoons cornstarch
¼	teaspoon salt
½	cup water
¼	cup lemon juice
2	tablespoons margarine or butter
1	teaspoon grated lemon peel
4	egg yolks, lightly beaten

MERINGUE

4	egg whites
¼	teaspoon cream of tartar
¾	cup granulated sugar

Heat the oven to 350°. Grease and flour two 8-inch or three 9-inch round cake pans. In a large bowl with an electric mixer on low speed combine the cake mix, water, oil, and eggs until moistened. After all is moistened, turn the mixer on high and beat 2 minutes. Pour the batter into the prepared pans. Bake 25 to 35 minutes or until the cake springs back when touched lightly in the center. Cool 15 minutes and remove from the pans. Cool completely.

For the **filling**, in a medium-size heavy saucepan combine the sugar, cornstarch, and salt. Gradually stir in the water, lemon juice, margarine, and lemon peel. Cook over medium heat until the mixture boils and thickens, stirring constantly. Remove from the heat. In a small bowl beat the egg yolks slightly and gradually blend about one-fourth of the hot lemon mixture into the egg yolks. Return the yolk mixture to the saucepan. Cook another 2 to 3 minutes, stirring constantly. Remove from the heat and set aside to cool.

For the **meringue**, heat the oven to 450°. In a large bowl with an electric mixer on high beat the egg whites with the cream of tartar until foamy. Gradually add the sugar, beating until stiff peaks form.

To assemble the cake, split each layer in half horizontally to form four layers. Place one layer on an ovenproof serving plate; spread with one-third of the filling. Repeat with the remaining layers and filling. Spread the meringue over the top and sides of the cake. Bake for 4 to 5 minutes or until the meringue is a light golden brown. Cool completely. Store in the refrigerator.

YIELD: 1 CAKE

Mascarpone Cheesecake

This recipe is a favorite of Kim Henry, first lady of Oklahoma, and is often prepared at the Oklahoma governor's mansion.

CRUST

10	tablespoons (1¼ sticks) unsalted butter, melted
2¼	cups finely ground vanilla wafers

FILLING

20	ounces cream cheese (room temperature)
8	ounces mascarpone cheese (room temperature)
¾	cup granulated sugar
3	large eggs
1	teaspoon vanilla extract
1	teaspoon fresh lemon juice
¼	teaspoon salt

TOPPING

1	cup sour cream
¼	cup granulated sugar
1	teaspoon vanilla extract
1	teaspoon fresh lemon juice
⅛	teaspoon salt

For the **crust**, preheat the oven to 350°. Spray a 9-inch springform pan with nonstick cooking spray. In a medium-size mixing bowl stir the butter and the ground vanilla wafers together. Reserve ¼ cup of the crumb mixture for the topping. Spread and pat the remaining crumb mixture in the bottom and 1½ inches up the side of the springform pan. Place in the oven and bake for 10 minutes or until golden brown. Cool on a rack for about 25 minutes.

For the **filling**, in a large bowl with an electric mixer at medium-high speed beat the cream cheese, mascarpone, and sugar together until fluffy. Turn the mixer speed to low and add the eggs one at a time. Add the vanilla, lemon juice, and salt. Beat at low speed until combined. Pour the filling into the crust and bake for 25 to 30 minutes or until the cheesecake is set and puffed around the edge, but still trembles when the pan is shaken. Cool in the springform pan on a rack for about 20 minutes.

For the **topping**, in a small bowl stir together the sour cream, sugar, vanilla, lemon juice, and salt. Spoon this mixture over the cheesecake, spreading evenly, leaving a ¼-inch border around the edge. Bake the cheesecake for about 10 minutes or until the topping is set. Sprinkle the top with the reserved ¼ cup crumb mixture. Cool on a rack and then chill for 8 hours loosely covered.

YIELD: 1 CHEESECAKE

Nell's Peanut Butter Cake

CAKE

1	cup all-purpose flour
1	cup plus 2 tablespoons granulated sugar
3½	teaspoons baking powder
¾	teaspoon salt
2	cups graham cracker crumbs
¾	cup peanut butter
½	cup (1 stick) margarine
1	cup plus 2 tablespoons milk
1½	teaspoons vanilla extract
3	eggs

CHOCOLATE FROSTING

2	cups granulated sugar
½	cup cocoa powder
½	cup (1 stick) butter
½	cup milk

PEANUT BUTTER FROSTING

1½	cups granulated sugar
1	(5-ounce) can evaporated milk
¼	cup (½ stick) butter
1	cup peanut butter

For the **cake**, preheat the oven to 375°. Sift the flour, sugar, baking powder, and salt together. Add the graham cracker crumbs, peanut butter, margarine, milk, and vanilla. Beat the mixture with an electric mixer on low until it is moistened and then beat on medium for 2 minutes. Add the eggs and beat for 1 minute. Pour into a greased 9 x 13-inch pan. Bake for 30 to 35 minutes. Do not remove from the pan. When cooled, frost the cake with either the chocolate or peanut butter frosting.

For the **chocolate frosting**, in a saucepan on medium heat combine the sugar, cocoa powder, butter, and milk. Heat and bring to a boil. Boil for 1 minute. Poke a few holes in the cake. Pour the warm frosting over it. For a chocolate-peanut butter taste you can add ½ cup peanut butter to this frosting, beating it in after removing the pan from the heat but before allowing it to cool.

For the **peanut butter frosting**, in a saucepan on medium heat combine the sugar, milk, and butter in a saucepan. Bring the mixture to a boil. Boil for 4 minutes. Add the peanut butter and beat until creamy. Spread quickly over the cake because this frosting hardens very quickly.

YIELD: 24 SERVINGS

Orange-Coconut Cake

This recipe from our original cookbook was given to us by Shirley C. Wood, whose husband was the pastor of the First Baptist Church in Social Circle. Both she and her husband were frequent guests at the Blue Willow Inn Restaurant. This recipe has been in Mrs. Wood's family for three generations. Her grandmother baked the Orange Coconut Cake for every Christmas dinner. Her mother then baked the same recipe for Christmas dinners at her home, and Mrs. Wood continued the family tradition by using this recipe for her family's Christmas dinner. The recipe is originally from a 1908 cookbook and is so old that no oven temperature was noted.

CAKE

1	cup (2 sticks) butter, softened
2	cups granulated sugar
5	egg yolks
½	cup water
	Juice and grated zest of 1 orange
3	egg whites
2	cups all-purpose flour
⅓	level teaspoon salt
1½	level teaspoons baking powder

ORANGE-COCONUT FROSTING

1	egg
1	cup whipped cream
½	cup confectioners' sugar
	Grated zest of 1 orange
1	cup grated coconut
	Juice of 1 orange

For the **cake**, beat the butter and sugar together. Add the egg yolks and water, then the juice and zest of the orange. Add the flour, salt, and baking powder sifted together. Beat the egg whites stiffly and fold them in very gently. Bake for 20 minutes in a hot oven (375°) in large (9-inch) layer cake pans. Cool and put the layers together with the frosting.

For the **orange-coconut-frosting**, beat the egg until light. Add the whipped cream and confectioners' sugar. Add the orange zest, coconut, and orange juice. Spread between the layers and on top of the cake.

YIELD: 1 CAKE

Peanut Butter Cake

If you have peanut allergies, this is not the cake for you. However, if you like what happens to the taste of peanuts when they are sweetened and baked, here is bliss on a dish.

CAKE

½	cup shortening
1	cup creamy peanut butter
1½	cups granulated sugar
3	eggs
2	cups all-purpose flour
1	teaspoon baking soda
1½	cups buttermilk
1	teaspoon vanilla extract

PEANUT BUTTER FROSTING

½ cup (1 stick) butter, softened

1 (16-ounce) box confectioners' sugar

1 cup peanut butter, creamy or chunky as desired

½ teaspoon vanilla extract

Milk, as needed

Grease and sprinkle with sugar three cake pans. Preheat the oven to 350°. For the **cake**, in a large mixing bowl beat the shortening, peanut butter, and sugar. Add the eggs one at a time, beating after each addition. In a separate bowl combine the flour with the baking soda, and add to the mixture alternately with the buttermilk, beating after each addition. Add the vanilla and mix well. Pour the batter into the prepared pans. Bake for 30 minutes. Remove from the oven and after the cakes have cooled for 5 to 10 minutes, remove them from the pans to a cooling rack.

For the **peanut butter frosting**, in a large mixing bowl beat together the butter, confectioners' sugar, peanut butter, and vanilla extract, adding just enough milk to make a creamy, spreadable frosting. Frost the layers as you add them one on top of the other and then frost the sides and top of the cake.

YIELD: 1 (3-LAYER) CAKE

POPULAR SOUTHERN SAYING

Grinning like a mule eating briars. (Proud)

Peppermint Chiffon Cake

2 cups sifted all-purpose flour

1½ cups granulated sugar

3 teaspoons baking powder

1 teaspoon salt

½ cup vegetable oil

7 egg yolks

¾ cup cold water

1 teaspoon peppermint extract

1 cup egg whites

½ teaspoon cream of tartar

½ teaspoon red food coloring

Seven-Minute Icing (recipe on page 356)

Peppermint candies, crushed

Preheat the oven to 325°. In a large bowl sift together the flour, sugar, baking powder, and salt. Make a well in the center of this mixture. Add the oil, egg yolks, water, and peppermint extract. Beat with a spoon until smooth. In a separate bowl beat the egg whites and cream of tartar until the whites are very stiff. Gently fold the egg whites into the batter just until blended. Do *not* stir. Sprinkle the food coloring over the top of the batter and fold in with only 3 or 4 strokes. Do *not* blend in the coloring completely. Pour into an ungreased 10-inch tube pan. Bake for 55 minutes. Increase the heat to 350° and continue baking for 10 to 25 minutes. Remove from the oven and set aside to cool. Frost with Seven-Minute Icing and sprinkle crushed peppermint candies over the icing.

YIELD: 1 CAKE

Melissa Hoganson
Port St. Lucie, Florida

Peppermint Angel Food Cake

1⅔   cups egg whites, about 12 large eggs

1   cup sifted confectioners' sugar

1   cup sifted cake flour or all-purpose flour

½   to 1 teaspoon cream of tartar

1   teaspoon vanilla extract

1   cup granulated sugar

¼   teaspoon peppermint extract

6   drops red food coloring

PINK PEPPERMINT FROSTING

2   egg whites

⅔   cup granulated sugar

2   tablespoons white corn syrup

¼   cup water

¼   teaspoon peppermint extract

      Red food coloring

Preheat the oven to 350°. Place the egg whites in a very large mixing bowl and allow them to stand at room temperature for 30 minutes. In another bowl sift the confectioners' sugar and flour together three times. Add the cream of tartar and vanilla to the egg whites. With an electric mixer on medium to high speed beat the egg white mixture until soft peaks form. Gradually add the granulated sugar, 2 tablespoons at a time, beating until stiff peaks form. Sift about one-fourth of the flour mixture over the beaten egg whites and gently fold it in. Repeat this procedure using only one-fourth of the flour at a time. Divide the batter in half. In one half, fold in the peppermint extract and the food coloring. Spoon the pink batter and white batter alternately into an ungreased 10-inch tube pan. Gently cut through the batters with a knife, swirling gently. On the lowest oven rack, bake the cake for 40 to 45 minutes or until the top springs back when lightly touched. After removing from the oven, invert the pan immediately onto its tube. Cool thoroughly. Remove the cake from the pan. Ice the cake with frosting.

For the **pink peppermint frosting**, place the egg whites in a mixing bowl and allow them to stand for 30 minutes to come to room temperature. In a 2-quart saucepan on medium heat mix the granulated sugar, corn syrup, and water. Cook the mixture and stir until it comes to a boil. Boil gently, without stirring, for 5 minutes. Remove from the heat. With an electric mixer on medium to high speed beat the egg whites until soft peaks form. Slowly add the hot syrup to the egg whites. Pour the syrup in a steady stream while continuing to beat the egg whites. Continue beating until stiff glossy peaks form. Beat in the peppermint extract and enough red food coloring to tint the frosting pink.

YIELD: 1 ANGEL FOOD CAKE

Petra's "Not Just Right" Pound Cake

Petra Broberg was a dear friend of Billie's. She was one of the first graduates of the Chicago School of Nursing in the early 1900s. When Petra was engaged to be married, her best friend became terminally ill. Before she died she asked Petra to raise her two small daughters. Petra agreed, but her beau flew from the altar at the prospect of a ready-made family. From that time on, Petra dedicated her life to taking care of other people and children whom no one else could care for or wanted. Billie and Petra met while Billie was in the children's home in Savannah and Petra was the director of the Fresh Air Home on Tybee Island, Georgia. Petra took Billie "under her wings." After Billie grew up and started her family, several years passed before she and Petra were reunited while visiting the same church in Savannah. This time Billie took Petra "under her wings," and Petra lived with Billie and Louis until her death in 1987.

One of Petra's favorite hobbies was cooking. She had mastered this recipe and made one of the best pound cakes anywhere. One reason may have been that after pouring the batter into the tube pan, she would bang the pan on the counter to "eliminate air pockets," an act that would often cause Louis to check on her to see if she was destroying the kitchen. When she served her pound cake, she would always say that "it's not just right" and enjoyed everyone telling her, "Oh, no, it's wonderful."

1	cup (2 sticks) butter
3	cups granulated sugar
6	eggs
1	cup sour cream
½	teaspoon baking soda
3	cups all-purpose flour, sifted
1	teaspoon vanilla extract

Grease and flour a tube pan. Preheat the oven to 350° degrees. In a large mixing bowl beat the butter and the sugar. Whip until creamy. Add the eggs, one at a time, beating at least 1 minute between each addition. In a small bowl mix the sour cream and baking soda. Alternately add the sour cream mixture and the flour to the egg mixture, beating 1 minute between each addition. Add the vanilla. Pour the batter evenly into the prepared tube pan, tapping the pan lightly on the counter to eliminate any air pockets. Bake for 1 hour and 15 minutes until light brown. Test to be sure the cake is done. A toothpick inserted in the center should come out clean. Cool the cake in the pan for 35 minutes before removing it.

YIELD: 1 LARGE POUND CAKE

Pineapple Nut Cake

Elaine Jones gave us this recipe. It is an old recipe that originally called for flour, baking soda, sugar, etc. Elaine modified it by using a cake mix to save time and money. Additionally, she found that by using the new "lite" cake mixes, you don't have to add oil or butter and that is another time and money saver.

CAKE

1	(18.25-ounce) box "lite" yellow cake mix
1	(14-ounce) can crushed pineapple with juice (do not drain)
¾	cup water
3	eggs

COCONUT ICING

¾	cup evaporated milk
½	cup (1 stick) butter
1	cup granulated sugar
1	cup coconut
1	cup chopped walnuts

For the **cake**, preheat the oven to 350°. Lightly grease a 9 x 13-inch pan. In a large mixing bowl combine the cake mix, crushed pineapple with juice, water, and eggs. Pour the batter into the prepared pan and bake for 30 minutes until golden brown and a toothpick inserted in the center comes out clean.

For the **coconut icing**, in a saucepan on medium heat, combine the milk, butter, and sugar. Bring to a boil, stirring frequently. Cook for 5 minutes on medium heat. Turn off the heat and stir in the coconut and walnuts. Pour the frosting over the cake.

Hint: If you do not have a "lite" mix available, you can use any yellow cake mix and follow the directions on the box except eliminate half a cup of water required to compensate for the juice of the pineapple.

YIELD: 24 SERVINGS

Pineapple Upside-Down Cake

1	(28-ounce) box yellow cake mix
1	(16-ounce) can pineapple rings, juice drained and reserved
	Maraschino cherries without stems
	Glaze (see recipe below)

GLAZE

1	cup reserved pineapple juice
¼	cup (½ stick) butter
½	cup packed light brown sugar

Preheat the oven to 350°. Prepared the cake according to the package directions, substituting pineapple juice for the water.

For the **glaze**, in a saucepan on medium heat combine the pineapple juice, butter, and brown sugar. Bring to a boil, stirring continuously.

Layer the bottom of a lightly greased 9 x 13-inch baking pan with the pineapple rings and place a cherry in the center of each ring. Pour the glaze over the pineapple rings. Pour the cake batter evenly over the pineapple rings. Bake for 35 minutes or until done when a wooden pick inserted in the cake comes out clean.

YIELD: 24 SERVINGS

Prune Spice Cake

1½	cups granuated sugar
1	cup vegetable oil
3	large eggs
1	cup cooked prunes
2	cups all-purpose flour
1	teaspoon baking soda
½	teaspoon salt
1	teaspoon ground cinnamon
½	teaspoon ground nutmeg
1	cup buttermilk
1	cup chopped nuts (optional)

FROSTING

½	cup granulated sugar
2	tablespoons butter
¼	teaspoon baking soda
¼	cup buttermilk
1	teaspoon vanilla extract

Preheat the oven to 300°. Grease a 9 x 13-inch pan. In a large bowl with an electric mixer beat together the sugar and oil. Add the eggs and beat. Add the prunes and beat well. In another bowl sift together the flour, baking soda, salt, cinnamon, and nutmeg. Add the dry ingredients alternately with the buttermilk to the prune mixture. Stir in the nuts if desired. Pour the batter into the prepared pan. Bake for 30 to 45 minutes. Have the frosting prepared when the cake comes out of the oven and pour it over the cake.

For the **frosting**, in a saucepan combine the sugar, butter, soda, buttermilk, and vanilla. Turn the heat to medium and cook for 2 minutes. Pour the frosting over the warm cake.

Hint: Self-rising flour can be used for this cake, omitting the baking soda and salt.

YIELD: 1 CAKE

Betty Hartzog
Loganville, Georgia

Punch Bowl Cake

On Thanksgiving and Mother's Day special-occasion dishes are featured at every station at the Blue Willow Inn from the salad bar to the dessert table. One of these extra-extravagant desserts is Punch Bowl Cake. It is a recipe brought to us by an employee, Keith Browning. The cake was served to Keith at a special function and it was a great hit. Keith asked for the recipe and brought it back to us. It is a wonderful easy-does-it recipe that requires very little kitchen drudgery, but turns out to be wonderfully majestic in appearance.

1	(18.25-ounce) box yellow cake mix
1	(12-ounce) package shredded coconut, divided in half
1	(20-ounce) can crushed pineapple
2	(12-ounce) containers whipped topping
¼	plus ¼ cup chopped pecans
1	(20-ounce) can cherry pie filling

Bake the cake according to the directions on the box and slice horizontally creating two layers. Allow the cake to cool. Crumble one layer into the bottom of a punch bowl along with half the coconut. Spread the crushed pineapple over the layer of coconut and cake. Layer 1 container of the whipped topping over the pineapple. Top this layer with ¼ cup of the pecans. Crumble the remaining layer of cake over the pecans. Spread the remaining half of the coconut and the cherry pie filling over the second layer of cake. Spread the second container of whipped topping over the cherry pie filling. Top

with the remaining ¼ cup pecans. Refrigerate for 6 to 8 hours to allow the flavors to mingle.

Yield: 1 cake

Red Velvet Cake

This old-fashioned bit of kitchen fun was popular throughout the country at one time, but has remained so only in places where traditions die hard—for example, the South. Yes, it is a vivid red. It has the flavor of a childhood birthday cake; and white cream cheese frosting is truly the order of the day.

1½	cups granulated sugar
1	cup shortening
2	large eggs
2	(2-ounce) bottles red food coloring
2	tablespoons cocoa powder
2¼	cups all-purpose flour
1	teaspoon salt
1	cup buttermilk
1	tablespoon vinegar
1	teaspoon baking soda

Frosting

1	(16-ounce) box confectioners' sugar
½	teaspoon vanilla extract
1	(8-ounce) package cream cheese, softened
½	cup chopped pecans
4	tablespoons margarine, softened

Preheat the oven to 350°. To make the cake cream the sugar and shortening in a large bowl. Add the eggs one at a time. In a separate bowl make a paste with the food coloring and cocoa powder. Add the paste to the shortening mixture. In another bowl combine the flour and salt and add it to the mixture. In a cup mix the buttermilk, vinegar, and baking soda, and add it to the mixture. Pour the batter into three greased and floured 8-inch cake pans. Bake for 25 to 30 minutes or until done. Let the cake cool in the pans before removing.

For the **frosting**, in a bowl cream together the sugar, vanilla, cream cheese, pecans, and margarine until light and fluffy. If the frosting is too thin, add more confectioners' sugar. Spread the frosting over the tops of the three layers, stack them, and then ice the sides.

YIELD: 1 (3-LAYER) CAKE

Rum Cake

It has always been a mystery to me how my mother-in-law could bake this cake yet never set foot in a liquor store.

CAKE

1	(18.25-ounce) yellow cake mix
1	(3-ounce) box vanilla instant pudding mix
4	eggs
½	cup cold water
½	cup vegetable oil
½	cup dark rum
1	cup chopped pecans

TOPPING

½	cup (1 stick) butter
¼	cup water
¼	cup granulated sugar
½	cup dark rum

For the **cake**, preheat the oven to 325°. Grease a tube pan. In a large mixing bowl with an electric mixer beat the cake mix, pudding mix, eggs, water, oil, and dark rum until smooth. Pour the batter into the tube pan. Sprinkle the pecans on the top of the batter. Bake for 1 hour. Set aside to cool. Using a fork, poke holes in the cake.

For the **topping**, in a saucepan on medium heat bring the butter, water, sugar, and rum to a boil, stirring continuously. Boil for 5 minutes. Pour over the cake.

YIELD: 1 CAKE

7-Up Cake

CAKE

1   (18.25-ounce) box lemon supreme cake mix

1   (3.4-ounce) package lemon instant pudding mix

¾   cup vegetable oil

4   large eggs

1   (12-ounce) can 7-Up

FROSTING

2   large eggs

2   cups granulated sugar

½   cup (1 stick) margarine, softened

1   (20-ounce) can crushed pineapple (do not drain)

1   cup chopped pecans

1   (7-ounce) can coconut

     Cornstarch

     Water

2   teaspoons vanilla extract

For the cake, preheat the oven to 350°. Grease and flour three 9-inch cake pans. In a large mixing bowl combine the cake mix, pudding mix, oil, eggs, and 7-Up. Mix well. Divide the batter evenly among three 9-inch cake pans. Bake for about 30 minutes or until a wooden pick inserted in the center comes out clean.

For the frosting, in a heavy saucepan combine the eggs, sugar, margarine, pineapple, pecans, and coconut. Place over medium heat and bring to a boil, stirring often. Boil for 1 minute, stirring continuously. Thicken with several tablespoons of cornstarch dissolved in water. Remove from the heat and stir in the vanilla. Frost the layers, the sides, and the top of the cake.

YIELD: 1 (3-LAYER) CAKE

Southern Delight Butter Pecan Cake

This is a very special cake. Toasting the pecans before adding them to this cake adds extra flavor and keeps the nuts crunchy in the cake and frosting.

CAKE

1⅓   cups chopped pecans

3   tablespoons plus ⅔ cup butter or margarine, softened

1⅓   cups granulated sugar

2   eggs

2   cups all-purpose flour

1½   teaspoons baking powder

¼   teaspoon salt

⅔   cup milk

1½   teaspoons vanilla flavoring

BUTTER PECAN FROSTING

3   tablespoons butter or margarine, softened

3   cups sifted confectioners' sugar

3   tablespoons milk

¾   teaspoon vanilla flavoring

Preheat the oven to 350°. To toast the pecans melt 3 tablespoons of the butter or margarine in a baking pan. Stir in the pecans. Bake for 10 minutes, stirring twice and watching closely because they burn easily. Set aside to cool.

For the **cake**, beat the remaining ⅔ cup butter and sugar in a large mixing bowl until it is light and fluffy. Add the eggs, one at a time, beating well after each addition. In a medium-size bowl combine the flour, baking powder, and salt. Add the dry ingredients alternately with the milk to the butter mixture. Stir in the vanilla and 1 cup of the toasted pecans. Pour the batter into two greased and floured 8-inch round baking pans. Bake for 30 to 35 minutes or until a toothpick inserted in the center comes out clean. Cool for 10 minutes and remove from the pans to wire racks to cool completely.

For the **butter pecan frosting**, beat the butter and sugar together in a mixing bowl. Add the milk and vanilla flavoring. Beat until it is light and fluffy. Add additional milk, if needed. Stir in the remaining ⅓ cup toasted pecans. Spread the frosting between the layers and over the top and sides of the cake.

Hint: If a greater amount of frosting is desired, increase the recipe to 4 tablespoons butter, 1 (16-ounce) box sifted confectioners' sugar, 4 tablespoons milk, and 1 teaspoon vanilla extract.

YIELD: 1 (2-LAYER) CAKE

Strawberry Cake

This is another scrumptious recipe from Nell Baines. This is a favorite of Billie's son, Chip, and either Billie or Nellie makes this cake for him every year for his birthday. Nell says that she normally makes the frosting for this cake first and uses the remaining strawberries in the cake.

1	(3-ounce) package strawberry gelatin
½	cup boiling water
1	(18.25-ounce) box butter recipe golden cake mix
¾	cup vegetable oil
4	large eggs
½	(10-ounce) box frozen strawberries, thawed

STRAWBERRY FROSTING

1	(16-ounce) box confectioners' sugar
½	cup (1 stick) butter or margarine, softened
½	(10-ounce) box frozen strawberries, thawed

Preheat the oven to 350°. In small bowl dissolve the gelatin in the boiling water. Set aside to cool. In a large mixing bowl combine the cake mix, vegetable oil, and the eggs one at a time. Beat to mix. Stir in half the box of strawberries and the gelatin mixture. Bake in two greased and sugared 9-inch cake pans for 25 to 30 minutes. Remove from the oven. Set aside to cool. Cover the top and sides with the strawberry frosting.

For the **strawberry frosting**, in a large bowl with an electric mixer beat the sugar and butter. Add the remaining ½ box strawberries one at a time and mix until the frosting is moistened.

YIELD: 1 (2-LAYER) CAKE

Strawberry Shortcake

Since Southerners are blessed with a long growing season, ripe fruits are available most of the year. When strawberries are at their largest and sweetest, it is time to make this shortcake.

1	quart plump and juicy fresh strawberries, sliced
⅓	cup plus 1½ tablespoons granulated sugar
2½	cups all-purpose flour
½	teaspoon baking powder
½	teaspoon salt
½	teaspoon baking soda
½	cup (1 stick) butter, softened
1	(¼-ounce) package active dry yeast
2	tablespoons lukewarm water
½	cup buttermilk
⅔	cup (1 stick plus 3 tablespoons) butter, melted
	Refrigerated whipped topping

Place the strawberries in a bowl. Sprinkle them with ⅓ cup of the sugar. Cover the strawberries and refrigerate while baking the cake.

For the dough, in a bowl combine the remaining 1½ tablespoons sugar, the flour, baking powder, salt, and baking soda. Cut in the butter until the mixture resembles coarse meal. In a small dish dissolve the yeast in the warm water. Add the dissolved yeast to the dry ingredients. Add the buttermilk and blend thoroughly. Preheat the oven to 450°. Turn the dough onto a lightly floured board and roll it out to a ¼-inch thickness. Cut the dough with a biscuit cutter. Dip the rounds in the melted butter. Place the rounds on an ungreased baking sheet and bake for 15 minutes. Top the cooled rounds with the strawberries and their juice. Top the strawberries with a generous portion of whipped topping.

YIELD: 12 TO 15 SHORTCAKES

Texas Sheet Cake

CAKE

2	cups granulated sugar
2	cups all-purpose flour
⅓	teaspoon salt
½	cup (1 stick) margarine
½	cup vegetable oil
1	cup water
3	tablespoons cocoa powder
2	eggs, beaten
½	cup buttermilk
1	teaspoon baking soda
1	teaspoon vanilla extract

FROSTING

½	cup (1 stick) butter or margarine, softened

6 tablespoons milk

4 tablespoons cocoa powder

½ cup creamy peanut butter (optional)

1 (16-ounce) box confectioners' sugar

1 teaspoon vanilla extract

For the **cake** preheat the oven to 350°. In a large mixing bowl mix together the sugar, flour, and salt. In a saucepan over medium heat mix the margarine, oil, water, and cocoa powder. Bring to a boil. Pour this over the sugar mixture. Add the eggs, buttermilk, baking soda, and vanilla. Mix with a spoon. Pour into a greased and floured 9 x 13-inch pan. Bake for 30 minutes.

For the **frosting**, in a saucepan on medium heat combine the butter or margarine, milk, and cocoa powder. Heat until boiling. Remove from the heat. Stir in the peanut butter if desired. Add the confectioners' sugar and the vanilla. Pour over the hot cake.

YIELD: ABOUT 24 SERVINGS

POPULAR SOUTHERN SAYING

He'd argue with a fence post! (Stubborn)

Watermelon Cake

This is a sweet, summery, light-as-air, delicious, and easy way to please your guests. This is a wonderful dessert for a cookout—especially the Fourth of July, when watermelon along with barbeque is the food of the day.

1 tablespoon all-purpose flour

1 (18.25-ounce) box white cake mix

1 (3-ounce) package mixed-fruit-flavored gelatin

¾ cup vegetable oil

1 cup chopped watermelon

4 eggs

ICING

½ cup (1 stick) margarine, softened

1 (16-ounce) box confectioners' sugar

½ to 1 cup watermelon

Red food coloring (optional)

Preheat the oven to 325°. In a large bowl sprinkle the flour over the cake mix. Add the gelatin, oil, and watermelon. Mix thoroughly with an electric mixer, adding the eggs one at a time. Divide the batter into two greased and floured 8 inch, cake pans. Bake for about 30 minutes.

For the **icing**, combine the margarine and confectioners' sugar. Blend in the watermelon gradually until a spreading consistency is reached. Red food coloring may be added for effect. Spread the icing generously over the cooled cake.

YIELD: 1 (2-LAYER) CAKE

Buttermilk Pralines

This recipe is so delicious and easy to make that I almost hate to give away its success story. Our first real friend in Georgia gave it to me after I moved here from south Florida. Dot was a grand lady from Cordele and the best candy maker ever. She showed me how she gathered pecans, shelled them, bought lots of sugar early — on sale — before the holidays and then began her annual candy making. Now that she is gone, I try to take her place by making lots of buttermilk pralines for gifts like she did. All say they enjoy them and ask to be sure to put them on my list for next year.

3	cups granulated sugar
1	teaspoon salt
1	cup buttermilk
¾	cup light corn syrup
2	tablespoons butter
2	cups pecan halves

In a saucepan on medium heat combine the sugar, salt, buttermilk, syrup, and butter. Cook, stirring often, until the mixture comes to the soft-ball stage (236° with a candy thermometer). Remove from the heat. Stir in the pecans. Beat by hand until the candy mixture loses its gloss. Drop by spoonfuls on wax paper. Allow to cool.

YIELD: 4½ DOZEN

Jean Elder
Covington, Georgia

Cranberry-Pear Fruit Jellies

These are great to add to your Thanksgiving celebration.

3	firm Comice or Bartlett pears (1½ pounds)
1	(12-ounce) bag fresh or frozen cranberries
1	cup water
2¾	plus 1 cups granulated sugar
2	tablespoons unsalted butter
1	(3-inch) cinnamon stick
2	(3-ounce) packages liquid pectin (not powdered)

Rinse an 8 x 8-inch baking pan with water and shake it dry. Line the bottom and the sides of the pan with plastic wrap, pressing it into the bottom and corners of the pan to smooth it out. (The water will help the plastic wrap adhere to the pan.) Quarter and core the pears. (Do NOT peel them.) Cut the pears into ½-inch pieces. In a 6-quart pot over medium high heat bring the pears, cranberries, water, 2¾ cups of the sugar, butter, and cinnamon stick to a boil, stirring occasionally. Reduce the heat to low and simmer, covered, stirring occasionally, until the cranberries burst and the pears are tender, about 10 minutes.

Remove and discard the cinnamon stick. Then carefully transfer the hot mixture to a food processor and purée until it is smooth, about 1 minute. The mixture will be thick. Force the mixture through a medium-mesh sieve back into the same pot, pressing on the solids with the back of a spoon and discarding the solids. Put a plate in the freezer to chill.

Bring the cranberry mixture to a boil over high heat and add the pectin. Reduce the heat to medium and cook, stirring frequently, until it is very thick and paste-like, about 45 minutes. To test, remove from the heat. Drop a teaspoonful on the chilled plate and chill in the freezer for 1 minute. Tilt the plate. The mixture should remain in a firm mound and not run. If the mixture runs, continue cooking and stirring and repeat the test every 5 minutes.

Remove from the heat and immediately pour the mixture into the prepared pan. Gently tap the sides of the pan to smooth the top and eliminate any air bubbles. Cool to room temperature, at least 1 hour; then cover the surface directly with plastic wrap and chill until firm, 2 hours up to 1 week.

Unmold the fruit mixture onto a cutting board and remove the plastic wrap. Using a sharp knife, cut into 1-inch squares. Spread the remaining 1 cup sugar in a shallow pan and coat the squares on all sides.

YIELD: 64 CANDIES

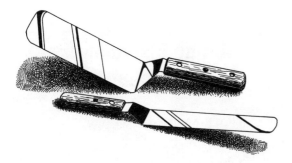

Cream Cheese Mints

1 **(3-ounce) package cream cheese, softened**

¼ **to ½ teaspoon flavoring (peppermint, butter, almond, wintergreen, or other) Food coloring or colored sugared (optional)**

2½ **to 3 cups confectioners' sugar Granulated sugar**

In a medium-size bowl mix the cream cheese until it is soft. Add the flavoring and food coloring. Gradually add the confectioners' sugar. Mix and knead until it is the consistency of pie dough or putty. Roll into balls the size of a marble. Dip in the granulated sugar and press firmly into a candy mold. Unmold at once onto waxed paper. Once firm, transfer the mints to a cake rack and let dry for a few hours. They will keep a long time if stored in an airtight container.

Hint: The food coloring in the cream cheese can be omitted and the mints can be rolled in colored sugar. If you don't have candy presses, roll the mints and then flatten with a fork for a pretty design.

YIELD: 6 DOZEN

Divinity

This wonderfully tasty confection should not be made on a rainy day.

2½	cups granulated sugar
½	cup water
½	cup light corn syrup
¼	teaspoon salt
2	egg whites
1	teaspoon vanilla extract
1	cup toasted chopped pecans
	Toasted pecan halves for garnish

In a heavy 2-quart saucepan over low heat cook the sugar, water, corn syrup, and salt until the sugar dissolves and a candy thermometer registers 248° (about 15 minutes). Remove the syrup mixture from the heat. In a bowl with an electric mixer on high speed beat the egg whites until stiff peaks form. Pour half of the hot syrup in a thin stream over the egg whites, beating constantly at high speed for about 5 minutes.

Cook the remaining half of the syrup over medium heat, stirring occasionally, until the candy thermometer registers 272° (4 to 5 minutes). Slowly pour the hot syrup and the vanilla extract over the egg white mixture, beating constantly at high speed until the mixture holds its shape, 6 to 8 minutes. Stir in the chopped pecans.

Drop the mixture quickly by the rounded teaspoonful onto lightly greased wax paper. Dip from the bottom of the bowl working gradually to the top. (The candy starts to harden first from the bottom of the bowl.) Garnish with a pecan half if desired. Cool.

YIELD: 4 DOZEN PIECES

Donna's Fudge

This recipe comes from Billie's daughter and is one of Louis' favorites. He requests that Donna makes him a tin of fudge for Christmas, Father's Day, and his birthday.

½	cup (1 stick) butter, softened
1	(16-ounce) package confectioners' sugar
½	cup cocoa powder
¼	cup milk
1	teaspoon vanilla extract
1	cup chopped pecans or walnuts (optional)

In a saucepan on medium heat melt the butter. Add the confectioners' sugar, cocoa powder, milk, vanilla, and nuts. Turn the heat to low. Stir until the sugar is completely dissolved and the mixture is smooth. Pour the mixture into an ungreased 9 x 9-inch pan. Set aside to cool. Cut into 1-inch squares.

YIELD: 18 (1-INCH) SQUARES

Mamie Eisenhower's Million-Dollar Fudge

4½	cups granulated sugar
	Pinch of salt
2	tablespoons butter
1	(12-ounce) can evaporated milk
1	(12-ounce) package semisweet chocolate bits

1   (12-ounce) box Baker's German's sweet chocolate

1   pint marshmallow creme

2   cups chopped pecans

In a saucepan on medium heat combine the sugar, salt, butter, and evaporated milk. Bring to a boil and boil for 6 minutes. In a mixing bowl mix together the semisweet chocolate, the German chocolate, marshmallow creme, and pecans. Pour the boiling syrup over the ingredients. Beat until the chocolate is melted. Pour into a 9 x 13-inch pan. Let stand a few hours before cutting. Cut into 1-inch squares.

YIELD: 117 SQUARES

Merry Cherry Fudge

Vegetable cooking spray

36   maraschino cherries with stems

1   (12-ounce) package semisweet chocolate morsels

6   (1-ounce) squares bittersweet chocolate, chopped

1   (14-ounce) can sweetened condensed milk

1   teaspoon maraschino cherry juice

2   cups chopped pecans

Lightly coat an 8 x 8-inch-square pan with cooking spray. Blot the cherries dry with paper towels. In a heavy saucepan on very low heat combine the semisweet and bittersweet chocolate. Stir constantly until the chocolate is melted and smooth. Remove from the heat. Stir in the sweetened condensed milk and cherry juice. Stir in the pecans. Spoon the mixture into the prepared pan. Immediately press the cherries into the fudge, leaving the top of each cherry with the stem exposed. Cover and chill for 2 hours or until firm. Cut into 1-inch squares with a cherry on each square.

YIELD: 36 SERVINGS

Mints

Mints are a must for Southern parties, receptions, and other special occasions. Store-bought mints can never compare with homemade mints.

⅓   cup light corn syrup

4   tablespoons butter, softened

1   teaspoon peppermint extract

½   teaspoon salt

1   (16-ounce) package confectioners' sugar, sifted

Food coloring

In a mixing bowl blend the corn syrup, butter, peppermint extract, and salt. Add the sugar and mix by hand with a spoon until smooth. Add 1 drop of food coloring for each ⅓ cup of the mixture. Press the mixture into desired mint molds. Let the molds stand for several hours to dry. Remove and store in a sealed container.

Hint: If mint molds are not available, roll a small amount of the mixture into a nickel-size ball and flatten with a fork onto wax paper.

YIELD: ABOUT 7 DOZEN

Peanut Brittle

3   cups granulated sugar
1   cup white corn syrup
½   cup water
3   cups raw Georgia peanuts
3   teaspoons margarine
1   teaspoon salt
1½   teaspoons baking soda

In a heavy 5 to 6-quart saucepan on medium heat combine the sugar, syrup, and water. Cook and stir until the sugar melts. Add the peanuts. Stir occasionally. Cook until a candy thermometer reaches 300° degrees or to the hard-crack stage. The syrup will be golden and the peanuts will pop because they have roasted. Remove from the heat and add the margarine, salt, and baking soda. Stir well. The candy will puff up. Pour the candy quickly onto greased aluminum foil. Stretch the mixture using a fork. You can stretch with your hands when it is cool enough. When completely cool, break into pieces.

YIELD: 12 TO 15 SERVINGS

Peppermint Brickle

This is a simple and unique treat that I enjoy making with my children during the Christmas holidays. It is a big hit at school and family events.

1   package peppermint candy canes (about 10)

1   (24-ounce) package white chocolate almond bark
1   tablespoon shortening

Place the candy canes in a plastic bag and crush them into small pieces. In a double boiler over low heat melt the almond bark. Stir in the shortening. Remove from the heat and stir in the crushed peppermint. Spread this onto a foil-covered cookie sheet. Place in the freezer long enough for the mixture to harden. Break into pieces.

YIELD: 12 TO 15 SERVINGS

Cherie Powell
Newborn, Georgia

Pralines

Pralines are beloved throughout the South, although they are most often associated with New Orleans. French-ancestry chefs originally pounded sugar and nuts into a fine paste that was supposed to be good for one's digestive tract.

1½   tablespoons light corn syrup
½   cup evaporated milk
3   tablespoons butter
½   cup firmly packed light brown sugar
1   cup granulated sugar
⅛   teaspoon salt
½   cup pecan halves, toasted
½   cup pecan pieces, toasted
1   teaspoon vanilla extract

Combine the corn syrup, milk, butter, brown sugar, granulated sugar, and salt in a buttered, heavy, 2-quart saucepan. Cook the mixture over medium heat, stirring frequently, until the temperature reaches 240° on a candy thermometer. Add the pecans and continue cooking until the temperature reaches 246°. Remove the mixture from the heat and let it cool for 2 minutes. Beat in the vanilla with a spoon until creamy. Immediately drop spoonfuls of the mixture onto wax paper, making 2-inch circles. The candy should drop easily from the spoon. If the candy hardens before you have finished, add a few drops of milk, reheat, and stir until creamy. Store in a sealed container, separating the layers with waxed paper.

YIELD: 2 TO 2½ DOZEN

Rocky Road

1   (12-ounce) package semisweet chocolate chips
1   (14-ounce) can sweetened condensed milk
2   tablespoons butter (not margarine)
2   cups dry roasted peanuts
1   (16-ounce) bag large white marshmallows

In the top of a double boiler over boiling water melt the chocolate chips. Stir in the milk and butter until well mixed with the chocolate. Remove from the heat. In a large bowl combine the peanuts and marshmallows. Fold these into the chocolate mixture. This hot mixture should only partially melt the marshmallows. Line the bottom of a 9 x 13-inch glass baking dish with waxed paper. Spread the mixture into the pan. Chill for 2 hours or until firm. Remove from the pan, peel off the waxed paper, and cut into 2-inch squares. Cover and store at room temperature.

YIELD: 24 SERVINGS

Strawberry Candies

1   (14-ounce) can sweetened condensed milk
1   pound finely ground coconut
2   (3-ounce) packages strawberry gelatin, divided
1   cup finely ground almonds
1   tablespoon granulated sugar
1   teaspoon vanilla extract
1   (4-ounce) can decorator icing

In a large mixing bowl combine the milk, coconut, two-thirds of the strawberry gelatin, the almonds, sugar, and vanilla. Mix thoroughly. Shape the mixture into strawberries. Spread the remaining one-third of the gelatin on wax paper. Roll the strawberry candies in the gelatin, coating thoroughly. Set aside to dry until firm. Form strawberry leaves with the icing. Store the finished product in the refrigerator in a covered container.

YIELD: 48 LARGE CANDIES

Banbury Tarts

Many years ago a dear friend gave me this recipe. It was her grandmother's favorite cookie and it soon became the favorite of our family and friends also. It is the perfect cookie served at any time of the year, whether for Valentine's Day tea, a Southern buffet, or a church Christmas cookie swap.

1½ cups (3 sticks) butter or margarine, softened
1 cup granulated sugar
2 egg yolks
1 teaspoon vanilla flavoring
4 cups all-purpose flour
1 jar tart red currant jelly

In a bowl using an electric mixer beat the butter and the sugar. Add the egg yolks one at a time, mixing after each addition. Add the vanilla. Add the flour gradually, stopping the mixer occasionally to hand stir because the mixture will be very stiff. Continue mixing with the electric mixer until the batter is well blended.

Preheat the oven to 350°. Cover several cookie sheets with parchment paper. Pinch off pieces of the batter large enough to form balls about 1-inch in diameter. Place the balls on the cookie sheets about 2 inches apart. Make a depression in each ball. Bake about 10 minutes. Remove from the oven and fill the depression with the red currant jelly, using about ¼ teaspoon of jelly for each cookie.

Return to the oven for 2 minutes or just long enough to melt the jelly and let the cookies turn golden brown. Cool on racks and store in airtight cookie tins.

YIELD: ABOUT 5 DOZEN

Bernice Wilson
Lawrenceville, Georgia

Chewy Oatmeal Cookies

¾ cup butter-flavored shortening
1¼ cups firmly packed light brown sugar
1 egg
⅓ cup milk
1½ teaspoons vanilla flavoring
3 cups oats, quick or old-fashioned
1 cup all-purpose flour
½ teaspoon baking soda
½ teaspoon salt
½ teaspoon ground cinnamon
1 cup raisins
1 cup coarsely chopped walnuts

Preheat the oven to 375° degrees. Lightly grease a baking sheet with a small amount of butter-flavored shortening. In a large bowl combine the shortening, brown sugar, egg, milk, and vanilla flavoring. Beat at medium speed with an electric mixer until well blended. In a medium-size bowl combine the oats, flour, baking soda, salt, and cinnamon. Mix these dry ingredients into the shortening mixture at low speed until blended. Stir in the raisins and walnuts. Drop by the rounded tablespoonful

2 inches apart the baking sheet. Bake for 10 to 12 minutes or until lightly browned.

YIELD: 2½ DOZEN COOKIES

Chocolate Chip Cookies

2¼	cups all-purpose flour
1	teaspoon baking soda
1	teaspoon salt
2	eggs
1	cup (2 sticks) butter, melted
¼	cup granulated sugar
¾	cup firmly packed light brown sugar
1	teaspoon vanilla extract
1	(3.4-ounce) package vanilla instant pudding
1	(12-ounce) package semisweet chocolate chips
1	cup chopped pecans (optional)

Preheat the oven to 375°. In a medium-size bowl combine the flour, baking soda, and salt. In a large bowl combine the eggs and butter. With an electric mixer beat on medium speed until the mixture is smooth and creamy. Add the granulated and brown sugars, vanilla extract, and vanilla pudding. Mix well. Slowly add the flour mixture. After the dough is well mixed, stir in the chocolate chips and the pecans if using. Drop by the heaping teaspoonful about 2 to 3 inches apart onto an ungreased cookie sheet. Bake for 8 to 10 minutes on the center rack of the oven.

YIELD: ABOUT 3 DOZEN

Chocolate Macaroons

Nancy East, a long-time hostess and friend of the Blue Willow Inn, was given this recipe at a U.S. Marine Corps officers' wives coffee in 1965 in Norfolk, Virginia. The customers at the Blue Willow love Nancy, and she loves the customers. She is truly a wonderful example of southern hospitality. We are all blessed to have her.

4	egg whites
1	cup granulated sugar
½	teaspoon salt
2	teaspoons vanilla extract
1	(12-ounce) package semisweet chocolate morsels (must be real chocolate)
2⅔	cups shredded coconut

In a large bowl beat the egg whites until they are stiff. Slowly add the sugar, salt, and vanilla while continuing to beat. Preheat the oven to 350°. In a saucepan on low heat melt the chocolate. Fold the melted chocolate and the coconut into the egg white mixture. Drop by the rounded teaspoonful onto lightly greased cookie sheets. Bake for 10 to 15 minutes.

YIELD: 4 DOZEN

Meringue Cookies

These light delights will melt in your mouth.

2   egg whites
⅛   teaspoon salt
⅛   teaspoon cream of tartar
¾   cup granulated sugar
1   teaspoon clear vanilla extract
1   (16-ounce) package chocolate chips
½   cup chopped pecans

Preheat the oven to 300°. In a mixing bowl with an electric mixer beat the egg whites until they are stiff. Add the salt, cream of tartar, and sugar and continue to constantly beat until the mixture is thick. Fold in the vanilla, chocolate chips, and pecans. Drop in small mounds onto parchment paper–lined cookie sheets. Bake for 25 minutes.

YIELD: 3 DOZEN

Noel Crisps

This is a great Christmas cookie. I often give them as gifts, and my friends love to receive them.

½   cup shortening
¾   cup granulated sugar
1   egg
½   teaspoon almond extract
1   cup all-purpose flour
½   teaspoon baking powder

½   teaspoon salt
1   cup semisweet chocolate chips
¾   cup flaked coconut
¾   cup chopped candied cherries

Preheat the oven to 325°. In a large bowl beat the shortening and sugar until it is light and fluffy. Beat in the egg and the almond extract. In a small bowl combine the flour, baking powder, and salt. Stir this mixture into the shortening mixture. When the mixture is again creamy, stir in the chocolate chips, coconut, and cherries. Drop the dough by the teaspoonful onto a greased cookie sheet. Bake for 12 to 15 minutes. Cool.

YIELD: 2 DOZEN

Oatmeal Cookies

This recipe is from my dear friend and neighbor, Mary Kitchens. She told me it was given to her years ago and was at least sixty years old at that time. The cookies are very light and crisp and delicious with hot tea. I changed the recipe slightly, substituting unsalted butter for the shortening. I also freeze the rolls to make them easier to slice thinly.

1½   cups all-purpose flour
1   teaspoon salt
1   teaspoon baking soda
1   cup (2 sticks) unsalted butter or margarine
1   cup packed light brown sugar
1   cup granulated sugar
2   eggs

1   teaspoon vanilla extract
3   cups rolled oats
½   cup chopped pecans

In a bowl sift together the flour, salt, and baking soda. In a large mixing bowl beat the butter, brown sugar, and granulated sugar thoroughly. Add the eggs and vanilla. Beat well. Beat in the flour mixture. Stir in the oats and pecans. Form the cookie dough into rolls. Wrap in wax paper and refrigerate overnight. Slice thinly and bake at 350° on a greased cookie sheet for 10 minutes.

YIELD: 4 TO 5 DOZEN

Barbara Sams
Social Circle, Georgia

Rolled-Out Cookies

I originally came by this recipe at a Delta Delta Delta recipe exchange party in Knoxville, Tennessee, way back in the late sixties. It has been a hit every holiday season. My children and I loved to gather together with all our cookie cutter collection and toppings and choose our favorites for decorating. Whether beautiful or weird in appearance, once our individual styles were sealed, they were always delicious. It was a bit of a mess, but full of wonderful smells and memories, and so worth it. All the children are grown now, but we still fill the kitchen with these special cookies once or twice each year.

4   cups all-purpose flour, sifted, plus more for rolling
½   teaspoon baking powder
½   teaspoon baking soda
1   teaspoon salt
1¼   cups (2½ sticks) butter
2   eggs
1¼   cups granulated sugar
1½   teaspoons vanilla extract
     Confectioners' sugar for rolling
     Colored sugar for baking
     Toppings (optional)

In a large bowl sift the flour, baking powder, baking soda, and salt together. Cut the butter into the flour mixture. In a small bowl beat the eggs, sugar, and vanilla together. Blend the sugar mixture into the flour mixture.

Sprinkle the rolling surface and rolling pin with a mixture of confectioners' sugar and flour. (Confectioners' sugar keeps from using too much flour and drying out the cookies.) The dough starts out a little soft, so keep the area well dusted and the more you and the kids fool with it and roll it out, the texture changes and the dough is easier for the kids to handle.

Preheat the oven to 400°. Roll out the dough and cut it into the desired shapes. Sprinkle with colored sugar before baking. Dust the cookie cutters with flour between cuttings to keep the dough from sticking. Top the cookies with nuts, cherries, or other favorite toppings before and/or after baking. Bake the cookies on a greased cookie sheet for approximately 8 minutes or until just delicately brown around the edges. After the cookies are done they can be brushed with confectioners' sugar glaze or sprinkled with colored powdered sugar. Cookies can be frosted and then decorated.

YIELD: 3½ DOZEN

Anne Galbraith
Knoxville, Tennessee

Granny's Sugar Cookies

When I think of a good Southern recipe, I think of something plain and simple, because times were hard and cooks used ingredients that were readily available. My mama, Susie Hodges, did just that. This plain and simple recipe brings great memories of my mother, special cookies made for my children, and fun times of baking and decorating them with my grandchildren. Bake up some memories with this recipe.

1	cup granulated sugar
½	cup (1 stick) butter or margarine, softened
1	egg
½	teaspoon vanilla flavoring
2	cups all-purpose flour
½	teaspoon salt
2	teaspoons baking powder

In a large bowl beat the sugar and butter together until fluffy. Add in the egg and vanilla. In a small bowl combine the flour, salt, and baking powder. Blend this into the first mixture. Mix well. Place the dough in a covered container and refrigerate for 6 to 8 hours or overnight for best results.

Preheat the oven to 400°. Roll out the dough to the desired thickness onto a well-floured board. Cut with favorite cookie cutters. Place the cookies on a lightly greased cookie sheet. Bake the cookies for 8 to 10 minutes or until the edges are golden. Carefully remove the baked cookies from the baking sheet using a metal spatula. Cool on wire racks. If desired, frost the cooled cookies with cream cheese, chocolate, or a favorite icing. Decorate as desired.

YIELD: 3½ DOZEN

Liz Allgood
Covington, Georgia

Sugar Cookies

This basic recipe can be colored and shaped to fit the season, the occasion, the mood, or the holiday.

1	cup (2 sticks) butter, melted
1½	cups granulated sugar
1	egg
1	teaspoon vanilla extract
½	teaspoon almond extract
2½	cups all-purpose flour
1	teaspoon baking soda
1	teaspoon cream of tartar

ICING (OPTIONAL)

⅓	cup butter, softened
3	cups confectioners' sugar
1½	teaspoons vanilla extract
2	tablespoons milk

In a large bowl thoroughly mix the butter, granulated sugar, egg, vanilla, and almond extract. Blend in the flour, baking soda, and cream of tartar. Cover and chill for 2 to

3 hours. Preheat the oven to 375°. Remove the dough from the refrigerator. Roll out the dough on a lightly floured surface. Cut into desired shapes and cook on a sheet pan for 9 to 11 minutes or until golden brown at the edges. Let the cookies cool before serving.

For the **icing**, in a mixing bowl blend the butter and confectioners' sugar. Stir in the vanilla. Add the milk to make a spreading consistency. Spread the icing over the cooled cookies. Add food colorings and toppings to fit the occasion or the season.

YIELD: ABOUT 6 DOZEN

Old-Fashioned Tea Cakes

This recipe comes to us from Betty Stephens of Monroe, Georgia, in memory of Annie Bell Light of Norcross, who passed away fifteen to twenty years ago. Betty says Mrs. Light was a leader of the senior group at church and was always happy, always laughing, and a joy to be around. She normally brought the tea cakes to covered-dish dinners. And if she did not, people asked her for them.

Betty says that this is the exact recipe, and when looking at the recipe she can almost taste the lovely tea cakes.

1	heaping teaspoon baking soda
1	cup buttermilk
¼	teaspoon salt
2½	cups granulated sugar
2	eggs
1	cup shortening
2	teaspoons vanilla flavoring
	All-purpose flour

Preheat the oven to 400°. In a large bowl dissolve the baking soda in the buttermilk. Add in the salt, sugar, eggs, shortening, vanilla, and enough flour to make a medium-fine dough (a fine dough is one that is not sticky). Using a big spoon, mix all the ingredients well. Separate the dough and work a little of the dough at a time on a well-floured cloth. Roll out the dough and cut it into desired shapes. It can be rolled ¼-inch or thinner. Bake on a greased baking sheet. When the tea cakes look a crispy medium-brown, take them out of the oven. Dump them on a clean cloth and grease the cookie sheet while it's hot for another batch.

YIELD: 2 DOZEN

Tea Cakes

This bite-size dainty is the simplest kind of cake to serve with tea because it requires no utensils, just plenty of napkins lest the powdered sugar falls all over the ladies' laps.

1　cup granulated sugar
1　cup (2 sticks) butter, softened
1　cup vegetable oil
2　large eggs
2　teaspoons vanilla extract
4½　cups all-purpose flour
1　teaspoon baking soda
1　teaspoon baking powder
1　teaspoon cream of tartar
1　cup confectioners' sugar
　　Sifted confectioners' sugar for topping

Preheat the oven to 325°. In a large bowl beat the granulated sugar, butter, oil, eggs, and vanilla. Add the flour, baking soda, baking powder, cream of tartar, and confectioners' sugar. Using a teaspoon, drop portions of the mixture onto a baking sheet. Bake for 15 minutes. Sprinkle with the sifted confectioners' sugar while still warm.

YIELD: ABOUT 5 DOZEN

White Chocolate Macadamia Nut Cookies

Louis and Billie's banker for a number of years, Sandra Conner, gave them this recipe. Sandra loves cookies, and the restaurant often sends her and her staff oatmeal and chocolate chip cookies. When the Blue Willow Inn was struggling to survive, Sandra often offered words of encouragement, telling Louis and Billie that she had faith in their ability to make the restaurant work. Sandra is loved and appreciated more than she can ever know.

½　cup (1 stick) butter
½　cup shortening
¾　cup packed brown sugar
½　cup granulated sugar
1　large egg
1½　teaspoons vanilla extract
2　cups all-purpose flour
1　teaspoon baking soda
6　ounces white chocolate chips
¾　cup chopped macadamia nuts

Preheat the oven to 350°. In a mixing bowl combine the butter, shortening, brown sugar, granulated sugar, egg, vanilla, flour, baking soda, white chocolate chips, and nuts. Mix well. Drop by the tablespoonful onto a lightly greased cookie sheet. Bake for 8 to 10 minutes. Cool.

YIELD: 2 TO 4 DOZEN

Boiled Custard Ice Cream

2½　cups granulated sugar
3　tablespoons all-purpose flour
　　Pinch of salt
3　quarts (12 cups) milk
6　eggs

1 cup cream

6 teaspoons vanilla extract

In a large bowl mix the sugar, flour, and salt. Stir in the milk. Cook in a double boiler over simmering water, stirring constantly, until slightly thickened. Cover and continue cooking for 10 minutes. In a medium-size bowl beat the eggs. Stir a little of the hot milk mixture into the beaten eggs and add it back to the milk mixture. Cook in the double boiler over hot—*not boiling*—water, stirring constantly, until the mixture coats a spoon, about 5 minutes. Strain and cool. Add the cream and vanilla. Freeze.

Hint: It is easier to fix the custard and allow it to cool 6 to 8 hours or overnight before adding the cream and vanilla. Store in the refrigerator.

YIELD: 3½ QUARTS

Martha Jane's Homemade Ice Cream

This recipe is made in an old-fashioned ice cream maker. My aunt in Tennessee made this as her special summer treat. Her backyard was the place to be on a hot summer day. My family moved to Mobile from the Sequatchie Valley in Tennessee and all of my childhood vacations were taken visiting with the family in Tennessee. Fifty years later this is still my favorite vacation spot to just relax and look at the mountains.

2 (4-ounce) boxes junket
Whole milk

2 (14-ounce) cans sweetened condensed milk

1 pint whipping cream
Peaches, mashed (optional)

In a large bowl combine the junket with enough milk to mix. Add the sweetened condensed milk, whipping cream, and peaches if using. Pour this mixture into the ice cream churn. Fill the churn with milk and freeze.

YIELD: 1 GALLON

Lynda Davis
Wilmer, Alabama

Cool Lemon Sherbet

7 lemons

3 cups granulated sugar

2 quarts (8 cups) whole milk

1 (12-ounce) can evaporated milk

Squeeze the lemons. In a large bowl pour the lemon juice over the sugar and mix together as well as possible. Add the milk to the sugar mixture, blending well. Add the evaporated milk. Freeze until firm.

YIELD: ABOUT 3 QUARTS

Barbara Nichols
Greenwood, Mississippi

Peppermint Ice Cream

1   (12-ounce) bag stick peppermints,
    crushed
1   quart (4 cups) milk
    Pinch of salt
4   tablespoons cornstarch

In a large bowl mix the crushed peppermints, milk, salt, and cornstarch. Blend thoroughly. Place in the freezer until frozen.

> Hint: This can be frozen in old-fashioned ice trays with the dividers removed.

YIELD: 1 QUART

Pineapple Sherbet

½   cup canned unsweetened pineapple juice
1   tablespoon lemon juice
½   teaspoon grated lemon rind
⅔   cup granulated sugar
2   cups whole milk, chilled

In a large pitcher combine the pineapple juice, lemon juice, lemon rind, and sugar. Stir to dissolve the sugar. Place in the refrigerator and chill. Pour the chilled milk into a large bowl. Pour the juice mixture into the chilled milk, stirring constantly. (Never pour the milk into the juice or it will curdle.). Place in ice trays with the dividers removed and freeze until hard. Remove from the freezer. Turn out into a bowl. Beat very lightly. Return to the freezer.

YIELD: ABOUT 1 QUART

Vanilla Ice Cream

This recipe is from Peggy Hawkins, catering director at Blue Willow's Magnolia Hall in Social Circle. It is one of the best homemade ice cream recipes we have tried.

4   cups granulated sugar
3   eggs
3   tablespoons vanilla extract
1   (12-ounce) can evaporated milk
    Whole milk

In a large bowl combine the sugar, eggs, vanilla, and evaporated milk and mix well. Pour this mixture into the cylinder of an ice cream maker and add whole make to the fill line. Put the lid on the cylinder and pack a layer of ice and rock salt around the cylinder. Crank the ice cream maker to freeze the ice cream.

> Hint: You can add 2 cups of any coarsely chopped sweetened fruit, such as strawberries, for a different flavor.

Vanilla Custard Ice Cream

8   cups milk
2   (12-ounce) cans evaporated milk
3   cups granulated sugar
6   large eggs
3   tablespoons vanilla extract

In a Dutch oven whisk the milk, evaporated milk, sugar, eggs, and vanilla extract together. Cook over medium heat, whisking constantly for 25 to 30 minutes or until the mixture thickens and coats a spoon. (Do NOT boil.) Cover, place in the refrigerator, and chill for 2 hours. Pour the custard into the freezer container of a 5-quart electric freezer. Freeze according to the manufacturer's directions. Allow the freezer to stand packed with additional ice and rock salt before serving.

Hint: To make strawberry or peach ice cream, stir in 4 cups mashed strawberries or 4 cups peeled and mashed fresh peaches before freezing.

YIELD: 12 CUPS

Amelia Mud Pie

PIE SHELL

21   Oreo cookies, chopped very finely
6   tablespoons butter, melted

FILLING

1   quart chocolate ice cream, softened
2   tablespoons ground coffee
2   tablespoons instant coffee (Sanka)
2   tablespoons brandy
2   tablespoons Kahlúa
4   tablespoons whipped cream
1   jar fudge topping

For the Pieshell, in a large mixing bowl mix the cookies and butter and press into a 9-inch pie pan. Freeze.

For the **filling**, whip the ice cream in a large bowl with the ground coffee, instant coffee, brandy, and Kahlúa. Add the whipped cream. Place in the pie shell. Freeze until very hard.

For the topping, dip a knife into hot water and spread the fudge topping over the pie. Work quickly. Return the pie to the freezer until ready to serve.

YIELD: 8 SERVINGS

Apple Pie

1   (14-ounce) can sliced apples or 1½ cups cooked apples
¼   cup light brown sugar
½   cup granulated sugar
2   tablespoons all-purpose flour
¼   teaspoon salt
½   teaspoon ground cinnamon
¼   teaspoon ground nutmeg
2   Pastry Piecrusts (recipe on page 340)
2   tablespoons butter, melted

Preheat the oven to 425°. In a large mixing bowl combine the apples, brown sugar, granulated sugar, flour, salt, cinnamon, and nutmeg. Line the bottom and sides of a 9-inch pie plate with 1 of the piecrusts. Pour the apples into the pie shell. Top with the second piecrust. Use a fork to seal the edges. Cut three or four 1½-inch slits in the top crust for ventilation. Brush the top of the pie with the melted butter. Bake for 40 to 45 minutes until a golden brown.

YIELD: 8 SERVINGS

The Best Banana Pie

1   (3.4-ounce) package banana instant pudding
1   Graham Cracker Piecrust (page 333)
1   (10-ounce) box frozen strawberries
1   (8-ounce) can crushed pineapple
5   bananas, sliced in small coin-size pieces
1   (12-ounce) container refrigerated whipped topping
    Chocolate syrup
    Maraschino cherries

In a medium-size bowl mix the instant pudding according to package instructions. Pour the pudding into the crust. Spread the strawberries on top of the pudding. Spread the crushed pineapple on top of the strawberries. Layer the bananas on top of the pineapple, piling them high and using all the bananas. Top the bananas with the whipped topping. Drizzle chocolate syrup over the top of the pie. Top with cherries.

Yield: 8 servings

Billie Sexton
Loganville, Georgia

Buttermilk Pie

3   eggs, lightly beaten
1   cup granulated sugar
2   tablespoons all-purpose flour
½   cup butter, melted
1   cup buttermilk
½   teaspoon vanilla extract
½   teaspoon lemon extract
1   unbaked (9-inch) Pastry Piecrust (recipe on page 340)

Preheat the oven to 350°. In a medium-size mixing bowl combine the eggs, sugar, flour, and butter. Mix well. Add the buttermilk, vanilla, and lemon extract. Mix well. Pour the filling into the pie shell. Bake for 45 to 50 minutes until the pie is set and golden brown.

Yield: 8 servings

Cherry Cheese Pie

1   (8-ounce) package cream cheese, softened
1   (14-ounce) can sweetened condensed milk
⅓   cup lemon juice from concentrate
1   teaspoon vanilla extract
1   Graham Cracker Piecrust (recipe on page 333)
1   (14-ounce) can cherry pie filling, chilled

In a large mixing bowl with an electric mixer beat the cream cheese until fluffy. Gradually add the condensed milk and continue to beat until the mixture is smooth. Stir in the lemon juice and vanilla. Pour the mixture into the graham cracker piecrust. Top with the pie filling. Chill until firm.

Hint: Other toppings that can be used on this pie are ambrosia, glazed strawberries, blueberry and cranberry nut. The recipes for each are at the end of this chapter.

YIELD: 8 SERVINGS

Chess Pie

This is a must-try pie. You would never know the ingredients unless you made the pie. Food historians speculate on its name. The best explanation we've found is that long ago a happy eater asked the cook what was in this delicious pie that contained no recognizable fruits or flavored fillings, but had such a satisfying character. The cook thought a while and said there was nothing spectacular in it. It was "just pie," which in the South sounds like "jes' pie" and it eventually became chess pie.

2	cups granulated sugar
1	tablespoon all-purpose flour
2	tablespoons yellow cornmeal
½	cup (1 stick) butter, melted
1	tablespoon white vinegar
½	teaspoon vanilla extract
4	eggs
¼	cup buttermilk

¼	teaspoon salt
1	unbaked (9-inch) Pastry Piecrust (recipe on page 340)

Preheat the oven to 350°. In a large bowl combine the sugar, flour, cornmeal, butter, white vinegar, vanilla, eggs, buttermilk, and salt. Mix well. Pour the mixture into the piecrust. Bake for 50 minutes. Cool on a wire rack before serving.

YIELD: 8 SERVINGS

Chocolate Chess Pie

2	cups granulated sugar
5	tablespoons unsweetened cocoa powder
2	tablespoons all-purpose flour
3	eggs, beaten
¾	cup evaporated milk
½	cup (1 stick) margarine, melted
1	unbaked pie shell (1 deep-dish or 2 regular)

Preheat the oven to 325°. In a medium-size mixing bowl combine the sugar, cocoa powder, and flour. Add the eggs, milk, and margarine. Blend well. Pour into the unbaked pie shell. Bake for 45 minutes for regular pies or about 1 hour for a deep-dish pie (or until a knife inserted in the center comes out clean).

YIELD: 8 SERVINGS

Jeanette Allen
Loganville, Georgia

Chocolate Lovers' Easy Pie

Chocolate pie has long been a southern favorite and is usually made with chocolate puddin' and whipped topping. This pie is an easy and delicious alternative.

½ pound chocolate almond bar
1 (8-ounce) container non-dairy whipped topping
1 (8-inch) chocolate pie shell
1 can chocolate whipped cream

In a microwavable bowl melt the chocolate bar. When the chocolate is cool, but not yet hardened, fold in the whipped topping. Pour the mixture into the pie shell and refrigerate. Before serving, top with the whipped cream and watch the chocoholics smile.

YIELD: 6 TO 8 SERVINGS

Kathy Walden
Monroe, Georgia

POPULAR SOUTHERN SAYING

What in the Sam Hill are you doin'?

Chocolate Meringue Pie

1 cup granulated sugar
3 heaping tablespoons all-purpose flour
3 heaping tablespoons cocoa powder
3 large eggs, separated (reserve whites at room temperature for making meringue)
1½ cups milk
1 teaspoon vanilla extract
1 (9-inch) baked pie shell
⅓ cup confectioners' sugar
½ teaspoon cream of tartar

In a medium-size saucepan combine the sugar, flour, and cocoa powder. Stir to remove any lumps. In a bowl beat the egg yolks and add to the dry ingredients. Gradually stir in the milk. Place over medium heat, stirring constantly so that the mixture does not burn. Cook until it thickens. Remove the mixture from the heat, add the vanilla, and stir well. Pour the mixture into the baked pie shell.

Preheat the oven to 475°. Make the meringue by beating the confectioners' sugar with the reserved egg whites and cream of tartar until light and fluffy, about 3 to 4 minutes. Spread the meringue over the pie, making sure it touches the crust all around. Bake the pie for 5 minutes or until the meringue is golden brown. Refrigerate the pie before serving.

YIELD: 8 SERVINGS

Coconut Cream Pie

1   cup granulated sugar
½   cup all-purpose flour
¼   teaspoon salt
3   cups milk
4   eggs, separated
3   tablespoons butter
1½ teaspoons vanilla extract
1   plus ⅓ cups flaked coconut
1   baked (9-inch) Pastry Piecrust (recipe on page 340)

In a medium-size saucepan on medium-high heat combine the sugar, flour, and salt. Gradually stir in the milk. Cook and stir the mixture until it is thickened and bubbly. Reduce the heat to low. Cook and stir 2 more minutes. Remove from the heat. In a small bowl slightly beat the egg yolks. Slowly stir 1 cup of the hot milk mixture into the yolks. Pour the egg yolks into the saucepan with the remaining milk mixture. Return to the heat on medium-high and bring to a slow boil. Cook and stir 2 more minutes. Preheat the oven to 400°. Remove the saucepan from the heat and stir in the butter, vanilla extract, and 1 cup of the coconut. Pour the mixture into the baked pastry pie shell. Toast the remaining ⅓ cup coconut on a baking sheet in the oven. Make a meringue (recipe on page 337) from the egg whites. Spoon the meringue over the pie and sprinkle with the toasted coconut. Place the pie under the broiler for a few seconds, just long enough for the meringue to brown. Refrigerate and serve cool.

YIELD: 8 SERVINGS

Double-Layer Pumpkin Pie

1   (8-ounce) package cream cheese, softened
1   cup plus 1 tablespoon milk
1   tablespoon granulated sugar
½   plus ½ (8-ounce) container refrigerated whipped topping, thawed
1   Graham Cracker Piecrust (page 333)
1   (15-ounce) can pumpkin
2   (3.4-ounce) packages vanilla instant pudding and pie filling
1   teaspoon ground cinnamon
½   teaspoon ground ginger
¼   teaspoon ground cloves
1½ teaspoons pumpkin pie seasoning

In a large mixing bowl with a wire whisk mix the cream cheese, 1 tablespoon of the milk, and the sugar until well blended. Gently stir in half the whipped topping. Spread this mixture into the piecrust. Into a large bowl pour the remaining 1 cup milk. Add the pumpkin, pudding mixes, cinnamon, ginger, cloves, and pumpkin pie seasoning. Beat with a wire whisk for 2 minutes or until well blended. The mixture will be thick. Spread the mixture over the cream cheese layer in the piecrust. Refrigerate for 4 hours or until set. Spread the remaining half of the whipped topping over the pie. Store in the refrigerator.

Hint: For a variation of this pie, use sweet potatoes and eliminate the pumpkin pie seasoning.

YIELD: 8 SERVINGS

Ada Vargas
Lawrenceville, Georgia

Coconut Pie

1	cup (2 sticks) butter, softened
2	cups shredded coconut
2	teaspoons vanilla extract
6	eggs
3	cups granulated sugar
½	cup buttermilk
2	tablespoons all-purpose flour
2	unbaked Pastry Piecrust (recipe on page 340)

Preheat the oven to 350°. In a large mixing bowl mix the butter, coconut, vanilla, eggs, sugar, buttermilk, and flour. Make sure the ingredients are mixed well. Pour into the pie shells. Bake for 20 to 25 minutes until the top is lightly browned.

YIELD: 2 PIES (16 SERVINGS)

Dried Apple & Egg Custard Pie

This recipe was given to me by Una King, not only a great cook, but a wonderful "one-of-a-kind" lady. My mother and I went to visit her after a tornado had killed her daughter, son-in-law, and two granddaughters. She said something I will never forget: "I don't know why this has happened, but according to Romans 8:28: 'And we know that all things work together for good to them that love God, to them who are called according to His purpose.'"

2	eggs, beaten
½	cup granulated sugar
1	scant tablespoon all-purpose flour
1½	cups milk
1	teaspoon vanilla extract
	Dried, cooked apples
1	(9-inch) Pastry Piecrust (recipe on page 340)

Preheat the oven to 400°. In a bowl with an electric mixer beat the eggs. Add the sugar and flour, continuing to beat. Add the milk and vanilla extract. Beat thoroughly. Spread the apples over the bottom of the piecrust. Pour the egg mixture over the apples. Cook for 5 minutes at 400°. Reduce the heat to 350° and bake until firm.

YIELD: 8 SERVINGS

Juanita Muse
Calhoun, Georgia

Easy Lemon Pie

This recipe has been in our family for a number of years. My mother has made it the most and her pie always seems to taste the best. It is something quick and easy to put together for unexpected company or those last-minute get-togethers.

	Vanilla wafers
1	(14-ounce) can sweetened condensed milk
3	egg yolks

⅓ cup lemon juice

1 (12-ounce) container refrigerated whipped topping

Layer the bottom and sides of a glass pie plate or container with the vanilla wafers. In a bowl stir together the sweetened condensed milk, egg yolks, and lemon juice. Pour over the vanilla wafers and top with the whipped topping. Chill and serve or serve immediately

YIELD: 8 SERVINGS

Ashlee Robinson

Gainesville, Georgia

Egg Custard Pie

2 tablespoons all-purpose flour

1¼ cups granulated sugar

3 eggs, beaten

½ cup (1 stick) butter, melted

¼ cup buttermilk

Pinch of salt

1 unbaked Pastry Piecrust (recipe on page 340)

Preheat the oven to 350°. In a mixing bowl combine the flour and sugar and mix well. Add the beaten eggs and butter. Mix well. Add the buttermilk and salt. Pour the egg mixture into the pie shell. Bake for 20 to 25 minutes until the custard is set.

YIELD: 8 SERVINGS

French Silk Chocolate Pie

A special friend and fellow caterer, Ruth Plympton, gave this recipe to Billie many years ago.

½ cup (1 stick) butter, softened

¾ cup granulated sugar

2 squares semisweet chocolate

1 teaspoon vanilla extract

2 eggs

1 (8-inch) baked pie shell
  Whipped cream

In a mixing bowl with an electric mixer beat the butter and sugar until light and fluffy. In a saucepan on low heat or in the microwave melt the chocolate. Add the melted chocolate to the butter mixture. Stir in the vanilla and beat until smooth. Add the eggs, one at a time, beating after each addition for 5 minutes. Pour into the baked pie shell. Refrigerate until set, about 3 to 4 hours. Top with the whipped cream. Serve cold.

YIELD: 8 SERVINGS

Fried Pies

This recipe was given to us by Ann Lowe, the first employee of the Blue Willow Inn, who is still giving her "special touch" to the cooking. We're not sure that your pies will have the same flavor, but maybe, just maybe.

1   (6-ounce) package dried peaches
1   cup granulated sugar
2   cups water
6   uncooked canned biscuits
1   cup all-purpose flour
2   cups vegetable oil

In a saucepan on low heat combine the peaches, sugar, and water. Cook until the peaches are tender. Drain the peaches. On a lightly floured surface roll out each canned biscuit into a thin sheet. Fill half of the side of each sheet with the peaches. Fold the other half over the peaches and seal with a fork. Dredge each little pie in the flour. In a large skillet heat the oil and cook the pies on each side until they are brown, turning each two times. Remove the pies from the skillet and drain on brown paper bags. (If drained on paper towels, the pies have a tendency to stick to the towels.)

> Hint: If substituting dried apples, follow the above directions but add 1/2 teaspoon cinnamon and 1/2 teaspoon nutmeg, apple pie spice, or your favorite spice.

YIELD: 6 SERVINGS

Fried Sweet Potato Pies

This recipe comes to us from Cheryl Lynn Wymbs, one of our cooks at Blue Willow Inn. The pies are mouth-watering, and we know you will enjoy them as much as we do.

2   large sweet potatoes
2   teaspoons butter, melted
2   teaspoons vanilla extract

FILLING
⅓   cup butter
½   cup vanilla extract
2½   cups granulated sugar
2   tablespoons ground cinnamon
2   tablespoons ground nutmeg
2   large eggs

DOUGH
3   cups all-purpose flour
½   cup shortening
1¼   cups buttermilk
     Vegetable oil

Preheat the oven to 350°. Peel the sweet potatoes and cut them into ½-inch slices. Arrange the slices in a 9 x 13-inch baking pan. Sprinkle the melted butter and vanilla extract over the potatoes. Bake for 1 hour.

For the **filling**, in a mixing bowl combine the butter, vanilla extract, sugar, cinnamon, nutmeg, and eggs. Mix well. Remove the sweet potatoes from the baking pan and with an electric mixer on medium speed mix them into the filling mixture.

For the **dough**, in a large mixing bowl combine the flour, shortening, and buttermilk. Mix well and roll the dough around until it clings together. Transfer the dough onto a lightly floured board and lightly sprinkle with flour . Knead gently for 10 to 12 strokes, curving your finger over the dough and pulling it towards you then pushing it down and away from you with the heels of your hands. Lightly spread more flour on the surface and roll the dough out with a rolling pin. Roll the dough out to about 1/4 inch thickness. Using a biscuit cutter cut two round shapes out of the dough. Place 1 teaspoon of the sweet potato mixture on 1 of the rounds of dough. Place the other round on top of the mixture. Using a fork, seal the edges of the dough. Heat vegetable oil in a deep fat fryer or at least a couple of inches deep in a skillet. Place the pies in the hot oil and fry until a golden brown.

YIELD: 24 CAKES

Frozen Lemonade Pie

This is great to make ahead and have on hand for dessert, especially in emergencies or to give to someone.

1   (14-ounce) can sweetened condensed milk (Eagle Brand preferred)

1   (6-ounce) can frozen lemonade concentrate, thawed and not diluted

1   (8-ounce) container whipped topping, thawed

2   Graham Cracker Piecrusts (recipe below)

In a large bowl fold the sweetened condensed milk and lemonade concentrate into the whipped topping. Spoon this mixture into the piecrusts. Freeze for 3 hours or until firm.

Hint: For variations, limeade or orange juice concentrate can be substituted.

YIELD: 8 SERVINGS

June Butler
Monroe, Georgia

Graham Cracker Piecrust

1½   cups graham cracker crumbs (about 18 crackers)

3   tablespoons sugar

⅓   cup butter, melted

Heat the oven to 350°. In a bowl mix the graham cracker crumbs and sugar. Add the butter and mix thoroughly. Press the mixture firmly and evenly against the bottom and sides of a pie pan. Bake for 10 minutes. Set aside to completely cool before adding any filling.

YIELD: 1 (9-INCH) PIECRUST

Ice Cream Pie

This is another great fix-ahead pie. In making this pie, you can use your favorite ice cream and drizzle it with your favorite topping. I always remember what my nephew said when he ate my ice cream pie. He said, "You are a good cooker!"

1   (6-ounce) package semisweet chocolate chips
¼   cup (½ stick) margarine
2   cups crisp rice cereal
1   tablespoon light corn syrup
    Chocolate ripple ice cream, slightly softened

In the top of a double boiler over hot water melt the chocolate chips and margarine. Remove from the heat. Reserve 3 tablespoons of the mixture. Add the Rice Krispies cereal to the remaining chocolate mixture and stir well. Press this mixture evenly around the sides and on the bottom of a 9-inch pie pan to form a crust. Chill.

In a small bowl add the corn syrup to the 3 tablespoons chocolate mixture. Spread the ice cream over the chilled pie shell and drizzle with the chocolate mixture. Freeze for about 2 hours or until firm. When ready to serve, set the pie on a hot, wet towel.

YIELD: 8 SERVINGS

Juanita Muse
Calhoun, Georgia

Julian's Pecan Pie

This pie is a favorite of Louis' dad. During the holiday season, Julian would bake pecan pies for friends and neighbors. He enjoyed delivering his fresh pies at Thanksgiving and Christmas. You will find pecan pie every day at the Blue Willow buffet tables; it is a staple throughout the South.

3   eggs, lightly beaten
½   cup light or dark corn syrup
½   cup pure maple syrup
½   cup granulated sugar
2½   tablespoons margarine, melted
1   teaspoon vanilla extract
1   teaspoon pure lemon extract
1   cup pecans
1   frozen (9-inch) pastry piecrust, thawed

Preheat the oven to 350°. In a large mixing bowl combine the eggs, corn syrup, maple syrup, sugar, margarine, vanilla extract, and lemon extract. Stir until well blended. Add the pecans and stir enough to spread evenly throughout the mixture. Pour into the thawed piecrust. Bake for 50 to 55 minutes.

Hint: If serving the pie warm, it can be topped with vanilla ice cream. If serving cooled, top the pie with whipped cream or whipped topping.

YIELD: 8 SERVINGS

Julian's Sweet Potato Pie

This recipe, too, comes from Louis' dad, Julian. Sweet potato pie usually appears regularly on the dessert menus of plate-lunch restaurants and barbecue shacks. As the autumn harvest approaches, sweet potatoes are on people's minds even more. They are a "must" at both Thanksgiving and Christmas dinners. Sweet potato pies are delicious served warm or cold. They make a wonderful midnight snack after the holiday dinner.

2   cups mashed cooked sweet potatoes

1   cup granulated sugar

¼   cup (½ stick) butter or margarine, melted

¼   teaspoon salt

1   teaspoon vanilla extract

1   teaspoon pure lemon extract

1   (14-ounce) can sweetened condensed milk

2   eggs, lightly beaten

1   teaspoon ground cinnamon

½   teaspoon ground ginger

1   teaspoon ground nutmeg

1   (9-inch) frozen flaky piecrust

Whipped cream (optional)

Nutmeg (optional)

Preheat the oven to 425°. In a large mixing bowl combine the sweet potatoes, sugar, butter, salt, vanilla and lemon extracts, condensed milk, eggs, cinnamon, ginger, and nutmeg. Mix well. Pour the mixture into the frozen piecrust. Bake for 15 minutes. Reduce the heat to 325° and bake for 35 to 40 minutes more. If desired, garnish each slice with a small amount of whipped cream and nutmeg.

YIELD: 8 SERVINGS

Key Lime Pie

Fresh lime juice is essential for a full-flavored pie. If you can secure real Key limes or their juice from Florida, they make a much better pie. A true Key lime pie is as yellow as lemons (that's a Key lime's juice color), but it has a mellow flavor all its own.

1	(14-ounce) can sweetened condensed milk
½	cup fresh lime juice
3	large egg yolks, lightly beaten
1	(9-inch) pie shell, cooked

MERINGUE

3	large egg whites, at room temperature
¼	teaspoon cream of tartar
6	tablespoons granulated sugar

Preheat the oven to 325°. In a medium-size bowl combine the condensed milk and lime juice. Blend in the egg yolks. Pour the mixture into the cooked pie shell. Bake for 10 to 15 minutes or until set. Let cool on a wire rack for 10 minutes.

For the **meringue,** in a medium-size bowl beat the egg whites with the cream of tartar until soft peaks form. Beat the sugar into the egg whites, one tablespoon at a time, until the egg whites form stiff glossy peaks. Spoon the egg whites over the pie filling and spread to the edge. Bake 15 minutes or until the topping is golden. Cool the pie on a wire rack before serving.

YIELD: 8 SERVINGS

Lemon Meringue Pie

1½	cups granulated sugar
½	cup cornstarch
⅛	teaspoon salt
1¾	cups cold water
4	large eggs, separated (reserve the whites at room temperature for meringue)
3	tablespoons butter
¼	cup lemon juice
2	tablespoons grated lemon zest
1	(9-inch) baked Pastry Piecrust (recipe on page 340)

MERINGUE

4	egg whites
½	teaspoon cream of tartar
⅓	cup sifted confectioners' sugar

In a medium-size heavy saucepan combine the sugar, cornstarch, and salt. Gradually add the water, stirring until smooth. Cook over medium heat, stirring continuously, until the mixture thickens and boils. Boil 1 minute, stirring continuously. Remove from the heat. In a bowl with an electric mixer beat the egg yolks at high speed until thick. Gradually stir about one-third of the hot mixture into the egg yolks. Add the warmed yolks to the remaining sugar mixture, stirring constantly. Return the pan to the heat and cook 2 to 3 minutes longer, continuing to stir. Remove from the heat. Add the butter, lemon juice, and lemon zest. Stir to mix. Pour the hot filling into the baked pie shell. Top with the meringue.

Preheat the oven to 350° degrees. Make the **meringue** by beating the egg whites, cream of tartar, and confectioners' sugar with an electric mixer on high speed until it is light and fluffy, about 3 to 4 minutes. Spread the meringue over the pie, making sure the meringue touches the crust all around. Bake for 12 to 14 minutes until the meringue is lightly browned. Remove from the oven and set aside to cool.

YIELD: 8 SERVINGS

Lemon Sponge Pie

I was planning a luncheon and searching for a simple dessert. A friend of mine who had gotten this recipe from the mother of a friend at college, gave me the recipe. It is an old recipe that keeps on satisfying the sweet tooth of lemon lovers. Needless to say, it was a big hit at my luncheon, and I have served it often since.

2   tablespoons butter, softened
½   plus ½ cup granulated sugar
3   eggs, separated
1   lemon, juice and grated rind
3   tablespoons all-purpose flour
1   cup milk
1   piecrust, not baked

Preheat the oven to 425°. In a medium-size bowl with an electric mixer beat the butter. Add ½ cup of the sugar. In a small bowl beat the egg yolks and add them to the butter mixture, continuing to beat. Add the lemon juice and rind. In another bowl, mix the remaining ½ cup sugar with the flour and add to the butter mixture. Add the milk and

stir well. In a clean bowl beat the egg whites and fold them into the mixture. Gently pour the filling into the unbaked pie shell. Bake at 425° for 10 minutes. Reduce the heat to 350° and bake for another 30 to 45 minutes.

YIELD: 8 SERVINGS

Ellen Hester
Monroe, Georgia

Meringue

3   egg whites
¼   teaspoon cream of tartar
6   tablespoons granulated sugar
½   teaspoon vanilla extract

In a mixing bowl with an electric mixer on high beat the egg whites with the cream of tartar until they are frothy. Gradually beat in the sugar, a little at a time. Continue beating until the whites are stiff and glossy. Do *not* under beat. Continue to beat until the sugar is dissolved. Beat in the vanilla extract. Pile the meringue onto a hot pie filling. Be careful to seal the meringue onto the edge of the piecrust to prevent shrinking or weeping. Swirl or pull up points for a decorative top. Either preheat the oven to 400° and bake the meringue for 8 to 10 minutes or until delicately brown, or place the pie under the broiler section of the oven for just a short while to allow the meringue to brown.

YIELD: MERINGUE FOR 1 (9-INCH) PIE

Mississippi Mud Pie

According to various food historians, this rich chocolate pie gets it name from the thick mud along the banks of the Mississippi River. Who cares where it got its name? Just enjoy.

1   cup (2 sticks) butter
     Dash of salt
½   cup cocoa powder
4   eggs, beaten
1½   cups all-purpose flour
2   cups granulated sugar
1½   cups pecans
1   bag small marshmallows

ICING

1   (16-ounce) package confectioners' sugar, sifted
¼   cup (½ stick) butter
½   teaspoon vanilla extract
½   cup milk
⅓   cup cocoa powder

Preheat the oven to 350°. In a saucepan on low heat melt the butter. Add the salt, cocoa powder, eggs, flour, and granulated sugar. Beat well. Add the pecans and continue to beat. Pour the batter into a greased 9 x 13-inch pan. Cook for 35 minutes. Arrange the marshmallows over the cake while it is hot and put it in the oven until the marshmallows partially melt.

For the icing, in a bowl with an electric mix combine the confectioners' sugar, butter, vanilla, milk, and cocoa powder. Mix well. Pour this mixture over the marshmallows. Cool and cut into squares.

YIELD: 24 SQUARES

Old South Berry Blue Pie

Born in 1929, I grew up as a sharecropper's daughter in the foothills of "Lost Mountain" (Kennesaw, Georgia). We ate what we grew and preserved canned, dried, or fresh produce. There were marvelous huckleberries growing wild for the picking. I would pick them and bring them to my mother, who transformed them into homemade-crust pies. Since I now live in Covington, there are no huckleberries to pick, so I planted six blueberry bushes.

2   (9-inch) frozen piecrusts, thawed
4   cups fresh blueberries, rinsed
½   plus ½ cup granulated sugar
2   cups all-purpose flour
½   cup packed brown sugar
¼   teaspoon salt
½   cup (1 stick) butter

Preheat the oven to 375°. In a medium-size bowl combine the blueberries and ½ cup of the sugar and stir gently. In another bowl, combine the flour, brown sugar, the remaining ½ cup granulated sugar, and the salt. Mix well with your hands. With two knives, cut the butter into the flour mixture. Set the two piecrusts on a large cookie sheet. Gently stir the blueberries and divide them between the piecrusts. Pour the flour/butter mixture into a mound on top of the berries. Bake for 40 to 50 minutes. When removing the pies from the oven, be very careful because the juice may spill onto the cookie sheet.

YIELD: 16 SERVINGS

Louise Cartwright
Covington, Georgia

Pawley's Island Pie

¾ cup granulated sugar
½ cup all-purpose flour
2 large eggs
1 teaspoon vanilla extract
½ cup (1 stick) butter, melted and cooled
1 cup walnuts
1 cup chocolate chips
1 (9-inch) Pastry Piecrust (recipe on page 340)

Preheat the oven to 350°. In a large bowl mix the sugar, flour, eggs, and vanilla. Stir until well blended. Add the cooled butter and stir until smooth. Add the walnuts and chocolate chips. Pour into a 9-inch piecrust and bake for 30 to 40 minutes.

YIELD: 8 SERVINGS

Lynn Grace
Grayson, Georgia

Peanut Butter Pie

Peanut butter pie is fundamental to the serious dessert repertoire of the South and that is especially true in the peanut-rich state of Georgia, where you might find peanut butter cake and peanut butter custard. This creamy peanut butter pie is on the dessert table every day at Blue Willow Inn. Louis says customers have been known to fight over what appears to be the last piece— usually it isn't. The kitchen usually has another pie ready to replace the pie when it gets down to the last couple of slices. A guest once asked, "Who made the peanut butter pie? I want to marry her."

1 (8-ounce) package cream cheese
1 cup confectioners' sugar
¾ cup crunchy peanut butter
1 plus 1 (12-ounce) cartons refrigerated whipped topping
2 Graham Cracker Piecrusts (recipe on page 333)

In a large bowl mix the cream cheese, confectioners' sugar, and peanut butter together. Fold in 1 carton of the whipped topping. Divide the mixture between the piecrusts and chill for several hours. Top each pie with half of the remaining carton whipped topping.

YIELD: 16 SERVINGS

Pastry Piecrust

2¼ cups all-purpose flour

1 teaspoon salt

⅔ cup shortening

⅓ cup ice cold water

In a large mixing bowl mix the flour, salt, and shortening to a coarse mixture. Add the water and mix until the dough forms a ball. Divide the dough into two equal portions. Roll each portion of dough out on a floured surface. Place one crust in the bottom of a pie shell with the crust slightly over the side of the shell. Place the second crust on top of the pie filling.

YIELD: 2 (9-INCH) PIECRUSTS

Pumpkin Pie

This pie is another "must have" on your holiday table.

1 (29-ounce) can 100% pure pumpkin

4 eggs

1½ cups granulated sugar

½ cup packed dark brown sugar

1 teaspoon salt

1 teaspoon ground cinnamon

2 cups milk

2 unbaked 9-inch Pastry Piecrusts (recipe on page 340)

Preheat the oven to 350°. In a large bowl combine the pumpkin, eggs, granulated sugar, brown sugar, salt, cinnamon, and milk. Mix well. Divide the pumpkin mixture between the two pie shells. Bake for 30 minutes. Serve warm or cold. If desired, top with whipped topping when ready to serve.

YIELD: 16 SERVINGS

Shirley's Chess Pie

Tennessee's first lady, Andrea Conte, requested that Hilda Pope, chef/manager of the governor's residence, send us this recipe. She has served this pie on many occasions and has even made it in individual, 4-inch, tart shells.

½ cup (1 stick) butter

1 cup granulated sugar

3 eggs

1 tablespoon white vinegar

1 tablespoon vanilla extract

1 tablespoon cornmeal

1 unbaked (8-inch) piecrust

Preheat the oven to 350°. In a large mixing bowl whisk together the butter, sugar, eggs, vinegar, vanilla, and cornmeal. Pour this mixture into the piecrust. Bake for 40 to 45 minutes or until set.

Hint: For a 9-inch deep-dish pie, double the ingredients.

YIELD: 8 SERVINGS

Snow-Capped Chocolate Pie

3   egg whites
1   teaspoon vanilla extract
¾   cup granulated sugar
1   teaspoon baking powder
4   ounces sweet cooking chocolate, grated
1   cup fine vanilla wafer crumbs
½   cup finely chopped pecans

TOPPING

1   cup whipping cream
2   tablespoons sugar
1   teaspoon vanilla extract

Preheat the oven to 350°. In a medium-size bowl with an electric mixer beat the egg whites with the vanilla to soft peaks. In a small bowl combine the sugar and baking powder. Gradually add this to the egg whites, beating continuously until stiff. In another small bowl combine the grated chocolate (reserving 1 tablespoon for decorating the top of the pie), vanilla wafer crumbs, and pecans. Fold this mixture gently into the egg whites. Spread the filling into a greased 9-inch pie plate and bake for 20 to 25 minutes. Do not overbake or the pie will become dry and hard. Remove from the oven and allow to cool.

For the **topping**, beat the whipping cream in a bowl with an electric mixer. Gradually add the sugar to the cream, continuing to beat. Add the vanilla. Be careful not to over beat. Spread the topping over the top of the pie. Sprinkle

the reserved 1 tablespoon of grated chocolate on top. Refrigerate and chill for 6 to 8 hours before serving.

YIELD: 8 SERVINGS

Patsy Joiner
Snellville, Georgia

Mock Apple Pie

This is a great favorite of Steve DeMoss, our neighbor.

3   egg whites
¾   cup granulated sugar
1   teaspoon baking powder
1   teaspoon vanilla
20 crumbled butter crackers
¾   cup chopped pecans
1   (8-ounce) container whipping cream
2   to 3 tablespoons sugar

Preheat the oven to 350°. In a medium-size mixing bowl beat the egg whites until stiff. With a spoon fold in the sugar and baking powder. Add the vanilla, crackers, and pecans. Stir until all the ingredients are moistened. Pour into a 9-inch pie pan. Bake at 350° for 25 minutes. Set aside to cool.

In a small mixing bowl beat the whipping cream and as it thickens add 2 to 3 tablespoons sugar until the cream reaches the desired consistency. Pour the whipped cream on top of the cooled pie.

YIELD: 8 SERVINGS

Alabama "Blue Ribbon" Banana Pudding

This recipe comes to us from Patsy Riley, first lady of the state of Alabama. She says, "During the summer of 1997 at the Annual Congressional Family Picnic, each spouse was asked to bring a dessert with a hint of her state. To my surprise, I won first place for my Alabama Banana Pudding. I was crowned with a chef's hat and my scepter was a wooden spoon. I'd like to add that members of my court, second through fourth-place winners, were all Southern spouses. Great Southern women are usually great cooks."

¾ cup granulated sugar
Dash of salt
¼ cup all-purpose flour
3 egg yolks, beaten
1 tablespoon vanilla flavoring
2 cups half-and-half
2 to 4 bananas, sliced across
15 vanilla wafers

MERINGUE

3 egg whites
2 dashes cream of tartar
6 tablespoons granulated sugar
½ teaspoon vanilla extract

In a small bowl combine the sugar, salt, and flour. In a double boiler over simmering water combine the egg yolks and vanilla. Add the sugar mixture to the egg yolks and vanilla. Slowly add the half-and-half, stirring frequently. Continue to heat until it thickens. In a 1½-quart baking dish layer the banana slices and vanilla wafers. Pour the pudding over these.

For the **meringue**, preheat the oven to 350°. In a medium-size bowl beat the egg whites and cream of tartar for 2 minutes. Slowly add the sugar and vanilla until the egg whites are very stiff. Spread this over the pudding and bake until the meringue is golden brown.

YIELD: 6 SERVINGS

Banana Pudding

6 tablespoons all-purpose flour
8 tablespoons granulated sugar
Dash of salt
2 eggs, beaten
4 cups milk
1 teaspoon vanilla flavoring
Vanilla wafer cookies
4 to 5 bananas, sliced crosswise
9 ounces whipped topping

In a medium-size saucepan combine the flour, sugar, salt, and eggs. Add the milk a little at a time and stir until the mixture is smooth. Add the vanilla. Cook this mixture on medium heat, stirring continuously, until the mixture thickens. Cool thoroughly. Line the bottom of a casserole dish with the vanilla wafers, then the bananas. Repeat this procedure until the dish is two-thirds full. Cover with the cooled pudding. Top with the whipped topping. Place in the refrigerator to chill. Be sure to refrigerate any leftover pudding.

YIELD: 8 TO 10 SERVINGS

Bread Pudding

Any time you have leftover buttermilk biscuits, make this great dish. It's good made with bread, but the biscuits give it a truly Southern flavor.

4	eggs
1¾	cups granulated sugar
¼	cup vanilla extract
1	teaspoon ground cinnamon
1	teaspoon ground nutmeg
1	quart (4 cups) milk
½	cup (1 stick) butter, softened
8	to 10 leftover biscuits or ½ loaf white bread, toasted
¾	cup raisins

Preheat the oven to 350°. In a large mixing bowl beat the eggs until frothy. Add the sugar, vanilla, cinnamon, and nutmeg. Beat well. Add the milk and butter. Mix well. Coarsely crumble the biscuits or bread and add these to the mixture. Add the raisins. Mix well but do not beat. Pour the mixture into an ungreased 9 x 13-inch pan. Bake for 40 to 45 minutes or until brown. Serve warm with Lemon Sauce (recipe on page 134).

YIELD: 8 TO 10 SERVINGS

River Club Bread Pudding

3	Pepperidge Farm hard rolls or equivalent
2	ounces seedless golden raisins
½	cup butter or margarine, melted
	Dash of salt
⅓	cup granulated sugar
4	eggs, whipped
½	pint half-and-half
½	pint milk
	Dash of vanilla flavoring
	Coconut

COLD SABAYON SAUCE

4	egg yolks
¾	cup granulated sugar
¾	cup dry sherry
¼	cup heavy cream, lightly whipped

Preheat the oven to 350°. In a large bowl slice or dice the rolls and combine with the raisins, butter or margarine, salt, and sugar. Mix well. In a medium-size bowl combine the whipped eggs, half-and-half, milk, and vanilla. Add this to the bread mixture. Toss lightly. Place in a 3-quart baking dish. Sprinkle the coconut on top. Bake for about 45 minutes. Serve with the sauce.

For the **cold sabayon sauce**, combine, beat, and heat the egg yolks, sugar, and sherry in the top of a double boiler over simmering water. Continue to beat with a whisk until the mixture is very thick. Remove from the heat and set the top of the boiler in a pan of cracked ice. Continue to beat with a whisk until the sauce is cold. Add the whipped cream to the sauce. Serve over the bread pudding.

YIELD: 4 SERVINGS

Chocolate Pudding

I inherited this fabulous pudding recipe from my mother.

1   cup all-purpose flour
1½   cups granulated sugar
2½   tablespoons cocoa powder
5   cups whole milk

In a small bowl combine the flour, sugar, and cocoa powder. In a large saucepan on medium heat combine the dry mixture with the milk. Mix well until the mixture is smooth. Cook, stirring continuously, until thick.

YIELD: 8 SERVINGS

Evelyn Chadwick
Cummings, Georgia

Indian Pudding

This is a recipe that my grandmother, Ellen Lincoln, brought with her from New England. It was always served as a winter dessert.

4   cups milk
⅓   cup cornmeal
¾   cup molasses
¼   cup (½ stick) butter
½   teaspoon salt
3   tablespoons granulated sugar
½   teaspoon ground ginger
½   teaspoon ground cinnamon

1   egg, well beaten
½   cup raisins
       Hard sauce or cream for serving

Place the milk and cornmeal in the top of a double boiler over simmer water. Stir and cook for 15 minutes. Add the molasses. Stir and cook for 5 more minutes. Remove from the heat and stir in the butter, salt, sugar, ginger, cinnamon, egg, and raisins. Preheat the oven to 325°. Pour the mixture into a greased 2-quart baking dish and bake for 1½ to 2 hours until set. Serve hot with hard sauce or cream.

Hint: You may substitute a scoop of vanilla ice cream for the hard sauce or cream when serving.

YIELD: 6 TO 8 SERVINGS

Jeanne Smith
Covington, Georgia

Rice Pudding

4   cups cooked rice
1½   cups granulated sugar
4   cups milk
1   cup raisins
½   teaspoon ground nutmeg
4   eggs, lightly beaten
       Dash of salt

Preheat the oven to 350°. In a large mixing bowl combine the rice, sugar, milk, raisins, nutmeg, eggs, and salt. Bake for 1½ hours until brown. Serve hot.

YIELD: 6 TO 8 SERVINGS

Strawberry Pudding

2   pints frozen sweetened strawberries
1   (6-ounce) package strawberry gelatin
3   cups cold milk
1   (5.1-ounce) box vanilla instant pudding
1   cup sour cream
1   (12-ounce) container whipped topping
1   large box vanilla wafers

In a saucepan on medium heat cook the strawberries and gelatin until the gelatin dissolves. Set this aside to cool. In a small bowl combine the milk and instant pudding. Stir until well mixed. Stir in the sour cream. Stir in the whipped topping. In a 9 x 13-inch pan layer the vanilla wafers, pudding mix, and strawberry mixture. Repeat until the ingredients are used. Chill before serving.

YIELD: ABOUT 24 SERVINGS

Blackberry Cobbler

2   to 3 cups fresh blackberries or 2 (16-ounce) packages frozen blackberries, thawed
1   cup plus 2 tablespoons granulated sugar
½   cup water
1   plus ¼ cups margarine
1   cup self-rising flour
1   plus ½ cups milk

Preheat the oven to 375°. In a medium-size bowl combine the berries, 1 cup of the sugar, and water. Pour the mixture in a 9 x 13-inch pan and dot with ¼ cup of the margarine. In a bowl combine the flour with the remaining 1 cup of the margarine and blend well with a fork. Add 1 cup milk and mix. The consistency of the mixture should be medium thin. If it is too thick, add the remaining ½ cup milk. Pour the mixture over the berries and sprinkle the remaining 2 tablespoons sugar over the batter. Bake for 35 to 40 minutes.

YIELD: 6 TO 8 SERVINGS

Delinda Kennedy
Conyers, Georgia

Blueberry Cobbler

3   cups fresh blueberries
1   plus ½ cup granulated sugar
½   cup (1 stick) butter, melted
1   cup self-rising flour

Preheat the oven to 350°. Pour the blueberries into a 2-quart baking dish and sprinkle ½ cup of the sugar over them. In another bowl combine the melted butter, the remaining 1 cup of sugar, and the flour. Mix well to form a pastry. Pour this over the blueberries and bake for 45 minutes.

YIELD: 8 SERVINGS

Cherry Cobbler

2½ cups pitted fresh cherries or 2 (16-ounce) cans pitted cherries
1   tablespoon grated lemon peel
3   tablespoons butter
3   tablespoons cornstarch
1   cup granulated sugar

Topping

1   cup all-purpose flour
¾   cup granulated sugar
1   teaspoon baking powder
½   teaspoon salt
1   cup milk
¼   cup shortening
1   teaspoon vanilla extract
1   egg

In a saucepan over medium-low heat, combine the cherries, lemon peel, and butter. Add the cornstarch and the sugar. Cook, stirring constantly, until thickened. Pour into a 10 x 6-inch baking dish. Set aside to stand while making the topping.

Preheat the oven to 350°. For the **topping**, in a mixing bowl sift the flour. Add the sugar, baking powder, and salt. Add the milk, shortening, vanilla, and egg. Beat at medium speed with an electric mixer for 2 to 3 minutes. Spoon this mixture over the fruit mixture. Bake for 40 minutes.

YIELD: 8 SERVINGS

Peach Cobbler

No meal at the Blue Willow Inn is complete without "a little taste" of peach cobbler. No matter what other desserts may be arrayed in the center of the buffet room, it is ever present on the side where bowls of it can supplement any other end-of-the-meal sweet.

¾   cup plus 2 tablespoons granulated sugar
1   cup self-rising flour
¼   plus ¼ cup (1 stick) butter, melted
1   (28-ounce) can sliced peaches, undrained

Preheat the oven to 350°. In a medium-size mixing bowl coarsely mix ⅔ cup of the sugar, the flour, and ¼ cup melted butter together. Sprinkle about one-third of this mixture on the bottom a baking dish. Add the peaches and juice. (If the juice from the peaches does not cover the peaches, add a small amount of water just to cover the peaches. Too little liquid will make the cobbler dry. Too much liquid will make it soupy.) Top the peaches with the remaining sugar/flour mixture. Sprinkle the top with the remaining 2 tablespoons sugar and the remaining ¼ cup butter. Bake for 30 to 40 minutes or until brown and bubbly. Serve hot.

Hint: Fresh peaches can be used. When using fresh peaches, peel and slice them, sprinkling the slices with an additional 1/2 cup sugar. Refrigerate them for 2 to 3 hours before using.

YIELD: 6 TO 8 SERVINGS

Apple Brown Betty

¾   plus ¾ cups graham cracker crumbs

6   tart baking apples, peeled, cored, and
     sliced

½   cup water

½   cup molasses

¼   cup packed brown sugar

½   cup (1 stick) butter, melted

½   teaspoon ground cinnamon

Preheat the oven to 350°. Sprinkle ¾ cup graham cracker crumbs onto the bottom of an 8 x 8-inch baking dish. Place half of the sliced apples on top of the crumbs, and repeat the layering with the remaining ¾ cup crumbs and remaining apple slices. In a small bowl mix the water, molasses, brown sugar, and butter. Add the cinnamon and mix. Pour this mixture evenly over the apples and graham cracker crumbs. Cover and bake for 40 minutes. Uncover and bake 15 minutes more.

YIELD: 8 SERVINGS

Apple Dumplings

These dumplings are even more delicious when topped with ice cream and nuts. This was a favorite of my grandmother at our family dinners. They are also requested at our church potluck dinners.

2   large Granny Smith apples

½   cup (1 stick) butter

1   cup granulated sugar

¾   cup water

1   teaspoon vanilla extract

1   (8-ounce) can crescent rolls
     Cinnamon-sugar mix for sprinkling

Preheat the oven to 350°. Peel, core, and quarter the apples. In a saucepan over medium heat melt the butter and sugar. Add the water and vanilla when the butter has melted.

Roll an apple quarter in a triangle of each of the crescent rolls. Press the dough together to cover most of the apple quarter. Repeat the rolling until you have used all eight apple quarters. Place the apple dumplings in a 9 x 13-inch baking dish. Cover with the butter mixture. Bake for 35 to 45 minutes or until a golden brown. Mix enough cinnamon and sugar together to lightly sprinkle each dumpling before cooling.

YIELD: 8 SERVINGS

Jane Saunders
Bethlehem, Georgia

First Place Winner—Sweets and Desserts
Blue Willow Inn Recipe Contest, 2004

Apple Fritters

1½ cups all-purpose flour
1 tablespoon granulated sugar
2 teaspoons baking powder
½ teaspoon salt
2 eggs, beaten
⅔ cup milk
3 cups plus 1 tablespoon vegetable oil
3 cups peeled, finely chopped apples
½ cup confectioners' sugar

In a large mixing bowl combine the flour, sugar, baking powder, and salt. Mix well. Add the eggs, milk, 1 tablespoon of the oil, and the apples. Mix by hand until combined and moist. Heat the remaining 3 cups oil in a heavy skillet or pot to 350°. To make the fritters, spoon about ¼ cup of the batter at a time into the hot oil and cook for 3 to 4 minutes until golden brown. Drain well. Roll in the confectioners' sugar while still hot.

YIELD 2½ TO 3 DOZEN

Old-Fashioned Blackberry Roll

My mother-in-law, Cornelia Lewis, was featured in a major area newspaper in October 1994 as one of Georgia's notable cooks. She often prepared this delicious old-fashioned fruit dessert. I have never known anyone else to make a berry pie this same way. She always called it a "roll." I guess that was because of the process of "rolling" the crust around the berries. Cornelia enjoyed cooking for her family until she was nintey-six years old.

4 cups fresh or frozen blackberries
1½ cups granulated sugar plus more for sprinkling
2 cups biscuit mix or homemade biscuit dough
  Butter
2 cups hot water

Wash the fresh blackberries and pour the sugar over them. Set them aside to allow the sugar time to release the juice from the berries. Preheat the oven to 350°.

Prepare the biscuit mix according to the package directions. Break off enough dough to make about two biscuits and roll this out until it is thin like a piecrust. Grease a 9 x 13-inch baking dish. Carefully lift the rolled-out dough and place it into the dish, allowing part of the crust to hang over the side of the dish. Spoon one-third of the berries onto the crust. "Roll" the crust over the berries. Repeat this process with the remainder of the dough and the berries. Dot the tops of the rolls with the butter and sprinkle with sugar. Pour the hot water into the dish around the rolls of dough. The water is necessary to make the rolls juicy. Bake for about 30 to 40 minutes until the rolls are golden brown on top.

Hint: Other berries may be used in this recipe

YIELD: 6 TO 9 SERVINGS

Rose Lewis
Covington, Georgia

Blueberry Dessert

The Hard Labor Creek Blueberry Farm in Social Circle gave the Blue Willow Inn this recipe.

1	cup all-purpose flour
½	cup (1 stick) butter, softened
1	cup packed dark brown sugar
1	chopped pecans
1	(8-ounce) package cream cheese, softened
1	(8-ounce) package refrigerated whipped topping
¾	plus ¼ cup granulated sugar
1	teaspoon vanilla extract
1	quart blueberries
2	heaping teaspoons cornstarch

Preheat the oven to 350°. In a large mixing bowl combine the flour, butter, dark brown sugar, and pecans. Mix well. Press this mixture into the bottom of a 9 x 13-inch baking dish. Bake for 15 to 20 minutes until slightly brown. Remove from the heat and set aside to cool.

In a large bowl mix together the cream cheese, whipped topping, ¾ cup of the sugar, and vanilla. Spread over the cooled base. In a saucepan combine the blueberries, cornstarch, and the remaining ¼ cup sugar. Cook over medium heat, stirring often, until thickened. Cool and spread over the cream cheese layer. Refrigerate until ready to serve.

YIELD: ABOUT 20 SERVINGS

Brownie Trifle

2	(21-ounce) packages chewy fudge brownie mix
1	(8-ounce) package cream cheese, softened
1	(7-ounce) jar marshmallow creme
2	(8-ounce) containers frozen whipped topping, thawed
3	cups milk
2	(3.4-ounce) packages white chocolate instant pudding mix
1	(12.5-ounce) jar caramel topping

Prepare each brownie mix according to package directions for chewy brownies in a 9 x 13-inch pan. After cooking, set aside to cool. Once the brownies are cool, break them into large pieces. In a large bowl with an electric mixer on medium speed beat the cream cheese until it is light and creamy. Beat in the marshmallow creme. Stir in 1 container of the whipped topping. In another large bowl stir together the milk and white chocolate pudding mix. Stir until thickened. Stir in the remaining container of whipped topping. In a 9 x 13-inch baking dish or a 3-quart bowl crumble half of the brownie pieces in an even layer. Pour the cream cheese mixture evenly over the brownies. Drizzle evenly with the caramel topping. Pour the pudding evenly over the caramel topping. Crumble the remaining brownie pieces on top. Cover and chill for at least 2 hours before serving.

YIELD: 15 SERVINGS

Betty Stephens
Monroe, Georgia

Cherry Dessert

1   cup all-purpose flour

¼   cup packed brown sugar

½   cup (1 stick) margarine, melted

1   cup chopped nuts

1   (8-ounce) package cream cheese, softened

⅔   cup confectioners' sugar

1   teaspoon vanilla flavoring

1   (16-ounce) container whipped topping, divided

1   (16-ounce) can cherry pie filling

Preheat the oven to 350°. In a medium-size bowl combine the flour, brown sugar, margarine, and nuts. Spread in a greased 9 x 13-inch baking dish. Bake for 15 minutes. Set aside to cool. In a large bowl combine the cream cheese, confectioners' sugar, vanilla, and ½ of the container whipped topping. Mix well. Spread this mixture over the cooled crust. Spread the cherry pie filling over this. Spread the remaining ½ container whipped topping over the pie filling. Place in the refrigerator to chill before serving.

YIELD: ABOUT 20 SERVINGS

Chocolate Delight

1   cup all-purpose flour

½   cup (1 stick) margarine, softened

½   cup chopped pecans

1   (8-ounce) package cream cheese, softened

1   cup confectioners' sugar

2   containers whipped topping

2   (3.4-ounce) chocolate instant pudding mixes

3   cups milk

Preheat the oven to 350°. In a medium-size bowl mix the flour, margarine, and pecans thoroughly to form a crust. Press into a 6 x 11-inch pan. Bake for 15 minutes. Remove from the oven and set aside to cool. In a medium-size bowl mix the cream cheese, confectioners' sugar, and 1 container of the whipped topping together. Spread this mixture over the cooled crust. Refrigerate for 15 minutes.

Mix the pudding with the milk according to package directions. Spread the pudding over the cream cheese mixture. Refrigerate for 15 minutes. Cover with the remaining container of whipped topping. Chill before serving.

YIELD: 12 SERVINGS

Chocolate Mousse

1   (12-ounce) package semisweet chocolate morsels

2   plus ½ cups whipping cream

1   teaspoon vanilla extract

1   tablespoon rum

Whipped cream for garnish

Grated chocolate for garnish

In a medium-size glass bowl microwave the chocolate morsels and ½ cup of the whipping cream on high for 1½ minutes or until the chocolate has melted, stirring two times. Stir in the vanilla and the rum, blending well. Cool for 5 minutes. In a medium-size bowl with an electric mixer on medium speed beat the remaining 2 cups whipping cream until soft peaks form. Fold the whipped cream into the chocolate mixture. Spoon into a large serving bowl or individual dessert dishes. Garnish with additional whipped cream and grated chocolate if desired. Chill 2 hours.

YIELD: 6 TO 8 SERVINGS

To bake, preheat the oven to 350°. Place the cups in a baking pan filled with water two-thirds up the sides of the custard cups. Bake for 25 to 40 minutes. Remove from the oven and chill. Before serving, sprinkle 1 to 2 teaspoons light brown sugar on top of each cup. Place under the broiler until bubbly and toasted.

A variation would be to use crystallized ginger mixed with granulated sugar for the topping.

YIELD: 8 CUSTARD CUPS

Crème Brulée

This recipe comes from Anita Perry, the first lady of the state of Texas. Sarah Bishop, the mansion chef, prepared this recipe for the special dinner honoring former governors and first ladies of Texas. Former governor Ann Richards raved about it. You will too.

8	egg yolks
1	pint heavy cream
¼	cup granulated sugar
¼	teaspoon vanilla flavoring
	Pinch of salt
	Light brown sugar

In a large bowl beat the egg yolks. In a heavy (non-aluminum) saucepan bring the cream, sugar, vanilla, and salt to a near boil but *do not boil*. Slowly add the hot cream mixture to the egg yolks while mixing continuously at low speed to avoid beating air into the mixture. Set up a cheesecloth to strain the mix. Pour into eight ovenproof custard cups (about 4 ounces).

Eggnog Mousse

This recipe comes from Peggy Hawkins, events manager at Magnolia Hall. She uses this as a holiday dessert.

2	cups cold eggnog
1½	cups cold milk
2	(3.4-ounce) packages vanilla instant pudding mix
¼	teaspoon ground nutmeg plus extra for garnish
1	(8-ounce) container French vanilla whipped topping, thawed and divided

In a large mixing bowl combine the eggnog, cold milk, pudding mixes, and nutmeg. Beat with a wire whisk for 2 minutes. Gently stir in ½ of the container whipped topping. Spoon evenly into dessert dishes or into a 1¼-quart serving bowl. Refrigerate for 2 hours. Garnish with the remaining ½ container whipped topping and additional nutmeg.

YIELD: 10 SERVINGS

Floating Islands

2   cups milk
3   eggs, separated
½   cup granulated sugar
     Pinch of salt
1   teaspoon vanilla flavoring
2   tablespoons confectioners' sugar

In the top of a double boiler over hot water scald the milk. In a small bowl lightly beat the egg yolks. Add these to the milk, stirring constantly. Add the granulated sugar and salt. Continue to cook and stir until the mixture thickens and coats the back of a spoon. Stir in the vanilla. Remove from the heat. Pour the custard into a serving dish and place in the refrigerator to chill. Serve topped with "floating islands," which are made by beating the egg whites with the confectioners' sugar. Drop this by the spoonful on top of the custard.

YIELD: 4 SERVINGS

Nancy Posner
Social Circle, Georgia

Hot Apple Crisp

This is a delicious dessert accompanied by vanilla ice cream. Yummy!

¾   cup self-rising flour
½   plus ¼ plus ¼ cup light brown sugar
¼   plus ¼ plus ¼ cup granulated sugar
¼   plus ¼ cup butter, melted
1   (16-ounce) can apple pie filling
¼   cup water
1   tablespoon lemon juice
¼   teaspoon ground cinnamon
¼   teaspoon ground nutmeg
¼   teaspoon apple pie spice

Preheat the oven to 350°. In a large mixing bowl, combine the flour, ½ cup of the light brown sugar, ¼ cup of the granulated sugar, and ¼ cup of the butter. Mix until coarse. Sprinkle half of this mixture on the bottom of a 9 x 13-inch baking dish. Gently and evenly spread the apple pie filling over the sugar and flour mixture. In a small bowl combine the water, lemon juice, cinnamon, nutmeg, and apple pie spice. Mix well. Sprinkle this mixture over the apples. In a small bowl mix together ¼ cup of the granulated sugar and ¼ cup of the light brown sugar. Cover the apples with this. Sprinkle the remaining half of the flour mixture on top of the sugars. In a small bowl combine the remaining ¼ cup brown sugar, ¼ cup granulated sugar, and ¼ cup butter. Sprinkle this as the final layer. Bake for 45 to 50 minutes or until golden brown and bubbly.

YIELD: ABOUT 24 SERVINGS

Lemon Lush

This recipe is a different take on the familiar Chocolate Delight (recipe on page 350). It is a great summer dessert.

½   cup (1 stick) margarine, melted
1   tablespoon granulated sugar
1   cup sifted all-purpose flour

½   cup chopped pecans

1   (8-ounce) package cream cheese, softened

1   cup sifted confectioners' sugar

1   (8-ounce) container whipped topping, divided

2   (3.4-ounce) packages lemon instant pudding mix

3   cups cold milk

2   tablespoons lemon juice

Preheat the oven to 350°.

For the first layer, combine the melted margarine, sugar, flour, and pecans in a medium-size bowl. Press this mixture into a 9 x 13-inch dish or pan. Bake for 15 minutes. Set aside to cool completely.

For the second layer, beat together the cream cheese, confectioners' sugar, and 1 cup of the whipped topping in a medium-size bowl. Spread this carefully over the cooled crust.

For the third layer, mix together the pudding mixes, milk, and lemon juice in a large bowl. Spread this over the cream cheese layer. Refrigerate for a few hours. Spread the remaining whipped topping over the top. Keep refrigerated.

YIELD: ABOUT 24 SERVINGS

Lemon Sponge Custard

2   eggs, separated

1   cup granulated sugar

3   tablespoons all-purpose flour

1   cup milk

1   lemon, juice and zest

Preheat the oven to 275°. In a small bowl beat the egg whites until stiff. In a large bowl slightly beat the egg yolks. Add the sugar, flour, milk, lemon juice, and lemon zest. Fold in the beaten egg whites. Pour this mixture into a small buttered casserole dish. Place the dish in a pan of hot water. Bake for 1 hour. Serve with whipped cream or whipped topping.

YIELD: 8 TO 10 SERVINGS

Joan McMillan
Social Circle, Georgia

Strawberry Delight

My great-great-grandfather on my mother's side, Constantine Shannon, brought the first strawberry plants from Shannon, Mississippi, to Plant City, Florida, in 1881. Today Plant City is know as the "World's Winter Strawberry Capitol." Every year there is a big strawberry festival and parade held in Plant City. My family is proud of this connection, so we use strawberries in a lot of recipes.

1	box vanilla wafers, crushed
½	cup (1 stick) margarine, softened
1½	cups confectioners' sugar
2	eggs
1	(16-ounce) package frozen strawberries
½	pint whipping cream or whipped topping
1	cup chopped pecans

Spread a layer of half the vanilla wafer crumbs in the bottom of a 9 x 13-inch dish. In a medium-size bowl beat the margarine and sugar. Add the eggs and mix well. Spread this mixture over the vanilla wafer crumbs. Next spread the strawberries over the butter mixture. Spread the whipped cream or topping over the strawberries. Spread the remaining crumbs on top of the whipped cream. Sprinkle the pecans on top. Refrigerate for 24 hours.

Note: This recipe contains raw eggs which can make you sick. To be safe substitute a pasteurized egg product for the eggs.

YIELD: ABOUT 22 SERVINGS

Nancy Posner
Social Circle, Georgia

Ambrosia Topping

This topping is delicious on top of Cherry Cheese Pie (page 326) and ice cream.

½	cup peach or apricot preserves
¼	cup flaked coconut
2	tablespoons orange-flavored liqueur
2	teaspoons cornstarch

In a small saucepan on medium-low heat combine the preserves, coconut, orange liqueur, and cornstarch. Cook, stirring continuously, until thickened. Chill thoroughly.

Hint: When using this to top a pie, arrange fresh orange slices on the top of the pie and drizzle with the sauce.

YIELD: ½ CUP

Blueberry Topping

This is another wonderful recipe from the Hard Labor Creek Blueberry Farm. The topping is good with ice cream when slightly cooled and is delicious on a loaf cake or pound cake.

½   cup granulated sugar
½   cup water
⅛   teaspoon salt
1   tablespoon cornstarch
1   cup blueberries, divided
1   tablespoon lemon juice
½   teaspoon grated fresh lemon peel

In a small saucepan over medium heat combine the sugar, water, salt, cornstarch, and a few blueberries. Cook, stirring often, until the mixture boils and thickens. Add the remaining blueberries. Heat the mixture until it is boiling again. Turn the heat to low. Simmer for 5 minutes. Stir in the lemon juice and lemon peel. Remove from the heat and cool.

YIELD: ABOUT 1½ CUPS

Cranberry Nut Topping

This colorful topping is a beautiful enhancement to Cherry Cheese Pie (recipe on page 326) or ice cream.

1   cup chilled Cranberry-Orange Relish
      (see page 126)

½   cup chopped walnuts
1   teaspoon grated orange rind

In a small bowl mix the relish, chopped walnuts, and grated orange rind. Place desired amount on top of pie or ice cream.

YIELD: ABOUT 1¼ CUPS

Pecan Topping

Ever wonder how to make a sweet potato soufflé extra special or to add a warm crunch topping to vanilla ice cream? This delicious topping is your answer to that dilemma.

1   cup cornflakes
½   cup firmly packed light brown sugar
⅓   cup butter, melted
¾   cup chopped pecans

Crush the cornflakes into small pieces. In a medium-size mixing bowl combine the cornflakes with the sugar, butter, and pecans and mix well.

If using on a sweet potato soufflé, top the just-cooked soufflé with this mixture and return it to the oven for 5 minutes to brown.

If using to top ice cream, preheat the oven to 350° and spread the topping onto a greased cookie sheet. Bake for 5 to 7 minutes, stirring so it doesn't stick or clump. Allow the topping to cool before spooning onto ice cream.

YIELD: 2 CUPS

Glaze for Strawberries

This makes a marvelous topping for fresh strawberries.

3   tablespoons apple jelly
1   teaspoon concentrated lemon juice
½   teaspoon cornstarch
1   teaspoon water
1   pint fresh strawberries

In a saucepan over medium heat combine the apple jelly and lemon juice. Cook, stirring continuously, until the jelly melts. In a small mixing bowl dissolve the cornstarch in the water. Add to the jelly mixture. Cook and stir until the glaze thickens. Wash and stem the strawberries. Drizzle the glaze over the strawberries.

YIELD: ABOUT 2 CUPS

Seven-Minute Icing

3   egg whites
1⅔ cups granulated sugar
¼   cup white corn syrup
¼   cup coconut milk (or water)
    Dash of salt
1   teaspoon vanilla or lemon juice (either ingredient accomplishes the desired flavor)
3   to 4 cups freshly grated coconut

In a double boiler over medium heat cook the egg whites, sugar, corn syrup, coconut milk, and salt for 7 minutes, beating with a hand mixer until peaks begin to drop off a spoon. Remove from the heat. Add the vanilla or lemon juice. Spread the icing between the layers and on the sides.

YIELD: ICING FOR 1 CAKE

Kids Korner

In the South, it is the custom for children to grow up in the kitchen. Many a great cook has learned at his or her mother's knee—standing on a stool, apron tied around his or her her waist—learning the secrets of family recipes that have been passed down for generations The following are some fun recipes to start children off in the kitchen. They are fun for Mom too!

Ants on a Log

Banana Boats

Blizzard Party Mix

Cherry Fluff

Chicken Feed

Cornflake Peanut Butter Balls

Dirt Cake

Double Strawberry-Banana Shake

Frozen Orange Balls

Garbage Bag Candy

Homemade Butter

Ice Cream Sandwich Dessert

Peanut Butter Balls

Pea-Choc

S'mores

Snow Ice Cream

Yummy Candy

Ants on a Log

A healthy snack for kids to make.

Celery ribs
Peanut butter
Raisins

Remove the ribs from a stalk of celery. Trim and clean. Cut into halves. Spread peanut butter on celery. Decorate with raisins.

YIELD: DEPENDS ON NUMBER OF RIBS USED

Banana Boats

1   banana
2   tablespoons peanut butter
1   tablespoon coconut
1   tablespoon granola

Peel the banana and slice in half lengthwise. Place on a salad plate. Spread peanut butter on each half. Sprinkle with coconut and granola. Make several to share.

YIELD: 1 SERVING

Blizzard Party Mix

2   cups oven-toasted cereal squares
2   cups small pretzel twists
1   cup dry roasted peanuts
1   cup (about 20) coarsely chopped caramels
2   cups white chocolate morsels

Spray a 9 x 13-inch baking pan with nonstick cooking spray. In a large bowl, combine the cereal, pretzels, peanuts, and caramels. In a microwavable bowl, microwave the white chocolate morsels for about 1 minute or until smooth. Pour this over the cereal mixture and coat evenly. Spread this mixture into the prepared baking pan. Let it stand for 20 to 30 minutes or until firm. Break into bite-size pieces.

YIELD: 8 TO 10 SERVINGS

Cherry Fluff

1   (8-ounce) container whipped topping
1   (20-ounce) can cherry pie filling
1   cup chopped walnuts

In a medium-size bowl mix the whipped topping, cherry pie filling, and walnuts. Refrigerate for 30 minutes.

YIELD: 6 SERVINGS

Chicken Feed

1   cup peanuts
½   cup sunflower seeds
½   cup raisins
1   cup M&Ms
2   cups Cheerios

In a large bowl combine the peanuts, sunflower seeds, raisins, and M&Ms. Add the Cheerios and stir gently.

YIELD: 6 TO 8 SERVINGS

Melissa Hoganson
Port St. Lucie, Florida

Cornflake Peanut Butter Balls

1   cup white Karo syrup
1   cup granulated sugar
6   cups cornflakes
1½ cups peanut butter

In a medium saucepan on medium heat bring the Karo syrup and sugar to a boil. In a large mixing bowl combine the cornflakes and peanut butter. Add the syrup mixture to the cornflake and peanut butter mixture, stirring to evenly coat. Drop by the teaspoonful onto wax paper until set.

YIELD: 36 PEANUT BUTTER BALLS

Dirt Cake

2   packages Oreo cookies
2   boxes French vanilla instant pudding
2   (12-ounce) containers frozen whipped topping, thawed

Place the Oreo cookies in a plastic bag and crush them. In a mixing bowl prepare the pudding according to the package directions. In a large mixing bowl place the 2 containers of frozen whipped topping. Fold in the pudding. In a 9 x 13-inch baking dish layer the crushed cookies and the pudding mixture. Began and end with a cookie layer.

YIELD: 24 SERVINGS

Kristen Osburn
Covington, Georgia

Double Strawberry-Banana Shake

2   cups strawberries, sliced and frozen
2   large ripe bananas, sliced and frozen
1   pint strawberry ice cream
2   cups milk
1   teaspoon vanilla extract

Process the strawberries, bananas, ice cream, milk, and vanilla in a blender until smooth, stopping to scrape down the sides. Serve immediately.

YIELD: 8 CUPS

Frozen Orange Balls

1   box vanilla wafers, finely crushed
1   (16-ounce) box confectioners' sugar
1   (12-ounce) can frozen orange juice
    concentrate
½   cup (1 stick) margarine, softened
1   cup chopped pecans
    Confectioners' sugar (optional)
    Coconut (optional)
    Cocoa powder (optional)

In a medium-size mixing bowl thoroughly mix the vanilla wafers, confectioners' sugar, orange juice, margarine, and pecans. Mix until a soft dough forms. Shape into balls and roll in confectioners' sugar, coconut, or cocoa powder if desired. Place in the freezer. Serve frozen.

YIELD: 36 ORANGE BALLS

Garbage Bag Candy

1   box Golden Graham cereal
1   can mixed nuts
¼   cup cashews
¼   cup pecan halves
¼   cup walnut halves
¼   cup raisins
1   (12-ounce) package semisweet
    chocolate
1   (12-ounce) jar crunchy peanut butter
1   (16-ounce) box confectioners' sugar

In a large bowl mix together the cereal, mixed nuts, cashews, pecan halves, walnut halves, and raisins. In a microwavable bowl on high melt together the semisweet chocolate and peanut butter. Fold into the cereal mixture until all the cereal and nuts are covered. Try not to crush the cereal squares. Pour into a 13-gallon garbage bag. Pour the confectioners' sugar over the mixture. Close and shake the garbage bag until all the ingredients are separated and coated. If clumps occur, shake to break up into pieces.

YIELD: ABOUT 14 TO 16 SERVINGS

Homemade Butter

    Heavy cream
    Salt

Allow the cream to come to room temperature. Pour into baby food jars, filling them about half full. Put the lid on tightly and allow children to shake heartily until the butter forms. Drain off the buttermilk. Rinse the butter with cold water. Add salt to taste before serving.

YIELD: DEPENDS ON THE AMOUNT OF
CREAM USED

Ice Cream Sandwich Dessert

14   mini ice cream sandwiches
1   (8-ounce) container whipped topping
3   Butterfinger candy bars, crushed

Lay the ice cream sandwiches in the bottom of 8 x 11-inch glass baking dish. Cover the ice cream sandwiches with the whipped topping. Sprinkle the crushed Butterfingers on top. Cover and place in the freezer until frozen.

YIELD: 14 SERVINGS

Peanut Butter Balls

2   egg yolks
1   teaspoon vanilla
⅛   teaspoon salt
1   cup crunchy peanut butter
1   cup plus 1 tablespoon confectioners' sugar
⅔   cup powdered milk plus some for rolling

In a medium-size bowl combine the egg yolks, vanilla, and salt. Mix well. Add the peanut butter, confectioners' sugar, and powdered milk. Mix thoroughly. Knead the mixture with your fingers until it is firm. Shape into 1-inch balls. Roll in powdered milk. Refrigerate for at least one hour before serving.

YIELD: 30 PEANUT BUTTER BALLS

Pea-Choc

This recipe from Lynn Kelley is a great snack recipe for children of all ages. By the way, you eat this with a spoon.

1   cup creamy peanut butter
1   cup chocolate milk mix
¼   cup milk

In a blender or large bowl combine the peanut butter, milk mix, and milk. Mix until smooth. For variety add M&M's, peanuts, graham cracker crumbs, mini marshmallows, or Rice Krispies. Mix well.

YIELD: 4 SERVINGS

S'mores

This is a favorite of William Dale, Billie's and Louis' grandson. We know your children will have fun making them too.

1   chocolate candy bar broken in half
2   graham crackers
1   large marshmallow

Place half the candy bar on a single graham cracker. Toast the marshmallow and place it on top of the candy. Place the remaining half candy bar on top of the toasted marshmallow. Place the second graham cracker on top of the candy bar.

YIELD: 1 SERVING

Snow Ice Cream

1 egg, beaten
¾ cup granulated sugar
1 cup evaporated milk
2 teaspoons vanilla extract
1 gallon clean, fresh snow

In a large mixing bowl combine the egg and sugar, stirring well with a wire whisk. Add the milk and vanilla and stir well. Place the snow in a large chilled bowl. Gradually add the milk mixture to the snow, gently stirring with a wooden spoon until blended.

Note: This recipe contains raw eggs which can make you sick. To be safe substitute a pasteurized egg product for the eggs.

YIELD: ABOUT 3 QUARTS

Yummy Candy

1 cup peanut butter
¼ cup mashed bananas
¼ cup cocoa powder
2 teaspoons vanilla extract
Crushed cereal
Chopped nuts

In a medium-size mixing bowl mix the peanut butter, mashed bananas, cocoa powder, and vanilla. After the ingredients are thoroughly mixed, roll the mixture into 1-inch balls. The balls can be rolled in the cereal or nuts if desired. Refrigerate or freeze.

YIELD: 24 CANDY BALLS

Charts & Tables

When people are planning a large function for family and friends, a church function, company picnic, or other event, they are often unsure of the amounts of food to prepare. We, at the restaurant, are then asked, "How much?" We hope this next section will be helpful in preparing for your next big function.

FOOD QUANTITIES FOR LARGE GROUPS

	25 servings	50 servings	100 servings
Beverages			
Coffee	½ pound plus 1½ gallons of water	1 pound plus 3 gallons of water	2 pounds plus 6 gallons of water
Lemonade	10 to 15 lemons plus 1½ gallons of water	20 to 30 lemons plus 3 gallons of water	40 to 60 lemons plus 6 gallons of water
Tea	2 ounces (¼ cup) tea plus 1½ gallons of water	4 ounces (½ cup) tea plus 3 gallons of water	8 ounces (1 cup) tea plus 6 gallons of water
Salads			
Cole Slaw	4¼ quarts	2¼ gallons	4½ gallons
Potato or Macaroni Salad	4¼ quarts	2¼ gallons	4½ gallons
Congealed Salad	3 quarts	1¼ gallons	2½ gallons
Vegetables			
Canned Vegetables	1 #10 can	2½ #10 cans	4 #10 cans
Scalloped Potatoes	4½ quarts	2¼ gallons	4½ gallons
Mashed Potatoes	9 pounds	18 to 20 pounds	25 to 35 pounds
Baked Beans	3 quarts	1¼ gallons	2½ gallons
Salad Vegetables			
Lettuce	4 heads	8 heads	15 heads
Carrots	6¼ pounds	12½ pounds	25 pounds
Tomatoes	3 to 5 pounds	7 to 10 pounds	14 to 20 pounds
Salad Dressings	1 pint	2 to 2½ pints	2 quarts

	25 servings	50 servings	100 servings
Pasta			
Lasagna	5 pounds	10 pounds	20 pounds
Spaghetti	13 pounds	26 pounds	52 pounds
Meats			
Hamburger	9 pounds	18 pounds	35 pounds
Weiners	6½ pounds	13 pounds	25 pounds
Ham	7 pounds	14 pounds	28 pounds
Chicken or Turkey	13 pounds	25 to 35 pounds	50 to 75 pounds
Fish - fillets/steaks	7½ pounds	15 pounds	30 pounds
Desserts			
Round Layer Cake	2 (9-inch) layer cakes	4 (9-inch) layer cakes	8 (9-inch) layer cakes
Sheet Cake	1 (10 x 12-inch) cake	1 (12 x 20-inch) cake	2 (12 x 20-inch) cake
Pies	4 (9-inch) pies	8 (9-inch) pies	16 (9-inch) pies
Whipping Cream	¾ to 1 pint	1½ to 2 pints	3 to 4 pints
Watermelon	37½ pounds	75 pounds	150 pounds
Fruit Cup (½ cup servings)	3 quarts	1½ gallons	3 gallons
Ice Cream			
Brick	3¼ quarts	6½ quarts	13 quarts
Bulk	2¼ quarts	1¼ gallons	2½ gallons

	25 servings	50 servings	100 servings
Sandwiches			
Bread	50 slices or 3 (1-pound) loaves	100 slices or 6 (1-pound) loaves	200 slices or 12 (1-pound loaves)
Rolls	4 dozen	8 dozen	16 dozen
Mayonnaise	1 cup	2 to 3 cups	4 to 6 cups
Butter	½ pound	1 pound	2 pounds
Ham	6¼ pounds	12½ pounds	25 pounds
Turkey	6¼ pounds	12½ pounds	25 pounds
Lettuce	1½ heads	3 heads	6 heads
Tomato	50 (¼-inch) slices	100 (¼-inch) slices	200 (¼-inch) slices
Cheese (2 ounce servings)	3¼ pounds	6½ pounds	13 pounds
Mixed Fillings			
Meat, Eggs, Fish	1½ quarts	3 quarts	6 quarts
Sweet Fruit	1 quart	2 quarts	4 quarts
Jams and Jellies	1 quart	2 quarts	4 quarts
Other			
Soup	1½ gallons	3 gallons	6 gallons
Crackers	½ pound	3 pounds	6 pounds

CAN CONTENTS

Can sizes were once standardized in the United States; numbered designations were printed on the label to indicate the weight and volume of the contents. Recipes in pre-World War II cookbooks often specified can sizes for quantities in their lists of ingredients. Today this practice has been abandoned, usually because manufacturers have taken to changing their can sizes rather than raising their prices. There is now a bewildering assortment of can and jar sizes on supermarket shelves. For the convenience of those who are adapting yesterday's recipes to today, the following table lists the most common standard sizes.

No. ¼	4 ounces	½ cup
No. ½	8 ounces	1 cup
No. 1 Tall	10½ ounces	1¼ cups
No. 300	14 to 16 ounces	1¾ to 2 cups
No. 303	16 to 17 ounces	2 cups
No. 2	20 ounces	2½ cups
No. 2½	29 ounces	3½ cups
No. 3	46 ounces	3¾ cups
No. 10	106 ounces	13 cups

GENERAL OVEN CHART

Very Slow Oven	250° to 300°F
Slow Oven	300° to 325°F
Moderate Oven	325° to 375°F
Medium Hot Oven	375° to 400°F
Hot Oven	400° to 450°F
Very Hot Oven	450° to 500°F

Equivalents Chart

Dash	=	less than ⅛ teaspoon
1 teaspoon	=	60 drops
3 teaspoons	=	1 tablespoon
2 tablespoons	=	⅛ cup or 1 fluid ounce
4 tablespoons	=	¼ cup
5 tablespoons + 1 teaspoon	=	⅓ cup
6 tablespoons	=	⅜ cup
8 tablespoons	=	½ cup
12 tablespoons	=	¾ cup
16 tablespoons	=	1 cup or 8 ounces
4 ounces	=	½ cup
½ cup + 2 tablespoons	=	⅝ cup
¾ cup + 2 tablespoons	=	⅞ cup
8 fluid ounces	=	1 cup or ½ pint
16 ounces	=	1 pound
1 pound	=	2 cups liquid
1 fluid ounce	=	2 tablespoons
1 ounce	=	1 dram
2 cups	=	1 pint or 16 ounces
2 pints	=	1 quart
1 quart	=	4 cups
4 quarts	=	1 gallon
8 quarts	=	1 peck
4 pecks	=	1 bushel
1 jigger or shot	=	1½ fluid ounces (3 tablespoons)
8 to 10 egg whites	=	1 cup
12 to 14 egg yolks	=	1 cup

1 cup unwhipped cream	=	2 cups whipped cream
1 pound shredded American cheese	=	4 cups shredded cheese
¼ pound crumbled bleu cheese	=	1 cup
1 (5-ounce) can almonds	=	1 cup slivered, toasted
1 pound unshelled walnuts	=	1½ to 1¾ cups shelled
1 pound unshelled pecans	=	about 2¼ cups shelled
2 cups fat	=	1 pound
1 pound butter	=	4 sticks or 2 cups
2 cups granulated sugar	=	1 pound
3½ to 4 cups unsifted confectioners' sugar	=	1 pound
2¼ cups packed brown sugar	=	1 pound
4 cups sifted flour	=	1 pound
4½ cups cake flour	=	1 pound
3½ cups unsifted whole wheat flour	=	1 pound
4 ounces (1 to 1¼ cups) uncooked macaroni	=	2¼ cups cooked
7 ounces spaghetti	=	4 cups cooked
4 ounces (1½ to 2 cups) uncooked noodles	=	2 cups cooked
1 cup long-grain rice	=	3½ to 4 cups cooked
4 slices bread	=	1 cup crumbs
14 square graham crackers	=	1 cup crumbs
28 saltine crackers	=	1 cup crumbs
22 vanilla wafers	=	1 cup crumbs
1 pound apples (3 medium)	=	3 cups sliced
3 medium bananas	=	1 cup mashed
1 pound whole dates	=	1½ cups, pitted and cut
1 lemon	=	3 tablespoons juice
1 orange	=	⅓ cup juice
1 pound peaches (4 medium)	=	2 cups sliced

1 pound pears (4 medium)	=	2 cups sliced
1 pound sweet potatoes (3 medium)	=	3 cups sliced
1 pound white potatoes (3 medium)	=	2 cups cubed cooked or 1¾ cups mashed
1 pound cabbage	=	4 cups shredded
1 large green bell pepper	=	1 cup diced
1 large carrot	=	1 cup grated raw carrot
4 medium ears corn	=	1 cup cut from the cob
1 pound tomatoes (4 medium)	=	2½ cups cooked
10 miniature marshmallows	=	1 large marshmallow
11 large marshmallows	=	1 cup

Missing Ingredients Substitutions

1 cup self-rising flour	=	1 cup all-purpose flour + 1 teaspoon baking powder + ½ teaspoon salt
1 cup sifted all-purpose flour	=	1 cup + 2 tablespoons sifted cake flour
1 cup sifted cake flour	=	1 cup minus 2 tablespoons sifted all-purpose flour
1 teaspoon baking powder	=	¼ teaspoon baking soda + ½ teaspoon cream of tartar
1 tablespoon cornstarch (for thickening)	=	2 tablespoons all-purpose flour
2 large eggs	=	3 small eggs
¾ cup cracker crumbs	=	1 cup breadcrumbs
3 cups dry corn flakes	=	1 cup crushed
1 (1-ounce) square chocolate	=	3 or 4 tablespoons cocoa powder + 1½ teaspoons fat
1 cup sour milk	=	1 cup sweet milk which has 1 tablespoon vinegar or lemon juice stirred into it
1 cup sweet milk	=	1 cup sour milk or buttermilk + ½ teaspoon baking soda
1 cup whole milk	=	½ cup evaporated milk + ½ cup water or 1 cup reconstituted nonfat dry milk + 1 tablespoon butter

1 cup sour heavy cream	=	⅓ cup butter + ⅔ cup milk in any sour milk recipe
1 teaspoon dried herbs	=	1 tablespoon fresh herbs or ¼ teaspoon ground herbs
1 tablespoon instant minced onion, rehydrated	=	1 fresh onion
¼ cup chopped fresh parsley	=	1 tablespoon dried parsley flakes
1 tablespoon prepared mustard	=	1 teaspoon dry mustard
⅛ teaspoon garlic powder	=	1 small pressed clove of garlic
2 ounces compressed yeast	=	3 (¼-ounce) packets of dry yeast

COOKING GUIDE

Cut	Weight (in pounds)	Approx time (325° oven)	Internal Temperature
Beef			
Standing Rib Roast - 10-inch ribs	4	1¾ hours	140° - rare
		2 hours	160° - medium
		2½ hours	170° - well done
Standing Rib Roast - 10-inch ribs	8	2½ hours	140° - rare
		3 hours	160° - medium
		4½ hours	170° - well done
Rolled Ribs	4	2 hours	140° - rare
		2½ hours	160° - medium
		3 hours	170° - well done
Rolled Ribs	6	3 hours	140° - rare
		3¾ hours	160° - medium
		4 hours	170° - well done
Rolled Rump (if high quality)	5	2¼ hours	140° - rare
		3 hours	160° - medium
		3¾ hours	170° - well done

Beef continued

Sirloin Tip	3	1½ hours	140° - rare
		2 hours	160° - medium
		2¼ hours	170° - well done

Lamb

Leg	6	3 hours	175° - medium
		3½ hours	180° - well done
Leg	8	4 hours	
		4½ hours	

Veal

Leg (piece)	5	2½ to 3 hours	180° - well done
Shoulder	6	3½ hours	180°- well done
Rolled Shoulder	3 to 5	3 to 3½ hours	180° - well done

Poultry

Chicken – unstuffed (if stuffed 5 minutes more per pound)	4 to 8	3 to 5 hours	185° - well done
Capon – unstuffed	4 to 7	2½ to 3	185° - well done
Duckling – unstuffed	3½ to 5½	2 to 3 hours	190° - well done
Turkey – stuffed (if unstuffed 5 minutes less per pound)	8 to 12	3¾ to 4½ hours	185° - well done

Pork

Ham (fully cooked)	5 to 7	18 to 24 minutes/pound	140°
	10 to 12	15 to 18 minutes/pound	140°
Ham (uncooked)	5 to 7	22 to 25 minutes/pound	160°
	10 to 14	18 to 20 minutes/pound	160°
Loin (Center Cut)	3 to 5	30 to 35 minutes/pound	150° to 155°
Boston Shoulder	4 to 6	40 to 45 minutes/pound	150° to 155°
Tenderloin	½ to 1	45 to 60 minutes/pound	150° to 155°

Baking Dishes and Pan Sizes

4-Cup Baking Dish

9-inch pie plate
8 x 1¼-inch cake pan
7⅜ x 3⅝ x 2¼-inch loaf pan

6-Cup Baking Dish

8 or 9 x 1½-inch cake pan
10-inch pie pan
8½ x 3⅝ x 2⅝-inch loaf pan

8-Cup Baking Dish

8 x 8 x 2-inch square pan
11 x 7 x 1½-inch baking pan
9 x 5 x 3-inch loaf pan

10-Cup Baking Dish

9 x 9 x 2-inch square pan
11¾ x 7½ x 1¾-inch baking pan
15 x 10 x 1-inch jelly-roll pan

12-Cup-or-More Baking Dish

13½ x 8½ x 2-inch glass baking dish
13 x 9 x 2-inch metal baking pan
14 x 10½ x 2½-inch roasting pan

Tube Pans

6 cups	7½ x 3-inch Bundt tube (scalloped sides)
9 cups	9 x 3½-inch Bundt tube
12 cups	9 x 3½-inch angel-food cake pan (smooth sides)
12 cups	10 x 3¾-inch Bundt tube
12 cups	9 x 3½-inch fancy tube pan (heavier pan with small scalloped sides)
16 cups	10 x 4-inch fancy tube pan
18 cups	10 x 4-inch angel food cake pan

Ring Molds

4 cups	8½ x 2¼-inch mold
9 cups	9¼ x 2¾-inch mold

Springform Pan

12 cups	8 x 3-inch mold
16 cups	9 x 3-inch mold

CANDY-MAKING TEMPERATURE STAGES AND TESTS

To determine if candy has been cooked to the correct consistency, use a fresh cupful of cold water each time you test. Place about ½ teaspoon of the candy in the cold water for the test. Pick up the candy and roll it into a ball with your fingers.

Soft-Ball – the candy will roll into a soft ball that quickly loses its shape when removed from the water.

Firm-Ball – the candy will roll into a firm, but not hard, ball. It will flatten out a few minutes after being removed from the water.

Hard-Ball – the candy will roll into a hard ball that has lost almost all flexibility and will roll around on a plate on removal from the water.

Light-Crack – the candy will form brittle threads that will soften on its removal from the water.

Hard-Crack – the candy will form brittle threads in the water that will remain brittle after having been removed from the water.

Caramelized – the sugar first melts then becomes a golden brown. It will form a hard brittle ball in cold water.

Types of Candy and Temperatures

Fondant, Fudge	Soft-Ball	234 to 238°
Divinity, Caramels	Firm-Ball	245 to 248°
Taffy	Hard-Ball	265 to 270°
Butterscotch	Light-Crack	275 to 280°
Peanut Brittle	Hard-Crack	285 to 290°
Caramelized Sugar	Caramelized	310 to 321°

Index

A

Abreo, Jo Ann, 244
Acorn squash
 Acorn Squash, 164
 Cinnamon Acorn Squash Rings, 174
Alexander, Georgianna, 149
Allen, Jeanette, 90, 148, 327
Allgood, Liz, 320
Almonds
 Almond and Orange Salad, 100
 Almond Chicken Casserole, 232
Appetizers. *See also* Dips; Spreads
 Asparagus Sandwiches, 38
 Bacon-Chestnut Appetizers, 38
 Bacon Roll-Ups, 39
 Bacon-Tomato Cocktail Rounds, 39
 Cheese Ball, 39
 Cheese Cookies, 40
 Cheese Mold, 40–41
 Chicken Bites with Sweet-Hot Tomato
  Chutney, 41
 Chocolate Chip Cheese Ball, 41
 Cream Cheese and Pineapple Finger
  Sandwiches, 42
 Cream Puffs, 43
 Cucumber Party Sandwiches, 43

 Double Oink Roll-Ups, 44
 Famous Tomato Sandwiches, 44–45
 Fruit Cheese Ball, 45
 Glorified Grapes, 46–47
 Granny Smith Apples with Caramel
  Fondue, 47
 Ham and Cheese Tarts, 47
 Jalapeño and Pimento Squares, 49
 Jezebel Sauce and Cream Cheese, 50
 Killer Sausage Balls, 50
 Lemon Tea Sandwiches, 51
 Olive Spread Tea Sandwiches, 51
 Salmon Ball, 52
 Sausage Balls in Cheese Pastry, 53
 Shrimp Mold, 54
 Shrimp Wrapped in Bacon, 54
 Spiced Olives, 54
 Spinach Balls, 55
 Spinach Roll-Ups, 55
 Stuffed Cherry Tomatoes, 56–57
 Sugared Nuts, 57
 Sweet and Sour Meatballs, 57
 Tea Sandwiches, 58
 Tomato Chutney, 127
 Tuna Salad Mini Sandwiches, 58
 Zucchini-Parmesan Appetizer Bread, 150

Apples
  Apple Brown Betty, 347
  Apple Butter, 80
  Apple Chutney, 124
  Apple Cole Slaw, 101
  Apple Dumplings, 347
  Apple Fritters, 348
  Apple-Mint Jelly, 80
  Apple Muffins, 153
  Apple Pie, 325
  Apple Walnut Cake, 274
  Baked Apples, 165
  Cheese Apples, 174
  Chunky Cranberry Applesauce, 132
  Crunchy Apple Salad, 106
  Dried Apple & Egg Custard Pie, 330
  Fresh Apple Cake, 287
  Granny Smith Apples with Caramel Fondue, 47
  Hot Apple Crisp, 352
  Hot Curried Fruit, 191
  "Not Apple Salad!", 118
  Oven Apple Butter, 84
  Stewed Apples, 202
  Waldorf Salad, 121
Apricots
  Apricot Baked Chicken, 233
Artichoke hearts
  Hot Artichoke Dip, 48
  Hot Spinach Artichoke Dip, 49
Asparagus
  Asparagus Casserole, 164
  Asparagus Chicken Casserole, 233
  Asparagus Sandwiches, 38
  Asparagus Vegetable Casserole, 164–165
  Asparagus with Ham, 221
  Jill's Asparagus, 191

B
BaBa (Billie Van Dyke's grandmother), 21
Bacon
  Bacon, Lettuce, and Tomato Dip, 38
  Bacon-Chestnut Appetizers, 38
  Bacon Roll-Ups, 39

  Bacon-Tomato Cocktail Rounds, 39
  Double Oink Roll-Ups, 44
  Fried Red Tomatoes and Creamed Gravy, 184–185
  Shrimp Wrapped in Bacon, 54
  Sophia's Green Beans in Blankets, 200
Bailey, Bobbi, 275
Baines, Nellie, 214
Baker, Charles, 21, 23
Baker, Dennis, 21, 22–23
Baker, Dorothy "Dot", 21, 22–23
Baker, Herman "Pop", 21
Baker, Jimmy, 21
Baker, Liz, 23
Baker, Nita Jean, 21
Baking dish sizes, 373–374
Bananas
  Alabama "Blue Ribbon" Banana Pudding, 342
  Banana Bars, 262–263
  Banana Boats, 358
  Banana-Nut Bread, 140
  Banana Pudding, 342
  Banana Split Cake, 274–275
  Best Banana Pie, The, 326
  Blueberry-Banana-Pecan-Nut Cake, 277
  Double Strawberry-Banana Shake, 359
  Spiced Mixed Fruit, 201
Bar cookies
  Banana Bars, 262–263
  Blue Willow Squares, 263
  Chewies, 264–265
  Chocolate Scotcheroos, 265
  Cream Cheese Peanut Bars, 265
  Deluxe Chocolate Marshmallow Bars, 267
  Easy Lemon Squares, 267
  Fudge Cuts, 268–269
  Lemon Squares, 270–271
  Pineapple Squares, 271
Beans. *See also* Green beans
  Baked Beans, 166
  Garbanzo Bean Soup (Chickpeas), 92
  Governor Mark Sanford's Favorite Butter Bean
      Casserole, 186–187
  Morgan & Seth's Wacky Beans, 194–195

Pinto Beans, 196
quantities for large groups, 365
Beaseley, Vivian, 41, 115, 143
Beef
Baked Beans, 166
Beef Hash, 212
Beef Stroganoff, 212
Betty Whitman's Hamburger Casserole, 212–213
Bob's Blue Ribbon Favorite, "Rileyhouse Beef Stew",
213
Brunswick Stew, 90
Chipped Beef with White Gravy, 213
cooking guide, 371–372
Country Fried Steak, 214
Dried Beef Dip, 44
Easy Oven Stew, 214
Ground Chuck Casserole, 215
Hamburger Stroganoff, 215
Hawkins Swiss Steak, 216
Hot Beef Dip, 48
Lasagna, 216–217
Liver and Onions, 217
Louis' Dad's North Carolina Brunswick Stew, 94
Meatloaf, 218
Morgan & Seth's Wacky Beans, 194–195
Picadillo with Capers, 52
Pot Roast, 220
President Ronald Reagan's Favorite Beef Stew, 219
quantities for large groups, 365
Roast Beef, 219
Steak Rolls with Sour Cream Sauce, 220–221
Sweet and Sour Meatballs, 57
Swiss Steak, 221
Beets
Harvard Beets, 189
Bertha Upshaw Club House, 19, 26
Beverages, cold and frozen. *See also* Punches
Bellini, 62
Cherry Jubilee Splash, 62
Chocolate Iced Coffee, 63
Classic Cola Float, 63
Coffee-House Slush, 63
Double Strawberry-Banana Shake, 359

labels for, 61
Low-Fat Cappuccino Cooler, 65
Magnolia Blossoms, 65
Mimosa, 66
Mint Julep, 66
Poppa's Eggnog, 66–67
quantities for large groups, 364
Scuppernong Juice, 85
Strawberry Lemonade, 69
Swamp Breeze, 67
Sweet Southern Tea, 68
Syllabub, 75
Three-Fruit Yogurt Shake, 68
Bevan, Diane, 157
Beverages, hot
Cherry Cordial Hot Chocolate, 62
Holiday or Spiced Tea, 64
Hot Chocolate, 64
quantities for large groups, 364
spiced tea or cider, 72
Winter Wassail, 77
Billie's at the American Legion, 25–26, 27, 29
Billie's Classic Country Dining, 23–25
Billie's Family Restaurant, 25
Biscuits
Angel Biscuits, 150–151
Blue Willow Buttermilk Biscuits, 151
Buttery Biscuit Rolls, 156
Cheesy Drop Biscuits, 151
Sweet Potato Biscuits, 152
Bish, Teresa, 291
Blackberries
Blackberry Cobbler, 345
Old-Fashioned Blackberry Roll, 348
Black-eyed peas
Black-Eyed Peas, 167
Hoppin' John, 190–191
North Georgia Caviar, 117
Blueberries
Blueberry-Banana-Pecan-Nut Cake, 277
Blueberry Cobbler, 345
Blueberry Dessert, 349
Blueberry Jam, 81

Blueberries *(continued)*
Blueberry Muffins, 156
Blueberry Salad, 102
Blueberry Sauce, 130
Blueberry Topping, 355
Bridge-Luncheon Frozen Fruit Salad, 103
Fresh Fruit and Cheese in Pineapple Wedges, 110–111
Old South Berry Blue Pie, 338–339
Blue-plate special, 17
Blue Willow china, 16–17, 20
Blue Willow Inn Restaurant, The
atmosphere of, 20
awards earned by, 31
banquet facilities, 20
buffet service at, 20
china collection, 20
Dining in Historic Georgia (Godbey), 30
early history of building, 17–19
food philosophy, 16
Lewis Grizzard appreciation of, 30–31
location of, 17–18
media interest in, 30–32
menu examples, 32–36
opening of, 19, 29
popularity of, 20, 31–32
Bowyer, Shirley Smith, 66, 135, 165, 175
Breads and rolls. *See also* Biscuits; Corn breads; Muffins
Banana-Nut Bread, 140
Beignets, 158
Bran Raisin Bread, 140
Buttery Biscuit Rolls, 156
Cinnamon Breakfast Rolls, 156–157
Gift of the Magi Bread, 142–143
Gingerbread, 143
Gramma's Rolls, 157
Grandma's Strawberry Nut Loaf, 144
Granny Julia's Sausage Bread, 144–145
Green Tomato Bread, 145
Hot Cross Buns, 160
Journey Cakes, 155
Knee Caps, 155
Sally Lunn Bread, 146–147
Skillet Corn Bread, 147

Sourdough Bread, 148
Sweet Potato Bread, 150
Yeast Rolls, 161
Zucchini-Parmesan Appetizer Bread, 150
Breakfast dishes
Beignets, 158
Christmas Breakfast Casserole, 223
Cinnamon Breakfast Rolls, 156–157
Company Breakfast Strata, 224
Eggs Golden, 182
French Toast, 161
Knee Caps, 155
Pancakes, 159
Sausage and Egg Casserole, 230
Waffles, 162
Broccoli
Broccoli Casserole, 170
Broccoli Salad, 103
Chicken Divine, 236–237
Ham & Broccoli Noodle Casserole, 227
Marinated Vegetable Salad, 112
Vegetable Pilaf, 207
Brownies
Aunt France's Brownie Recipe, 262
Babe's Brownie Stuff, 262
Brownie Trifle, 349
Buttermilk Brownies, 264
Crème de Menthe Squares, 266
Grandmother Alice's Brownies, 269
Louis' Brownies, 271
Triple-Layer Brownies, 272–273
Butler, Deborah, 289
Butler, June, 333
Butler, Rhett, 18

C
Cabbage
Cabbage Casserole, 172
Cabbage Relish, 125
Chow-Chow, 125
Cole Slaw, 105
Cooked Cabbage, 175
Fried Cabbage, 183

Red Cabbage and Cranberry Relish, 127
Cakes
Amy's Orange Pineapple Layer Cake, 273
Apple Walnut Cake, 274
Banana Split Cake, 274–275
Birthday Cake, 275
Bishop's Cake, 277
Blueberry-Banana-Pecan-Nut Cake, 277
Brown Sugar Pound Cake, 278
Burnt Sugar Cake, 276
Cameo Cake with White Chocolate Frosting, 278–279
Caramel Cake, 280
Celestial Snow Cake, 279
Chocolate Cherry Cake, 281
Chocolate Pound Cake, 282–283
Coca-Cola Cake with Broiled Peanut Butter Frosting, 283
Country Lane Cake, 284
Dirt Cake, 286, 359
Dutch Chocolate Cake, 285
Eight-Layer Butter Cake, 286
Feud Cake, 287
Fresh Apple Cake, 287
Fresh Coconut Cake from Scratch, 288
Frosted Creams, 268
Fruit Cake, 290
Grasshoppers, 270
Green Velvet Cake, 289
Hershey's Syrup Cake, 291
Hummingbird Cake, 290–291
Ice Cream Cake, 292
Italian Cream Cake, 292–293
Lane Cake, 294
Lemon Meringue Cake, 295
Nell's Carrot Cake, 282
Nell's Peanut Butter Cake, 297
1-2-3-4 Cake, 293
Orange-Coconut Cake, 298
Peanut Butter Cake, 298–299
Peppermint Angle Food Cake, 300
Peppermint Chiffon Cake, 299
Petra's "Not Just Right" Pound Cake, 301

Pineapple Nut Cake, 302
Pineapple Upside-Down Cake, 302–303
Prune Spice Cake, 303
Punch Bowl Cake, 304
quantities for large groups, 365
Red Velvet Cake, 304–305
Rum Cake, 305
7-Up Cake, 306
Southern Delight Butter Pecan Cake, 306–307
Strawberry Cake, 307
Texas Sheet Cake, 308–309
Watermelon Cake, 309
Candies
Buttermilk Pralines, 310
Cranberry-Pear Fruit Jellies, 310–311
Cream Cheese Mints, 311
Divinity, 312
Donna's Fudge, 312
Garbage Bag Candy, 360
Mamie Eisenhower's Million-Dollar Fudge, 312–313
Merry Cherry Fudge, 313
Mints, 313
Peanut Brittle, 314
Peppermint Brickle, 314
Pralines, 314–315
Rocky Road, 315
Strawberry Candies, 315
temperature stages and tests, 374
temperature stages by type, 375
Yummy Candy, 362
Canning and pickling fruits and vegetables, 88
Can size chart, 367
Carrots
Carrot Casserole, 173
Carrot-Raisin Salad, 104
Carrots au Gratin, 172
Carrots Vichy, 174
Glazed Carrots, 186
Nell's Carrot Cake, 282
quantities for large groups, 365
Cartwright, Louise, 339
Casseroles
Almond Chicken Casserole, 232

Casseroles *(continued)*
Asparagus Chicken Casserole, 233
Baked Pineapple Casserole, 168
Betty Whitman's Hamburger Casserole, 212–213
Blue Willow Chicken Casserole, 234
Blue Willow Corn Pudding, 169
Broccoli Casserole, 170
Cabbage Casserole, 172
Carrot Casserole, 173
Carrots au Gratin, 172
Casserole of Chops, 222–223
Cauliflower-Cheese Casserole, 173
Cheese Apples, 174
Cheese Casserole, 175
Cheesy Ham Potato Casserole, 223
Chicken and Dressing Casserole, 236
Chicken and Rice, 234
Chicken and Rice Casserole, 235
Chicken Casserole, 235
Chicken Divine, 236–237
Chicken Macaroni, 237
Chicken Noodle Delight, 238
Chicken Pecan Pasta, 238–239
Chicken Pot Pie, 240
Chicken Spectacular, 241
Chicken Tetrazzini, 240–241
Christmas Breakfast Casserole, 223
Company Breakfast Strata, 224
Corn Casserole, 176
Corn Pudding, 177
Crab Casserole, 249
Crabmeat Casserole, 250
Eggplant Casserole, 181
Governor Mark Sanford's Favorite Butter Bean
    Casserole, 186–187
Green Bean and Corn Casserole, 187
Green Bean Casserole, 188
Green Pea Casserole, 188
Grits Casserole, 189
Ground Chuck Casserole, 215
Ham & Broccoli Noodle Casserole, 227
Lee's Baked Garlic Cheese Grits, 192

Lynn's Sausage Casserole, 218
Macaroni and Cheese and Corn Bake, 192
Martha Washington's Turkey Potpie, 242–243
Mom's Sweet Potato Casserole, 194
Poppy Seed Chicken, 244
Potatoes au Gratin, 196
Potato Soufflé, 196–197
Sausage and Egg Casserole, 230
Sausage Casserole, 231
Savannah Red Rice, 198
Savannah Shrimp and Rice, 252
Scalloped Potatoes, 198
Seafood au Gratin, 254
Sherried Fruit, 198–199
Shrimp & Wild Rice Casserole, 254–255
Sophia's Squash Casserole, 200
Squash Casserole, 201
Tomato-Corn Casserole, 205
Tuna Casserole, 255
Vegetable Casserole, 207
Vidalia Onion Casserole, 208
Vidalia Onion Shortcake, 209
Cast iron, seasoning, 147
Catholic Church ban on tomatoes, 15
Cauliflower
Cauliflower-Cheese Casserole, 173
Marinated Vegetable Salad, 112
Chadwick, Evelyn, 344
Cheese
Baked Corn Chex and Cheese, 167
Blender Soufflé, 168
Blue Willow Inn's Mac & Cheese, 169
Cauliflower-Cheese Casserole, 173
Cheese Apples, 174
Cheese Ball, 39
Cheese Casserole, 175
Cheese Cookies, 40
Cheese Mold, 40–41
Cheese Sauces, 131
Cheese Spread, 85
Cheesy Drop Biscuits, 151
Cheesy Ham Potato Casserole, 223

Chocolate Chip Cheese Ball, 41
Chutney-Onion Cheese Spread, 86
Fresh Fruit and Cheese in Pineapple Wedges, 110–111
Fruit Cheese Ball, 45
Ham and Cheese Pie, 226
Ham and Cheese Tarts, 47
Lee's Baked Garlic Cheese Grits, 192
Macaroni and Cheese and Corn Bake, 192
quantities for large groups, 366
Slow-Cooker Macaroni and Cheese, 199
Zucchini-Parmesan Appetizer Bread, 150

Cheesecakes
Cheesecake, 280–281
Cherry Cheese Pie, 326–327
Mascarpone Cheesecake, 296

Cherries
Cherry Cheese Pie, 326–327
Cherry Cobbler, 346
Cherry Cordial Hot Chocolate, 62
Cherry Dessert, 350
Cherry Fluff, 358
Cherry Jubilee Splash, 62
Chocolate Cherry Cake, 281
Frozen Bing Cherry Salad, 102
Merry Cherry Fudge, 313
Roast Pork with Spiced Cherry Sauce, 229

Chicken
Almond Chicken Casserole, 232
Ann Lowe's Chicken Stew, 90
Apricot Baked Chicken, 233
Asparagus Chicken Casserole, 233
Baked Chicken, 233
Blue Willow Chicken Casserole, 234
Chicken and Dressing Casserole, 236
Chicken and Dumplings, 90–91
Chicken and Rice, 234
Chicken and Rice Casserole, 235
Chicken Bites with Sweet-Hot Tomato Chutney, 41
Chicken Casserole, 235
Chicken Divine, 236–237
Chicken Fry-Bake, 237

Chicken Macaroni, 237
Chicken Noodle Delight, 238
Chicken Pecan Pasta, 238–239
Chicken Pie with Sweet Potato Crust, 239
Chicken Pot Pie, 240
Chicken Salad, 104
Chicken Spectacular, 241
Chicken Tetrazzini, 240–241
Company Chicken Salad, 106
cooking guide, 372
Dried Fruit Pilaf, 180
Elegant Chicken Salad, 108
Fried Chicken Livers, 242
Grilled Lemon Pepper Chicken, 242
Hot Chicken Salad, 111
Louis' Dad's North Carolina Brunswick Stew, 94
Mama's Fried Chicken, 244
Orange-Pecan Glazed Chicken and Wild Rice, 245
Oven-Fried Chicken, 244–245
Pecan-Encrusted Chicken, 246
Poppy Seed Chicken, 244
quantities for large groups, 365
Southern Fried Chicken, 247
Stuffed Chicken Breast, 247
Chlapowski, Ann, 272

Chocolate
Aunt France's Brownie Recipe, 262
Buttermilk Brownies, 264
Cameo Cake with White Chocolate Frosting, 278–279
Chocolate Cherry Cake, 281
Chocolate Chess Pie, 327
Chocolate Chip Cheese Ball, 41
Chocolate Chip Cookies, 317
Chocolate Delight, 350
Chocolate Iced Coffee, 63
Chocolate Lovers' Easy Pie, 328
Chocolate Macaroons, 317
Chocolate Meringue Pie, 328
Chocolate Mousse, 350–351
Chocolate Pound Cake, 282–283
Chocolate Pudding, 344

Chocolate *(continued)*
    Chocolate Scotcheroos, 265
    Crème de Menthe Squares, 266
    Death by Chocolate, 284–285
    Deluxe Chocolate Marshmallow Bars, 267
    Donna's Fudge, 312
    Dutch Chocolate Cake, 285
    Eight-Layer Butter Cake, 286
    French Silk Chocolate Pie, 331
    Fudge Cuts, 268–269
    Grandmother Alice's Brownies, 269
    Grasshoppers, 270
    Hershey's Syrup Cake, 291
    Louis' Brownies, 271
    Mamie Eisenhower's Million-Dollar Fudge, 312–313
    Merry Cherry Fudge, 313
    Mississippi Mud Pie, 338
    Pea-Choc, 361
    Rocky Road, 315
    S'mores, 361
    Snow-Capped Chocolate Pie, 341
    Texas Sheet Cake, 308–309
    Triple Chocolate Clusters, 272
    Triple-Layer Brownies, 272–273
    White Chocolate Macadamia Nut Cookies, 322
Chowders. *See* Soups, stews, and chowders
Christmas dinner menu, 35–36
Chutney. *See* Relishes
Clack, Jimmy, 114, 213
Clams
    Quick-and-Easy Clam Chowder, 97
Coconut
    Chocolate Macaroons, 317
    Coconut Cream Pie, 329
    Coconut Pie, 330
    Fresh Coconut Cake from Scratch, 288
    Orange-Coconut Cake, 298
Cookies
    Banbury Tarts, 316
    Chewy Oatmeal Cookies, 316–317
    Chocolate Chip Cookies, 317
    Chocolate Macaroons, 317
    Date Balls, 266

    Granny's Sugar Cookies, 320
    Meringue Cookies, 318
    Noel Crisps, 318
    Oatmeal Cookies, 318–319
    Old-Fashioned Tea Cakes, 321
    Peanut Butter Balls, 361
    Rolled-Out Cookies, 319
    Sugar Cookies, 320–321
    Tea Cakes, 322
    Triple Chocolate Clusters, 272
    White Chocolate Macadamia Nut Cookies, 322
Corasaniti, Amy, 273
Corn
    Baked Corn Chex and Cheese, 167
    Blue Willow Corn Pudding, 169
    Corn, 176
    Corn Casserole, 176
    Corn Chowder, 91
    Corn Pudding, 177
    Corn Salsa, 126
    Creamed Corn, 178
    Fried Corn, 183
    Green Bean and Corn Casserole, 187
    importance of in Southern cooking, 14–15
    Macaroni and Cheese and Corn Bake, 192
    Tomato-Corn Casserole, 205
    Vegetable Casserole, 207
Corn breads
    Cheddar Corn Bread, 142
    Corn Bread Dressing, 177
    Corn Bread or Corn Muffins, 154
    Corn Bread Salad, 105
    Crackling Bread, 142
    Red and Green Confetti Corn Bread, 146
Cornmeal
    Hushpuppies, 145
    importance of in Southern cooking, 15
    Southern Spoon Bread, 149
    Spoon Bread, 149
Crabmeat
    Crab Cakes, 249
    Crab Casserole, 249
    Crab Chowder, 92

Crab Dip, 42
Crabmeat Casserole, 250
Maryland Vegetable Crab Soup, 95
Mildred's Imperial Crab, 250–251
Pine-Bark Stew, 251
Seafood au Gratin, 254
Seafood Gumbo, 253
She-Crab Soup, 97

Cranberries
Baked Cranberry Sauce, 130
Cabernet Cranberries, 131
Chunky Cranberry Applesauce, 132
Cranberry-Ambrosia Cream Cheese Spread, 86
Cranberry Nut Topping, 355
Cranberry-Orange Relish, 126
Cranberry-Pear Fruit Jellies, 310–311
Red Cabbage and Cranberry Relish, 127

Cucumbers
Bread and Butter Pickles, 124
Cucumber Party Sandwiches, 43
Marinated Vegetable Salad, 112

D
Dally, Becky, 48
Dalton, Lois, 103, 233, 266
Davis, Lynda, 323
DeMoss, Sophia, 182
Desserts. *See also* Bar cookies; Brownies; Cakes; Cookies;
        Frozen desserts and salads; Pies; Puddings
Ambrosia, 100–101
Apple Brown Betty, 347
Apple Dumplings, 347
Apple Fritters, 348
Blackberry Cobbler, 345
Blueberry Cobbler, 345
Blueberry Dessert, 349
Blueberry Salad, 102
Brownie Trifle, 349
Cheesecake, 280–281
Cherry Cobbler, 346
Cherry Dessert, 350
Chocolate Delight, 350
Chocolate Mousse, 350–351

Crème Brulée, 351
Crêpes, 158–159
Death by Chocolate, 284–285
Eggnog Mousse, 351
Floating Islands, 352
Frozen Lemon Squares, 268
Gingerbread, 143
Hot Apple Crisp, 352
Lemon Lush, 352–353
Lemon Sponge Custard, 353
Mascarpone Cheesecake, 296
Old-Fashioned Blackberry Roll, 348
Peach Cobbler, 346
quantities for large groups, 365
Sherry Soup, 98
Stewed Apples, 202
Strawberry Delight, 354
Strawberry Pretzel Delight, 272
Strawberry Shortcake, 308
Dina, Joyce, 42, 58, 98, 140, 167, 173
Dining in Historic Georgia (Godbey), 30
Dinner, 14
Dips. *See also* Fruit dips
Bacon, Lettuce, and Tomato Dip, 38
Crab Dip, 42
Dried Beef Dip, 44
Flamingo Floyd's Spinach Dip, 45
Hot Artichoke Dip, 48
Hot Beef Dip, 48
Hot Shrimp Dip, 48–49
Hot Spinach Artichoke Dip, 49
Marshmallow Fruit Dip, 46
Oyster Dip, 51
Picadillo with Capers, 52
Shrimp Dip, 53
Spinach Dip, 55
Virginia's Vidalia Onion Dip, 58
Watercress Dip or Spread, 59
Dressing or stuffing
Corn Bread Dressing, 177
Mincemeat Stuffing, 193
Squash Dressing, 202
Dykes, Joanne 194, 231

E

Easter Sunday menu, 32–33
Edgerly, Dale, 22, 23
Edgerly, Donna, 22
Edgerly, William "Bill", Jr, 21–22
Edgerly, William "Chip", III, 22, 25
Eggplants
    Eggplant and Tomatoes, 181
    Eggplant Casserole, 181
    Farmer's Garden Stew, 182–183
    Stuffed Eggplant, 203
Eggs
    Blender Soufflé, 168
    Christmas Breakfast Casserole, 223
    Company Breakfast Strata, 224
    Deviled Eggs, 179
    Deviled Ham Stuffed Eggs, 180
    Eggs Golden, 182
    Molded Egg Salad, 116
    Sausage and Egg Casserole, 230
    Sweet Potato Soufflé, 204
Elder, Jean, 91, 130, 151, 310
Equivalents chart, 368–371
Exley, Annie Laura, 21
Exley, Marvin, 21

F

Father's Day menu, 33–34
Figs
    Fig Preserves, 81
    Fig-Strawberry Preserves, 81
First Prize Winners
    Appetizers and Hors d'Oeuvre (Vivian Beasley), 41
    Beverages and Punches (Shirley Smith Bowyer), 66
    Breads (Judy Suggs), 144
    Jellies and Sauces (Nancy Posner), 83
    Meats and Main Dishes (Nancy Morris), 232
    Soups and Salads (Buddy Logan), 109
    Vegetables and Side Dishes (Mary Landress), 202
Fish
    Baked Flounder, 248
    Catfish Stew, 248
    Fried Catfish, 250

    Pine-Bark Stew, 251
    quantities for large groups, 365
    Salmon Ball, 52
    Salmon Croquettes, 252
    Seafood au Gratin, 254
Fourth of July menu, 34
Franks, Chris, 45
Fried green tomatoes, 15
Fritters
    Apple Fritters, 348
    Fritters, 141
    Hushpuppies, 145
Frostings
    Broiled Peanut Butter Frosting, 283
    Burnt Sugar Frosting, 276
    Butter Pecan Frosting, 306–307
    Cameo Cake with White Chocolate Frosting, 278–279
    Coconut Icing, 302
    Cream Cheese Frosting, 282, 291, 292–293
    Frosting, 279, 281, 284, 285, 286, 287, 289, 294, 303, 304–305, 306, 308–309
    Icing, 309, 320–321, 338
    Orange-Coconut Frosting, 298
    Peanut Butter Frosting, 297, 299
    Pink Peppermint Frosting, 300
    Seven-Minute Icing, 288, 356
    Strawberry Cake Frosting, 307
Frozen desserts and salads
    Amelia Mud Pie, 325
    Babe's Brownie Stuff, 262
    Boiled Custard Ice Cream, 322–323
    Bridge-Luncheon Frozen Fruit Salad, 103
    Cool Lemon Sherbet, 323
    Frozen Bing Cherry Salad, 102
    Frozen Lemonade Pie, 333
    Frozen Lemon Squares, 268
    Frozen Orange Balls, 360
    Ice Cream Cake, 292
    Ice Cream Pie, 334
    Ice Cream Sandwich Dessert, 360–361
    Martha Jane's Homemade Ice Cream, 323
    Peppermint Ice Cream, 324

Pineapple Sherbet, 324
quantities for large groups, 366
Snow Ice Cream, 362
Vanilla Custard Ice Cream, 324–325
Vanilla Ice Cream, 324
Fruit
Bridge-Luncheon Frozen Fruit Salad, 103
Fresh Fruit and Cheese in Pineapple Wedges,
110–111
Fritters, 141
Fruit Cake, 290
Fruit Cheese Ball, 45
Hot Curried Fruit, 191
pickling and canning, 88
quantities for large groups, 365
Sherried Fruit, 198–199
Spiced Mixed Fruit, 201
Fruit dips
Fruit Dip, 46
Marshmallow Fruit Dip, 46
Strawberries with Fluffy Cream Cheese Dip, 56
Strawberries with Mint Yogurt Dip, 56
Fuller, Frances Hawkins, 216

G
Galbraith, Anne, 50, 98, 319
Gasaway, Juanita, 177
Godbey, Marty, 30
Goose
Stuffed Wild Goose, 258
Goucher, Marilyn, 67, 190, 224
Grace, Lynn, 218, 273, 339
Grapes. *See also* Muscadine grapes; Scuppernong grapes
Fresh Fruit and Cheese in Pineapple Wedges,
110–111
Glorified Grapes, 46–47
Grape Salad, 110
Gravies
Chipped Beef with White Gravy, 213
Creamy Gravy, 257
Fried Ham with Redeye Gravy, 224–225
Giblet Gravy, 137
Pan or Cream Gravy, 137

Roux, 137
Sausage and Gravy, 231
Sausage Gravy, 138
Tomato Gravy, 138
Green beans
Barbecued Green Beans, 165
Green Bean and Corn Casserole, 187
Green Bean Casserole, 188
Green Beans, 188
Sophia's Green Beans in Blankets, 200
Vegetable Casserole, 207
Greens
Collard Greens, 175
Turnip Greens, 206
Watercress Dip or Spread, 59
Green tomatoes
Blue Willow Inn's Famous Fried Green Tomatoes,
170
Chow-Chow, 125
fried green tomatoes, 15
Green Tomato Bread, 145
Green Tomato Marmalade, 82
Green Tomato Pie, 188–189
Grits
Grits Casserole, 189
Lee's Baked Garlic Cheese Grits, 192
Grizzard, Lewis, 30–31
Guerine, Nancy, 146

H
Ham
Asparagus with Ham, 221
Cheesy Ham Potato Casserole, 223
Company Breakfast Strata, 224
cooking guide, 372
Deviled Ham Stuffed Eggs, 180
Fresh Ham, 225
Fried Ham with Redeye Gravy, 224–225
Grilled Ham, 226
Ham & Broccoli Noodle Casserole, 227
Ham and Cheese Pie, 226
Ham and Cheese Tarts, 47
Hawaiian Grilled Ham, 226

Ham *(continued)*
    Hawaiian Pineapple Ham Steaks, 227–228
    Pineapple Ham, 228
    quantities for large groups, 365, 366
    Shredded Potato & Ham Pie, 232
    Sugar-Cured Ham, 231
Harvey, Homer, 19, 26–27
Harrison, Elaine, 46
Hartzog, Betty, 264, 271, 287, 303
Hawkins, Peggy, 111
Hester, Ellen 208, 255, 337
Hicks, Stacey, 195
Hoganson, Melissa, 145, 174, 299, 359

I
Ice cream desserts. *See* Frozen desserts and salads
Ingredient equivalents chart, 368–370
Ingredient substitutions chart, 370–371

J
Jacobs, Kitty, 116, 125, 269
Jams and jellies
    Apple Butter, 80
    Apple-Mint Jelly, 80
    Blueberry Jam, 81
    Fig Preserves, 81
    Fig-Strawberry Preserves, 81
    Green Tomato Marmalade, 82
    Guava Jelly, 82
    Kudzu Blossom Jelly, 83
    Muscadine Marmalade, 84
    Oven Apple Butter, 84
    Peach Preserves, 83
    Scuppernong Jelly, 84–85
    Strawberry Preserves, 85
Jenkins, Joanne, 150
Johnston, Ginny, 192
Joiner, Patsy, 235, 341

K
Kennedy, Delinda, 345
Kids' recipes
    Ants on a Log, 358
    Banana Boats, 358
    Blizzard Party Mix, 358
    Cherry Fluff, 358
    Chicken Feed, 359
    Cornflake Peanut Butter Balls, 359
    Dirt Cake, 359
    Double Strawberry-Banana Shake, 359
    Frozen Orange Balls, 360
    Garbage Bag Candy, 360
    Homemade Butter, 360
    Ice Cream Sandwich Dessert, 360–361
    Pea-Choc, 361
    Peanut Butter Balls, 361
    S'mores, 361
    Snow Ice Cream, 362
    Yummy Candy, 362
Kitchen, Carolyn, 187

L
Lamb
    cooking guide, 372
    Roast Leg of Lamb with Mint Sauce, 257
Landress, Mary, 202
Lee, Harper, 12–13
Lee, Joyce, 80
Lemons
    Cool Lemon Sherbet, 323
    Easy Lemon Pie, 330–331
    Easy Lemon Squares, 267
    Frozen Lemonade Pie, 333
    Frozen Lemon Squares, 268
    Lemonade, 65
    Lemon Lush, 352–353
    Lemon Meringue Cake, 295
    Lemon Meringue Pie, 336–337
    Lemon Sauce, 134
    Lemon Sponge Custard, 353
    Lemon Sponge Pie, 337
    Lemon Squares, 270–271
    Lemon Tea Sandwiches, 51
    Luscious Lemon Cream Salad, 114–115
    Strawberry Lemonade, 69
Lewis, Rose, 181, 236, 348

Limes
Key Lime Pie, 336
Logan, Buddy, 109

M
Massey, Deborah, 69
Marks, Dot, 171, 181, 193, 210
McDowell, Nada, 165, 172, 199
McLendon, Gena, 197
McMillan, Joan, 205, 353
McMillan, Yvonne, 43, 159
Measurement equivalents chart, 368
Menu examples, 32–36
Miller, Marilyn, 183, 245
Minton, Thomas, 16
Mitchell, Margaret, 18
Morris, Nancy, 232
Mother's Day menu, 33
Muffins
Apple Muffins, 153
Blueberry Muffins, 156
Bran Muffins, 154
Corn Bread or Corn Muffins, 154
Muscadine grapes
Muscadine Marmalade, 84
Muse, Juanita, 64, 207, 265, 330, 334

N
Native Americans, contributions of, 15
New Southern Cuisine, 15–16
New Year's Day menu, 32
Nichols, Barbara, 323
Nicholson, Jill, 95, 191
Nuts and seeds. *See also* Pecans; Walnuts
Banana-Nut Bread, 140
Chicken Feed, 359
Cranberry Nut Topping, 355
Grandma's Strawberry Nut Loaf, 144
Pineapple Nut Cake, 302
storage tip, 62
Sugared Nuts, 57
White Chocolate Macadamia Nut Cookies, 322

O
O'Kelley, Sue, 215
Okra
Boiled Okra, 171
Fried Okra, 184
Georgia Okra, 186
Okra and Tomatoes, 195
Olives
Olive Spread Tea Sandwiches, 51
Spiced Olives, 54
Onions
Baked Vidalia Onions, 166–167
Chutney-Onion Cheese Spread, 86
Fried Onion Rings, 184
Georgia Okra, 186
Onion Pie, 195
Roasted Vidalia Onion Salad, 117
Vidalia Onion Casserole, 208
Vidalia Onion Pie, 208
Vidalia Onion Shortcake, 209
Virginia's Vidalia Onion Dip, 58
Oranges
Almond and Orange Salad, 100
Ambrosia, 100–101
Amy's Orange Pineapple Layer Cake, 273
Cranberry-Orange Relish, 126
Frozen Orange Balls, 360
Orange-Coconut Cake, 298
Orange Fluff, 119
Orange-Pecan Glazed Chicken and Wild Rice, 245
Spiced Mixed Fruit, 201
Osburn, Kristen, 359
Oven chart, 367
Oysters
Oyster Dip, 51
Pine-Bark Stew, 251
Scalloped Oysters, 252–253
Seafood Gumbo, 253
Southern Fried Oysters, 255

P
Pace, Dorothy, 153
Page, Donna, 119

Pancakes
    Crêpes, 158–159
    Pancakes, 159
Pan sizes, 373–374
Pasta
    Blue Willow Inn's Mac & Cheese, 169
    Chicken Macaroni, 237
    Chicken Noodle Delight, 238
    Chicken Pecan Pasta, 238–239
    Chicken Tetrazzini, 240–241
    Ham & Broccoli Noodle Casserole, 227
    Lasagna, 216–217
    Macaroni and Cheese and Corn Bake, 192
    Pasta Salad, 113
    quantities for large groups, 365
    Rice-A-Roni Salad, 118
    Slow-Cooker Macaroni and Cheese, 199
Peaches
    Bridge-Luncheon Frozen Fruit Salad, 103
    Fried Pies, 332
    Georgia Peach Champagne Punch, 71
    Georgia Peach Soup, 93
    Hot Curried Fruit, 191
    Peach Cobbler, 346
    Peach Preserves, 83
    Pickled Peaches, 126–127
    Sherried Fruit, 198–199
    Texas Governor's Mansion Summer Peach Tea
        Punch, 76
Peanut butter
    Coca-Cola Cake with Broiled Peanut Butter
        Frosting, 283
    Cornflake Peanut Butter Balls, 359
    Cream Cheese Peanut Bars, 265
    Nell's Peanut Butter Cake, 297
    Pea-Choc, 361
    Peanut Butter Balls, 361
    Peanut Butter Cake, 298–299
    Peanut Butter Pie, 339
    Peanut Soup, 93
    Yummy Candy, 362
Pears
    Cranberry-Pear Fruit Jellies, 310–311

Hot Curried Fruit, 191
Mama Smith's Pear Delight, 114
Sherried Fruit, 198–199
Peas
    Creamed Peas, 178
    Green Pea Casserole, 188
    Minted Peas, 193
Pecans
    Banana-Nut Bread, 140
    Blueberry-Banana-Pecan-Nut Cake, 277
    Buttermilk Pralines, 310
    Feud Cake, 287
    Julian's Pecan Pie, 334
    Orange-Pecan Glazed Chicken and Wild Rice, 245
    Pecan-Encrusted Chicken, 246
    Pecan Topping, 355
    Pralines, 314–315
    Ranch House Salad with Pecan Vinaigrette, 115
    Southern Delight Butter Pecan Cake, 306–307
    Sugared Nuts, 57
Pickles
    Bread and Butter Pickles, 124
    Watermelon Pickles, 128
Pickling and canning fruits and vegetables, 88
Pies
    Amelia Mud Pie, 325
    Apple Pie, 325
    Best Banana Pie, The, 326
    Buttermilk Pie, 326
    Cherry Cheese Pie, 326–327
    Chess Pie, 327
    Chicken Pie with Sweet Potato Crust, 239
    Chocolate Chess Pie, 327
    Chocolate Lovers' Easy Pie, 328
    Chocolate Meringue Pie, 328
    Coconut Cream Pie, 329
    Coconut Pie, 330
    Double-Layer Pumpkin Pie, 329
    Dried Apple & Egg Custard Pie, 330
    Easy Lemon Pie, 330–331
    Egg Custard Pie, 331
    French Silk Chocolate Pie, 331
    Fried Pies, 332

Fried Sweet Potato Pies, 332–333
Frozen Lemonade Pie, 333
Graham Cracker Piecrust, 333
Green Tomato Pie, 188–189
Ham and Cheese Pie, 226
Ice Cream Pie, 334
Julian's Pecan Pie, 334
Julian's Sweet Potato Pie, 335
Key Lime Pie, 336
Lemon Meringue Pie, 336–337
Lemon Sponge Pie, 337
Meringue, 337
Mississippi Mud Pie, 338
Old South Berry Blue Pie, 338–339
Onion Pie, 195
Pastry Piecrust, 340
Pawley's Island Pie, 339
Peanut Butter Pie, 339
Pumpkin Pie, 340
quantities for large groups, 365
Shirley's Chess Pie, 340
Shredded Potato & Ham Pie, 232
Snow-Capped Chocolate Pie, 341
Steve's Favorite Pie, 341
Vidalia Onion Pie, 208

Pineapples
Amy's Orange Pineapple Layer Cake, 273
Baked Pineapple Casserole, 168
Cream Cheese and Pineapple Finger Sandwiches, 42
Fresh Fruit and Cheese in Pineapple Wedges, 110–111
Hawaiian Grilled Ham, 226
Hawaiian Pineapple Ham Steaks, 227–228
Pineapple Ham, 228
Pineapple Nut Cake, 302
Pineapple Sherbet, 324
Pineapple Squares, 271
Pineapple Upside-Down Cake, 302–303
Sherried Fruit, 198–199

Pork
Baked Pork Chops, 222
Baked Pork Chops and Rice, 222
Casserole of Chops, 222–223
cooking guide, 372
Fried Fatback (also know as Streak O'Lean), 224
Fried Pork Chops, 225
importance of in Southern cooking, 14
Pork Roast, 228
Pork Tenderloin, 228–229
Roast Pork Creole, 230
Roast Pork with Spiced Cherry Sauce, 229

Posner, Nancy, 49, 83, 352, 354

Potatoes
Cheesy Ham Potato Casserole, 223
Creamed Potatoes or Mashed Potatoes, 179
Dandelion Potato Salad, 107
Gourmet Potato Salad, 112–113
Holiday Mashed Potatoes, 190
Louis' Potato Salad, 114
Mashed Potato Cakes, 192–193
Potatoes au Gratin, 196
Potato Soufflé, 196–197
Potato Soup, 96
quantities for large groups, 365
Red New Potatoes, 197
Roasted New Potatoes, 197
Scalloped Potatoes, 198
Shredded Potato & Ham Pie, 232
Twice-Baked Potatoes, 206

Poultry, 372
Powell, Cherie, 38, 241, 314
Preserves. See Jams and jellies
Pressley, Susan, 23
Price, Reynolds, 13, 15

Puddings
Alabama "Blue Ribbon" Banana Pudding, 342
Banana Pudding, 342
Blue Willow Corn Pudding, 169
Bread Pudding, 343
Chocolate Pudding, 344
Corn Pudding, 177
Indian Pudding, 344
Rice Pudding, 344
River Club Bread Pudding, 343
Strawberry Pudding, 345

Pumpkin
Double-Layer Pumpkin Pie, 329

Pumpkin (*continued*)
Pumpkin Pie, 340
Punches
Auntie Lucille's Punch, 68–69
Bourbon-Tea Punch, 67
Champagne Punch, 70
Chatham Artillery Punch, 70
Coffee Punch, 71
Georgia Peach Champagne Punch, 71
Ice Mold, 73
labels for, 61
Magnolia Punch, 72
Minted Tea Punch, 72
Miss Betty Rob's Southern Punch, 73
Peppermint Punch, 74
Punch for a Crowd, 74
Request Punch, 74
Sweet Tart Punch, 75
Texas Governor's Mansion Summer Peach Tea
    Punch, 76
tips, 61
Veranda Tea Punch, 76

Q
Quail
John Lowe's Quail, 256–257
Sautéed Quail, 258
Quantities for large groups, 364–366

R
Rabbit
Fried Young Rabbit, 256
Raisins
Bran Raisin Bread, 140
Carrot-Raisin Salad, 104
Raisin Sauce, 134–135
Raspberries
Raspberry Sauce, 135
Sexy Raspberry Salad, 119
Relishes
Apple Chutney, 124
Cabbage Relish, 125

Chow-Chow, 125
Corn Salsa, 126
Cranberry-Orange Relish, 126
Red Cabbage and Cranberry Relish, 127
Tomato Chutney, 127
Tomato Relish, 128
Rice
Baked Pork Chops and Rice, 222
Chicken and Rice, 234
Chicken and Rice Casserole, 235
Dried Fruit Pilaf, 180
Green Rice, 187
Journey Cakes, 155
Rice-A-Roni Salad, 118
Rice Pudding, 344
Savannah Red Rice, 198
Savannah Shrimp and Rice, 252
Vegetable Pilaf, 207
Robinson, Ashlee, 331
Rushing, Jeannie, 230
Rutabagas
Rutabagas, 197

S
Salad dressings. *See also* Vinaigrettes
quantities for large groups, 365
Salads
ABC Salad, 99
Al Fresco Watermelon Salad, 100
Almond and Orange Salad, 100
Ambrosia, 100–101
Amy's Salad, 101
Apple Cole Slaw, 101
Blueberry Salad, 102
bowl recommendation, 89
Bridge-Luncheon Frozen Fruit Salad, 103
Broccoli Salad, 103
Buttermilk Congealed Salad, 104
Carrot-Raisin Salad, 104
Chicken Salad, 104
Cole Slaw, 105
Company Chicken Salad, 106

Corn Bread Salad, 105
Cottage Cheese Salad, 105
Crunchy Apple Salad, 106
Curried Sweet Potato Salad, 107
Dandelion Potato Salad, 107
Daylily Salad, 108
Elegant Chicken Salad, 108
Family-Favorite Layered Salad, 108–109
Fresh Fruit and Cheese in Pineapple Wedges,
    110–111
Friendship, or Doug's Favorite, Salad, 109
Frozen Bing Cherry Salad, 102
Gourmet Potato Salad, 112–113
Grape Salad, 110
Holiday Mincemeat Salad, 111
Horseradish Salad, 112
Hot Chicken Salad, 111
Kraut Salad, 113
Louis' Potato Salad, 114
Luscious Lemon Cream Salad, 114–115
Mama Smith's Pear Delight, 114
Marinated Vegetable Salad, 112
Millionaire Salad, 116
Molded Egg Salad, 116
North Georgia Caviar, 117
"Not Apple Salad!", 118
Orange Fluff, 119
quantities for large groups, 364, 365
Ranch House Salad with Pecan Vinaigrette, 115
Rice-A-Roni Salad, 118
Roasted Vidalia Onion Salad, 117
Sexy Raspberry Salad, 119
Spinach-Strawberry Salad, 120
Tomato Zucchini Salad, 120
Waldorf Salad, 121
Watergate Salad (also known as Green Stuff), 121
Sams, Barbara, 118, 209, 319
Sandwiches
Asparagus Sandwiches, 38
Cream Cheese and Pineapple Finger Sandwiches, 42
Cucumber Party Sandwiches, 43
Famous Tomato Sandwiches, 44–45
Lemon Tea Sandwiches, 51
Olive Spread Tea Sandwiches, 51
quantities for large groups, 366
Tea Sandwiches, 58
Tuna Salad Mini Sandwiches, 58
Sauces
Baked Cranberry Sauce, 130
Blueberry Sauce, 130
Bourbon Sauce, 130
Cabernet Cranberries, 131
Carolina Low Country Dressing, 131
Cheese Sauce, 131, 223
Chunky Cranberry Applesauce, 132
Classic Hollandaise Sauce, 132
Cold Sabayon Sauce, 343
Cream Sauce, 254
Creole Sauce, 230
Dijon Sauce, 133
Dill Sauce, 133
Ginger Sauce, 133
Lemon Sauce, 134
Marchand de Vin Sauce, 134
Mint Sauce, 257
Raisin Sauce, 134–135
Raspberry Sauce, 135
Shrimp Sauce for Vegetables, 135
Sour Cream Sauce, 220–221
Tartar Sauce, 136
White Sauce, 136, 164–165, 182
Sauerkraut
Kraut Salad, 113
Saunders, Jane, 347
Sausage
Baked Beans, 166
Christmas Breakfast Casserole, 223
Double Oink Roll-Ups, 44
Granny Julia's Sausage Bread, 144–145
Lasagna, 216–217
Lynn's Sausage Casserole, 218
Sausage and Egg Casserole, 230
Sausage and Gravy, 231
Sausage Balls in Cheese Pastry, 53

Sausage *(continued)*
Sausage Biscuits, 152
Sausage Casserole, 231
Sausage Gravy, 138
Scallops
Pine-Bark Stew, 251
Scuppernong grapes
Scuppernong Jelly, 84–85
Scuppernong Juice, 85
Sears, Janice "Sams", 119
Sears, Richard, 227
Seiler, Lee, 192
Sexton, Billie, 326
Shrimp
Hot Shrimp Dip, 48–49
Pine-Bark Stew, 251
Savannah Shrimp and Rice, 252
Seafood au Gratin, 254
Seafood Gumbo, 253
Shrimp & Wild Rice Casserole, 254–255
Shrimp Dip, 53
Shrimp Mold, 54
Shrimp Sauce for Vegetables, 135
Shrimp Wrapped in Bacon, 54
Smith, Alma K.,46, 73, 155
Smith, Jeanne, 75, 268, 344
Smith, Robin, 45
Social Circle, Georgia, 19, 26
Social Circle Church of God, 19, 26–27
Sommerville, Sherrie, 69
Soups, stews, and chowders
Ann Lowe's Chicken Stew, 90
Bob's Blue Ribbon Favorite, "Rileyhouse Beef Stew", 213
Brunswick Stew, 90
Catfish Stew, 248
Chicken and Dumplings, 90–91
Corn Chowder, 91
Crab Chowder, 92
Easy Oven Stew, 214
Garbanzo Bean Soup (Chickpeas), 92
Georgia Peach Soup, 93
Jill's Vegetable Soup, 94–95

Louis' Dad's North Carolina Brunswick Stew, 94
Maryland Vegetable Crab Soup, 95
Minestrone Soup, 96
Peanut Soup, 93
Pine-Bark Stew, 251
Potato Soup, 96
President Ronald Reagan's Favorite Beef Stew, 219
quantities for large groups, 366
Quick-and-Easy Clam Chowder, 97
Seafood Gumbo, 253
She-Crab Soup, 97
Sherry Soup, 98
Tomato-Basil Cream Soup, 98
Vegetable Soup, 99
Venison Stew, 259
Southern cooking
definition, 14
down-home cuisine, 14
evolution of, 16
methods for preparing, 15
New Southern Cuisine, 15–16
passing down recipes, decline in, 16
staples of, 15
Southern culture
hospitality, 11–12
manners, 12
pace of life, 12–13
speech patterns, 13
vocabulary, 13–14
Spinach
Flamingo Floyd's Spinach Dip, 45
Hot Spinach Artichoke Dip, 49
Spinach Balls, 55
Spinach Dip, 55
Spinach Roll-Ups, 55
Spinach-Strawberry Salad, 120
Spoon breads
Southern Spoon Bread, 149
Spoon Bread, 149
Spreads
Cheese Spread, 85
Chutney-Onion Cheese Spread, 86

Cranberry-Ambrosia Cream Cheese Spread, 86
Garlic Cheese Spread, 86–87
Nasturtium Spread, 87
Pepper Jelly Spread, 88
Pimento Cheese Spread, 87
Watercress Dip or Spread, 59
Squash
Fried Squash, 185
Marinated Vegetable Salad, 112
Skillet Squash, 200
Sophia's Squash Casserole, 200
Squash Casserole, 201
Squash Dressing, 202
Stuffed Zucchini Squash, 203
Yellow Squash and Tomatoes, 210
Squirrel
Fried Squirrel, 256
Stanhope, Debra, 199
Staples, Sue, 237
Stephens, Betty, 207, 349
Stews. *See* Soups, stews, and chowders
Strawberries
Bridge-Luncheon Frozen Fruit Salad, 103
Double Strawberry-Banana Shake, 359
Fig-Strawberry Preserves, 81
Fresh Fruit and Cheese in Pineapple Wedges, 110–111
Glaze for Strawberries, 356
Grandma's Strawberry Nut Loaf, 144
Spinach-Strawberry Salad, 120
Strawberries with Fluffy Cream Cheese Dip, 56
Strawberries with Mint Yogurt Dip, 56
Strawberry Cake, 307
Strawberry Candies, 315
Strawberry Delight, 354
Strawberry Lemonade, 69
Strawberry Preserves, 85
Strawberry Pretzel Delight, 272
Strawberry Pudding, 345
Strawberry Shortcake, 308
Stewart, Fran, 120
Stone, Ariann, 110
Stuffing. *See* Dressing or stuffing

Substitutions chart, 370–371
Sugar snap peas
Sugar Snap Peas with Bacon Dressing, 205
Suggs, Judy, 144
Supper, 14
Sweet potatoes
Candied Yams, 171
Chicken Pie with Sweet Potato Crust, 239
Cornwallis Yams, 178
Curried Sweet Potato Salad, 107
Fried Sweet Potato Pies, 332–333
Julian's Sweet Potato Pie, 335
Mom's Sweet Potato Casserole, 194
Sweet Potato Biscuits, 152
Sweet Potato Bread, 150
Sweet Potato Crust, 239
Sweet Potato Puffs, 204
Sweet Potato Soufflé, 204
Yams Louie, 209

T
Thanksgiving dinner menu, 34–35
Tomatoes. *See also* Green tomatoes
Catholic Church ban on, 15
Eggplant and Tomatoes, 181
Famous Tomato Sandwiches, 44–45
Fried Red Tomatoes and Creamed Gravy, 184–185
Okra and Tomatoes, 195
quantities for large groups, 365, 366
Skillet Tomatoes and Zucchini, 199
Stewed Tomatoes, 202
Stuffed Cherry Tomatoes, 56–57
Tomato-Basil Cream Soup, 98
Tomato Chutney, 127
Tomato-Corn Casserole, 205
Tomato Gravy, 138
Tomato Relish, 128
Tomato Zucchini Salad, 120
Yellow Squash and Tomatoes, 210
Toppings
Ambrosia Topping, 354
Blueberry Topping, 355

Toppings *(continued)*
    Cranberry Nut Topping, 355
    Pecan Topping, 355
Trammel, Karol, 113, 117, 284
Tribble, Mildred, 100
Tuna
    Tuna Casserole, 255
    Tuna Salad Mini Sandwiches, 58
Turkey, 372
    Martha Washington's Turkey Potpie, 242–243
    quantities for large groups, 365, 366
    Roast Turkey, 246
Turner, Carole, 262
Twain, Mark, 13

U

Upshaw, Bertha, 17, 18
Upshaw, John Phillips, Jr., 17–19
Upshaw, John Phillips, Sr., 18
Upshaw, Redd, 18
Upshaw, Sanders, 18
Upshaw Gannon, Nell, 17, 19

V

Van Dyke, Billie
    Billie's at the American Legion, 25–26, 27, 29
    Billie's Classic Country Dining, 23–25
    Billie's Family Restaurant, 25
    catering business, 23
    childhood of, 21
    children of, 22
    china collection, 17, 20
    death of son, 23
    financial problems, 29–30
    food, interest in, 21, 22
    marriage to Bill Edgerly, 21–22
    marriage to Louis, 22
    media interest in, 31
    meeting Louis, 22
    move from Atlanta, 23
    prayers about restaurant, 28, 30
    reunion with Dennis Baker, 22–23
    Upshaw mansion, interest in, 26–28

Upshaw mansion, purchase of, 19, 29
    Upshaw mansion, renovation of, 19–20, 29
    volunteer work of, 22
Van Dyke, Louis
    Billie's at the American Legion, 25–26, 27, 29
    Billie's Classic Country Dining, 23–25
    Billie's Family Restaurant, 25
    career change, 23
    china collection, 17, 20
    financial problems, 29–30
    friendship with Edgerly family, 22
    Lewis Grizzard meeting, 30–31
    marriage to Billie, 22
    move from Atlanta, 23
    prayers about restaurant, 28
    Upshaw mansion, interest in, 26–28
    Upshaw mansion, purchase of, 19, 29
    Upshaw mansion, renovation of, 19–20, 29
    U.S. Navy service of, 22
Vargas, Ada, 329
Veal, 372
Vegetables
    Asparagus Vegetable Casserole, 164–165
    Farmer's Garden Stew, 182–183
    Fritters, 141
    Jill's Vegetable Soup, 94–95
    Marinated Vegetable Salad, 112
    Maryland Vegetable Crab Soup, 95
    pickling and canning, 88
    quantities for large groups, 364
    Vegetable Casserole, 207
    Vegetable Pilaf, 207
    Vegetable Soup, 99
Venison
    Venison Stew, 259
Vinaigrettes
    Garlic Vinaigrette, 117
    Pecan Vinaigrette, 115

W

Walden, Kathy, 291, 328
Walker, Marilyn 106, 152
Walnuts

Apple Walnut Cake, 274
Pineapple Nut Cake, 302
Water chestnuts
Bacon-Chestnut Appetizers, 38
Watermelons
Al Fresco Watermelon Salad, 100
quantities for large groups, 365
Watermelon Cake, 309
Watermelon Pickles, 128
Wild rice
Orange-Pecan Glazed Chicken and Wild Rice, 245
Shrimp & Wild Rice Casserole, 254–255
Wilson, Bernice, 128, 185, 251, 316

Y

Yams. *See* Sweet potatoes
Yogurt
Strawberries with Mint Yogurt Dip, 56

Z

Zucchini
Farmer's Garden Stew, 182–183
Skillet Tomatoes and Zucchini, 199
Stuffed Zucchini Squash, 203
Tomato Zucchini Salad, 120
Zucchini-Parmesan Appetizer Bread, 150